# LOBSTER

# LOBSTER

## 75 Recipes Celebrating the World's Favorite Seafood

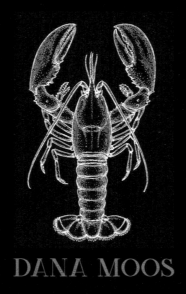

DANA MOOS

Down East Books

Camden, Maine

**Down East Books**

Published by Down East Books
An imprint of The Rowman & Littlefield Publishing Group, Inc.
4501 Forbes Blvd., Suite 200
Lanham, MD 20706
www.rowman.com

Distributed by NATIONAL BOOK NETWORK

British Library Cataloguing in Publication Information Available

**Library of Congress Cataloging-in-Publication Data Available**

Names: Moos, Dana, author.
Title: Lobster : 75 recipes celebrating the world's favorite seafood / Dana Moos.
Description: Camden, Maine : Down East Books, [2021] | Summary: "With recipes for everything from tasty breakfast bites to brunch, lunch, and hearty entrees, all incorporating lobster, this collection will have family and friends asking to eat in every day of the week"— Provided by publisher.
Identifiers: LCCN 2020047854 (print) | LCCN 2020047855 (ebook) | ISBN 9781608937349 (cloth) | ISBN 9781608937356 (ebook)
Subjects: LCSH: Cooking (Lobsters) | LCGFT: Cookbooks.
Classification: LCC TX754.L63 M66 2021 (print) | LCC TX754.L63 (ebook) | DDC 641.6/95—dc23
LC record available at https://lccn.loc.gov/2020047854
LC ebook record available at https://lccn.loc.gov/2020047855

♾ ™ The paper used in this publication meets the minimum requirements of American National Standard for Information Sciences—Permanence of Paper for Printed Library Materials, ANSI/NISO Z39.48-1992.

# CONTENTS

## STARTERS AND SMALL BITES

## DIPS AND SPREADS

## SOUPS AND SALADS

## SANDWICHES AND HANDHELDS

## TACOS

# MAIN COURSES

# LOBSTER—IT'S WHAT'S FOR BREAKFAST

# BLOODY MARYS

# INTRODUCTION

Lobster can be so much more than just steamed with drawn butter and a roll of paper towels. You might ask, "Why bother with something so pure and delicious as a simple lobster with butter?" As I often do, I challenged myself to come up with some creative ways to incorporate lobster into a wide variety of dishes that still allow for the lobster to shine. Some dishes you will find here are complex and require some advance preparation, while others are much simpler. Some of the components in these dishes can be used in other recipes, and versatility is always a good thing. Several of the sauces are repeated in a number of my recipes and can be used on salads, sandwiches, eggs, grilled meats, and more.

This cookbook is about combining creativity with versatility and focuses on loads of flavor. There are recipes that are perfect for two as well as entertaining a crowd, from breakfast, brunch, and lunch to appetizers and dinner. And two varieties of lobster Bloody Marys!

# THE BASICS

The North Atlantic lobster, once considered bait, is among the most prized of all crustaceans. A good majority of lobster is harvested from the great state of Maine, the wonderful place I have been fortunate to call home since 2004. Lobsters are harvested throughout the year in Maine, but the majority are caught between June and December. Although they are harvested during the winter and early spring months, the catch is smaller. Lobsters are more abundant in summer because they come in closer to shore and shallow, warmer water, where they often shed their shells. Soft-shell lobsters are generally found July through sometime in October; during the remainder of the year they are hard shell.

So what really is the difference between hard-shell and soft-shell lobster meat? My punctured fingers can tell you that soft shells are much easier to pick and draw less blood! But aside from that, the meat from a soft shell is smaller than hard shell but tends to be a bit more tender. But then some will say they like hard-shell lobster meat better because it doesn't absorb water since the shells aren't porous like the soft shells are. Any way you look at it, lobster meat is delicious; it's all how you cook it and what you do with it!

# The Yield from a Lobster

Depending on the size of the lobster you buy, generally speaking, one (1¼- to 1½-pound) lobster will yield 3–4 ounces of meat. In this cookbook, you will see recipes that call for raw picked lobster, live lobster, and cooked lobster meat. You can find cooked lobster meat at many grocers and nearly all lobster retailers and wholesalers. Claw and knuckle are usually sold together for one price per pound, and tail meat is sold at a higher price per pound. You can decide based on the quantity needed for any given recipe whether you want to cook live lobster and shuck the meat yourself or buy cooked meat. If they are soft shell, they are much easier to pick than hard shell; for hard shell, I recommend having Band-Aids at the ready! I'd also recommend wearing kitchen or medical-grade vinyl gloves (even though the spiny crustacean can sometimes puncture them anyway)!

The prize is worth the effort. Forget picking crabs (I'm from Maryland)—there's not enough meat for that amount of effort! With lobster, there certainly is.

---

One 1¼–1½-pound lobster = 4 ounces or ½ cup
Two 1¼–1½-pound lobsters = 8 ounces or 1 cup
Three 1¼–1½-pound lobsters = 12 ounces or 1½ cups
Four 1¼–1½-pound lobsters = 1 pound or 2 cups

*Note:* The yield will depend on whether you are using soft-shell lobster or hard-shell (soft-shell lobsters yield less meat).

# Steaming versus Boiling

Steaming tends to be a better process for cooking the lobster, as it cooks it more gently. Boiling lobster introduces more water into the lobster, which, in all likelihood, will cause a slight loss in flavor. Steaming preserves the flavor and yields more tender meat. Generally speaking, for 1¼–1½ pound lobsters, you will fill a large stockpot with about 2 inches of water and bring to a boil. Place a steamer basket upside down, and then add the lobsters and cover. Cook for about 11–12 minutes.

If you are going to be using cooked lobster in a dish that will be further cooked for any period of time beyond just warmed, you will want to par-cook the lobster (using the steaming method) for about 5–6 minutes, and then proceed with the recipe.

# Grilling Lobster

Grilling lobster imparts some smoky flavor but also yields a very nice texture when cooked. The best way to grill them is to boil for 3 or 4 minutes, drain, and let them cool enough to handle. Then turn the lobster on its back and cut down the middle of the belly to halve the lobster. Crack the claws, but leave them intact. Discard any unwanted parts. Drizzle a mixture of olive oil and melted butter all over the lobster, and start grilling cut side down, turning halfway through, for a total of 8–10 minutes. This is one of my favorite ways to enjoy the crustacean!

# Poaching Raw Lobster

**Dana's Tip:** If you do poach raw lobster in butter, be sure to strain the lobster cooking butter/liquid and cool in the refrigerator. The "lobster butter" will float to the top, and the lobster cooking juices will remain on the bottom. SAVE this. Both can be used in other dishes!

Often recipes call for cooking lobster meat that has already been cooked, which could easily result in overcooked, chewy meat. If you can find a source that sells raw picked lobster meat, give it a try. I get mine from Shucks Maine Lobster. But if you can't find a source, you'll parcook the lobsters about 6 minutes and then continue with the recipe as written for poaching the lobster.

Bring a large stock pot of water to a boil. Put the lobster into the boiling water head first and cook until bright red all over (about 5 minutes). Transfer the lobster to a large rimmed baking sheet and let cool. Twist the tail from the lobster body and break off the claws. With scissors, cut down the tail shell and remove the meat. Cut down the center of the tail and remove the dark intestinal vein. Crack the claws and knuckles and remove the meat.

If you want to take a shortcut in any recipe in this cookbook, you can substitute with already-picked lobster meat you've purchased; just warm it for 2–3 minutes in the butter or brown butter per the recipe.

# Picking a Lobster

1. Twist off the claws.

2. Crack each claw and knuckle with a lobster or nut cracker (although you can also do this by hand). Remove the meat with a small fork or with your fingers.

3. Separate the tail from the body by twisting at the tail-body joint. Break off the tail flippers.

4. Holding the tail as straight as you can, insert a fork or, with your finger at the flipper end, push the tail meat in one piece.

5. Remove and discard the black "vein" that runs the entire length of the tail meat. The easiest way is to butterfly the tail, or score the back of the tail with a knife, exposing the vein, and then remove.

When using picked cooked lobster meat in a recipe, allow for chef sampling—it's a must!

# MY FAVORITES

I'm always asked what my favorite recipes are in my cookbooks. A few are simple, and a few are more involved. But I can tell you, the more involved dishes are flavor bombs and well worth the effort! For some recipes, there are time-saving steps where sauces or components can be made ahead of time or can be used in various recipes throughout the book.

My preferred flavor profile tends to be Asian fusion, and I think that will become evident as you browse the recipes. I also enjoy mixing regions of the country, such as Maine lobster with cheddar jalapeño grits or with fried green tomatoes.

**Lobster-Topped Wontons** *(see page 12)*

**Lobster and Fried Green Tomatoes with Spicy Remoulade** *(see page 37)*

**Panko-Fried Lobster Bites with Garlic Mayo** *(see page 39)*

**Creamy Lobster, Shrimp, and Parmesan Dip** *(see page 77)*

**Pacific Rim Lobster Salad with Napa Cabbage, Carrots, Scallions, Mango, Red Pepper Aioli, Soy Glaze, and Wonton Chips** *(see page 97)*

Lobster, Mango, and Avocado Salad with Citrus Vinaigrette
*(see page 105)*

Lobster and Black Pepper Candied Bacon Slider on Brioche with
Brown Butter Wasabi Mayo and Pickled Red Onions and Carrots
*(see page 117)*

Lobster Panini with Roasted Shallots, Creamy Fontina, Smoked
Red Pepper Aioli, and Arugula *(see page 119)*

Fried Lobster Po'Boy with Garlic Mayo, Roasted Shallots, Lettuce,
and Tomatoes *(see page 127)*

Asian Fusion Lobster Tacos *(see page 149)*

Lobster Mac and Cheese with Truffle Oil and Shaved Truffles
*(see page 164)*

Lobster and Scallops Hamayaki Style with Soy Glaze *(see page 203)*

Egg Roulade with Lobster and Sherry Butter *(see page 209)*

Lobster Fried Rice with Candied Pork Belly and Fried Egg
*(see page 215)*

Savory Scallion Waffles Topped with Brown Butter–Poached Lobster,
Poached Egg, Brown Butter Wasabi Mayo, and Sweet Soy Glaze
*(see page 221)*

My favorite sauces in the dishes above are the Smoked Red Pepper Aioli,
Smoked Truffle Aioli, Soy Glaze, and Brown Butter Wasabi Mayo. You'll
find they're versatile and delicious with a variety of other recipes in this
cookbook or elsewhere!

# STARTERS AND SMALL BITES

# Lobster-Topped Wontons

Fried wontons, smoked truffle aioli with charred scallions and truffle oil, lobster, and a soy glaze—this is a double-award-winning recipe! First place in Judge's and People's Choice for Best Lobster Bite at the 2018 Boothbay Harbor, Maine Claw Down competition. This win automatically entered me in the 2018 Harvest on the Harbor Lobster Chef of the Year competition in Portland, Maine, and I won the People's Choice for my Lobster Scallion Crepes *(page 198)*. The sauces in this recipe are so good that I've used them in several dishes throughout this cookbook.

*Makes 32 wontons*

Black and white sesame seeds

Vegetable oil (for frying)

16 wonton wrappers, cut in half

Kosher salt to taste

1 pound fresh-picked lobster meat, portioned into 32 (½-ounce) portions

Smoked Truffle Aioli *(see recipe below)*

Soy Glaze *(see recipe below)*

Minced chives (for garnish)

1.  Toast the sesame seeds on a parchment-lined sheet pan in a 300°F oven until the white sesames have a light golden hue, about 10–12 minutes. Let cool.

2.  Add an inch or so of vegetable oil to a deep fry or sauté pan. When the oil is 375°F, add 4 or 5 wontons at a time and cook for about a minute, until golden brown on each side. Set aside on a towel and season with kosher salt. Let cool and store in an airtight container.

# Smoked Truffle Aioli

*Makes about 2 cups*

1 bunch of scallions (about 6–8), bottoms trimmed

1 tablespoon olive oil (for grilling scallions)

1½ cups Japanese "Kewpie" mayonnaise *(This is made from egg yolks, not whole eggs like traditional American mayonnaise, so it's creamier. You can find it online or in Asian markets.)*

½ stick butter

½ teaspoon kosher salt plus ¼ teaspoon for tossing on scallions

1 teaspoon black pepper

1 tablespoon white truffle oil *(I only use Fiore brand, a Maine company, and their truffle oil is the best!)*

1. Drizzle the scallions with the olive oil, sprinkle with salt, and grill over medium heat until really well charred, about 10 minutes. Roughly chop and set aside.

2. For the smoking, you can use either an outdoor smoker or a stove-top smoker. I used a Cameron stovetop smoker, but I used it on the grill since I had to grill my scallions and the grill was already hot.

3. Place 1 cup of the mayonnaise and butter in an ovenproof dish and put in smoker (following the manufacturer's instructions). Smoke for about 30 minutes. If it has been adequately smoked, you'll see browned bits along the edge of the baking dish and a light brown tint to the mayo and butter. Let cool.

4. Add to blender with the remaining mayonnaise, salt, black pepper, and truffle oil. Add the scallions and blend until scallions are in small bits but still very visible. Store in a squeeze bottle.

# Soy Glaze

*Makes 1 cup*

1. Add the brown sugar, soy sauces, garlic, ginger, rice wine, sherry, and rice wine vinegar to a small saucepan and heat until brown sugar is dissolved. Remove from heat.

2. Stir in mirin and fish sauce. Let cool and store in a squeeze bottle.

> **Dana's Tip:** A similar bottled alternative can be found in supermarkets or Asian grocers—Kikkoman makes a nice "Unagi" sweet sauce as well as "Sweet Soy Sauce for Rice." Throughout the cookbook, you'll find I use a soy glaze, and it freezes well. So make a big batch and freeze in squeeze bottles. Or purchase one of the suggested prepared versions.

- ¼ cup dark brown sugar
- ¼ cup sweet soy sauce *(which is thicker, similar to molasses, and can be found in Asian markets)*
- ¼ cup regular soy sauce
- 1 garlic clove, finely minced
- ½ teaspoon fresh grated ginger
- 2 tablespoons rice cooking wine (Shaoxing)
- 2 tablespoons medium sherry
- 1 teaspoon rice wine vinegar
- 1 tablespoon mirin
- 1 teaspoon fish sauce

# To Assemble

Squeeze the aioli onto the wonton, from end to end. Top with ½ ounce of lobster chunks, a drizzle of soy glaze, a sprinkling of chives, and toasted sesames. Don't be shy on the sauces—they are key to the flavor explosion!

# Lobster and Pork Pot-Stickers, Pan Fried

I can make a meal of just dumplings! These can be prepared ahead and frozen prior to cooking. Then pull out as many as you want and cook them off.

*Makes 48*

1. Combine pork, lobster, cabbage, ginger, garlic, scallion whites, and 2 tablespoons soy sauce in a bowl. Lay a wrapper on a clean, dry surface, and, using your finger or a brush, spread a bit of egg along half of the wrapper. Place a rounded teaspoon of filling in center, fold over, and seal by pinching edges together. (Do not overfill.) Place dumplings on a plate; if you want to wait a few hours before cooking, cover plate with plastic wrap and refrigerate. Or freeze for up to two weeks.

2. To cook, place water and chicken stock in a saucepan and bring to a boil. Drop in pot-stickers, no more than 6 or 8 at a time, and boil for 3 minutes. Remove to plate. Repeat with remaining pot-stickers.

3. Put about 2 tablespoons oil in a large nonstick skillet and turn heat to medium-high. A minute later, add dumplings—about 8–10 in a 10- or 12-inch sauté pan. Cook about 4 minutes, or until bottoms are lightly browned. Lower heat to medium and let cook on the other side about 2 minutes.

4. To make the dipping sauce, combine remaining soy sauce, green parts of scallions, mirin, and rice vinegar.

½ pound ground pork

½ pound finely chopped cooked lobster meat

½ cup minced Napa cabbage

1 tablespoon minced ginger

1 tablespoon minced garlic

6 scallions, the white and green parts separated, both minced

½ cup plus 2 tablespoons soy sauce

48 dumpling or wonton wrappers

1 egg, lightly beaten in a bowl

1 quart chicken broth

2 cups water

4 tablespoons vegetable oil

1 tablespoon mirin

2 tablespoons rice vinegar

# Lobster and Pork Pot-Stickers, Deep Fried

This is the same pot-sticker as the pan-fried version, just deep fried. That crunch is irresistible!

*Makes 48*

½ pound ground pork

½ pound finely chopped cooked lobster meat

½ cup minced Napa cabbage

1 tablespoon minced ginger

1 tablespoon minced garlic

6 scallions, the white and green parts separated, both minced

½ cup plus 2 tablespoons soy sauce

48 dumpling or wonton wrappers

1 egg, lightly beaten in a bowl

1½ quarts vegetable oil

1 tablespoon mirin

2 tablespoons rice vinegar

1. Combine pork, lobster, cabbage, ginger, garlic, scallion whites, and 2 tablespoons soy sauce in a bowl. Lay a wrapper on a clean, dry surface, and, using your finger or a brush, spread a bit of egg along half of the wrapper. Place a rounded teaspoon of filling in center, fold over, and seal by pinching edges together. (Do not overfill.) Place dumplings on a plate; if you want to wait a few hours before cooking, cover plate with plastic wrap and refrigerate. Or freeze for up to two weeks.

2. Heat vegetable oil to 375°F. Once hot, add about 6 pot-stickers at a time and deep fry until golden, about 2 minutes, flipping to ensure even cooking. Remove to paper towel and salt lightly before serving.

3. To make the dipping sauce, combine remaining soy sauce, green parts of scallions, mirin, and rice vinegar.

# Fried Lobster Rangoon

Any time I get Chinese carryout, I order crab Rangoon, and it NEVER makes it home. It's just the perfect car snack! But these are elevated with lobster. And like the pot-stickers, these can be made and frozen prior to frying. They're perfect for entertaining or game day snacks.

*Makes about 36*

1. In a bowl, combine the cream cheese, olive oil, chives, garlic, Parmesan cheese, black pepper, seafood seasoning, and red pepper flakes until well combined. Add the lobster and fold until combined.

2. Set aside a small bowl of water.

3. On a flat surface, lay out several wonton wrappers to work in batches. Dollop a teaspoon of the filling in the center of each wonton square.

4. Using your fingers, wet the wrapper all along the edges. Bring all four corners upward and pinch the edges together to seal. Continue until all wrappers are filled.

5. Once all of the wontons have been filled, heat a deep saucepan with oil over medium-high heat (until the oil shimmers). When it is very hot, place about 8 wontons in at a time. Fry the wonton purses until they are golden brown and blistered, about 2 minutes.

6 ounces cream cheese, softened to room temperature

2 tablespoons olive oil

A bunch of chives, finely diced

2 garlic cloves, finely diced

4 tablespoons grated Parmesan cheese

Freshly ground black pepper (to taste)

¼ teaspoon Chesapeake Bay seasoning (seafood seasoning)

¼ teaspoon red pepper flakes

2 cups chopped lobster meat

Small bowl of water

1 (14-ounce) package wonton wrappers (a 48-count package)

Vegetable oil (for frying)

# Fresh Lobster Spring Roll

*Makes 6*

6 rice wrappers

6–8 butter lettuce leaves

¼ cup julienned carrot

¼ cup fried shallots

1 avocado, cut into ½-inch slices

8 ounces cooked lobster meat, cut into small chunks

1 ripe mango, cut into ½-inch sticks

2 tablespoons Kikkoman "Sweet Soy Sauce for Rice"

1.  Follow instructions on the rice wrapper package to soften.

2.  Lay out 1 rice paper wrapper and top with butter lettuce leaves.

3.  Evenly distribute the carrots, shallots, avocado, lobster, and mango on the butter lettuce leaves. Top with soy sauce.

4.  Roll bottom toward the middle. Fold in both sides and continue rolling. Individually wrap each roll with plastic wrap. Will hold for 2 hours in the refrigerator. Slice in the middle and serve.

# Lobster Sushi Roll with Roasted Shallots, Smoked Red Pepper Aioli, Brown Butter Wasabi Mayo, and Soy Glaze

I'm a big fan of real sushi with raw fish. But this is a fun way to use a small amount of lobster. Besides, it's really as much about the sauces here.

*Makes 1 roll*

1. Preheat oven to 375°F. Roast shallots drizzled with olive oil on sheet pan until lightly browned on all sides, about 30 minutes. Cool to room temperature, slice, and set aside.

2. Lay the sheet of nori on a bamboo sushi mat, with the long side of nori closest to you.

3. With wet hands, spread the rice over the nori in an even layer.

4. Distribute the roasted shallot evenly over the rice.

5. Arrange the lobster across the rice from side to side, just a bit closer to you than the middle.

6. Using the edge of the nori and the mat closest to you, fold the bottom over the filling and roll up, jelly-roll style, pressing down slightly with each rotation.

7. Using a sharp, slightly dampened knife, slice into 6 portions.

8. Serve with the Smoked Red Pepper Aioli, Brown Butter Wasabi Mayonnaise, and soy sauce.

2 small shallots

1–2 teaspoons olive oil, for roasting shallots

1 sheet nori

¼ cup cooked sushi rice

2 ounces cooked lobster meat, cut into chunks

Smoked Red Pepper Aioli, for dipping *(see recipe below)*

Brown Butter Wasabi Mayonnaise, for dipping *(see recipe below)*

Soy sauce, for dipping

# Smoked Red Pepper Aioli

This aioli is a recipe I've used in many of the dishes throughout this cookbook. It's great on salads, sandwiches, grilled meats, and vegetables, too.

*Makes about 1½ cups*

1 red bell pepper, quartered, ribs and seeds removed

1 tablespoon olive oil (for smoking)

Sprinkle of salt (for smoking)

2 egg yolks

½ teaspoon kosher salt

½ teaspoon sugar

½ teaspoon black pepper

½ cup good-quality olive oil (mild)

1. Drizzle the cut pepper with the olive oil, sprinkle with salt, and place in smoker. For the smoking, you can use either an outdoor smoker or a stovetop smoker. I use a Cameron stovetop smoker, but I use it on the grill to keep the smoke outdoors. Smoke for about 25–30 minutes over medium heat. If it has been adequately smoked, you'll see a slight golden brown tint to the pepper slices. Remove, let cool, and remove skin from peppers.

2. Add peppers to food processor and process until smooth.

3. Add the egg yolks, salt, sugar, and black pepper. Turn on processor, and then add the oil in a slow stream to blend. Adjust salt or pepper if needed. Store in a squeeze bottle. (You can use a good-quality prepared mayonnaise instead of making your own.)

# Brown Butter Wasabi Mayonnaise

*Makes about 1 cup*

Mix all ingredients and let meld for a couple of hours.

1 cup mayonnaise

2 teaspoons prepared wasabi

1 teaspoon honey

3 tablespoons brown butter, melted or softened

Dana's Tip: Kikkoman makes a creamy wasabi that you can use as your base. It's delicious, and it's what gave me the idea for this mayo.

# Brown Butter

1. In small saucepan, add 1 stick butter and cook over medium-low heat until lightly brown in color and milk solids have fully separated, about 8–10 minutes.

2. Strain through a fine-mesh sieve and place brown butter in a container and keep at room temperature.

1 stick butter

# Lobster Egg Roll

This is very simply lobster and scallions wrapped in my favorite egg roll wrapper and fried, but elevated by serving them with a couple of my favorite sauces.

*Makes 16*

16 egg roll wrappers

1 pound fresh-picked lobster meat, portioned into 16 portions

1 bunch of scallions, thinly sliced

Vegetable oil (for frying)

Smoked Truffle Aioli *(see recipe below)*

Soy Glaze *(see recipe below)*

Chives (for garnish)

1. Place a large egg roll wrapper on a diagonal and dampen each corner with a drop of water.

2. Place about 2 tablespoons chopped lobster and a good scattering of scallions in the center, fold the bottom up (tucking it into a tight roll), and then fold each side in and roll up, sealing the edge tightly.

3. Fry in vegetable oil (in a small sauté pan with enough oil to come up about halfway) until golden brown on all sides, about a minute each side. Drain on paper towel.

4. Serve the egg roll drizzled with the Smoked Truffle Aioli and Soy Glaze. Top with chives and enjoy!

# Smoked Truffle Aioli

1½ cups Japanese "Kewpie" mayonnaise *(This is made from egg yolks, not whole eggs like traditional American mayonnaise, so it's creamier. You can find it online or in Asian markets.)*

½ stick butter

½ teaspoon kosher salt

1 teaspoon black pepper

1 tablespoon white truffle oil

*Makes about 2 cups*

1. For the smoking, you can use either an outdoor smoker or a stove-top smoker. I use a Cameron stovetop smoker, but I use it on the grill so I could keep the smoke out of the house.

2. Place 1 cup of the mayonnaise and butter in an ovenproof dish and place in smoker (following the manufacturer's instructions). Smoke for about 30 minutes. If it has been adequately smoked, you'll see browned bits along the edge of the baking dish and a light brown tint to the mayo and butter. Let cool completely. Add to blender with the remaining mayonnaise, salt, black pepper, and truffle oil. Store in a squeeze bottle.

# Soy Glaze

*Makes 1 cup*

1. Add the brown sugar, soy sauces, garlic, ginger, rice wine, sherry, and rice wine vinegar to a small saucepan and heat until brown sugar is dissolved. Remove from heat.

2. Stir in mirin and fish sauce. Let cool and store in a squeeze bottle.

**Dana's Tip:** A similar bottled alternative can be found in supermarkets or Asian grocers—Kikkoman makes a nice "Unagi" sweet sauce, as well as "Sweet Soy for Sushi."

¼ cup dark brown sugar

¼ cup sweet soy sauce *(which is thicker, similar to molasses, and can be found in Asian markets)*

¼ cup regular soy sauce

1 garlic clove, finely minced

½ teaspoon fresh grated ginger

2 tablespoons rice cooking wine (Shaoxing)

2 tablespoons medium sherry

1 teaspoon rice wine vinegar

1 tablespoon mirin

1 teaspoon fish sauce

# Lobster Bread Pudding

I had a dish at a seafood restaurant many years ago and thought one day I'd try to replicate what I remembered it to be. This recipe is rich, decadent, and everything you want in a small side dish or starter. And it pairs really well with a glass of white Burgundy wine.

*Serves 4*

1. Butter individual 1-cup baking dishes.

2. Coarsely chop the lobster tail and knuckle meat. Finely chop the claw meat and keep it separate.

3. Sauté the shallots in butter and olive oil over medium heat until lightly browned, about 10 minutes. Add the cognac and either ignite to burn off alcohol or cook for 5 minutes to allow most of it to cook off. Add the claw meat and tomato paste during the last 2 minutes of cooking. Let cool 5–10 minutes.

4. Mix mascarpone with sherry, chives, ½ teaspoon salt, and pepper.

5. In a blender, mix the eggs, yolks, cream, half and half, and 1 teaspoon salt until well blended. Fold in thyme leaves.

6. In a large bowl, mix the egg/cream mixture with the bread cubes. Add the shallot/cognac/lobster mixture and toss.

7. Place some of the bread/custard mixture in each baking dish, filling about halfway. Dollop some mascarpone mixture and some lobster chunks, and then top with more bread custard mixture and a few more lobster chunks.

8. Bake covered at 325°F for 35 minutes; then uncover and bake for another 10 minutes. Top with more diced chives.

8 ounces cooked lobster meat (claw separated from tail and knuckle)

2 large shallots, finely diced

2 tablespoons butter plus 2 tablespoons for buttering the ramekins

1 tablespoon olive oil

½ cup cognac

1 tablespoon tomato paste

4 ounces mascarpone, softened

1 tablespoon medium dry sherry

1 tablespoon chives plus some for garnish

1½ teaspoons kosher salt, divided

½ teaspoon pepper

3 large eggs

2 egg yolks

1½ cups heavy cream

½ cup half and half

1 teaspoon fresh thyme leaves

8 ounces of brioche bread or challah, cubed (preferably day old and stale)

# Lobster and Roasted Tomatoes with Ricotta, Mascarpone, and Parmesan

**Roasting the tomatoes before putting this recipe together really enhances the flavor of this rich dish.**

*Serves 3–4*

5 plum tomatoes, halved

2 tablespoons olive oil

½ teaspoon kosher salt, divided

Freshly ground black pepper (to taste)

2 tablespoons butter

½ cup Panko breadcrumbs

1 cup ricotta cheese

2 tablespoons mascarpone

2 garlic cloves, finely minced

¼ cup grated Parmesan cheese

1 cup cooked lobster meat, cut into small chunks

¼ cup shredded Parmesan cheese

1. Preheat oven to 375°F.

2. Place the tomato halves on a baking sheet, sprinkle on 1 tablespoon of the olive oil, ¼ teaspoon salt, and pepper, and roast for an hour.

3. Meanwhile, melt the butter and place into a baking dish. Add Panko to coat the bottom.

4. Mix the ricotta, mascarpone, garlic, remaining ¼ teaspoon of salt, and grated Parmesan cheese together until well blended and place over Panko crumbs. Fold in lobster. Top with the tomato halves and shredded Parmesan cheese. Drizzle remaining tablespoon of olive oil.

5. Bake until hot and cheese is melted, about 20 minutes.

6. Serve with crackers or crusty Italian bread.

# Lobster and Fried Green Tomatoes with Spicy Remoulade

This was the cover dish for my cookbook *The Art of Breakfast*, but that version had shrimp and a poached egg. The shrimp was delicious, but lobster is the best!

*Serves 4*

In a medium bowl, whisk 4 eggs with the milk and set aside.

## To prepare the tomatoes

1. Slice tomatoes into 3–4 equally thick slices, about ¼ inch. Lightly salt and dust with flour.

2. Heat vegetable oil in large, deep pan to about 375°F.

3. Dip each slice of floured tomato into the egg mixture and then into the Panko breadcrumbs, pushing the crumbs onto the surface and coating completely.

4. Add a few tomatoes at a time to the oil, but don't overcrowd. They'll take only 3–4 minutes. Remove and let sit on a paper towel. (You can keep them warm by then moving them to a dry sheet pan and placing in a 225°F oven until ready to serve.)

5. Cook bacon until crisp, drain, and set aside.

6. Add lobster to a small saucepan with 2 tablespoons butter just to warm over low heat 3–4 minutes.

4 large eggs (for dredging)

2 tablespoons milk

2 or 3 large green tomatoes

¼ teaspoon kosher salt

½ cup flour (for dusting)

Vegetable oil (for frying)

2 cups Panko breadcrumbs

4 slices thick-cut bacon, diced and cooked until crisp

8 ounces cooked lobster meat, cut into large chunks

2 tablespoons butter

2 cups loosely packed baby greens or butter lettuce

Remoulade (*see recipe below*)

2 tablespoons thinly sliced scallions (for garnish)

1 tablespoon Fiore
brand chipotle-
flavored olive oil

1 cup mayonnaise

2 tablespoons Dijon
mustard

1 tablespoon
horseradish

1 teaspoon pickle relish

1 tablespoon minced
shallots

1 teaspoon fresh dill

1 teaspoon
Worcestershire sauce

1 teaspoon ketchup

1 teaspoon smoked
paprika

½ teaspoon seafood
seasoning

1 tablespoon fresh diced
chives

¼ teaspoon kosher salt

¼ teaspoon cayenne

1 teaspoon fresh lemon
juice

Freshly ground black
pepper (to taste)

# Remoulade

*Makes about 1¼ cups*

Place all ingredients in blender and mix well. Place in a squeeze bottle and let sit in the refrigerator at least an hour to allow flavors to meld.

# To Assemble

Place a small handful of baby greens on the plate, and then top with fried green tomatoes. Drizzle remoulade on top. Add crumbled bacon and warm lobster. Garnish with a sprinkling of scallions.

# Panko-Fried Lobster Bites with Garlic Mayo

**This recipe seems too simple to be so good, but it is. Sometimes simplicity wins!**

*Serves 2–4 but hard not to eat it all yourself*

1. Bring a large stockpot filled with about 2 inches of water to a boil. Place a steamer basket upside down, and then add the lobsters and cover. Cook for about 5–6 minutes. Pick meat and proceed with the recipe.

2. Add oil to 2- or 3-quart saucepan and fill halfway. Heat to 365–375°F.

3. Beat eggs with heavy cream and set aside.

4. Add Panko to large bowl and set aside.

5. Split lobster tail meat down the center and cut in half, so you end up having long pieces to fry. Try to keep the knuckles in one piece (when they often come out in two separate pieces). The larger the pieces, the easier to fry.

6. Season lobster with salt and dust with flour.

7. Dip lobster into egg and then into Panko.

8. Drop into hot oil and fry until browned, about 3–4 minutes. Drain on paper towel. Lightly salt once fried.

9. Serve with Garlic Mayo.

Four 1¼–1½-pound lobsters (to yield about 1 pound of parcooked meat)

Vegetable oil (for frying)

3 eggs

1 tablespoon heavy cream

2 cups Panko breadcrumbs

Kosher salt (for seasoning lobster)

Flour (for dusting)

Garlic Mayo, for dipping *(see recipe below)*

# Garlic Mayo

*Makes about 1 cup*

Mix all ingredients and let meld for about an hour.

1 cup mayonnaise

2 garlic cloves, minced

1 tablespoon Fiore brand garlic-flavored olive oil

2 teaspoons water

# Coconut-Fried Lobster with Sweet Curry Mango Aioli

I have always enjoyed making coconut-fried shrimp, and I make a curry salad dressing. Why not combine the two? A bit of the tropics to enjoy in this version of a crunchy lobster bite.

*Serves 2–4*

Four 1¼–1½-pound lobsters (to yield about 1 pound of parcooked meat)

Vegetable oil (for frying)

3 eggs

1 tablespoon heavy cream

1¼ cups Panko breadcrumbs

¾ cup shredded sweetened coconut

Kosher salt (for seasoning)

Flour (for dusting)

Sweet Curry Mango Aioli, for dipping *(see recipe below)*

1. Bring a large stockpot filled with about 2 inches of water to a boil. Place a steamer basket upside down, and then add the lobsters and cover. Cook for about 5–6 minutes. Pick meat and proceed with the recipe.

2. Add oil to 2- to 3-quart saucepan and fill halfway. Heat to 365–375°F.

3. Beat eggs with heavy cream and set aside.

4. Add Panko and coconut to large bowl and set aside.

5. Split lobster tail meat down the center and cut in half, so you end up having long pieces to fry. Try to keep the knuckles in one piece (they often come out in two separate pieces). The larger the pieces, the easier to fry.

6. Season lobster with salt and dust with flour.

7. Dip lobster into egg and then into Panko.

8. Drop into hot oil and fry until browned, about 3–4 minutes. Drain on paper towel. Lightly salt once fried. Serve with Sweet Curry Mango Aioli for dipping.

# Sweet Curry Mango Aioli

*Makes about 1 cup*

Mix all ingredients and let meld for about an hour.

1 cup mayonnaise

2 teaspoons curry powder

2 tablespoons Mango Coulis *(see recipe below)*

# Mango Coulis

*Makes 2 cups*

1.  Combine the mango, sugar, and lemon juice in a blender and puree for about 20 seconds.

2.  Push through a fine-mesh sieve or a strainer.

3.  Store in a plastic airtight container or squeeze bottles up to 1 week in the refrigerator or 4 weeks in the freezer (if you freeze it, leave room at the top for expansion).

1 (24-ounce) bag frozen mango, thawed, draining most of the visible excess liquid

½ cup powdered sugar

1 tablespoon fresh lemon juice

# Grilled Bacon-Wrapped Lobster Skewers with Garlic Mayo for Dipping

I will warn you that wrapping the bacon around the lobster and grilling isn't easy, but it's worth the results for the taste. Not all dishes are perfect for plating!

*Serves 4 (as small bites)*

1. If you use bamboo skewers, soak in water for 30 minutes.

2. Precook bacon at 350°F for about 15 minutes until some fat is rendered but bacon is still very pliable. Set aside.

3. Steam lobster for 6 minutes. When cool enough to handle, twist off tail and slice down the middle lengthwise. Remove meat from claws and knuckles.

4. Wrap bacon over sections of lobster and place on skewers, using the skewer to secure the ends of the bacon.

5. Grill lobster over medium heat, flesh side down first, for 5 minutes. Flip and grill another 4 minutes. Serve with Garlic Mayo.

6–8 skewers depending on length

8 slices bacon

2 lobsters, about 1¼–1½ pounds each

Garlic Mayo, for dipping *(see recipe below)*

## Garlic Mayo

*Makes about 1 cup*

Mix all ingredients and let meld for about an hour.

1 cup mayonnaise

2 garlic cloves, minced

1 tablespoon Fiore brand garlic-flavored olive oil

2 teaspoons water

# Lobster Bruschetta with Fresh Tomato, Corn, Scallions, and Roasted Tomato Aioli

Crunchy toasted sourdough or baguette topped with this fresh mixture is a nice alternative to traditional bruschetta.

*Makes 4–6*

1. Thinly slice baguette on a bias and toast until lightly golden. Set aside.

2. Mix corn, tomatoes, and scallions and season with salt and pepper. Set aside.

3. Spread some Roasted Tomato Aioli on each slice of crostini, top with tomato/corn mixture and some lobster chunks. Garnish with microgreens.

1 small baguette

2 tablespoons cooked fresh corn from the cob

8 cherry tomatoes, thinly sliced

2 scallion stalks, thinly sliced

⅛ teaspoon kosher salt

Freshly ground black pepper (to taste)

Roasted Tomato Aioli *(see recipe below)*

8 ounces cooked lobster meat

Microgreens (for garnish)

# Roasted Tomato Aioli

*Makes about 1½ cups*

1. Preheat oven to 375°F.

2. Season tomatoes and shallots with salt and pepper.

3. Drizzle both with olive oil and roast (cut side up) for 40 minutes (remove the shallot if it cooks and caramelizes faster than the tomatoes). Let cool 15 minutes.

4. In a blender, add the tomatoes, shallots, garlic, smoked paprika, and mayonnaise, and blend until smooth. Add salt to taste.

3 Roma tomatoes, halved

1 large shallot, quartered

¼ teaspoon kosher salt

¼ teaspoon black pepper

1 tablespoon olive oil, for roasting

2 garlic cloves, minced

1 teaspoon smoked paprika

1 cup mayonnaise

# Lobster and Sliced Filet Mignon with Horseradish Cream on Crostini

**This surf-and-turf bruschetta is reminiscent of prime rib with horseradish sauce. I love the simplicity of sliced tenderloin, the creamy sauce, and lobster. The flavors work so nicely together.**

*Makes 8–10*

1 baguette

⅓ cup mayonnaise

1 tablespoon prepared horseradish

½ teaspoon kosher salt, plus some for seasoning filet

¼ teaspoon white pepper

1 (4-ounce) petite filet mignon

Black pepper (for seasoning filet)

Olive oil (for seasoning filet)

8 ounces cooked lobster meat

1. Thinly slice baguette on a bias and toast until lightly golden. Set aside.

2. Mix mayonnaise, horseradish, salt, and white pepper and let meld in the refrigerator for at least an hour.

3. Season both sides of filet with salt and black pepper, and drizzle a small amount of olive oil. Grill over medium-high heat, about 10–12 minutes (if about 1 inch thick) for medium rare. Let rest and cool for at least 20 minutes before slicing.

4. Spread some horseradish cream on crostini, and top with a couple slices of filet and a few chunks of lobster. Very simple and a delicious way to have your surf and turf!

# Potato and Scallion Latkes Topped with Butter-Poached Lobster, Lemon Zest, Sour Cream, Red Onion, and Fresh Dill

Potato latkes are one of my favorite dishes to make for any time of day. I used to make them at the inn and use them as the vessel for a poached egg in lieu of an English muffin. Topped with creamed spinach and lemon, they're a delicious breakfast or brunch. I came up with this version for a catered dinner, and they're perfect because it isn't crucial they be served hot. In fact, they are better closer to warm/room temperature so that the sour cream doesn't just melt.

*Makes 16 latkes*

1. In a small saucepan, add 1 stick butter and cook over medium-low heat until milk solids have fully separated, about 6–7 minutes.

2. Strain through a fine-mesh sieve and place in large sauté pan. Add lobster, reduce heat to a low simmer, and cook until lobster is fully opaque, but cook slowly to avoid overcooking—about 7–8 minutes. Remove lobster and set aside and let cool to room temperature.

3. Mix sour cream, salt, lemon zest, lemon juice, and fresh dill and let meld for at least 30 minutes.

1 stick butter

16 ounces raw lobster meat

½ cup sour cream

½ teaspoon kosher salt

Zest from 1 lemon

Juice from ½ lemon

1 tablespoon fresh dill (for garnish)

1 tablespoon minced red onion (for garnish)

# Potato Latkes

*Makes about 16 three-inch latkes*

- 3 large Russet or Idaho potatoes
- 1 medium yellow or sweet onion
- ½ cup thinly sliced scallions
- 3 eggs
- ¾ cup flour
- 1½ teaspoons baking powder
- 1½ teaspoons kosher salt
- ¼ teaspoon freshly ground black pepper
- ½ teaspoon onion powder
- 2 cups vegetable oil for frying (or enough to come up about ¼ inch from the bottom of the pan)

1. In a food processor, using the medium shredding disc, process the potatoes and onion and set into a large mixing bowl.

2. Add the scallions, eggs, flour, baking powder, salt, pepper, and onion powder, and mix until well blended.

3. In a large frying pan, heat vegetable oil until hot.

4. Take about ⅓ cup of the mixture and shape it into a flat disc as best you can; then carefully add to the oil, trying to keep its round shape. Fry for 3–4 minutes, until brown on one side. Flip, cooking another 3 minutes until browned. Remove to a paper towel. Repeat until all the latkes are fried.

5. You can keep them warm in a 250°F oven on a rack placed on a sheet pan (so they are elevated and air can circulate under) until ready to serve. Or keep them at room temperature for an hour or so and reheat before serving.

# To Assemble

Place a couple teaspoons of the lemon zest sour cream atop each potato latke. Divide the lobster among the latkes. Top with a scattering of red onion and a sprig of fresh dill.

# Jerk-Spiced Sweet Potato Latkes Topped with Butter-Poached Lobster and Mango Jalapeño Salsa

Because I like to combine sweet, spicy, and savory, this recipe was a twist on the regular potato latkes I came up with based on my love of jerk chicken.

*Makes 18–20 mini latkes*

## Butter-Poached Lobster

In a small saucepan, add 1 stick butter and cook over medium-low heat until milk solids have fully separated, about 6 or 7 minutes. Strain through a fine-mesh sieve and place clarified butter in large sauté pan. Add 1 pound of raw, picked lobster meat, reduce heat to a low simmer, and cook until lobster is fully opaque, but cook slowly to avoid overcooking—about 7–8 minutes. Remove lobster and set aside to cool to room temperature. If using cooked meat instead of raw, warm lobster in 1 tablespoon of butter over low heat for just 2 minutes to bring the lobster to room temperature.

1 stick butter

1 pound raw lobster meat

Sweet Potato Latkes *(see recipe below)*

Mango Jalapeño Salsa *(see recipe below)*

## Sweet Potato Latkes

1. In a food processor, using the medium shredding disc, process the potatoes and onion and set into a large mixing bowl.

2. Add the eggs, flour, baking powder, salt, pepper, cinnamon, thyme, cayenne, nutmeg, paprika, and sugar, and mix until well blended.

3. In a large frying pan, heat vegetable oil until hot. Take about ⅓ cup of the mixture and shape it into a flat disc as best you can; then carefully add to the oil, trying to keep its round shape.

4. Fry for 3–4 minutes, until brown on one side. Flip, cooking another 3 minutes until browned. Remove to a paper towel. Repeat until all the latkes are fried.

5. You can keep them warm in a 250°F oven on a rack placed on a sheet pan (to elevate and allow air to circulate under) until ready to serve. Serve with Mango Jalapeño Salsa for dipping.

2 large sweet potatoes

1 medium yellow or sweet onion

3 eggs

¾ cup flour

1½ teaspoons baking powder

1 teaspoon kosher salt

¼ teaspoon freshly ground black pepper

¼ teaspoon cinnamon

¼ teaspoon thyme

⅛ teaspoon cayenne

⅛ teaspoon nutmeg

¼ teaspoon smoked paprika

1 teaspoon sugar

2 cups vegetable oil for frying (or enough to come up about ¼ inch from the bottom of the pan)

## Mango Jalapeño Salsa

*Makes about 1 cup*

Mix all ingredients and refrigerate until ready to use.

2 ripe mangoes, cut into a medium-small dice

1 small jalapeño, finely diced

1 small red bell pepper, finely diced

⅛ teaspoon kosher salt

# Chilled Lobster Meat Cocktail with Smoked Red Pepper Aioli

**Classic, unadulterated lobster meat. But instead of cocktail sauce, give it a try with this Smoked Red Pepper Aioli.**

*Serves 4*

4 (1½-pound) live lobsters (or if you want to serve all tail meat, it's up to you how generous you want to be!)

Smoked Red Pepper Aioli, for dipping *(see recipe below)*

Parsley or diced chives (for garnish)

1. Steam the lobsters for 12 minutes.

2. When cool, pick and chill the meat.

3. Serve with the Smoked Red Pepper Aioli and garnish with parsley or diced chives.

# Smoked Red Pepper Aioli

*Makes about 1½ cups*

1 red bell pepper, quartered, ribs and seeds removed

1 tablespoon olive oil (for smoking)

2 egg yolks

½ teaspoon kosher salt (plus some for sprinkling on the pepper)

½ teaspoon sugar

½ teaspoon black pepper

½ cup good-quality olive oil (mild)

1. Drizzle the cut pepper with the olive oil, sprinkle with salt, and place in smoker. For the smoking, you can use either an outdoor smoker or a stovetop smoker. I use a Cameron stovetop smoker, but I use it on the grill to keep the smoke outdoors. Smoke for about 25–30 minutes over medium heat. If it has been adequately smoked, you'll see a slight golden brown tint to the pepper slices. Remove, let cool, and remove skin from peppers.

2. Add peppers to food processor and process until smooth. Add the egg yolks, salt, sugar, and black pepper and turn on processor, and then add the oil in a slow stream to blend. Adjust salt or pepper if needed. Store in a squeeze bottle.

**Dana's Tip:** You can also use a good-quality prepared mayonnaise instead of making your own.

# Lobster Panna Cotta

Panna cotta is an Italian dessert made of sweetened cream and gelatin and flavored in a variety of ways. I used to make various sweet panna cottas to serve with berries at the inn. But I am most intrigued by a savory variety. And this one is a bit firmer than a mousse and has a nice smoky flavor from the smoked red pepper mayo, not unlike a smoked salmon pâté. But with lobster!

*Serves 8*

1. For the smoking, you can use either an outdoor smoker or a stovetop smoker. I use a Cameron stovetop smoker, but I use it on the grill to keep the smoke outdoors.

2. Place butter in an ovenproof dish and place in smoker (following the manufacturer's instructions). Smoke for about 25 minutes. If it has been adequately smoked, you'll see browned bits along the edge of the baking dish and a light golden tint to the butter. Let cool.

3. Add lobster to a saucepan with smoked butter and heat to a simmer. Cook until lobster is fully opaque, but cook slowly to avoid overcooking—about 7–8 minutes. Remove lobster and set aside. When cool, cut ½ cup into a small dice, leaving the remaining ½ cup in larger pieces to top the dish.

4. Mix the gelatin and water in a small saucepan and let soften for 2 minutes. Heat over low until the gelatin is dissolved, about 1 minute. Remove from heat.

5. In a medium saucepan, add the cream and half and half. Bring to a boil over medium heat. Once just boiling, remove the pan from the heat and add the cream cheese, poached lobster, smoked butter from poaching lobster, Smoked Red Pepper Mayo, salt, and melted gelatin mixture. Mix well with a whisk. Cool 15 minutes.

½ stick butter

1 cup raw lobster

1 envelope unflavored gelatin

2 tablespoons cold water

1 cup heavy cream

½ cup half and half

4 ounces whipped cream cheese

2 tablespoons Smoked Red Pepper Mayo *(see recipe below)*

½ teaspoon kosher salt

Vegetable oil (for coating ramekins)

6. Coat individual ramekins or a baking dish with vegetable oil and divide/fill evenly with the cream mixture. Cover with plastic wrap and chill overnight, or at least 6 hours.

7. Run a sharp knife around the edge to loosen the suction. Carefully pop out onto plates and serve with microgreens and top with remaining chunks of lobster.

## Smoked Red Pepper Mayo

*Makes about 1½ cups*

1. Drizzle the cut pepper with the olive oil, sprinkle with salt, and place in smoker. For the smoking, you can use either an outdoor smoker or a stovetop smoker. I use a Cameron stovetop smoker, but I use it on the grill to keep the smoke outdoors. Smoke for about 25–30 minutes over medium heat. If it has been adequately smoked, you'll see a slight golden brown tint to the pepper slices. Remove, let cool, and remove skin from peppers.

2. Add peppers to a food processor and process until smooth. Add the mayo and process to blend. Adjust salt or pepper if needed. Store in a squeeze bottle.

1 red bell pepper, quartered, ribs and seeds removed

1 tablespoon olive oil (for smoking)

1 cup prepared mayonnaise

½ teaspoon kosher salt

# Lobster and Scallion Cream Cheese Hand Pies

This is the kind of dish that is born from another creation. The Lobster Scallion Cream Cheese Spread that I love on a bagel or crackers found its way into pastry dough for these adorable little hand pies!

*Makes 8–10*

Pastry Crust *(see recipe below)*

1 cup Lobster Scallion Cream Cheese Spread *(see page 74)*

½ cup chopped cooked lobster meat

½ teaspoon granulated garlic

½ teaspoon sweet paprika

4 ounces plain whipped cream cheese

1 egg plus 1 teaspoon milk for egg wash

Kosher salt (for dusting)

1. Prepare Pastry Crust rounds and set aside.

2. Prepare Lobster Scallion Cream Cheese Spread and set aside.

3. Fold lobster meat, garlic, paprika, and whipped cream cheese into the Lobster Scallion Cream Cheese Spread. Place a tablespoon of the mixture on the center of each pastry round and fold over. Crimp the edges with a fork to seal.

4. Brush edges with egg wash, sprinkle with salt, and bake at 400°F for about 18 minutes, until golden brown.

# Pastry Crust

1½ sticks very cold
  unsalted butter

3 cups all-purpose flour

1 teaspoon kosher salt

1 tablespoon sugar

⅓ cup very cold
  vegetable shortening

6–7 tablespoons (about
  ½ cup or less) ice
  water

1.  Preheat oven to 400°F.

2.  Dice the butter and return it to the refrigerator while you prepare the flour mixture.

3.  Place the flour, salt, and sugar in the bowl of a food processor fitted with a blade and pulse a couple times to incorporate.

4.  Add the butter and shortening. Pulse 8–12 times, until the butter is the size of peas.

5.  With the machine running, pour the ice water down the feed tube and pulse the machine until the dough begins to form a ball. Place dough on a floured board and roll into a ball. Wrap in plastic and refrigerate for 30 minutes.

6.  Cut the dough in half. Roll each piece on a floured board into a circle, turning and flouring the dough as needed to make sure it doesn't stick to the board.

7.  Using a biscuit cutter, cut into 4-inch rounds and set aside.

# Sweet and Spicy Chili Glazed Lobster

This is my interpretation of a dish I've had at a chain restaurant. I love the flavors and the light coating on the lobster.

*Serves 3–4 as a small appetizer*

1. Bring a large stockpot filled with about 2 inches of water to a boil. Place a steamer basket upside down, and then add the lobsters and cover. Cook for about 5–6 minutes. Pick meat, set aside, and proceed with the recipe.

2. In a small bowl, add the Chili Sauce.

3. In a second bowl, add the lobster and buttermilk and stir to coat all the lobster.

4. Remove from the buttermilk and let excess drain away.

5. Coat the lobster in cornstarch.

6. In a 2- to 3-quart heavy saucepan, add 2–3 inches of vegetable oil and heat to 375°F. Fry the lobster until light golden brown, about 3 minutes.

7. Once fried, coat with the Chili Sauce and serve immediately.

Four 1¼–1½-pound lobsters (to yield about 1 pound of parcooked meat)

¼ cup Chili Sauce *(see recipe below)*

½ cup buttermilk

¾ cup cornstarch

Vegetable oil (for frying)

# Chili Sauce

*Makes about 1 cup*

1. Add the rice vinegar, sugar, water, and sambal oelek to a small sauce pot. Heat and stir the mixture over medium heat until the sugar fully dissolves.

2. Stir the cornstarch into 1 tablespoon water until dissolved, and then pour it into the sauce pot with the sweet chili sauce. Continue stirring and heating until the mixture comes up to a boil. Continue to cook for 1 minute and then let cool.

3. Mix in mayonnaise.

½ cup rice vinegar

½ cup sugar

¼ cup water

1½ tablespoons sambal oelek

½ tablespoon cornstarch plus 1 tablespoon water

½ cup mayonnaise

# DIPS AND SPREADS

# Chilled Lobster Butter

This delicious recipe results from poaching lobster in butter. It's packed with flavor and perfect for use in soups, stews, sauces, and more. (In the photo, the green lobster is the wasabi brown butter found in other recipes; the orange is the lobster butter.)

1. In a small saucepan, add 1 stick butter and cook over medium-low heat until milk solids have fully separated, about 6 or 7 minutes. Strain through a fine-mesh sieve and place in a large sauté pan.

2. Add lobster, reduce heat to a low simmer, and cook until lobster is fully opaque, but cook slowly to avoid overcooking—about 7–8 minutes. Remove lobster and set aside.

3. Strain the lobster cooking butter/liquid and cool in the refrigerator. The resulting "lobster butter" will float to the top and the lobster cooking juices will remain on the bottom. *SAVE* the juices, too. Both can be used in a variety of dishes. Lobster butter on a popover with lobster stew or bisque is wonderful!

1 stick of butter

1 pound raw lobster meat

# Lobster and Scallion Cream Cheese Spread

This spread is my idea of the perfect bagel topping for a change of pace from smoked salmon and cream cheese.

*Makes about 1 cup*

½ stick butter

½ cup raw lobster

6 ounces whipped cream cheese

2 tablespoons scallions, thinly sliced

½ teaspoon Old Bay seasoning

½ teaspoon kosher salt

¼ teaspoon freshly ground black pepper

1.  For the smoking, you can use either an outdoor smoker or a stove-top smoker. I use a Cameron stovetop smoker, but I use it on the grill to keep the smoke outdoors.

2.  Place butter in an ovenproof dish and place in smoker (following the manufacturer's instructions). Smoke for about 25 minutes. If it has been adequately smoked, you'll see browned bits along the edge of the baking dish and a light golden tint to the butter. Let cool.

3.  Add lobster to a saucepan with smoked butter and heat to a simmer. Cook until lobster is fully opaque, but cook slowly to avoid over-cooking—about 7–8 minutes. Remove lobster and set aside. When cool, cut into small bite-size chunks.

4.  Mix poached lobster and smoked butter used for poaching, cream cheese, scallions, Old Bay, salt, and pepper, and mix well.

5.  Chill in refrigerator until ready to use.

6.  Serve with toasted bagels, crusty bread, or crackers.

# Creamy Lobster, Shrimp, and Parmesan Dip

This recipe is a real crowd pleaser that's perfect for a happy hour get-together, a football game snack, or a great topping for poached eggs.

*Serves 2–4*

1. Preheat oven to 375°F.

2. Bring a large stockpot filled with about 2 inches of water to a boil. Place a steamer basket upside down, and then add the lobster and cover. Cook for about 5–6 minutes. Pick meat and proceed with the recipe.

3. Mix all ingredients and put into greased baking dish. Bake until lightly browned and bubbly, about 25 minutes.

One 1¼–1½-pound lobster (to yield about ½ cup of parcooked meat, diced)

½ cup Parmesan cheese

3 ounces Fontina cheese, cut into small cubes

1 garlic clove, minced

2 tablespoon raw shrimp, diced

1 cup mayonnaise

# Fondue with Grilled Lobster, Asparagus, and Baby Potatoes

**Because fondue. And lobster. Enough said? Along with lobster, crusty bread and fondue are two of my favorite foods. I think I have cheese in my DNA!**

*Serves 4*

12 baby potatoes (white, red, or purple)

8 asparagus spears

3 lobsters, about 1½ pounds each

Olive oil (for grilling lobster and potatoes)

8 ounces shredded Swiss cheese

8 ounces shredded Gruyère cheese

1 tablespoon cornstarch

1 garlic clove, minced

½ cup dry white wine (I like a crisp Sauvignon Blanc)

½ teaspoon kosher salt

1. Halve the potatoes and boil until tender. Remove potatoes and set aside.

2. Boil asparagus in the same pot of water for 2 minutes. Remove from water and set aside.

3. Steam lobster for 6 minutes. When cool enough to handle, place lobster shell side down, and slice into the tail but don't cut all the way through. You're just trying to expose the meat to the heat/flame. Crack the claw sections slightly. Brush with olive oil.

4. Grill lobster over medium heat, flesh side down first, for 5 minutes. Flip and grill another 4 minutes.

5. Brush potato halves with oil and grill for a few minutes cut side down. You can skip this step, but the grill adds such nice flavor.

6. Mix cheeses with cornstarch in a large bowl.

7. Add the garlic and wine to the fondue dish or saucepan and increase the heat until the wine comes to a boil.

8. Lower heat and slowly add cheese, ½ cup at a time, stirring constantly over low heat, until melted. Add salt to taste.

9. Serve cheese with grilled lobster, potatoes, and asparagus.

# SOUPS AND SALADS

# Lobster Stock

Many good dishes begin with a good homemade stock, including my Lobster Bloody Marys. Making your own is worth the effort. You can also freeze it in ice cube trays, and when you need a pop of lobster flavor, you have it at the ready.

*Makes about 4 cups*

1. Heat oven to 375°F.

2. With the back of a heavy knife, crush the lobster shells and heads. Chop carrot and onion roughly.

3. Roast lobster shells with the onions with a drizzle of olive oil for 30 minutes.

4. In an 8-quart heavy stockpot, heat oil and butter over medium heat; add carrot, onion, tomato paste, and wine, and simmer until most of wine is evaporated. Add water, bay leaves, and peppercorns, and simmer until liquid is reduced to about 4 cups, about 1½ hours.

5. Pour stock through a fine-mesh sieve into a heatproof bowl. Stock may be made three days ahead. Stock keeps frozen for three months.

Shells and heads from 3 cooked (1¼-pound) lobsters

1 large carrot

2 onions

Olive oil (for drizzling lobster shells)

2 tablespoons vegetable oil

½ stick butter

3 tablespoons tomato paste

1 cup dry white wine

8 cups water

2 bay leaves

1 tablespoon black peppercorns

A few thyme sprigs

1 stick butter

1 large onion

1 large poblano pepper, finely diced

4 strips bacon, chopped

8 ounces frozen corn

1 small can green chiles

¾ cup flour

5 cups chicken stock

1 tablespoon "Better than Bouillon Lobster Base" for soups (alternatively, add 1 cup of homemade Lobster Stock [see page 83] with 4 cups chicken stock)

1 tablespoon chile oil or more to taste (I use Fiore's "Green Baklouti" olive oil—a Maine company)

1 cup milk (2 percent or whole)

1 cup half and half

1 cup sweet/spicy pepper mustard

16 ounces shredded sharp cheddar cheese (shred from a block for the best quality)

1 pound cooked lobster meat, cut into chunks, reserving a couple pieces for garnish

1 tablespoon freshly ground pepper

Kosher salt to taste

Red bell pepper, diced (for garnish)

Minced chives (for garnish)

# Sweet and Spicy Lobster, Bacon, and Poblano Corn Chowder

I won the People's Choice award in a cooking competition at Cellardoor Winery in Lincolnville, Maine, with this dish! It's creamy, rich, sweet, and spicy. Great comfort food.

*Makes approximately 4 quarts*

1. In large soup or stock pot, melt butter, add onions, poblano, and bacon, and sauté over medium-high heat for about 15 minutes.

2. Stir in corn and canned chiles and cook another few minutes. Add flour and stir for 2 minutes.

3. Add stock, lobster base, chile oil, milk, and half and half, and stir until thickened over medium heat, about 10 minutes.

4. Lower heat to a simmer (do not boil, or milk solids will separate). Add mustard and cheese, stir, and cover until fully melted and soup is hot, about 10 minutes.

5. Add the lobster meat and cook another 5 minutes. Garnish with remaining lobster chunks, diced red bell pepper, and chives.

# Lobster Bisque

Cream, butter, sherry, lobster. Is there anything more comforting? This is a classic pureed soup, but my version leaves some of the vegetables out prior to pureeing for a bit more texture within the silky smooth bisque.

*Serves 4*

1. Toast baguette cubes in a 350°F oven until crispy, about 15 minutes. Set aside.

2. In a large sauté pan, add butter and heat over a low simmer. Add lobster, lower heat to a simmer, and cook until lobster is fully opaque, but cook slowly to avoid overcooking—about 7–8 minutes. Remove lobster and set aside. When cool, cut into small bite-size chunks.

3. Strain the lobster cooking butter/liquid and cool in the refrigerator. The resulting "lobster butter" will float to the top, and the lobster cooking juices will remain on the bottom. SAVE the juices to add back to this bisque along with the Lobster Stock.

4. Add the remaining butter from poaching the lobster to a clean sauté pan over medium flame.

5. Add onion and shallot, and cook until translucent.

6. Add carrots and celery and continue to sauté until vegetables are softened and lightly browned, about 10 minutes. Season with salt and pepper to taste. Set half of the mixture aside.

7. Add the tomato paste to the pan and cook for 2 minutes.

8. Add the flour and cook another 2 minutes.

9. Add the sherry, Lobster Stock, along with juices from the poaching liquid, half and half, heavy cream, and thyme leaves, and lower heat to simmer and stir regularly. Cook 20 minutes.

1 small baguette, cubed

6 tablespoons butter

1 pound raw lobster meat

1 small onion, finely diced

1 large shallot, finely diced

2 carrots, cut into small dice

2 celery ribs, cut into small dice

1 tablespoon tomato paste

2 tablespoons flour

1 cup medium dry sherry

2 cups Lobster Stock (*see page 83*)

1 cup half and half

1 cup heavy cream

2 thyme sprigs

Parsley or diced chives (for garnish)

Kosher salt and freshly ground black pepper to taste

10. Add half of the cooked lobster to the pan (reserving tails if you've used them) and cook for 1 minute.

11. Pour soup into a blender, or using a stick blender, puree soup until smooth.

12. Add soup back to the pan, stir in the reserved vegetables and remaining lobster, and heat for 3 minutes. Season again with salt and pepper to taste.

Serve with garlic croutons and garnish with parsley or diced chives.

# Lobster Wonton Soup with Lobster- and Pork-Filled Wontons and Lobster and Pork Meatballs

Another way to enjoy filled wontons! Make a big batch and freeze them uncooked. Then you can choose whether to enjoy them pan fried *(see page 17)*, deep fried *(see page 18)*, or boiled as I've done in this recipe. Versatility in the kitchen is good!

*Makes approximately 2½ quarts of soup and 48 wontons*

## Lobster- and Pork-Filled Wontons

1.  Combine pork, lobster, cabbage, ginger, garlic, scallion whites, and soy sauce in a bowl. Roll about 2 teaspoons to make 8 miniature meatballs, and set the rest of the mixture aside.

2.  Cook the 8 meatballs in a sauté pan with a couple teaspoons of vegetable oil over medium heat for 5 minutes and then set aside until ready to add to the broth.

3.  Lay a wrapper on a clean, dry surface, and, using your finger or a brush, spread a bit of egg along half of the wrapper. Place a rounded teaspoon of remaining filling in center, fold over, and seal by pinching edges together. (Do not overfill.) Place wontons on a plate; if you want to wait a few hours before cooking, cover plate with plastic wrap and refrigerate. Freeze the wontons you aren't ready to cook (they'll last up to two weeks). You'll have about 10 wrappers left over after you've filled them, which are perfect for making your own fried wontons for garnish. Set aside until ready to cook in soup broth (recipe to follow).

½ pound ground pork

½ pound finely chopped cooked lobster meat

½ cup minced Napa cabbage

1 tablespoon minced ginger

1 tablespoon minced garlic

6 scallions, white parts only, minced

2 tablespoons soy sauce

48 dumpling or wonton wrappers (standard package size)

1 egg, lightly beaten in a bowl

# Wonton Soup Broth

1.  Place all broth ingredients (and only half of the scallions) in a large stockpot and bring to a boil. Reduce heat to medium low and cook for 20 minutes. Remove ginger.

2.  Add the number of filled wontons you intend to serve along with the meatballs and simmer 3–4 minutes.

3.  Serve 2–3 wontons and 2 meatballs per bowl. Garnish with remaining scallions and fried wontons (you can use the store-bought version, but wonton wrappers fried at home are much better!).

32 ounces chicken stock

32 ounces mushroom stock

12 ounces shiitake mushrooms

1 bunch of scallions, thinly sliced on a bias

2 tablespoons soy sauce

2 teaspoons chile oil

1-inch piece of peeled ginger

1 garlic clove, sliced

¼ cup Shaoxing rice cooking wine

2 teaspoons kosher salt

½ teaspoon ground white pepper

12 purple and white baby potatoes

2 teaspoons kosher salt for boiling potatoes

½ pound fresh green beans, trimmed

Ice water for green beans and eggs

4 large eggs, room temperature

¼ cup red wine vinegar

1 tablespoon Dijon mustard

1 small shallot, finely diced

2 small garlic cloves, minced

1 teaspoon fresh thyme leaves

¼ teaspoon kosher salt

½ teaspoon honey

1 cup extra-virgin olive oil

1 head of Bibb lettuce

1 small head of Baby Gems lettuce (preferably a purple/red variety)

1 pound cooked lobster meat, cut into chunks, kept chilled *(let sit at room temperature before assembling the salad)*

¼ cup mixed whole olives

Freshly ground black pepper (to taste)

1 tablespoon minced chives

# Lobster Salad Niçoise

**With green beans, baby potatoes, olives, hard-cooked eggs, cherry tomatoes, and Bibb and Baby Gems lettuce. A bright vinaigrette and briny olives bring the perfect balance to the eggs and potatoes in this elegant salad.**

*Serves 4*

1. Bring a large pot of water to a boil. Add salt and potatoes, and cook for 12 minutes or until tender when tested with a sharp knife. Remove and let cool.

2. Add green beans to the salted water and cook 3 minutes. Transfer to a bowl of ice water and let sit for 3 minutes. Drain and dry green beans.

3. In a clean pot, add water and eggs and bring to a boil. Cook 11 minutes. Drain and transfer to a bowl of ice water. Let sit 4–5 minutes. Peel and slice eggs.

4. In a bowl, whisk red wine vinegar, Dijon mustard, shallot, garlic, thyme, salt, and honey.

5. Slowly add the olive oil while whisking to emulsify. Adjust salt and pepper to taste.

6. Clean and tear lettuce leaves, toss with a couple tablespoons of dressing, and add to platter.

7. Place lobster, green beans, sliced eggs, and olives atop lettuce. Add dressing over the top and sprinkle with freshly ground black pepper and chives.

# Lobster Louie Salad with Snap Peas, Tomatoes, Hard-Cooked Eggs, and Avocado

One of my favorite salad experiences was in San Francisco, where I had a classic crab Louie salad. The dressing could not be easier to make, and the combination of flavors is a classic. I used snap peas instead of green beans in this version.

*Serves 4*

1. Cut iceberg lettuce into 4 wedges, removing the very outer leaves.

2. Blanch snap peas for 3 minutes in boiling water and then shock in ice water to stop the cooking.

3. Add eggs to the boiling water and cook for 11 minutes. When done, place in a bowl of ice water to cool. Peel eggs and set aside until ready to assemble.

4. Halve cherry tomatoes.

5. Slice avocado.

6. Slice eggs.

7. Finely mince chives.

1 head of iceberg lettuce

1 cup snap peas

Ice water for snap peas and eggs

4 hard-cooked eggs

½ cup cherry tomatoes, halved.

1 avocado, sliced

Chives (for garnish)

Louie Dressing *(see recipe below)*

12 ounces cooked lobster meat, cut into large chunks

## Louie Dressing

1 cup mayonnaise

3 tablespoons ketchup

1 teaspoon
 Worcestershire sauce

1 tablespoon lemon
 juice

1 teaspoon prepared
 horseradish

1 teaspoon sweet
 paprika

⅛ teaspoon cayenne

Mix all ingredients and let meld for at least an hour before serving.

## To Assemble

Place a wedge on each plate. Top with a couple tablespoons of dressing, scatter the tomatoes and snap peas. Then place sliced eggs and avocado beside the wedge. Add lobster over the top and garnish with chives. *If you're like me, add more dressing!*

# Pacific Rim Lobster Salad with Napa Cabbage, Carrots, Scallions, Mango, Red Pepper Aioli, Soy Glaze, and Wonton Chips

These flavors are some of my favorites combined into one dish. The steps are worth the effort for the flavor explosion your taste buds will enjoy!

*Serves 4*

1. Fry wonton triangles in 375°F oil until browned, about 30 seconds per side.

2. Drain, salt, and cool completely. Keep in an airtight container until ready to use.

3. Thinly slice shallots and fry in 375°F oil until browned. Drain on towel until ready to use.

12 wonton wrappers, cut on a diagonal

Vegetable oil (for frying shallots and wontons)

¼ teaspoon sea salt

2 large shallots

Brown Butter–Poached Lobster *(see recipe below)*

1 cup thinly sliced Napa cabbage, leafy parts only

¼ cup thinly julienned carrots

1 bunch of scallions, thinly sliced on a bias

4 cups baby greens

1 fresh mango, finely diced

1 red bell pepper, finely diced

1 small jalapeño, finely diced

Smoked Red Pepper Aioli *(see recipe below)*

Soy Glaze *(see recipe below)*

Sesame seeds (for garnish)

# Brown Butter–Poached Lobster

1. In small saucepan, add 1 stick butter and cook over medium-low heat until lightly brown in color and milk solids have fully separated, about 8–10 minutes, watching very carefully not to burn the butter.

2. Strain through a fine-mesh sieve, place in large sauté pan, and heat butter over medium low for 1 minute.

3. Add lobster, lower heat to a simmer, and cook until lobster is fully opaque, but cook slowly to avoid overcooking—about 7–8 minutes.

4. Remove lobster and set aside.

5. When cool, cut into small bite-size chunks.

**1 stick butter (for poaching)**

**8 ounces raw picked lobster meat**

# Smoked Red Pepper Aioli

*Makes about 1½ cups*

1 red bell pepper,
   quartered, ribs and
   seeds removed

1 tablespoon olive oil
   (for smoking)

2 egg yolks

½ teaspoon kosher salt

½ teaspoon sugar

½ teaspoon black
   pepper

½ cup good-quality
   olive oil (mild)

1.  Drizzle the cut pepper with 1 tablespoon of the olive oil, sprinkle with salt, and place in smoker. For the smoking, you can use either an outdoor smoker or a stovetop smoker. I use a Cameron stovetop smoker, but I use it on the grill to keep the smoke outdoors. Smoke for about 20 minutes over medium heat. If it has been adequately smoked, you'll see a slight golden brown tint to the pepper slices. Remove, let cool, and remove skin from peppers.

2.  Add peppers to food processor and process until smooth. Add the egg yolks, salt, sugar, and black pepper and turn on processor, and then add the oil in a slow stream to blend. Adjust salt or pepper if needed. Store in a squeeze bottle.

# Soy Glaze

*Makes about 1 cup*

1. Add the brown sugar, soy sauces, garlic, ginger, rice wine, sherry, and rice wine vinegar to a small saucepan, and heat until brown sugar is dissolved. Remove from heat.

2. Stir in mirin and fish sauce.

3. Let cool and store in a squeeze bottle.

**Dana's Tip: A very good store-bought alternative is "Sweet Soy for Sushi" by Kikkoman.**

# To Assemble

Mix the cabbage, carrots, scallions, greens, fried shallots, mango, red pepper, and jalapeño and mix well. Place a serving into dish, and add a good drizzle of the Red Pepper Aioli and drizzle of Soy Glaze. Top with lobster and a touch more Soy Glaze and sesame seeds. Serve with fried wonton triangles.

¼ cup dark brown sugar

¼ cup sweet soy sauce *(which is thicker, similar to molasses, and can be found in Asian markets)*

¼ cup regular soy sauce

1 garlic clove, finely minced

½ teaspoon fresh grated ginger

2 tablespoons rice cooking wine (Shaoxing)

2 tablespoons medium sherry

1 tablespoon rice wine vinegar

1 tablespoon mirin

1 teaspoon fish sauce

# Lemon Zest Lobster Salad with Shallots and Fresh Dill in Puff Pastry

Puff pastry can elevate anything that goes on it or in it! In this dish, the lemon zest and fresh dill really enhance the lobster salad without overpowering the lobster. The puff pastry is the perfect crispy vessel.

*Serves 4*

1. Mix lobster, mayonnaise, lemon juice, the zest from half of the lemon, shallot, 1 tablespoon dill, paprika, salt, and pepper and refrigerate. Keep refrigerated to meld for at least 1 hour.

2. Preheat oven to 400°F.

3. Cut 4 five-inch squares from the puff pastry sheet and reserve remaining dough for another use (or double the recipe for the lobster salad). Place squares of puff pastry on a sheet pan lined with parchment or a silicone baking sheet. With a knife, score the dough around the edge and use a fork to prick holes in the center. Doing so will keep the center from puffing up too much.

4. Bake until lightly browned, 12–15 minutes. Let cool 15 minutes. Top each puff pastry with lobster salad, zest from the remaining half lemon, and a sprinkling of dill from the remaining ½ tablespoon.

12 ounces cooked lobster meat, cut into ½-inch chunks

¼ cup mayonnaise

Juice from 1 lemon plus the zest from the lemon

1 large shallot, finely diced

1½ tablespoons fresh dill, minced

½ teaspoon sweet paprika

¾ teaspoon kosher salt

¼ teaspoon coarse black pepper

1 sheet of frozen puff pastry, thawed

# Lobster, Mango, and Avocado Salad with Citrus Vinaigrette

Not just beautiful but also light and full of fresh flavor. Be sure to get a ripe mango. If it's extremely ripe, I'll cut the mango, let it sit in a strainer, and use the juices in the vinaigrette.

*Serves 4*

1. Prepare dressing. Set aside.

2. Cut avocados into chunks and coat with some dressing to keep them from browning.

3. Coat the lobster with some of the dressing.

4. Mix the mango and red bell pepper.

## Dressing

Add lemon juice, orange juice, honey, Dijon mustard, shallots, salt, and pepper, and whisk while slowly adding the olive oil to incorporate and emulsify. Set aside.

## To Stack

Using a ring mold, place avocado on the bottom to cover the surface of the plate. Add lobster, followed by some microgreens, and then mango and red pepper. Remove ring mold and garnish with either lobster claw or split tail and chives. Drizzle dressing over the stack.

Dressing *(see recipe below)*

2 ripe avocados

12 ounces cooked lobster meat, cut into chunks, leaving a split tail or whole claw for the top

1 ripe mango, diced

1½ teaspoons finely diced red bell pepper

2 tablespoons microgreens

Minced chives (for garnish)

Juice from 1 lemon

2 tablespoons orange juice

1 teaspoon honey

1½ teaspoons Dijon mustard

1 small shallot, minced

¼ teaspoon kosher salt

A few grinds of freshly ground black pepper

2 tablespoons olive oil

# Chilled Lobster and Calamari Salad with Olives, Capers, White Wine, Garlic, Olive Oil, and Lemon

1½ pounds cleaned squid, tubes and tentacles

1 small leek, thinly sliced (white parts only)

½ cup extra-virgin olive oil (plus 1 tablespoon for sautéing leeks)

1 tablespoon butter (for sautéing leeks)

2 tablespoons fresh lemon juice

1 tablespoon white wine

1 tablespoon red wine vinegar

1 large garlic clove, minced

½ teaspoon kosher salt

¼ teaspoon black pepper

1 small shallot, very thinly sliced

1 pound cooked lobster meat, cut into chunks

¼ cup pitted Kalamata olives, thinly sliced

1 cup orange and red cherry tomatoes, halved or quartered if large

2 celery ribs, cut into ¼-inch-thick slices

1 tablespoon capers

1 cup loosely packed fresh flat-leaf parsley leaves

The inspiration for this dish came from a local Maine seafood purveyor who offers some packaged seafood salads to go. I'd stop in and the calamari salad wasn't always available, so I knew I needed to make my own. The bright, acidic dressing is so addictive, and the dish is super easy to make.

*Serves 4*

1. Rinse squid under cold running water and pat dry between paper towels. Cut tubes into ½-inch rings.

2. Cook squid, uncovered, in a 4- to 6-quart stock pot of boiling salted water uncovered until just cooked, about 90 seconds. Drain in a colander and let cool.

3. Sauté leeks in 1 tablespoon olive oil and butter over low-medium heat until softened and slightly golden, about 5–7 minutes. Let cool completely.

4. Whisk together lemon juice, white wine, vinegar, ½ cup olive oil, garlic, salt, and pepper in a small bowl; then add shallot and let stand 15 minutes.

5. Combine squid, lobster, leeks, olives, tomatoes, celery, capers, and parsley in a large bowl. Toss with dressing, and season with salt and pepper. Let stand at least 45 minutes to allow flavors to develop. Serve over baby greens.

# Grilled Lobster Caesar Salad

I could eat Caesar salad every other day, I love it so much. Grilling the heads of lettuce adds great flavor to the dish, but without losing all of the crispness. And grilled lobster is one of my favorite ways to enjoy it!

*Serves 4 as small salad course*

1. Prepare croutons and set aside.

2. Rinse, dry, and halve lettuce hearts end to end. Drizzle with olive oil and sprinkle with salt and a heavy dose of freshly ground pepper. Grill on a gas or charcoal grill, cut side down over medium-high heat until the lettuce wilts and you see some char, about 3–4 minutes. Let sit at room temperature until you are ready to serve.

3. Prepare dressing. Set aside.

4. Split tails, drizzle cut side with olive oil, and place cut side down over medium-hot grill.

5. Flip tails, spread softened butter (which remains spreadable at room temperature), and grill another 5 minutes.

Croutons *(see recipe below)*

2 small heads of Romaine (or 3 hearts)

Olive oil (for drizzling lettuce) plus some for lobster tails

½ teaspoon coarse kosher salt

Freshly ground black pepper (to taste)

Dressing *(see recipe below)*

4 small lobster tails, raw (or steamed 5 minutes if you don't have raw)

4 tablespoons softened butter

4 tablespoons grated Parmesan cheese

4 ounces shredded or shaved Parmesan cheese

## Croutons

2 tablespoons butter

2 tablespoons olive oil

1 garlic clove, minced

Dash of kosher salt

1 small baguette, cut into ½-inch cubes

1. Preheat oven to 350°F.

2. Melt butter with olive oil over low heat, add garlic, and then simmer for 2 minutes. Add salt.

3. Spread bread cubes on a cookie sheet and drizzle with butter/oil mixture.

4. Bake until crisp and lightly browned, about 15–20 minutes.

## Dressing

2 garlic cloves, minced

1 large egg yolk

4 tablespoons mayonnaise

Juice from ½ lemon

1 teaspoon Worcestershire sauce

1 teaspoon red wine vinegar

1 teaspoon honey

½ cup extra-virgin olive oil

Coarse kosher salt, to taste

Freshly ground black pepper (to taste)

1. In a large mixing bowl, add the garlic, egg yolk, mayo, lemon juice, Worcestershire sauce, vinegar, and honey, and whisk until smooth.

2. Slowly drizzle olive oil while whisking to incorporate until very smooth. Add salt and pepper to taste. If you like it thicker, add more mayo. If you like it thinner, add more lemon or vinegar (or even a drop of water).

## To Assemble

Add one wedge of grilled lettuce to a plate. Toss croutons and grated Parmesan cheese, and add to lettuce. Add a generous amount of dressing, and finish with shredded or shaved Parmesan cheese and a generous amount of ground pepper. Top with grilled lobster tail meat.

# Lobster and Chilled Udon Noodles with Pickled Red Onions and Carrots, Soy Glaze, Wasabi Cream, and Blistered Shishito Peppers

This is a great dish with a nice balance of textures and flavors with sweet, savory, spicy, and crunchy.

*Serves 4*

1. Mix mayo, wasabi, honey, and milk, and let meld for about an hour before using.

2. Cook udon noodles according to package directions. Let cool and toss with Soy Glaze and 1½ tablespoons sesame seeds, reserving ½ tablespoon for garnish.

3. Add olive oil to sauté pan and cook peppers over high heat until blistered, about 5 minutes. Season with salt.

1 cup mayonnaise

2 teaspoons prepared wasabi

1 teaspoon honey

1 tablespoon milk

8 ounces udon noodles

½ cup Soy Glaze *(see recipe below)* plus some for drizzling

2 tablespoons black and white sesame seeds

1 tablespoon olive oil

12 shishito peppers

Kosher salt to taste

8 ounces cooked lobster meat, cut into chunks

½ very thinly sliced red onion

1 carrot, cut into thin matchsticks

# Soy Glaze

*Makes about 1 cup*

1. Add the brown sugar, soy sauces, garlic, ginger, rice wine, sherry, and rice wine vinegar to a small saucepan and heat until brown sugar is dissolved. Remove from heat.

2. Stir in mirin and fish sauce.

3. Let cool and store in a squeeze bottle.

**Dana's Tip: A very good store-bought alternative is "Sweet Soy for Sushi" by Kikkoman.**

- ¼ cup dark brown sugar
- ¼ cup sweet soy sauce *(which is thicker, similar to molasses, and can be found in Asian markets)*
- ¼ cup regular soy sauce
- 1 garlic clove, finely minced
- ½ teaspoon fresh grated ginger
- 2 tablespoons rice cooking wine (Shaoxing)
- 2 tablespoons medium sherry
- 1 tablespoon rice wine vinegar
- 1 tablespoon mirin
- 1 teaspoon fish sauce

# To Assemble

Divide noodles among plates. Top with lobster, red onion, and carrots, and then drizzle more Soy Glaze over top. Sprinkle remaining sesame seeds and garnish plate with peppers and wasabi mayo.

# SANDWICHES AND HANDHELDS

# Lobster and Black Pepper Candied Bacon Slider on Brioche with Brown Butter Wasabi Mayo and Pickled Red Onions and Carrots

This is one flavor bomb of a sandwich full of mixed textures. Crunchy, soft, and creamy, this one is going to become a favorite!

*Makes 4*

1. Preheat oven to 350°F.

2. Lay bacon strips flat on a sheet pan and spread brown sugar directly over each piece. Run the pepper mill over each piece to lightly cover.

3. Cook bacon, rotating pan if needed to cook evenly, until bacon is dark brown/burgundy in color, just shy of burned. Remove to clean pan (do not use a towel or paper towel, as the bacon will stick). It will harden as it cools to yield a crackling exterior like the top of crème brûlée. Cut each piece in half.

4. Mix vinegar, water, and sugar in a small saucepan and heat over medium until sugar is completely dissolved. Then pour into a bowl with onions and carrots, and let sit at least 1 hour or more before using.

4 slices thick-cut bacon

½ cup light brown sugar

Freshly ground black pepper (to taste)

¼ cup white vinegar

¼ cup water

¾ cup sugar

¼ red onion, thinly sliced

1 medium carrot, julienned or cut into matchsticks

4 mini brioche buns

½ cup pea shoots or microgreens

12 ounces cooked lobster meat, cut into chunks

2 tablespoons Brown Butter Wasabi Mayo *(see recipe below)*

# Brown Butter Wasabi Mayo

1 cup mayonnaise

2 teaspoons prepared wasabi

1 teaspoon honey

3 tablespoons brown butter, melted or softened *(see recipe below)*

*Makes about 1 cup*

Mix all ingredients.

> **Dana's Tip:** Kikkoman makes a creamy wasabi that you can use as your base. It's delicious, and it's what gave me the idea for this mayo.

# Brown Butter

1. In small saucepan, add 1 stick butter and cook over medium-low heat until lightly brown in color and milk solids have fully separated, about 8–10 minutes, watching very carefully not to burn the butter.

2. Strain through a fine-mesh sieve and place in container to store at room temperature.

# To Assemble

Place pea shoots on the bottom half of each brioche, top with candied bacon, lobster, and ½ tablespoon of wasabi mayo, followed by a tablespoon of the pickled onions and carrots.

# Lobster Panini with Roasted Shallots, Creamy Fontina, Smoked Red Pepper Aioli, and Arugula

The combination of flavors here makes this sandwich one of my most favorites. Be sure to get the shallots nice and brown. Color equals flavor!

*Makes 4*

1. Preheat oven to 375°F.

2. Place quartered shallots and red pepper on a sheet pan and drizzle with olive oil. Sprinkle with salt and pepper. Roast for about 20 minutes, flipping the pieces midway through, until caramelized, about 20–25 minutes.

3. Place a good amount of the Smoked Red Pepper Aioli on each side of the bread. Add the Fontina cheese. Then divide the lobster among the sandwich bottoms, and add the top piece of bread or roll.

4. Melt butter in large frying pan (or use a panini press if you have one) over medium heat, and add each sandwich. Using a large heavy plate, add to the top, and place a couple of large cans (I use two [28-ounce] cans of tomatoes) and cook for about 5 minutes. Flip sandwiches and cook another 3–4 minutes until bread has browned and gotten crispy and cheese has melted.

Remove top bun and add arugula.

---

5 large shallots, quartered

1 small red bell pepper, cut into ½-inch-wide strips

Olive oil for roasting shallots and red pepper

Kosher salt

Freshly ground black pepper (to taste)

4 crusty mini baguettes, sliced in half (along the equator)

Smoked Red Pepper Aioli *(see recipe below)*

4 slices of Fontina cheese

8 ounces of cooked lobster meat

4 tablespoons butter

1½ cups baby arugula

# Smoked Red Pepper Aioli

*Makes about 1½ cups*

1.  Drizzle the cut pepper with the olive oil, sprinkle with salt, and place in smoker. For the smoking, you can use either an outdoor smoker or a stovetop smoker. I use a Cameron stovetop smoker, but I use it on the grill to keep the smoke outdoors. Smoke for about 25–30 minutes over medium heat. If it has been adequately smoked, you'll see a slight golden brown tint to the pepper slices. Remove, let cool, and remove skin from peppers.

2.  Add peppers to food processor and process until smooth. Add the egg yolks, salt, sugar, and black pepper and turn on processor, and then add the oil in a slow stream to blend. Adjust salt or pepper if needed. Store in a squeeze bottle.

1 red bell pepper, quartered, ribs and seeds removed

1 tablespoon olive oil (for smoking)

2 egg yolks

½ teaspoon kosher salt

½ teaspoon sugar

½ teaspoon black pepper

½ cup good-quality olive oil (mild)

# Lobster BLT with Candied Black Pepper Bacon

**The Smoked Red Pepper Aioli** *(see page 121)* **is a perfect substitution instead of plain mayo. And a little cayenne would be nice sprinkled on the candied bacon!**

*Makes 4*

8 slices of thick-cut slab bacon

¼ cup light brown sugar

Freshly ground black pepper (to taste)

8 slices of thick-cut white bread such as brioche

Prepared mayonnaise *(or Smoked Red Pepper Aioli)*

8 ounces cooked lobster meat

1 small head of Bibb lettuce

1 large ripe tomato sliced into quarters (preferably heirloom)

1. Preheat oven to 350°F.

2. Lay bacon strips flat on a sheet pan and spread brown sugar directly over each piece. Run the pepper mill over each piece to lightly cover.

3. Cook bacon, rotating pan if needed to cook evenly, until bacon is dark brown/burgundy in color, just shy of burned. Remove to clean pan (do not use a towel or paper towel, as the bacon will stick). It will harden as it cools to yield a crackling exterior like the top of crème brûlée.

4. Toast bread to your liking.

5. Add a good amount of mayonnaise to each side of the bread, layer on the bacon, and then lobster, followed by lettuce and sliced tomato.

# Lobster Sliders with Lobster Poached in Brown Butter, Roasted Tomato Mayo, Bibb Lettuce, Roasted Tomatoes, and Crispy Fried Shallots

These adorable handhelds are full of flavor and texture with the crunch of the lettuce and fried shallots. And the Roasted Tomato Aioli is nice on a salad or as a fresh veggie dip.

*Serves 4*

1. Preheat oven to 375°F.

2. Quarter tomatoes and place cut side up on a sheet pan. Drizzle with olive oil and sprinkle with salt. Roast for about 30 minutes and lower oven to 300°F, flip tomatoes onto a cut side, and roast another 15 minutes. Let cool. *Note: Set aside one half to make the Roasted Tomato Aioli and the other half to put on the slider.*

3. In a sauté pan, heat olive oil and add shallots. Pan fry until browned. Set aside on a paper towel.

4. In small saucepan, add 1 stick butter and cook over medium-low heat until lightly brown in color and milk solids have fully separated, about 8–10 minutes, watching very carefully not to burn the butter. Strain through a fine-mesh sieve and place in large sauté pan.

5. Heat the browned butter over medium low for 1 minute. Add lobster, lower heat to a simmer, and cook until lobster is fully opaque, but cook slowly to avoid overcooking—about 7–8 minutes. Remove lobster and set aside. When cool, cut into small bite-size chunks.

6 Roma tomatoes, quartered and roasted, reserving half after roasting for the Roasted Tomato Aioli

Olive oil for drizzling tomatoes

Kosher salt for the tomatoes

2 tablespoons olive oil (for frying shallots)

2 large shallots, thinly sliced

1 stick butter

8 ounces of raw lobster meat

4 mini brioche buns

3 tablespoons Roasted Tomato Aioli *(see recipe below)*

4 pieces of Bibb lettuce

## Roasted Tomato Aioli

½ of the roasted
  tomatoes

1 cup mayonnaise

½ teaspoon kosher salt

Freshly ground black
  pepper (to taste)

Place the roasted tomatoes in a blender or food processor with mayonnaise, salt, and pepper until well blended. Let meld for at least an hour or longer before using.

## To Assemble

Place some Roasted Tomato Aioli on the brioche buns, add lettuce, top with lobster, a roasted tomato quarter, and some fried shallots.

# Fried Lobster Po'Boy with Garlic Mayo, Roasted Shallots, Lettuce, and Tomatoes

If I have to choose a favorite sandwich, this one is *IT*. The Panko-fried lobster is . . . well . . . fried—and there's lobster. Enough said? Add garlic mayo and caramelized shallots with a crusty ciabatta, and this becomes addictive—and messy (don't go easy on the garlic mayo)!

*Makes 4*

1. Bring a large stock pot of water to a boil. Plunge the lobsters into the boiling water head first and cook until bright red all over, about 6 minutes. Transfer the lobsters to a large rimmed baking sheet and let cool. Twist the tails from the lobster bodies and break off the claws. With scissors, cut down the tail shell and remove the meat. Cut down the center of the tail and remove the dark intestinal vein. Crack the claws and knuckles and remove the meat. Let cool.

2. To make the garlic mayo, mix mayonnaise, garlic, 1½ teaspoons olive oil, and water and let sit to meld while shallots are roasting.

3. Place quartered shallots on a sheet pan and drizzle with olive oil. Sprinkle with salt and pepper. Roast for about 20 minutes, flipping the pieces midway through, until caramelized, about 20–25 minutes. Set aside when done.

4. Toast ciabatta in oven for about 5 minutes. Then slice in half along the equator.

5. Mix eggs with milk in a large bowl and whisk well.

6. Add Panko to a large bowl.

3 live 1¼-pound lobsters

⅓ cup mayonnaise

2 garlic cloves

1½ teaspoons olive oil plus some for roasting shallots

½ teaspoon water

5 large shallots, quartered

Kosher salt (for seasoning)

Freshly ground black pepper (for seasoning)

4 crusty mini Ciabatta loaves, toasted and sliced

2 large eggs

2 tablespoons milk

2 cups Panko breadcrumbs

Vegetable oil (for frying)

Flour (for dredging lobster)

1 large tomato, sliced (preferably heirloom)

8 pieces of Bibb lettuce

7.  Add enough vegetable oil to a deep 2½- to 3-quart saucepan to come up halfway or so. Heat to 370°F.

8.  Dredge pieces of lobster in flour, then into the egg mixture, and then once into Panko, coating completely.

9.  Fry lobster until golden brown, about 4 minutes. Remove to paper towel and sprinkle with salt.

## To Assemble

Place a good amount of garlic mayo mixture on each side of the bun, add fried lobster, and top with roasted shallots, lettuce, and tomato.

# Lobster Imperial on English Muffin with Melted Fontina, Fried Shallots, Heirloom Tomato, Avocado, and Fresh Baby Spinach

Four 1¼–1½-pound lobsters (to yield about 1 pound of parcooked meat, chopped)

1 large shallot, thinly sliced

2 tablespoons vegetable oil

½ cup mayonnaise

1½ teaspoons Worcestershire sauce

1 tablespoon lemon juice

1 tablespoon capers

1½ teaspoons Dijon mustard

¼ teaspoon Old Bay seasoning

½ teaspoon kosher salt

Paprika (for dusting)

4 English muffins

1 cup fresh baby spinach

4 slices Fontina cheese

1 ripe heirloom tomato

1 ripe avocado

**Royalty! Another rich combination of flavors and textures, this makes a lovely lunch with vinaigrette-dressed greens.**

*Makes 4*

1. Bring a large stockpot filled with about 2 inches of water to a boil. Place a steamer basket upside down, and then add the lobsters and cover. Cook for about 5–6 minutes. Pick meat and proceed with the recipe.

2. Pan fry shallots in vegetable oil until golden brown, about 6–7 minutes. Drain and set aside.

3. Mix mayonnaise, Worcestershire sauce, lemon juice, capers, Dijon mustard, Old Bay, and salt.

4. Fold in lobster, and then top with paprika. Bake in a small ramekin or baking dish at 350°F for about 25 minutes, but no longer, or the sauce will "break," which means it will become translucent and will appear oily rather than creamy. (This is not so bad if it happens, however, and will not affect flavor.) Keep covered for a few minutes until you are ready to assemble the dish.

5. Toast English muffins.

6. Place a few spinach leaves and then about ¼–½ cup of the warm Lobster Imperial on the bottom half of the toasted muffin. The butter from the dish will seep in and flavor it nicely.

7.  Place a slice of Fontina cheese over the lobster and broil until cheese is melted, just about 2 minutes.

8.  Top with sliced tomato, avocado, and fried shallots.

Be sure to have extra napkins at the ready!

# TACOS

The taco recipes in this section are quite similar, but they have just enough subtle nuances to make each one special.

# Lobster Street Corn Tacos

**Don't skip grilling the corn. It's worth the extra step!**

*Makes 4 tacos*

1.  To make the corn salsa, drizzle corn with olive oil and grill over medium-high heat until lightly charred. Cut from cob when cool. Mix with cherry tomatoes, salt, lime juice, and smoked paprika. Let sit an hour so flavors develop.

2.  Prepare the Smoked Onion Aioli.

3.  Drizzle scallions with olive oil and grill over medium-high heat until lightly charred. Cut into 1-inch pieces. Set aside.

4.  Warm tortillas in a dry pan on the stovetop, or grill.

5.  Warm lobster in a small saucepan with 1 tablespoon butter over low heat for 3–4 minutes.

Olive oil (for grilling corn and scallions)

1 large ear of corn

¼ cup cherry tomatoes, quartered

¼ teaspoon kosher salt

1 teaspoon lime juice

¼ teaspoon smoked paprika

Smoked Onion Aioli *(see recipe below)*

1 bunch of scallions

8 small (street-taco-size) corn tortillas (2 per taco)

8 ounces cooked lobster meat, cut into small chunks

1 tablespoon butter

2 tablespoons crumbled queso fresco

# Smoked Onion Aioli

*Makes about 1 cup*

1 medium onion cut into quarters

1 tablespoon olive oil (for smoking)

2 egg yolks

½ teaspoon kosher salt, plus some for sprinkling on onion

½ teaspoon sugar

½ teaspoon black pepper

½ cup good-quality olive oil (mild)

1.  Drizzle the cut onion with the olive oil, sprinkle with salt, and place in smoker. For the smoking, you can use either an outdoor smoker or a stovetop smoker. I use a Cameron stovetop smoker, but I use it on the grill to keep the smoke outdoors. Smoke for about 25–30 minutes over medium heat. If it has been adequately smoked, you'll see a slight golden brown tint to the onion. Remove and let cool.

2.  Add cut onion to food processor and process until smooth. Add the egg yolks, salt, sugar, and pepper, and turn on processor; then add the oil in a slow stream to blend. Adjust salt or pepper if needed. Store in a squeeze bottle.

> **Dana's Tip:** You can use a good-quality prepared mayonnaise instead of making your own.

# To Assemble

Place 2 tortillas together. Add about ½ tablespoon Smoked Onion Aioli to each; then divide the lobster among the 8 tacos. Top with some corn salsa, some queso fresco, and grilled scallions.

# Lobster Wonton Tacos

A fried wonton shell with lobster, Smoked Scallion Truffle Aioli, Napa cabbage, carrots, scallions, Soy Glaze, and Soy Caviar Pearls. This recipe is a riff on my award-winning Lobster-Topped Wontons *(see page 12)*.

*Makes about 12 mini wonton tacos*

1. Add enough vegetable oil to a deep stock pot or saucepan to fill ⅔ of the way.

2. When the oil is 375°F, add 1 wonton at a time. To obtain the taco shell shape (this might take some practice), you can hold each side with tongs for about 15 seconds until it sets in the oil (or buy taco shell–shaped tongs like I did!) and cook for about a minute, until golden brown. Repeat with remaining wonton wrappers.

3. Set aside on a towel and season with salt. Let cool and store in an airtight container.

4. Warm lobster in a small saucepan with 1 tablespoon butter over low heat for 3–4 minutes.

Vegetable oil (for frying)

12 round wonton wrappers (if you can only find square, use a biscuit cutter or top of a wide glass to trim into a round shape)

Kosher salt (for seasoning)

1 pound picked lobster meat, cut into small chunks

1 tablespoon butter

1½ cups shredded Napa cabbage (very thinly sliced)

½ cup julienned or shredded carrots

1 bunch scallions, thinly sliced on a bias

Smoked Scallion Truffle Aioli *(see recipe below)*

Soy Glaze *(see recipe below)*

Soy Caviar Pearls *(see recipe below)*

# Smoked Truffle Aioli

*Makes about 2 cups*

1. Drizzle the scallions with the olive oil, sprinkle with salt, and grill over medium heat until really well charred, about 10 minutes. Roughly chop and set aside.

2. For the smoking, you can use either an outdoor smoker or a stovetop smoker. I used a Cameron stovetop smoker, but I used it on the grill since I had to grill my scallions and the grill was already hot.

3. Place 1 cup of the mayonnaise and butter in an ovenproof dish and place in smoker (following the manufacturer's instructions). Smoke for about 30 minutes. If it has been adequately smoked, you'll see browned bits along the edge of the baking dish and a light brown tint to the mayo and butter. Let cool. Add to blender with the remaining mayonnaise, salt, black pepper, and truffle oil. Add the scallions and blend until scallions are in small bits but still very visible. Store in a squeeze bottle.

1 bunch of scallions (about 6–8), bottoms trimmed

1 tablespoon olive oil (for grilling scallions)

½ teaspoon kosher salt, plus ¼ teaspoon for tossing on scallions

1½ cups Japanese "Kewpie" mayonnaise *(This is made from egg yolks, not whole eggs like traditional American mayonnaise, so it's creamier. You can find it online or in Asian markets.)*

½ stick butter

1 teaspoon black pepper

1 tablespoon white truffle oil

**Dana's Tip:** If you want to omit the grilled scallion step, you'll still have great flavor with the remaining ingredients. I'm all about time savers if the quality of the dish is not compromised!

# Soy Glaze

*Makes 1 cup*

¼ cup dark brown sugar

¼ cup sweet soy sauce
*(which is thicker,
similar to molasses,
and can be found in
Asian markets)*

¼ cup regular soy sauce

1 garlic clove, finely
minced

½ teaspoon fresh grated
ginger

2 tablespoons rice
cooking wine
(Shaoxing)

2 tablespoons medium
sherry

1 teaspoon rice wine
vinegar

1 tablespoon mirin

1 teaspoon fish sauce

1.  Add the brown sugar, soy sauces, garlic, ginger, rice wine, sherry, and rice wine vinegar to a small saucepan and heat until brown sugar is dissolved. Remove from heat.

2.  Stir in mirin and fish sauce. Let cool and store in a squeeze bottle.

**Dana's Tip: A similar bottled alternative can be found in supermarkets or Asian grocers. Kikkoman makes a nice "Unagi" sweet sauce as well as "Sweet Soy Sauce for Rice." Sometimes shortcuts are more than acceptable!**

## Soy Caviar Pearls

*Precise measurements are important for this recipe, so it would be best to use a scale to weigh each ingredient.*

1.  Place vegetable oil container in freezer for 30 minutes.

2.  To a small saucepan, add soy and agar; mix well with stick blender, and bring to a boil. Remove from heat and let cool a few minutes.

3.  While soy is cooling, remove oil from freezer. Using a squeeze bottle or dropper, carefully drop the soy into the oil. They will form pearls and sink to the bottom.

4.  Once you've dropped all of the soy, strain and rinse the pearls and store in a container until ready to use (best within a day or two).

1 (2- or 3-cup) measuring cup filled ¾ full with vegetable oil

250 milliliters soy of your choice (I prefer Kikkoman's "Sweet Soy Sauce for Rice")

2 grams agar

## To Assemble

Place about 1½ teaspoons of Smoked Truffle Aioli onto the wonton; top with some cabbage, carrots, and lobster, and then add a drizzle of Soy Glaze and scallions. Top with ½ teaspoon of soy pearls. Be sure to get enough of the sauces, as they are a big part of the flavor explosion!

# Lobster Soft Tacos

A soft corn taco with Bibb lettuce, Napa cabbage, carrots, scallions, lobster, Smoked Red Pepper Aioli, sweet Soy Glaze, and crispy fried shallots. A nice balance of textures and flavors.

*Makes 4 tacos*

1 tablespoon good-quality olive oil (mild)

4 shallots, quartered

4 taco-size soft corn tortillas

8 ounces of cooked lobster meat, cut into small chunks

1 tablespoon butter

4 pieces of Bibb lettuce

½ cup finely shredded Napa cabbage

¼ cup julienned or shredded carrots

2 scallions, thinly sliced on a bias

2 tablespoons Smoked Red Pepper Aioli *(see recipe below)*

4 teaspoons Soy Glaze *(see recipe below)*

1. In a sauté pan, heat olive oil and add shallots. Pan fry until browned. Set aside on a paper towel.

2. Heat tortillas in a dry pan or on the grill just a minute or two so they are more pliable.

3. Warm lobster in a small saucepan with 1 tablespoon butter over low heat for 3–4 minutes.

# Smoked Red Pepper Aioli

*Makes about 1 cup*

1 red bell pepper, quartered, ribs and seeds removed

1 tablespoon olive oil (for smoking)

2 egg yolks

½ teaspoon kosher salt

½ teaspoon sugar

½ teaspoon black pepper

½ cup good-quality olive oil (mild)

1. Drizzle the cut pepper with the olive oil, sprinkle with salt, and place in smoker. For the smoking, you can use either an outdoor smoker or a stovetop smoker. I use a Cameron stovetop smoker, but I use it on the grill to keep the smoke outdoors. Smoke for about 25–30 minutes over medium heat. If it has been adequately smoked, you'll see a slight golden brown tint to the pepper slices.

2. Remove, let cool, and remove skin from peppers.

3. Add peppers to food processor and process until smooth. Add the egg yolks, salt, sugar, and black pepper and turn on processor, and then add the oil in a slow stream to blend. Adjust salt or pepper if needed. Store in a squeeze bottle.

**Dana's Tip: You can use a prepared mayonnaise instead of making your own and still achieve great flavor and texture.**

# Soy Glaze

*Makes 1 cup*

1.  Add the brown sugar, soy sauces, garlic, ginger, rice wine, sherry, and rice wine vinegar to a small saucepan and heat until brown sugar is dissolved. Remove from heat.

2.  Stir in mirin and fish sauce. Let cool and store in a squeeze bottle.

**Dana's Tip:** A similar bottled alternative can be found in supermarkets or Asian grocers. Kikkoman makes a nice "Unagi" sweet sauce as well as "Sweet Soy Sauce for Rice." Sometimes shortcuts are more than acceptable!

- ¼ cup dark brown sugar
- ¼ cup sweet soy sauce *(which is thicker, similar to molasses, and can be found in Asian markets)*
- ¼ cup regular soy sauce
- 1 garlic clove, finely minced
- ½ teaspoon fresh grated ginger
- 2 tablespoons rice cooking wine (Shaoxing)
- 2 tablespoons medium sherry
- 1 teaspoon rice wine vinegar
- 1 tablespoon mirin
- 1 teaspoon fish sauce

# To Assemble

Place about ½ tablespoon of Smoked Red Pepper Aioli on each of the tortillas. Divide the lettuce, cabbage, scallions, and carrots among the 4 tortillas. Divide the lobster meat among the 4 tortillas. Top each with about 1 teaspoon of Soy Glaze (or more to taste since the sauces make this dish!) and the crispy fried shallots.

# Crispy Corn Lobster Tacos

A house-fried corn tortilla, Bibb lettuce, grilled corn, lobster, mango jalapeño relish, smoked onion aioli, and fried shallots. It's worth frying your own corn tortillas.

*Makes 4 tacos*

1. In a sauté pan, heat olive oil and add shallots. Pan fry until browned. Set aside on a paper towel.

2. Add enough vegetable oil to a deep stock pot or saucepan to fill ⅔ of the way.

3. When the oil is 375°F, add 1 tortilla at a time. To obtain the taco shell shape (this might take some practice), hold each side with tongs for about 15 seconds until it sets in the oil (or buy taco shell–shaped tongs like I did!) and cook for about a minute, until golden brown. Repeat with remaining tortillas.

4. Set aside on a towel and season with kosher salt. Let cool and store in an airtight container.

5. Brush corn with olive oil and grill on medium heat until corn is lightly charred, about 6–8 minutes. Cut from cob and set aside.

6. To make the mango salsa, mix the mango, jalapeño, and lime juice and let meld for 30 minutes until ready to use.

7. Warm lobster in a small saucepan with 1 tablespoon butter over low heat for 3–4 minutes.

1 tablespoon good-quality olive oil (mild)

1 large or 2 medium-small shallots, diced

Vegetable oil (for frying tortillas)

4 corn tortillas

Kosher salt (for seasoning)

1 ear of corn

Olive oil to brush on corn for grilling

1 ripe mango, diced

1 small jalapeño, very finely diced

1 teaspoon fresh lime juice

8 ounces cooked lobster meat, cut into small chunks

1 tablespoon butter

4 pieces of Bibb lettuce

Smoked Onion Aioli *(see recipe below)*

# Smoked Onion Aioli

*Makes about 1½ cups*

1½ cups mayonnaise

1 large onion, peeled and quartered

½ teaspoon kosher salt

¼ teaspoon black pepper

1.  Place half of the mayonnaise in a small, shallow baking dish and place in smoker. Drizzle the cut onion quarters with the olive oil, sprinkle with salt, and place in smoker (on the rack, but line the base of the smoker with foil to capture the juices). For the smoking, you can use either an outdoor smoker or a stovetop smoker. I use a Cameron stovetop smoker, but I use it on the grill to keep the smoke outdoors. Smoke for about 25–30 minutes over medium heat. If it has been adequately smoked, you'll see a slight golden brown tint to the onion and to the mayonnaise. Let both cool.

2.  In a food processor, blend the smoked onion, the smoked mayonnaise, and the unsmoked mayonnaise. Season with salt and pepper.

# To Assemble

Place a piece of Bibb lettuce in the taco shell. Add about ½ tablespoon or so of the Smoked Onion Aioli, and then top with 2 ounces of lobster, about a tablespoon of corn, about a tablespoon of mango salsa, and top with some fried shallots.

# Asian Fusion Lobster Tacos

A flour tortilla, Smoked Truffle Aioli, Soy Glaze, lobster, microgreens, and frizzled leeks. The Smoked Truffle Aioli was a component (and one of my favorites) of my award-winning Lobster-Topped Wontons *(see page 12)*.

*Makes 4 tacos*

1. Add enough vegetable oil to a deep stock pot or saucepan to fill ⅔ of the way.

2. When the oil is 375°F, add the leeks and fry until light golden brown. Drain on a paper towel.

3. Warm lobster in a small saucepan with 1 tablespoon butter over low heat for 3–4 minutes.

Vegetable oil (for frying leeks)

1 small leek, white parts only, thinly sliced

8 ounces of cooked lobster meat, cut into small chunks

1 tablespoon butter

4 taco-size flour tortillas

2 tablespoons Smoked Truffle Aioli *(see recipe below)*

4 teaspoons Soy Glaze *(see recipe below)*

Microgreens (for garnish)

# Smoked Truffle Aioli

*Makes about 2 cups*

1.  Drizzle the scallions with the olive oil, sprinkle with salt, and grill over medium heat until really well charred, about 10 minutes. Roughly chop and set aside.

2.  For the smoking, you can use either an outdoor smoker or a stovetop smoker. I used a Cameron stovetop smoker, but I used it on the grill since I had to grill my scallions and the grill was already hot.

3.  Place 1 cup of the mayonnaise and butter in an ovenproof dish and place in the smoker (following the manufacturer's instructions). Smoke for about 30 minutes. If it has been adequately smoked, you'll see browned bits along the edge of the baking dish and a light brown tint to the mayo and butter. Let cool. Add to blender with the remaining mayonnaise, salt, black pepper, and truffle oil. Add the scallions and blend until scallions are in small bits but still very visible. Store in a squeeze bottle.

- 1 bunch of scallions (about 6–8), bottoms trimmed
- 1 tablespoon olive oil for grilling scallions
- 1½ cups Japanese "Kewpie" mayonnaise *(This is made from egg yolks, not whole eggs like traditional American mayonnaise, so it's creamier. You can find it online or in Asian markets.)*
- ½ stick butter
- ½ teaspoon kosher salt plus ¼ teaspoon for tossing on scallions
- 1 teaspoon black pepper
- 1 tablespoon white truffle oil

# Soy Glaze

*Makes 1 cup*

¼ cup dark brown sugar

¼ cup sweet soy sauce *(which is thicker, similar to molasses, and can be found in Asian markets)*

¼ cup regular soy sauce

1 garlic clove, finely minced

½ teaspoon fresh grated ginger

2 tablespoons rice cooking wine (Shaoxing)

2 tablespoons medium sherry

1 teaspoon rice wine vinegar

1 tablespoon mirin

1 teaspoon fish sauce

1.  Add the brown sugar, soy sauces, garlic, ginger, rice wine, sherry, and rice wine vinegar to a small saucepan and heat until brown sugar is dissolved. Remove from heat.

2.  Stir in mirin and fish sauce. Let cool and store in a squeeze bottle.

**Dana's Tip:** A similar bottled alternative can be found in supermarkets or Asian grocers. Kikkoman makes a nice "Unagi" sweet sauce as well as "Sweet Soy Sauce for Rice."

# To Assemble

On a flour tortilla, place about a tablespoon of the aioli, and then about 2 ounces of lobster meat, followed by a good drizzle of the soy glaze and top with a scattering of frizzled leeks and microgreens.

# Lobster Banh Mi Tacos

You had me at banh mi. If I see any variation of a banh mi on a menu, I order it. So I wanted to create a lobster version in which I keep with tradition and used pickled veggies, a sauce, cucumber, and cilantro.

*Makes 4 tacos*

4 taco-size soft corn tortillas

8 ounces cooked lobster meat, cut into chunks

Pickled Vegetables *(see recipe below)*

12 thin slices of cucumber

2 tablespoons cilantro leaves

Habanero peppers (optional)

# Pickled Vegetables

1. Add sugar, salt, and vinegar to a small saucepan and heat until sugar is dissolved.

2. Remove from heat and add vegetables. Let chill for at least 30 minutes.

⅛ cup sugar

½ teaspoon kosher salt

1 cup white vinegar

¼ of a small onion, thinly sliced pole to pole

1 carrot, julienned

3 radishes, thinly sliced

# Sauce

Mix all ingredients to combine.

¼ cup mayonnaise

2 teaspoons fish sauce

1 tablespoon coconut milk

1 teaspoon sugar

½ teaspoon kosher salt

# To Assemble

Spread some of the sauce on each tortilla. Divide the lobster among the tacos. Top each with pickled vegetables, 3 slices of cucumber, and cilantro. Add some thinly sliced habanero peppers for a spicy kick.

# MAIN COURSES

# Lobster and Sausage Jambalaya

A classic New Orleans staple, but with a touch of Maine and our favorite crustacean.

*Serves 6*

1.  Bring a large stockpot filled with about 2 inches of water to a boil. Place a steamer basket upside down, and then add the lobsters and cover. Cook for about 5–6 minutes. Pick meat and proceed with the recipe.

2.  Heat the oil in a large Dutch oven or cast-iron pot over medium heat.

3.  Season the chicken with about ¼ teaspoon of salt and a few grinds of freshly ground pepper and sauté for 8–10 minutes, until browned. Remove to a bowl, and set aside.

4.  Add the butter, onion, celery, and peppers to the same pot and sauté for 8–10 minutes, until the onion is translucent.

5.  Add the sausage, cooked chicken, lobster, tomatoes, garlic, jalapeño, oregano, thyme, smoked paprika, and tomato paste, and cook until all the vegetables and herbs are blended well.

6.  Add the chicken and lobster stock and hot sauce, and bring to a rolling boil.

7.  Stir in the rice and return to a boil, add remaining salt and pepper, reduce the heat to low, and simmer, covered, for 20 minutes.

8.  Add ¼ cup of the scallions, parsley, lemon juice, and shrimp and stir well. Cover the pot, remove it from the heat, and allow the jambalaya to rest, covered, for 10 minutes before serving.

9.  Garnish with the remaining scallions.

Two 1¼–1½-pound lobsters (to yield about 1 cup of parcooked meat)

2 tablespoons olive oil

6 ounces chicken breast

2 teaspoons kosher salt

1 teaspoon freshly ground black pepper

1 tablespoon butter

1 medium onion, diced

1 cup diced celery

1 poblano pepper, cored and diced

1 red bell pepper, cored and diced

2 smoked, cured, or spicy Andouille sausages, sliced

1 can fire roasted tomatoes

4 garlic cloves, minced

1 jalapeño pepper, seeded and minced

2 teaspoons diced fresh oregano

1 teaspoon diced fresh thyme

1 teaspoon smoked paprika

3 tablespoons tomato paste

3 cups chicken stock

2 cups Lobster Stock *(see page 83)*

6–8 dashes hot sauce, optional *(I prefer Cholula)*

2½ cups long-grain rice

½ cup chopped scallions, divided

¼ cup chopped fresh parsley

¼ cup freshly squeezed lemon juice

1 pound medium shrimp, deveined

# Lobster Cakes with Creamy Dijon Sauce and Fresh Dill

Four 1¼–1½-pound lobsters (to yield about 1 pound of parcooked meat, cut into a small chop)

2 ounces shredded mozzarella

3 ounces shredded Parmesan cheese

1 egg

¼ cup mayonnaise

1 teaspoon Worcestershire sauce

½ teaspoon kosher salt

¼ teaspoon black pepper

1 tablespoon minced chives

3 tablespoons flour

3 tablespoons butter for pan frying

Fresh dill (for garnish)

Creamy Dijon Sauce (for garnish) *(see recipe below)*

**The addition of cheese in this version makes the cakes ever so slightly gooey.**

*Serves 4*

1. Bring a large stockpot filled with about 2 inches of water to a boil. Place a steamer basket upside down, and then add the lobsters and cover. Cook for about 5–6 minutes. Pick meat and let cool 15 minutes and then proceed with the recipe.

2. Mix all ingredients and let sit in refrigerator for 30 minutes to an hour.

3. Heat butter in sauté pan over medium-high heat.

4. Using a 2½- to 3-inch cookie scoop, scoop out the lobster mixture and place in sauté pan, gently flattening down some with the scoop. Cook without moving until the edges appear golden, about 3 minutes, and then flip carefully. Cook another 3 minutes.

5. Garnish with fresh dill and Creamy Dijon Sauce.

## Creamy Dijon Sauce

¼ cup sour cream

¼ cup mayonnaise

2 teaspoons fresh lemon juice

½ teaspoon kosher salt

¼ teaspoon black pepper

½ teaspoon fresh dill

Mix and let meld for at least 30 minutes before serving.

# Lobster Risotto with Grilled Asparagus

If you're like me, you really enjoy a good risotto. Creamy, but not by added cream—rather by proper slow cooking and using good-quality rice.

*Serves 4*

1. In a medium pot, heat both stocks and keep warm.

2. In a large sauté pan, melt the butter and olive oil over medium-high heat. Add the onion and shallot, and sauté about 5 minutes. Add a large pinch of salt, and then add the rice and stir constantly for about 2 minutes. Add the wine and cook for 3–4 minutes. Add 1 cup of broth and simmer, stirring until the broth is almost absorbed. Add more broth, a cup at a time, allowing each addition to be absorbed before adding the next. Stir often. Cook until the rice is tender and the mixture is creamy, about 20–25 minutes.

3. While rice is cooking, drizzle asparagus with olive oil and grill asparagus on either an outdoor grill or a grill pan until tender-crisp, about 6–8 minutes.

4. Stir in the lobster meat until heated through; then add the chives and ¼ cup of the Parmesan cheese. Season to taste with salt and pepper. Serve immediately, topped with grilled asparagus and remaining Parmesan cheese.

About 4 cups chicken stock

2 cups Lobster Stock *(see page 83)*

½ stick of butter

¼ cup extra-virgin olive oil, plus some to drizzle on asparagus

1 medium onion, finely diced

1 large shallot, finely diced

Large pinch of kosher salt

2 cups arborio rice

½ cup dry white wine

1 pound asparagus

12 ounces cooked lobster meat, cut into chunks

2 tablespoons minced chives

½ cup grated Parmesan cheese

Kosher salt to taste

Freshly ground black pepper (to taste)

Three 1¼–1½-pound
lobsters (to yield
about 1½ cups of
parcooked meat,
chopped)

Vegetable oil

8 ounces pasta—use
a shape that can
hold the sauce, such
as lumache (snail
shell shape) or
campanelle (tubular
shape)

1 cup whole milk

1 cup half and half

½ stick plus 1
tablespoon unsalted
butter

¼ cup all-purpose
flour

¾ cup Parmesan
cheese, shredded

1 cup extra-sharp
white cheddar,
shredded

2 cups Fontina cheese,
shredded

1 teaspoon kosher
salt and to taste (as
some cheeses taste
saltier than others)

½ teaspoon freshly
ground black pepper

1 tablespoon white
truffle oil

2 teaspoons shaved
truffles (sold in olive
oil in small jars), plus
some for garnish

# Lobster Mac and Cheese with Truffle Oil and Shaved Truffles

*THIS* is one of my favorite dishes ever with the shaved truffles and lobster! Using the shaved truffles instead of just truffle oil makes a difference.

*Serves 4*

1.  Preheat oven to 375°F.

2.  Bring a large stockpot filled with about 2 inches of water to a boil. Place a steamer basket upside down, and then add the lobsters and cover. Cook for about 5–6 minutes. Pick meat and proceed with the recipe.

3.  Add a couple teaspoons of vegetable oil to a large pot of boiling salted water. Add the pasta and undercook by 2 minutes from the directions on the package. Drain well.

4.  Heat the milk and half and half in a small saucepan, but don't allow it to boil. Once warm, turn off heat.

5.  In a large pot, melt the butter and add the flour. Cook over low heat for 3 minutes, whisking constantly.

6.  Continue to whisk and add the hot milk mixture and cook for a couple more minutes, until thickened and smooth.

7.  Remove from the heat, add the cheeses, salt, pepper, truffle oil, and shaved truffles, and mix well.

8.  Add the cooked pasta and lobster, and stir well. Place the mixture into a baking dish (or individual gratin dishes).

9.  Bake for 30–35 minutes until bubbly.

10.  Add a drizzle of truffle oil and a few shaved truffle slices as garnish (truffle oil and truffles mellow while cooking, so they are best fresh and added for a boost before serving).

# Lobster and Shellfish Stew

*Serves 3–4*

1. Bring a large stockpot filled with about 2 inches of water to a boil. Place a steamer basket upside down, and then add the lobsters and cover. Cook for about 5–6 minutes. Pick meat and proceed with the recipe.

2. In a large stock pot, heat the olive oil.

3. Add the shallots and cook over medium-high heat until lightly golden, about 5 minutes.

4. Add the garlic and cook another 2 minutes.

5. Add the wine and boil for 2–3 minutes.

6. Add the two stocks, tomatoes, thyme, and bay leaf, and season with salt and pepper. Bring to a boil over high heat and cook until slightly reduced, about 10 minutes.

7. Add the clams, cover and cook 3 minutes, and then add the mussels, just until most of them open, about 5 minutes.

8. Add the lobster and shrimp. Cover and simmer until they are cooked through and the remaining clams and mussels have opened, about 3–4 minutes. Using a slotted spoon, transfer the seafood to serving bowls.

9. Add the squid and butter and cook for 2 more minutes. Spoon the broth over the seafood, garnish with parsley, and serve with toasted sourdough bread for dunking.

Four 1¼–1½-pound lobsters (to yield about 1 pound of parcooked meat, cut into large chunks)

2 tablespoons olive oil

2 large shallots, finely diced

3 large garlic cloves, minced

½ cup dry white wine (Sauvignon Blanc)

1½ cups chicken stock

1 cup Lobster Stock *(see page 83)*

1½ cups San Marzano tomatoes, crushed

2 thyme sprigs

1 bay leaf

Kosher salt and freshly ground pepper

1 dozen littleneck clams, scrubbed

1 pound mussels, beards removed

½ pound shelled and deveined medium shrimp

½ pound squid (calamari) tubes and tentacles, tubes sliced into ¼-inch rings

2 tablespoons unsalted butter

2 tablespoons coarsely chopped flat-leaf parsley

Sourdough toast (for serving)

# Lobster Seafood Paella with Grilled Octopus

1 small octopus, about 2 pounds, cleaned and beak removed

3 cups dry white wine (Sauvignon Blanc) divided

1 onion, quartered, skin on

2 lemons, halved

3 whole garlic cloves for the octopus

Olive oil for grilling the octopus

3 cups chicken stock

1½ cups Lobster Stock (see page 83)

¼ cup extra-virgin olive oil

½ cup smoked duck breast or duck bacon (you can substitute pork bacon or chorizo)

2 cups onion, finely diced

5 cloves garlic, finely minced

1 28-ounce can San Marzano tomatoes, crushed

One 14-ounce can diced tomatoes

*(continued)*

I cannot stress how much I love octopus. If I see it on a menu, there's no need to look further. Combine it with lobster, and it's become a serious favorite. And cooking octopus is easier than you might think.

*Serves 6*

1. Bring a large stockpot filled with about 2 inches of water to a boil. Place a steamer basket upside down, and then add the lobsters and cover. Cook for about 5–6 minutes. Pick meat and proceed with the recipe.

2. Prepare octopus. To a large stockpot (about 4–6 quarts), add enough water to allow octopus to be fully submerged. Add 1 cup of the white wine, onion, lemons, and garlic cloves, and bring to a boil. Add the octopus and cook until tender, about 45 minutes to an hour. You can test whether it's done by seeing how easily a tentacle separates from the body. If it's tender, it will pretty much cut with a butter knife.

3. Remove and let rest for 20 minutes or so. Drizzle with olive oil and grill until charred, about 3–4 minutes each side.

4. Combine the chicken stock, Lobster Stock, and 2 cups of white wine and bring to simmer just to warm it up before using.

5. Put the olive oil in a heavy 12- to 14-inch paella pan. Ideally, place over a charcoal or gas grill and heat until hot but not smoking. (You can use the pan on a stovetop with a large burner, but it won't cook as evenly.)

6. Add the duck, bacon, or sausage, and cook for about 5 minutes.

Four 1¼–1½-pound lobsters (to yield about 1 pound of parcooked meat, cut into chunks, tails split in half)

½ cup medium dry sherry

1 tablespoon smoked paprika

1 tablespoon fresh thyme leaves

1 bay leaf

½ tablespoon saffron threads

4 cups Bomba rice (or substitute other short-grained rice)

2 dozen littleneck clams

2 pounds mussels

1 pound large shrimp, peeled and deveined

1 pound squid (calamari) tubes and tentacles, tubes sliced into ¼-inch rings

1 roasted red pepper, peeled and cut into strips (for garnish)

Fresh parsley (for garnish)

Smoked Red Pepper Aioli (see recipe below)

7.  Add the onions and cook, stirring frequently, until soft and light golden, about 5 minutes.

8.  Add the garlic and cook another minute.

9.  Add the tomatoes, sherry, smoked paprika, thyme, bay leaf, saffron, and half the stock mixture. Bring to simmer and then add the rice. Stir well to combine and allow to come back to a slow simmer. The rice should be submerged; if it isn't, add more of the stock.

10.  Push the clams and mussels down into the rice/sauce so they are covered by the liquid, being careful not to stir. Move the paella pan around on the grill if needed, to ensure even cooking and so the liquid continues to simmer. Add more stock as needed to maintain a thin layer for about 20 minutes, but do not move the rice around. You're trying to achieve a light crust on the bottom, being careful not to burn the rice. After 20 minutes, stop adding liquid. Add the shrimp, calamari, lobster, and grilled octopus, and continue to cook until all visible liquid is absorbed and rice is tender and not overcooked (another 5–10 minutes). Remove from the grill and lay peppers on top.

11.  Garnish with parsley and Smoked Red Pepper Aioli.

# Smoked Red Pepper Aioli

*Makes about 1½ cups*

1.  Drizzle the cut pepper with the olive oil, sprinkle with salt, and place in smoker. For the smoking, you can use either an outdoor smoker or a stovetop smoker. I use a Cameron stovetop smoker, but I use it on the grill to keep the smoke outdoors. Smoke for about 25–30 minutes over medium heat. If it has been adequately smoked, you'll see a slight golden brown tint to the pepper slices. Remove, let cool, and remove skin from peppers.

2.  Add peppers to food processor and process until smooth.

3.  Add the egg yolks, salt, sugar, and black pepper and turn on processor, and then add the oil in a slow stream to blend. Adjust salt or pepper as desired. Store in a squeeze bottle.

1 red bell pepper, quartered, ribs and seeds removed

1 tablespoon olive oil (for smoking)

2 egg yolks

½ teaspoon kosher salt

½ teaspoon sugar

½ teaspoon black pepper

½ cup good-quality olive oil (mild)

**Dana's Tip: You can use a good-quality prepared mayonnaise instead of making your own.**

# Lobster Newburg Pasta

This rich classic is made from some of my favorite things: cream, butter, cognac (brandy in my version), and sherry. I serve mine over campanelle, a tube-shaped pasta (because I could never tire of pasta), but it's often served over toast points or puff pastry.

*Serves 4*

1. Bring a large stockpot filled with about 2 inches of water to a boil. Place a steamer basket upside down, and then add the lobsters and cover. Cook for about 5–6 minutes. Pick meat, cut into chunks, and set aside.

2. Boil pasta in heavily salted water according to instructions and drain a minute shy of al dente. Put back in pan with a tablespoon of butter and keep covered.

3. In a heavy saucepan, heat ½ stick butter, add the shallot, and sauté over medium-low heat until translucent and light golden—about 6 minutes.

4. Add the lobster and cook in the butter over medium heat, stirring regularly, for 2 minutes.

5. Add 3 tablespoons of the sherry and 2 tablespoons of the brandy, and cook the mixture, stirring, for 2 minutes. Transfer the lobster meat with a slotted spoon to a bowl. Add the cream to the sherry mixture and boil the mixture until it is reduced to about 1 cup. Reduce the heat to low and stir in the remaining 1 teaspoon sherry, the remaining 1 teaspoon brandy, nutmeg, cayenne, and salt to taste. Whisk in the yolks, and cook the mixture, whisking constantly, until it registers 140°F on a thermometer; continue to cook, whisking for another 3 minutes. Stir in the lobster meat and serve over pasta.

6. Garnish with sliced cherry tomatoes, parsley, and chives.

3 live lobsters, about 1½ pounds each

1 pound preferred pasta

Kosher salt, for boiling the pasta and to taste

½ stick plus 1 tablespoon unsalted butter

1 large shallot, finely minced

3 tablespoons plus 1 teaspoon medium-dry sherry

2 tablespoons plus 1 teaspoon brandy

1½ cups heavy cream

¼ teaspoon freshly grated nutmeg

Cayenne to taste

4 large egg yolks, beaten well

1 cup cherry tomatoes, halved (for garnish)

1 tablespoon minced parsley

1 tablespoon minced chives

# Lobster and Squid Ink Pasta with Pureed Delicata Squash, Caramelized Shallots, Crispy Jerusalem Artichokes, and Brown Butter

1 stick butter

1 small Delicata squash

Olive oil, for drizzling squash and asparagus

1 bunch of asparagus (12–16 spears)

½ cup heavy cream

¼ teaspoon turmeric

½ teaspoon sweet paprika

½ teaspoon kosher salt (plus salt to taste for artichoke)

12 ounces squid ink pasta

1 medium Jerusalem artichoke

2 large shallots, sliced

1½ pounds cooked lobster meat

Microgreens (for garnish)

This is a surprisingly beautiful plate of dramatic colors and flavors. The briny-earthy squid ink pasta is balanced nicely by the rich squash puree. And the brown butter over the lobster and entire dish brings it all together. The result is worth the work!

*Serves 4*

1. Preheat oven to 375°F.

2. In small saucepan, add 1 stick butter and cook over medium-low heat until lightly brown in color and milk solids have fully separated, about 8–10 minutes, watching very carefully not to burn the butter. Strain through a fine-mesh sieve and place in large sauté pan. Set aside.

3. Halve squash lengthwise, remove seeds, and drizzle with olive oil. Roast cut side down until soft, about 40 minutes.

4. Place asparagus on sheet pan drizzled with olive oil and roast in oven until al dente, about 10–12 minutes (depending on how thick).

5. Scrape squash meat into a blender. Add 2 tablespoons brown butter, heavy cream, turmeric, paprika, and salt, and blend until smooth. Add more heavy cream if you want a thinner consistency. Place in small saucepan, cover, and keep warm over a simmer.

6. Cook pasta until al dente, drain, and place back in pan; cover to keep warm.

7.  Thinly slice Jerusalem artichoke. Add 2 tablespoons brown butter to a large sauté pan and pan fry over medium-high heat and cook until browned and crispy, about 10 minutes. Salt to taste. Remove to plate and cover to keep warm.

8.  Add remaining 4 tablespoons brown butter to the same sauté pan and cook shallots over medium low until light golden brown, about 10–12 minutes.

9.  Add lobster to pan with shallots and warm for just a couple minutes. Remove lobster and shallots, and set aside.

10.  Add pasta to the pan with the brown butter and toss to warm for a couple minutes.

11.  To serve, place some of the squash puree on the plate. Twirl pasta and divide among plates. Add lobster, asparagus spears, and shallots. Drizzle any remaining butter from the pan. Garnish with microgreens and crispy artichokes.

# Lobster Piccata with Capers, Lemon, White Wine, and Caramelized Shallots over Bucatini

Move over, Chicken Piccata—lobster is here to steal the show! If you tend to favor the bright, lemony style of a piccata, you'll love this dish.

*Serves 4*

1. Bring a large stockpot filled with about 2 inches of water to a boil. Place a steamer basket upside down, and then add the lobsters and cover. Cook for about 5–6 minutes. Pick meat and proceed with the recipe.

2. Cook bucatini in salted water 1 minute shy of instructions on the package. Drain, put back into pan, and drizzle with olive oil so pasta doesn't stick together.

3. Heat a large sauté pan over medium heat. Melt 2 tablespoons butter and add the shallots. Cook until golden, about 8–10 minutes. Add the garlic and cook for another 2 minutes.

4. Pour in the white wine and allow to reduce to half, while scraping any bits off of the bottom of the pan.

5. Reduce heat to medium low, add the cream, and bring to a gentle simmer, stirring occasionally. Cook for about 5 minutes. Then add the lobster. Season with salt and pepper.

6. Add in the Parmesan cheese and allow sauce to gently simmer for a further minute or so until the cheese melts through the sauce.

7. Add the lemon juice, capers, and parsley; stir through.

Four 1¼–1½-pound lobsters (to yield about 1 pound of parcooked meat)

1 pound bucatini

1 tablespoon olive oil

1 stick unsalted butter, divided

2 shallots

6 garlic cloves, minced

½ cup dry white wine (such as Sauvignon Blanc or unoaked Pinot Grigio)

3 tablespoons heavy cream

Kosher salt and pepper to taste

½ cup fresh-grated Parmesan cheese

2 tablespoons fresh lemon juice or more to taste

3 tablespoons rinsed and drained capers

2 tablespoons fresh minced parsley

Lemon slices, to serve

Fresh chopped parsley (extra), to garnish

8. Mix bucatini into sauce and cook for another minute.

9. Reduce heat to the lowest simmer and add remaining 6 tablespoons butter and stir to incorporate. Once it has mostly melted, turn off heat and continue to stir.

10. Add lemon slices and extra parsley to garnish.

# Lobster Carbonara with Bacon, Peas, and Parmesan

Lobster, bacon, and cream? *YES*, please.

*Serves 4*

Kosher salt, for cooking pasta

16 ounces thick spaghetti

1 tablespoon olive oil

½ cup bacon, diced

1 shallot, minced

3 garlic cloves, minced

¼ cup fresh English peas

1 pound lobster meat, cooked

2 egg yolks

¼ cup heavy cream

¼ cup Parmesan cheese, ground

Freshly ground black pepper (to taste)

Chives (for garnish)

1.  Bring a large pot of salted water to a boil. Place pasta in water and cook 1 minute shy of al dente. Drain, reserving ¼ cup of the pasta water. Put pasta back into pan and drizzle with olive oil so pasta doesn't stick together.

2.  In a large sauté pan over medium heat, cook bacon and shallots until bacon is shy of crisp and shallots are golden.

3.  Add garlic and English peas and cook until peas begin to soften.

4.  Add lobster and heat for another minute.

5.  Mix eggs with ¼ cup of the reserved pasta water and heavy cream, and whisk well.

6.  Lower the heat to simmer and add egg mixture; toss gently to combine. You want the eggs to become the sauce, not scrambled. Stir in the Parmesan cheese and add the pasta. Mix well.

7.  Finish with black pepper and garnish with chives.

# Butter-Poached Lobster on Filet Mignon with Crispy Fried Shallots, Parsnip-Potato Puree, and Brown Butter Drizzle

This is a simple, elegant dish that's elevated by a silky parsnip-potato puree and decadent lobster brown butter.

*Serves 4*

1. In small saucepan, add 1 stick butter and cook over medium-low heat until milk solids have fully separated, about 6–7 minutes.

2. Strain through a fine-mesh sieve and place in a large sauté pan. Add lobster, reduce heat to a low simmer, and cook until lobster is fully opaque, but cook slowly to avoid overcooking—about 7–8 minutes. Remove lobster and set aside and let cool to room temperature. Strain butter through a fine-mesh sieve and save for the next step.

3. Add strained lobster butter to a sauté pan and cook shallots over medium heat until golden, about 7–8 minutes. Turn off heat and set aside until ready to use.

4. Bring steak to room temperature before cooking (at least 30 minutes up to 1 hour).

5. Add the olive oil and 3 tablespoons butter to a cast iron skillet and turn heat to medium high. Salt and pepper the filets, and place the filets facedown and sear undisturbed for 4 minutes. Flip the filets and sear for an additional 3 minutes. If steaks are small enough (not too thick), or you cut them into smaller medallions, you can use the stovetop for 4 minutes on each side and not transfer them to an oven.

1 stick plus 3 tablespoons butter

4 raw lobster tails*

2 large shallots, thinly sliced

4 small (5–6 ounce) filets, about 1½ inches thick

1 tablespoon olive oil

Kosher salt and pepper (for seasoning)

Parsnip-Potato Puree *(see recipe below)*

6.  Transfer your skillet directly to the oven (for medium rare, 5–6 minutes; medium, 6–7 minutes). Let rest before slicing.

*If you can't find raw lobster tails, steam 2 lobsters (about 1½ pounds each) for 6 minutes and remove meat from shells. Proceed with recipe for poaching lobster. Cooking time may be reduced by 2–3 minutes.*

## Parsnip-Potato Puree

½ stick butter

1 pound parsnips, peeled and cut into 1-inch pieces

1 pound Yukon gold potatoes, peeled and cut into 2-inch pieces

1 tablespoon plus ½ teaspoon kosher salt

1 cup heavy cream

½ stick unsalted butter

¼ teaspoon black pepper

1.  Cover parsnips and potatoes with cold water by 1 inch in a 6- to 8-quart pot; then add 1 tablespoon salt and bring to a boil. Reduce heat and simmer vegetables, until very tender but not falling apart, about 30–35 minutes.

2.  Bring cream, butter, pepper, and remaining ½ teaspoon salt to a simmer in a 3- to 4-quart heavy pot over medium heat.

3.  Drain vegetables. Force warm vegetables through ricer fitted with a medium disc into cream mixture, and then stir to combine well. For a silky-smooth puree, place in blender and pulse a few times, being careful not to overblend to avoid the mixture becoming gummy. Keep covered until ready to plate. Puree can be made a day ahead and chilled in a baking dish, covered. Bring to room temperature and reheat, covered, in a preheated 400°F oven until hot (about 20–25 minutes).

## To Serve

Place some of the parsnip-potato puree on the plate, top with sliced filet, a lobster tail, some fried shallots, and the brown butter. Garnish with microgreens and some freshly ground black pepper. This recipe pairs well with steamed fresh green beans.

# Grilled Lobster Tails, Corn Puree, and Queso Fresco, with Smoked Paprika Oil and Fried Shallots

**Once you try grilled lobster, you might agree it's hard to beat. The smoky flavor of the grilled lobster in this dish is nicely complemented by the sweet corn puree and cornbread "crouton."**

*Serves 2*

1. To make brown butter, in a small saucepan, add ½ stick butter and cook over medium-low heat until lightly brown in color and milk solids have fully separated, about 8–10 minutes, watching very carefully not to burn the butter. Strain through a fine-mesh sieve and set aside.

2. Thinly slice shallot and pan fry in 2 tablespoons olive oil over medium-high heat until browned, about 5 minutes.

3. In a small saucepan, add 4 tablespoons brown butter and sauté corn 3 minutes.

4. Add heavy cream and salt and simmer 5 minutes.

5. Put corn mixture in blender and puree until smooth. For a really smooth sauce, strain through a fine-mesh sieve. Add chives and put back into saucepan to keep warm or to reheat before serving.

6. Split tails, drizzle cut side with olive oil, and place cut side down over medium hot grill.

7. Flip tails, spread 4 tablespoons softened brown butter (which remains spreadable at room temperature), and grill another 5 minutes.

4 Cornbread "Croutons" *(see recipe below)*

½ cup brown butter, divided

1 large shallot

2 tablespoons olive oil

2 ears of corn, cut from the cob

¾ cup heavy cream

¼ teaspoon kosher salt

1 tablespoon minced chives

4 small lobster tails, raw (or steamed 5 minutes if you don't have raw)

Olive oil for grilling

¼ crumbled queso fresco cheese

1 tablespoon thinly sliced scallions (for garnish)

1 tablespoon finely diced red bell pepper (for garnish)

Smoked Paprika Oil, for garnish *(see recipe below)*

# Smoked Paprika Oil

1. Heat the olive oil over medium heat in a small skillet or saucepan until warm and the oil begins to shimmer.

2. Remove from heat and stir in smoked paprika and a good pinch of salt. Whisk really well to combine. Let meld for 1 hour.

3. Strain through a fine-mesh sieve. Set aside.

¼ cup extra-virgin olive oil

1½ teaspoons smoked paprika

Kosher salt

1 cup corn meal

1 cup flour

1 cup milk

1 egg

⅓ cup vegetable oil

⅔ cup sugar

3½ teaspoons baking
  powder

## Cornbread "Croutons"

1.  Preheat oven to 350°F.

2.  Mix cornbread ingredients and bake in 9-inch by 9-inch glass baking dish for 25 minutes. Let cool. Using biscuit cutter, cut into 2- to 3-inch rounds. Lower oven to 300°F and crisp "croutons" in oven for 20 minutes.

## To Assemble

Place 2 cornbread croutons on each plate. Top each with a tablespoon or so of corn puree. Top each with 2 tail halves. Sprinkle queso, scallions, and red pepper. Drizzle plate with Smoked Paprika Oil.

# Lobster Pot Pie

Chicken pot pie is one of my most favorite food dishes to make, so it was a no-brainer that I was going to make a lobster version for this cookbook. The base flavor is similar to a lobster bisque. And don't skimp on the sherry!

*Makes 4–6 individual pot pies*

1. Preheat oven to 375°F.

2. Prepare Pastry Crust and set aside. In a large sauté pan, add Chilled Lobster Butter and sauté shallots over medium heat for 3–4 minutes.

3. Add carrots and celery, and sauté another 3–4 minutes.

4. Lower heat and add tomato paste, and cook 2 minutes.

5. Add flour and incorporate thoroughly, and cook 2 minutes.

6. Add stock, wine, sherry, salt, pepper, parsley, and thyme, and simmer while stirring for 5 minutes.

7. Add heavy cream and milk, and stir.

8. Add lobster, reserving the claw for garnish.

9. Place bottom crust in dish, divide filling among dishes and top with crust, crimping edges together.

10. Cut steam vent in each.

11. Brush with egg wash and bake until brown and filling is bubbling, about 45 minutes for individual pies, or 1 hour or so for one large pie.

12. Garnish top with lobster claw coming up out of vent hole in crust.

Pastry Crust *(see recipe below)*

6 tablespoons Chilled Lobster Butter *(see page 73)*

2 large shallots, diced

3 small carrots, diced

2 celery ribs, diced

1 tablespoon tomato paste

½ cup flour

2½ cups Lobster Stock *(see page 83)*

½ cup dry white wine

¼ cup medium dry sherry

½ teaspoon kosher salt

¼ teaspoon white pepper

1 tablespoon chopped parsley

Leaves from 3 thyme sprigs

½ cup heavy cream

1 cup whole milk

8 ounces lobster, cut into chunks, leaving 1 whole claw for garnish

1 egg plus 1 teaspoon milk (for egg wash for top crust)

# Pastry Crust

1. Dice the butter and return it to the refrigerator while you prepare the flour mixture.

2. Place the flour, salt, and sugar in the bowl of a food processor fitted with a blade and pulse a couple times to incorporate.

3. Add the butter and shortening. Pulse 8–12 times, until the butter is the size of peas.

4. With the machine running, pour the ice water down the feed tube and pulse the machine until the dough begins to form a ball. Place dough on a floured board and roll into a ball. Wrap in plastic and refrigerate for 30 minutes.

5. Cut the dough in half. Roll each piece on a floured board into a circle, turning and flouring the dough as needed to make sure it doesn't stick to the board.

6. Cut portions of the dough large enough to fit your pot pie baking dish (if individual) or to fit one large dish. Repeat with the top crust. Set aside until ready to put together.

1½ sticks very cold unsalted butter

3 cups all-purpose flour

1 teaspoon kosher salt

1 tablespoon sugar

⅓ cup very cold vegetable shortening

6–7 tablespoons (about ½ cup or less) ice water

# Lobster Imperial

Having moved to Maine from Maryland, I was used to buying jumbo lump crab (from the Chesapeake Blue crab) and making Crab Imperial. Now that I'm in Maine, why not make this dish with the king of crustaceans?

*Serves 4*

Six 1¼–1½-pound lobsters (to yield about 1½ pounds of parcooked meat, chopped)

½ cup mayonnaise

1½ teaspoons Worcestershire sauce

1 tablespoon lemon juice

1 tablespoon capers

1½ teaspoons Dijon mustard

¼ teaspoon Old Bay seasoning

½ teaspoon kosher salt

Paprika (for dusting)

1. Bring a large stockpot filled with about 2 inches of water to a boil. Place a steamer basket upside down, and then add the lobsters and cover. Cook for about 5–6 minutes. Pick meat and proceed with the recipe.

2. Mix mayonnaise, Worcestershire sauce, lemon juice, capers, Dijon mustard, Old Bay seasoning, and salt.

3. Fold in lobster, and then dust with paprika. Bake in individual ramekins or baking dishes at 350°F for about 22–25 minutes, but no longer, or the sauce will "break," which means it will become translucent and appear oily rather than creamy. (This is not so bad if it happens, however, and will not affect flavor.)

# Lobster, Mushroom, and Asparagus Crepes with Lemon Brown Butter

Savory crepes make a perfect light dinner or lunch with a mixed-greens salad. This version might become a regular in your recipe rotation.

## Basic Savory Crepes

*Makes 12 (serves 4)*

1. Mix the milk, eggs, flour, and salt in a blender, scraping down the sides to incorporate all the ingredients.

2. Pour the melted butter through the opening in the lid and mix for another few seconds. Let the batter sit in the refrigerator at least 30 minutes or up to one day.

3. Remove the batter from the refrigerator.

4. You'll need a shallow nonstick frying pan or crepe pan, 8–9 inches in diameter. Heat over medium high. Once hot, coat with nonstick cooking spray or butter.

5. Add a small amount of batter (about ⅓ cup) to coat the pan, swirling the batter around to spread to ensure it stays thin. Heat until the edges just turn brown, about 2 minutes, and flip to cook for another 30 seconds or so. Remove to a piece of wax paper and repeat with remaining batter, stacking the crepes.

1⅓ cups whole or 2 percent milk

4 large eggs

1⅓ cups flour

A pinch of kosher salt

½ stick butter, melted

Nonstick cooking spray

## Filling the Crepes

36 stems of asparagus, cut in half

Olive oil (optional; for grilling asparagus)

2 cups mixed wild mushrooms, chopped

6 tablespoons butter, divided

Leaves from 2 thyme sprigs

8 ounces ricotta cheese

1 egg yolk

½ teaspoon kosher salt

½ cup grated Parmesan cheese

1 pound cooked lobster meat, chopped (plus some for garnish)

Lemon Brown Butter (*see recipe below*)

Microgreens (for garnish)

1. Preheat oven to 350°F.

2. Blanch the asparagus in boiling water for 3 minutes. Alternatively, brush with olive oil and grill until lightly charred.

3. Sauté mushrooms in 3 tablespoons butter and thyme until mushrooms are lightly browned, about 10 minutes.

4. Put the ricotta, egg yolk, salt, and grated Parmesan cheese in a food processor and mix until very smooth.

5. Place 2 tablespoons of filling in the center of each crepe. Add 3 stalks of asparagus, about 2 tablespoons of chopped lobster, and 1 tablespoon of mushrooms. Roll and place seam side down onto a parchment-lined, rimmed baking sheet. Repeat with remaining crepes.

6. Add 3 tablespoons butter to a sauté pan and brown crepe on both sides, about 2–3 minutes per side. Place on a sheet pan and place in a 300°F oven for 10 minutes, to fully warm the inside. Lower oven to 180–190°F until ready to serve to keep warm.

7. Top with Lemon Brown Butter.

8. Garnish with a couple pieces of lobster, a few mushrooms, and microgreens.

# Lemon Brown Butter

1.  Add butter to a small saucepan set over medium heat.

2.  Add shallot and cook, stirring and swirling the pan every few seconds, until the foam subsides, the butter begins to turn golden brown and smells nutty, and the shallots soften—about 5 minutes.

3.  Then stir in garlic and let it sizzle for about 30 seconds and turn off the heat.

4.  Add lemon juice and zest. Season with salt and pepper; keep warm until ready to serve.

5 tablespoons unsalted butter

1 shallot, minced

1 garlic clove, minced

1 tablespoon fresh lemon juice

Zest from ½ lemon

Kosher salt and freshly ground black pepper (to taste)

# Lobster Scallion Crepes

2 bunches of scallions

Olive oil for grilling scallions

5 large eggs

1¼ cups milk (2 percent)

1 cup all-purpose flour

1 teaspoon salt

1 teaspoon sugar

½ teaspoon mustard powder

1 teaspoon onion powder

1 teaspoon dried chives

½ teaspoon black pepper

½ cup plus 1 tablespoon Soy Glaze (see recipe below)

2 sticks butter, separated

16–20 wonton skins (the more crunch, the better!)

About 2 cups of vegetable oil, for frying wontons

1 pound lobster meat, raw and picked

½ cup Smoked Truffle Aioli (see recipe below)

**Garnishes:**

microgreens

chives, finely minced

black and white sesame seeds

Charred scallion crepes with brown butter–poached lobster, Smoked Truffle Aioli, sweet Soy Glaze, fried wonton bits, toasted sesame seeds, chives, and microgreens—another award-winning recipe, this one from the 2018 Maine Lobster Chef of the Year competition at Harvest on the Harbor in Portland, Maine!

*Makes about 14 crepes*

1. Heat grill and cook scallions, tossed in olive oil, with lid closed on medium-low heat, flipping halfway through, until very charred, about 8–10 minutes. Set aside to cool. Chop into small pieces, about an inch.

2. In a blender, add eggs, milk, flour, salt, sugar, mustard powder, onion powder, dried chives, black pepper, and 1 tablespoon Soy Glaze. Blend on medium, scrape down the sides, and blend another few seconds.

3. Melt ½ stick of butter and add through the blender lid opening, and blend another few seconds. On medium-low, add scallions and blend until scallions are in very small bits, about 5 seconds. Let the batter rest at least 4 hours or as long as overnight. Bring to room temperature before making crepes.

4. Heat a crepe pan or a very shallow 8- to 9-inch sauté pan on medium-low until hot. Add about ½ tablespoon butter. After butter has melted, pour ⅓ cup of batter into the center of the pan. Immediately pick up the pan and tilt and swirl it to spread the batter evenly over the bottom. Cook for 1½–2 minutes, or until the crepe is golden on the bottom. When you see the edge begin to brown, you know it's time to flip. Cook another 30 seconds on the other side. Set aside on wax paper.

5. Cook remaining crepes, adding butter to pan as needed (at least every other crepe or more). I stack mine without wax paper between

and have never found the need to place wax paper between crepes—and I've stacked nearly 100 crepes in a stack!

6.  Toast sesame seeds on a parchment-lined sheet pan in a 300°F oven until the white sesames have a light golden hue, about 10–12 minutes. Let cool.

7.  Cut wontons into small ⅛-inch to ¼-inch squares and fry in vegetable oil at 360°F until golden. Drain on a paper towel and store in an airtight container.

8.  In a small saucepan, add 1 stick butter and cook over medium-low heat until lightly brown in color and milk solids have fully separated, about 8–10 minutes, watching very carefully not to burn the butter. Strain through a fine-mesh sieve and place in clean saucepan.

9.  In a clean saucepan, add the strained brown butter and heat over medium low for 1 minute. Add lobster and cook until lobster is fully opaque, but cook slowly to avoid overcooking—about 6–8 minutes. Set aside.

**Dana's Tip:** Be sure to strain the lobster cooking butter/liquid and cool in the refrigerator. The "lobster butter" will float to the top, and the lobster cooking juices will remain on the bottom. Both can be used in other dishes!

## To Assemble

Quarter-fold the warm crepe. Top with the butter-poached lobster. Drizzle both the aioli and remaining ½ cup of Soy Glaze over top. Garnish with microgreens, minced chives, toasted sesames, and a nice scattering of the wonton bits. If your crepes are cool, quarter-fold them and warm in a sauté pan with butter, 2 minutes per side, before topping.

# Soy Glaze

*Makes about 1 cup*

1. Add the brown sugar, soy sauces, garlic, ginger, rice wine, sherry, and rice wine vinegar to a small saucepan and heat until brown sugar is dissolved. Remove from heat.

2. Stir in mirin and fish sauce. Let cool and store in squeeze bottle.

> A similar bottled alternative can be found in supermarkets or Asian grocers—Kikkoman makes a nice "Unagi" sweet sauce as well as a "Sweet Soy for Sushi."

¼ cup dark brown sugar

¼ cup sweet soy sauce *(which is thicker, similar to molasses, and can be found in Asian markets)*

¼ cup regular soy sauce

1 garlic clove, finely minced

½ teaspoon fresh grated ginger

2 tablespoons rice cooking wine (Shaoxing)

2 tablespoons medium sherry

1 teaspoon rice wine vinegar

1 tablespoon mirin

1 teaspoon fish sauce

# Smoked Truffle Aioli

*Makes about 2 cups*

1. For the smoking you can use either an outdoor smoker or a stove-top smoker. I used a Cameron stovetop smoker, but I used it on the grill to keep the smoke out of the house!

2. Place 1 cup of the mayonnaise and butter in an ovenproof dish and place in smoker (following manufacturer instructions). Smoke for about 30 minutes. If it has been adequately smoked, you'll see browned bits along the edge of the baking dish and a light brown tint to the mayo and butter. Let cool completely. Add to blender with the remaining mayonnaise, salt, black pepper, and truffle oil. Store in squeeze bottle.

1½ cups Japanese "Kewpie" mayonnaise *(This is made from egg yolks, not whole eggs like traditional American mayonnaise, so it's creamier. You can find it online or in Asian markets.)*

½ stick butter

½ teaspoon kosher salt

1 teaspoon black pepper

1 tablespoon white truffle oil

# Lobster and Scallops Hamayaki Style with Soy Glaze

This dish is an absolute umami bomb and one of my favorite dishes. I had a dish with crab at a Japanese restaurant and knew I had to re-create it at home with lobster. It's simple but rich and full of flavor.

*Serves 4*

1. Preheat oven to 350°F.

2. Cook rice according to your rice cooker and/or directions on the bag of rice.

3. Mix Kewpie with truffle oil, salt, and pepper.

4. In a large sauté pan, heat Chilled Lobster Butter over high heat; when hot, add scallops. Cook to sear and cook until just opaque, about 4 minutes.

5. Lower heat and add lobster to the same pan just to warm 1 minute.

6. Using large scallop shells (which can be purchased online), top each with the rice and shape into a rounded mound. Alternatively, you can use shallow gratin or baking dishes.

7. Place lobster and scallops over the top.

8. Spread a thick layer of Kewpie over each, covering most of the surface.

9. Place on a baking sheet and bake in middle oven for 20 minutes.

10. Top each with a tablespoon of Soy Glaze and broil just until bubbly.

11. Garnish with lobster claw.

2 cups cooked sushi rice (*I use Kokuho brand*)

1½ cups Kewpie Japanese mayonnaise

1½ teaspoons truffle oil

¼ teaspoon kosher salt

¼ teaspoon Sichuan pepper

2 tablespoons Chilled Lobster Butter (*see page 73*)

6 ounces dry sea scallops, cut into large chunks

8 ounces cooked lobster meat, cut into chunks

4 large scallop shells

4 tablespoons Soy Glaze (*see page 201*)

# LOBSTER— IT'S WHAT'S FOR BREAKFAST

# Lobster and Corn Quiche with Fontina and Basil

Primarily a crustless quiche, this version uses cornbread crumbs as the base instead of a pie crust. It's a nice combination with the corn, lobster, and basil.

*Makes 4 individual quiches*

1. In small saucepan, add 1 stick butter and cook over medium-low heat until lightly brown in color and milk solids have fully separated, about 8–10 minutes, watching very carefully not to burn the butter. Strain through a fine-mesh sieve and set aside.

2. In saucepan, sauté corn with 2 tablespoons brown butter for 3 minutes. Add half and half, and simmer over low for 10 minutes. Strain and set both aside to cool.

3. Coat baking dishes with nonstick cooking spray.

4. Add about 2 tablespoons Panko/cornbread crumb mixture *(see page 208)* to each dish and press into bottom. Divide lobster meat, corn, Fontina cheese, and basil among the baking dishes.

5. In blender, mix strained half and half with eggs, salt, and pepper. Pour into baking dishes.

6. Bake until set, but not browned—about 20 minutes. Time will vary based on the size and depth of your baking dishes.

1 stick butter

1 ear of corn, kernels cut from the cob

1¾ cups half and half

Cooking spray

¾ cup cooked lobster, cut into small chunks

½ cup Fontina cheese, cut into a small dice

½ tablespoon fresh basil, minced

½ cup cornbread crumbs

¼ cup Panko crumbs

4 eggs

½ teaspoon kosher salt

¼ teaspoon freshly ground black pepper

# Cornbread (for Crumbs)

1 cup corn meal

1 cup flour

1 cup milk

1 egg

⅓ cup vegetable oil

⅔ cup sugar

3½ teaspoons baking powder

1.  Preheat oven to 350°F.

2.  Mix cornbread ingredients and bake in 9-inch by 9-inch glass baking dish for 25 minutes. When cool enough to handle, remove about ¼ of the bread and crumble into a bowl. Place on a cookie sheet and put back into the oven until crumbs get crisp, about 10–12 minutes. Mix with Panko crumbs and 2 tablespoons brown butter. Use remaining cornbread for the croutons in the Grilled Lobster Tails, Corn Puree, and Queso Fresco, with Smoked Paprika Oil and Fried Shallots *(see page 185)*, or make croutons for a salad or turkey stuffing/dressing.

# Egg Roulade with Lobster and Sherry Butter

**This dish has long been a favorite enjoyed by inn guests, friends, and family alike. And it's absolutely worth the effort.**

*Serves 6*

1.  Preheat oven to 350°F.

2.  Grease a rimmed heavy-duty half sheet pan with butter or vegetable oil. Line the pan with parchment paper and grease the parchment, making sure to press it flat to the surface of the pan, leaving at least an inch of overhang. This is critical to the rolling of the egg "sponge."

3.  In a blender (critical to use the blender to create air in the egg mixture), mix the eggs, 2 cups of cream, and ½ teaspoon salt on high speed for 4–5 seconds. Pour the mixture into the lined baking sheet. Bake until you begin to see the surface of the egg start to lightly brown, about 25–30 minutes. Remove and let cool.

4.  While cooling, heat the olive oil and 3 tablespoons of butter in a pan over medium-high heat. Sauté the leeks, covered, until soft, about 10–12 minutes. When soft, add the cream cheese, Worcestershire sauce, the remaining 2 tablespoons of cream, lemon juice, and the remaining ½ teaspoon of salt and stir. When the cream cheese is thoroughly incorporated, remove from heat. Let cool for a few minutes.

5.  Dollop small amounts of the leek filling onto the egg. Using an offset spatula, carefully spread the mixture over the entire egg sponge, trying not to tear the egg, as it is very delicate. Sprinkle the Parmesan cheese over the filling.

6.  With the short edge of the pan closest to you, and using the parchment as a guide, roll the egg up onto itself (like a jelly roll cake) until you end up with the egg seam on the underside of the roll. Keep the egg covered with the parchment left after rolling, as doing so will help

## Ingredients

- Butter or vegetable oil, for greasing pan
- 8 eggs
- 2 cups plus 2 tablespoons heavy cream
- 1 teaspoon kosher salt, divided
- 2 tablespoons extra-virgin olive oil
- 1 stick plus 3 tablespoons butter
- 3 large leeks, washed and thinly sliced
- 1 (8-ounce) package cream cheese
- 1 teaspoon Worcestershire sauce
- Juice from ¼ lemon
- 1½ cups shredded Parmesan cheese
- ½ cup medium dry sherry
- 16 ounces fresh, cooked lobster meat, cut into small chunks
- 1 (10-ounce) package baby spinach, washed and dried
- Fresh chopped chives (for garnish)

keep the egg moist. Cover the entire roll with aluminum foil and bake for another 20 minutes.

7. While baking, melt the remaining stick of butter in a pan with the sherry and cook for about 5 minutes, allowing much of the alcohol to burn off. Then add the lobster, lower the heat, and cover. Simmer for 3–4 minutes.

## To Serve

Place a pile of fresh baby spinach on a plate. Slice the roulade into 6 pieces, layer onto the spinach, and top with a couple spoonfuls of the lobster butter. Garnish with fresh chives.

# Lobster and Poached Egg on Crispy Potato Latkes with Lemon Brown Butter and Wilted Baby Spinach

**Crispy potato latkes replace the English muffin for a creative twist on eggs Benedict.**

*Serves 6*

1 stick butter

Juice from ½ lemon

¼ teaspoon kosher salt

6 cups baby spinach

1 cup cooked lobster meat, cut into chunks

¼ cup white vinegar

12 eggs

1.  In small saucepan, add 1 stick butter and cook over medium-low heat until lightly brown in color and milk solids have fully separated, about 8–10 minutes, watching very carefully not to burn the butter. Strain through a fine-mesh sieve and set aside in a small bowl. Add the juice from ½ of a lemon and salt and mix.

2.  In a large sauté pan, add 2 tablespoons of the lemon brown butter and wilt spinach over medium heat for 3 minutes. Set aside.

3.  Warm lobster in 1 tablespoon of lemon brown butter in small saucepan for 3–4 minutes. Turn off heat and keep covered while preparing the rest of the dish.

4.  Fill a saucepan (3 quart) ¾ full with water and add the white vinegar.

5.  Bring to a slow rolling boil.

6.  Crack 1 egg into a small bowl or ramekin and lower into the boiling water. Repeat with remaining eggs. Cook for 3–4 minutes for a softer yolk.

7.  Remove the eggs with a slotted spoon and place on a paper towel to dry before plating.

# Potato Latkes

*Makes about 12 (4-inch) latkes*

3 large Russet or Idaho
potatoes

1 medium yellow or
sweet onion

½ cup thinly sliced
scallions

3 eggs

¾ cup flour

1½ teaspoons baking
powder

1½ teaspoons salt

¼ teaspoon freshly
ground black pepper

½ teaspoon onion
powder

2 cups vegetable oil for
frying (or enough to
come up about ¼ inch
from the bottom of
the pan)

1.  In a food processor, using the medium shredding disc, process the potatoes and onion and set into a large mixing bowl.

2.  Add the scallions, eggs, flour, baking powder, salt, pepper, and onion powder and mix until well blended.

3.  In a large frying pan, heat vegetable oil until hot.

4.  Take about ⅓ cup of the mixture and shape it into a flat disc as best you can; then carefully add to the oil, trying to keep its round shape. Fry for 3–4 minutes, until brown on one side. Flip, cooking another 3 minutes until browned. Remove to a paper towel. Repeat until all the latkes are fried.

5.  You can keep them warm in a 250°F oven on a rack placed on a sheet pan (so they are elevated and air can circulate under) until ready to serve. Or keep them at room temperature for an hour or so and reheat before serving.

# To Assemble

Divide spinach among plates. Add 2 latkes and top with lobster and poached egg. Drizzle with remaining lemon brown butter.

**Dana's Tip:** For a time saver, poach your eggs ahead of time by cooking 3 minutes and placing them into ice water. Then, when ready to plate and serve, warm the eggs in a pan of clean simmering water for 2 minutes. Then remove eggs from the water, place onto a towel to drain and serve!

# Lobster Fried Rice with Candied Pork Belly and Fried Egg

This recipe will obviously make a great dinner entrée, but I wanted to change it up a bit and offer it for breakfast with a nice fried egg. Another flavor bomb!

*Serves 4*

## Fried Rice

1. Add the Chilled Lobster Butter and vegetable oil to a large sauté pan and heat over medium high until melted. Add onion and cabbage and season with a generous pinch of salt and pepper. Sauté for about 5 minutes or until the onion is soft.

2. Increase heat to high and add the rice, about ¾ of the scallions, bean sprouts, and soy sauce; stir until combined. Continue stirring for an additional 4 minutes to fry the rice. Add the garlic and continue to cook for 2 minutes.

3. Add the lobster and braising juices and cook another 2 minutes. Turn down to the lowest simmer and cover until ready to serve.

4. In a separate frying pan over medium heat, add 2 tablespoons butter and fry 4 eggs until edges are lightly browned, whites are set, and yolk is still soft, about 4 minutes.

2 tablespoons Chilled Lobster Butter *(see page 73)*

2 tablespoons vegetable oil

1 large onion, diced

1 cup shredded Napa cabbage

Kosher salt and freshly ground black pepper (for seasoning)

4 cups cooked medium or long-grain white rice

1 bunch of scallions, thinly sliced, divided

½ cup bean sprouts

2–3 tablespoons soy sauce

2 garlic cloves, minced

1 pound cooked lobster meat

2 tablespoons reserved pork belly braising juices *(see page 217)*

2 tablespoons butter

4 large eggs

1 tablespoon Soy Glaze *(see page 201)* for garnish

# Pork Belly

1. In a large plastic bag or container, combine the soy sauce, mirin, rice wine, brown sugar, scallions, ginger, and garlic.

2. Add the pork belly to the marinade and seal the bag. Refrigerate for 8 hours.

3. Preheat oven to 325°F.

4. Add 1 tablespoon vegetable oil and chopped onion to a 5- to 6-quart Dutch oven. Season lightly with salt and cook over moderate heat, stirring, until softened, about 5 minutes. Add the pork belly and marinade and bring to a boil. Cover and braise in the oven for 2 hours, until the meat is nearly tender. Uncover and braise for 1 hour longer, until the meat is very tender and nicely browned.

5. Transfer the pork to a cutting board. Let cool to room temperature. Strain braising juice and set aside for the fried rice.

6. Slice into ⅓- to ½-inch slices.

7. Add 2 tablespoons vegetable oil to a sauté pan and sear on both sides over medium-high heat until crispy, about 3 minutes per side. Set aside until ready to plate.

- ¼ cup soy sauce
- ¼ cup mirin
- ¼ cup rice wine (Shaoxing)
- 3 tablespoons light brown sugar
- 2 scallions, thinly sliced, reserving some for garnish
- 2 tablespoons fresh grated ginger
- 2 garlic cloves, minced
- 1½ pounds skinless pork belly
- 3 tablespoons vegetable oil, divided
- 1 large onion, coarsely chopped
- Kosher salt (for seasoning)

# To Serve

Divide fried rice among the plates and top with 2 slices of pork belly and a fried egg. Garnish with remaining scallions and a drizzle of Soy Glaze (you can also use Kikkoman's sweet soy sauce as a substitute).

# Lobster Frittata with Leeks, Parmesan, and Roasted Tomatoes

Three 1¼–1½-pound lobsters (to yield about 1½ cups of parcooked meat, chopped)

3 Roma tomatoes

Kosher salt and pepper (for seasoning)

Olive oil (for roasting)

18 large eggs

2 cups heavy cream

1 teaspoon dry mustard

½ teaspoon granulated onion powder

1 teaspoon salt

2 tablespoons extra-virgin olive oil

2 tablespoons butter

2 leeks, white and pale green parts, diced

2 shallots, diced

¼ cup grated Parmesan cheese

1 cup Fontina cheese, shredded

½ cup shredded Parmesan cheese

Freshly ground black pepper (for seasoning)

*My method for making a frittata results in a much fluffier and creamier texture than many I've tried.*

*Serves 6–8*

1.  Preheat oven to 325°F.

2.  Bring a large stockpot filled with about 2 inches of water to a boil. Place a steamer basket upside down, and then add the lobsters and cover. Cook for about 5–6 minutes. Pick meat and proceed with the recipe.

3.  Cut the tomatoes in quarters and sprinkle with salt and pepper and a drizzle of olive oil. Roast for 35–40 minutes.

4.  Mix the eggs, cream, dry mustard, onion powder, and salt in a blender for about 4–5 seconds. (A blender really incorporates air and increases the volume dramatically.)

5.  In a large ovenproof sauté pan over medium heat, add the olive oil and butter, and sauté the leeks and shallots until very lightly caramelized, about 10 minutes. Set aside about ⅓ of the mixture.

6.  Reduce heat to medium low, add the egg mixture, and stir constantly with a heatproof rubber spatula until curds form. Once you see curds just begin to form, add 1 cup of the lobster, grated Parmesan cheese, and shredded Fontina cheese. Lower the heat and continue to move the eggs around, never stopping, almost as if to scramble. Remove from heat when the eggs are about half set. Doing so helps the bottom from cooking in place and browning. A traditional frittata is intentionally browned; mine is not and remains fluffy and creamy.

7. Top with roasted tomato quarters and shredded Parmesan cheese and a few cracks of black pepper.

8. Place on the center rack in the oven for about 10 minutes.

9. Remove from the oven and top with remaining ½ cup of lobster and remaining leek and shallot mixture. Finish in the oven for another 10 minutes, just until the toppings warm slightly but the egg does not overcook.

10. Let sit 5 minutes before slicing and serving (as you would a lasagna) so it will hold together, as the egg is very tender.

# Savory Scallion Waffles Topped with Brown Butter–Poached Lobster, Poached Egg, Brown Butter Wasabi Mayo, and Sweet Soy Glaze

This is my absolute new favorite way to eat a savory waffle! The balance between sweet, savory, and umami is perfectly addictive.

*Makes 6 (4-inch) waffles (serves 2 or 3)*

## Brown Butter–Poached Lobster

1. In a small saucepan, add 1 stick butter and cook over medium-low heat until lightly brown in color and milk solids have fully separated, about 8–10 minutes, watching very carefully not to burn the butter.

2. Strain through a fine-mesh sieve, place in large sauté pan, and heat butter over medium low for 1 minute.

3. Add lobster, lower heat to a simmer, and cook until lobster is fully opaque, but cook slowly to avoid overcooking—about 7–8 minutes.

4. Remove lobster and set aside.

5. When cool, cut into small bite-size chunks.

1 pound raw lobster meat

1 stick butter (for poaching)

# Waffle Batter

1. Toast sesames on a sheet pan at 325°F for 10 minutes.

2. Mix oils, salt, sugar, baking powder, and seasoning spices with egg and oil, and whisk.

3. Add milk and mix well.

4. Add flour and mix gently (to avoid developing gluten).

5. Fold in scallions.

6. Heat waffle iron on highest setting. Coat lightly with cooking spray. When hot, add batter to cover. Cook about 5 minutes, and then open to release steam. Close and cook another 2 minutes or until crispy to your liking.

2 tablespoons black and white toasted sesames (for garnish)

1 egg

¼ cup vegetable oil

¼ teaspoon sesame oil

1 teaspoon kosher salt

½ teaspoon sugar

½ tablespoon baking powder

¼ teaspoon garlic powder

¼ teaspoon onion powder

¼ teaspoon powdered ginger

¼ teaspoon coriander

¼ teaspoon ancho chile powder

½ teaspoon Sichuan pepper powder

½ teaspoon Skordo powdered soy sauce (*Skordo is a Maine spice company, and they ship!*)

¾ cup milk (2 percent)

1 cup flour

½ cup thinly sliced scallions

Cooking spray

# Brown Butter Wasabi Mayo

2 teaspoons prepared wasabi

½ cup brown butter, melted *(see recipe below)*

1 tablespoon mayonnaise

⅓ teaspoon kosher salt

*Makes about ¾ cup*

Whisk all ingredients in small bowl and serve warm.

# Brown Butter

*Makes about ¾ cup*

1.  In small saucepan, add 1 stick butter and cook over medium-low heat until lightly brown in color and milk solids have fully separated, about 8–10 minutes, watching very carefully not to burn the butter.

2.  Strain through a fine-mesh sieve and place in a container to store at room temperature.

# Poached Eggs

¼ cup white vinegar

3 large eggs

1.  Fill a *3*-quart saucepan ¾ the way up with water and add the white vinegar.

2.  Bring to a slow rolling boil.

3.  Crack 1 egg into a small bowl or ramekin and lower into the boiling water. Repeat with remaining eggs. Cook for 3–4 minutes for a softer yolk.

4.  Remove the eggs with a slotted spoon and place on a paper towel to dry before plating.

# Soy Glaze

*Makes about 1 cup*

1.  Add the brown sugar, soy sauces, garlic, ginger, rice wine, sherry, and rice wine vinegar to a small saucepan and heat until brown sugar is dissolved.

2.  Remove from heat. Stir in mirin and fish sauce.

3.  Let cool and store in a squeeze bottle.

> **Dana's Tip: A very good store-bought alternative is "Sweet Soy for Sushi" by Kikkoman.**

# To Assemble

Stack waffles, place poached egg on top, and then add lobster, Soy Glaze, and Brown Butter Wasabi Mayo. Garnish with sesames.

> **Dana's Tip: For a time saver, poach your eggs ahead of time by cooking 3 minutes and placing them into ice water. Then, when ready to plate and serve, warm the eggs in a pan of clean simmering water for 2 minutes. Then remove eggs from the water, place onto a towel to drain, and serve!**

- ¼ cup dark brown sugar
- ¼ cup sweet soy sauce *(which is thicker, similar to molasses, and can be found in Asian markets)*
- ¼ cup regular soy sauce
- 1 garlic clove, finely minced
- ½ teaspoon fresh grated ginger
- 2 tablespoons rice cooking wine (Shaoxing)
- 2 tablespoons medium sherry
- 1 tablespoon rice wine vinegar
- 1 tablespoon mirin
- 1 teaspoon fish sauce

# Lobster and Andouille Sausage with Jalapeño Cheddar Grits Topped with Scallions, Fried Egg, and Smoked Tomato Butter

The inspiration for this dish came from a restaurant in New Orleans where I had the best grits I've ever eaten. Southern food and shellfish make for a nice pair, and I wanted to create a hearty breakfast or brunch dish around it. Pair with one of the Lobster Bloody Mary recipes!

*Serves 4*

1 large or 2 small jalapeños, finely diced

1 large shallot, finely diced

5 tablespoons unsalted butter, divided

2½ cups good-quality lobster or shellfish stock, divided (or ½ chicken stock / ½ vegetable stock if preferred)

2½ cups heavy cream

1 cup grits

1½ cups sharp cheddar cheese, shredded

Kosher salt and ground black pepper (to taste)

## Grits

1. Sauté the jalapeño and shallot with 1 tablespoon of butter over medium heat until soft and lightly caramelized, about 10–12 minutes.

2. Bring 2 cups of the lobster stock, the heavy cream and 4 tablespoons of the butter to a simmer in a heavy saucepan. Gradually whisk in the grits. Reduce the heat and simmer until the grits have thickened, 15–20 minutes, stirring occasionally to avoid lumps. Once the grits are thick and creamy, adjust the consistency with stock or more cream, if necessary. Add the sautéed jalapeños and the cheese and mix until combined and melted. Season with salt and pepper to taste.

2 tablespoons olive oil

1 pound smoked
  Andouille sausage,
  sliced ¼ inch thick on
  a bias

2 garlic cloves, minced
  on a zester

1 red bell pepper,
  chopped

1 yellow bell pepper,
  chopped

1 poblano pepper,
  chopped

1 large sweet onion,
  small dice

Meat from 3 (1¼-1 ½
  pound) lobsters

2 tablespoons butter

½ teaspoon garlic
  powder

½ teaspoon onion
  powder

½ teaspoon smoked
  paprika

½ teaspoon sweet
  paprika

¼ teaspoon oregano

¼ teaspoon thyme

¼ teaspoon black pepper

¼ teaspoon cayenne

½ teaspoon kosher salt

1 tablespoon chopped
  fresh parsley

½ bunch of scallions,
  thinly sliced (reserve
  some for garnish)

# Lobster and Sausage

1. Heat the olive oil in a large skillet. Add the sausage and brown, and then transfer to a plate, leaving all of the fat in the pan.

2. Add the peppers, onions, and some salt and pepper, and sauté over medium heat until tender and lightly browned, about 10–12 minutes.

3. Add the spices, salt, reserved sausage, scallions, and remaining ½ cup lobster stock (from the grits) to the skillet and reduce for a few minutes.

4. Add lobster to small saucepan with butter to warm, 2–3 minutes.

## Eggs

1. Heat olive oil in sauté pan over medium heat; when hot, carefully crack each egg into the pan.

2. Cook until edges are browned and whites are set, about 4 minutes.

3. Top with salt and coarsely cracked black pepper to taste.

1 tablespoon olive oil

4 large eggs

Kosher salt to taste

Coarsely cracked black pepper to taste

# Smoked Tomato Butter

*Makes about 2 cups*

10 plum tomatoes

Kosher salt and pepper (for seasoning tomatoes)

1 28-ounce can San Marzano tomatoes

2 tablespoons olive oil

1 large sweet onion, finely chopped

Kosher salt to taste

1 pinch red pepper flakes

3 garlic cloves

2 tablespoons sugar

1 teaspoon smoked paprika

½ stick butter, melted

2 tablespoons flat-leaf parsley

1.  Smoke the tomatoes in a stovetop smoker: Cut the core of the tomatoes with a paring knife, and then cut the tomatoes in half through the core end. Line the tomato halves cut side up on the smoking rack. Line the bottom pan with foil to catch the juices. Season the cut side of the tomatoes with salt and pepper. Smoke the tomatoes until they are softened and have a golden hue, about 35–40 minutes over the heat after closing the smoker lid. Then turn off heat and let sit another 10 minutes with the smoker lid closed.

2.  Cool the tomatoes a few minutes and set aside.

3.  Heat the olive oil in a heavy saucepan over medium heat. Add the onion, season lightly with salt, and add the red pepper flakes. Continue to cook, stirring occasionally, until the onion is lightly browned, about 15 minutes. Stir in the garlic and cook about 2 minutes. Add the tomatoes to the pan, lower the heat, add the sugar and paprika, and cook another 5 minutes.

4.  Add sauce to a blender (or use immersion blender) and puree until smooth. Add butter and parsley and season to taste. For a smoother sauce, push through a fine-mesh sieve.

# To Assemble

Add the grits to a serving dish, top with the sausage and onion/pepper mixture. Then top with a fried egg, ¼ of the lobster meat, and Smoked Tomato Butter. Garnish with parsley and scallions.

# BLOODY MARYS

Both of these recipes call for vodka, simply because vodka's absence of distinct flavor allows the Bloody Mary ingredients to shine through. But go ahead and play with the recipes and decide for yourself which spirit you like best with each base recipe.

## Homemade Bloody Mary Base Recipe

*Makes just over 2 cups*

Mix all ingredients together and keep refrigerated until ready to use.

2 cups tomato juice

2 teaspoons lemon juice

2 teaspoons red wine vinegar

2 tablespoons Worcestershire sauce

½ tablespoon Cholula hot pepper sauce

1 teaspoon kosher salt

1 teaspoon sugar

¼ teaspoon celery salt

# BLT Bloody—Bacon, Lobster Stock, Roasted Tomatoes

4 medium Roma tomatoes

6 strips of bacon (2 for roasting tomatoes, 2 for garnish, 2 for the chef!)

2 tablespoons light brown sugar

Freshly ground black pepper

1 tablespoon plus ½ ounce lemon juice

Old Bay seasoning (for the rim)

Ice

1 cup homemade Bloody Mary mix, chilled

¼ cup Lobster Stock (see page 83)

4 ounces vodka

¼ teaspoon sweet paprika

1 teaspoon kosher salt

**Garnishes:**

olives

cherry tomatoes

cornichon or dill pickle

celery stalk

lobster claw

lemon wedge

candied bacon strip

*Makes 2*

1. Preheat oven to 350°F.

2. Halve tomatoes and place on baking sheet, cut side up. Sprinkle with kosher salt and freshly ground black pepper. Add bacon strips to the pan. Roast for 35–40 minutes. Set aside to chill. Watch that bacon doesn't burn, and remove if it starts to before the tomatoes are done.

3. Lay bacon strips flat on a sheet pan and spread brown sugar directly over each piece. Run the pepper mill over each piece to lightly cover.

4. Cook bacon, rotating pan if needed to cook evenly, until bacon is dark brown/burgundy in color, just shy of burned. Remove to clean pan (do not use a towel or paper towel, as the bacon will stick). It will harden as it cools to yield a crackling exterior like the top of crème brûlée. Cut each piece in half. Reserve bacon grease.

5. Mix 1 teaspoon of bacon grease with 1 tablespoon lemon juice and run around the rim of 2 glasses.

6. Dip the rim into the Old Bay spice mixture. Add ice to the glasses.

7. To a blender, add the base mix, lobster stock, and roasted tomatoes along with the tomato roasting pan juice and 1 tablespoon of bacon grease.

8. In a shaker over ice, add stock/roasted tomato mixture, vodka, sweet paprika, ½ ounce lemon juice, salt, and additional pepper, and shake well. Strain and pour into the glasses. For the loaded version, garnish with olives, cherry tomatoes, cornichon, celery, lobster claw, lemon wedge, and candied bacon strip!

# Smokin' Bloody—Smoked Tomatoes, Smoked Horseradish, Lobster Stock

*Makes 2*

1. Prepare stovetop smoker per manufacturer's instructions. I use a Cameron's smoker and sometimes use it on the grill outside instead of the stovetop to keep the smoke outdoors.

2. Slice tomatoes in half lengthwise, drizzle with olive oil, and lightly salt and pepper. Add to smoker.

3. Add prepared horseradish to a small oven-safe bowl or dish, and place in smoker.

4. Smoke both for 25 minutes. Let cool.

5. Add white vinegar to the smoked horseradish.

6. Rim the glasses with a cut lemon. Dip the rim into the Old Bay spice mixture. Add ice to the glasses.

7. To a blender, add the smoked tomatoes, base mix, Lobster Stock, vodka, and smoked horseradish.

8. In a shaker over ice, add the pureed mixture, smoked paprika, lemon juice, salt, and pepper, and shake well. Strain and pour into the glasses. Garnish with cherry tomatoes, celery, lobster claw, lemon wedge, and pepperoncini for added spice.

4 medium Roma tomatoes

Olive oil for smoking tomatoes

Kosher salt and pepper (for seasoning tomatoes)

2 tablespoons prepared horseradish

1 teaspoon white vinegar

½ ounce lemon juice

Old Bay seasoning (for the rim)

Ice

1 cup homemade Bloody Mary mix, chilled

¼ cup Lobster Stock *(see page 83)*

4 ounces vodka

¼ teaspoon smoked paprika

1 teaspoon kosher salt

¼ teaspoon black pepper

**Garnishes:**

cherry tomatoes

celery stalk

lobster claw

lemon wedge

pepperoncini

# ABOUT THE AUTHOR

**Dana Moos** is a hospitality investment broker, cookbook author, cooking instructor, and former innkeeper living in Midcoast Maine. Believing the plate is her canvas, she is all about lots of flavor and putting simple ingredients together in sophisticated ways.

Dana won the 2018 Maine Lobster Chef of the Year People's Choice at Harvest on the Harbor in Portland, Maine, and she won both first-place Judge's and People's Choice for her Best Lobster Bite at the 2018 Boothbay Harbor Claw Down competition in Boothbay Harbor, Maine. These achievements led to the creation of this cookbook and her passion for lobster!

## Also by Dana Moos

***The Art of Breakfast: B&B Style Recipes to Make at Home***

A Maine breakfast is more than just blueberries. Dana Moos, the former innkeeper of the Kingsleigh Inn in Southwest Harbor, Maine, has great advice on serving a breakfast that not only tastes great but also looks good. Perfect for hosting out-of-town guests, or just having friends and family over, *The Art of Breakfast* makes it easy to create artful and tasty meals.

Ask for it wherever books are sold.

Hardcover, 232 pages, ISBN: 978-1-60893-596-3, $29.95

# MODERNO

Design for Living in Brazil,
Mexico, and Venezuela,
1940-1978

Visual Arts of the Americas
Modern and Contemporary Publication Series

Lina Bo Bardi in the Glass House, São Paulo, 1952. Courtesy
Chico Albuquerque/Convênio Museu da Imagem e do Som
- SP/Instituto Moreira Salles.

This publication is produced in conjunction with the exhibition *Moderno: Design for Living in Brazil, Mexico, and Venezuela, 1940–1978,* on view at the Americas Society Art Gallery from February 11 to May 16, 2015, guest curated by Maria Cecilia Loschiavo dos Santos, Ana Elena Mallet, and Jorge F. Rivas Pérez.

The publication *Moderno: Design for Living in Brazil, Mexico, and Venezuela, 1940–1978* is made possible by the generous support of PRISA/Santillana USA; and Furthermore: a program of the J. M. Kaplan Fund.

The exhibition and accompanying public programs were made possible, in part, by an award from the National Endowment for the Arts; the New York State Council on the Arts with the support of Governor Andrew Cuomo and the New York State Legislature; by public funds from the New York City Department of Cultural Affairs, in partnership with the City Council; and by the generous support of Mercantil; the Ministry of Foreign Affairs/Mexican Agency for International Development Cooperation (SRE/AMEXCID), The National Council for Culture and the Arts (CONACULTA), the National Institute of Fine Arts (INBA), and the Mexican Cultural Institute of New York; Jaime and Raquel Gilinski; Mex-Am Cultural Foundation; Grupo DIARQ; and Colección Patricia Phelps de Cisneros.

**EDITORS**
Gabriela Rangel
Jorge F. Rivas Pérez

**ASSOCIATE EDITORS**
Maria Cecilia Loschiavo dos Santos
Ana Elena Mallet

**MANAGING EDITOR**
Christina L. De León

**ASSISTANT EDITOR**
Amanda York

**PROJECT MANAGEMENT SANTILLANA USA**
Jacqueline Rivera

**GRAPHIC DESIGNER**
Kate Johnson

**COPYEDITORS**
Tanya Heinrich
Richard Koss

**TRANSLATORS**
Anthony Beckwith
Clifford Landers
Christopher Leland Winks
Alexis Levitin

**PHOTOGRAPHY**
Francisco Kochen
Walter Otto
Wilson Santiago

**EXHIBITION DESIGNER**
Theodora Doulamis

**PRINTING**
Printed in United States by
Thomson-Shore, Inc.

**PUBLISHING**
© 2015, the authors, photographers,
artists, and designers for their work

We apologize if for reasons beyond our control any photographic sources have not been listed.

ISBN: 978-1-879128-79-8

**PUBLISHED BY:**
Americas Society
680 Park Avenue, New York, NY 10065

Prisa/Santillana USA
2023 NW 84th Avenue , Miami, FL 33122

Living room of the Quinta Perla house with a chair by Miguel Arroyo and three BKF chairs produced by Tienda Gato, with the Mendoza-Guardia's Dalmatian, 1954. Photo by Sara Guardia de Mendoza. Courtesy of Centro de Estudios de Archivos Audiovisuales y Artísticos and the Mendoza Guardia Family.

# FOREWORD

## SUSAN S. SEGAL, CEO AND PRESIDENT

The Americas Society is proud to present *Moderno: Design for Living in Brazil, Mexico, and Venezuela, 1940–1978.* This outstanding visual arts exhibition is a multinational initiative based on three years of research, documented and expanded upon in this book. *Moderno* is the result of close collaboration between the publisher PRISA/Santillana USA; three outstanding international curators and scholars, Maria Cecilia Loschiavo dos Santos, Ana Elena Mallet, and Jorge F. Rivas Perez; and the Americas Society's Department of Visual Arts. It is an examination of the field of design, an emerging discipline in Latin America during an important period of economic and political change.

*Moderno* continues the Americas Society's longstanding tradition of innovation and investigation while shedding light on aspects of the visual arts that have been previously overlooked. Both the exhibition and the publication focus on the creation of objects designed in Latin America that were compatible with local tastes and customs, but influenced by international trends. *Moderno* examines how designers of domestic objects rethought everyday life, in turn testing and creating new designs that featured local materials. This exploration aided the introduction and acceptance of new living standards in the region. We believe *Moderno* makes an important contribution to this historical topic while also introducing it to audiences in the United States.

The complexity and ambition of this exhibition and catalogue required the generous partnership of numerous individuals and institutions that, together, made possible the assembly of more than eighty objects loaned from public and private collections in Brazil, Mexico, Venezuela, Europe, and the United States. We extend our deep gratitude to the following people for their trust and commitment: Juan Luis Cebrián Echarri, José Luis Sainz, and Marcus Vinicius Ribeiro of Prisa/Santillana USA; Gustavo Vollmer, Tahia Rivero, and Luis Calvo of Banco Mercantil and Colección Mercantil; the Ministry of Foreign Affairs/Mexican Agency for International Development Cooperation (SRE/AMEXCID); the National Council for Culture and the Arts (CONACULTA); the National Institute of Fine Arts (INBA); the Mexican Cultural Institute of New York; Ambassador Sandra Fuentes Berain; Lizeth Galván Cortés; Caterina Toscano; Jaime and Raquel Gilinski; Mex-Am Cultural Foundation; Grupo DIARQ; Furthermore, a program of the J. M. Kaplan Fund; and the Colección Patricia Phelps de Cisneros with Patricia Phelps de Cisneros, Rafael Romero, and Gabriel Perez Barreiro. The Americas Society is also grateful for the support, in part, by an award from the National Endowment for the Arts, by the New York State Council on the Arts with the support of Governor Andrew Cuomo and the New York State Legislature, and by public funds from the New York City Department of Cultural Affairs, in partnership with the City Council.

The Americas Society would like to acknowledge the outstanding commitment and intellectual generosity of the curators for their dedication to the project, as well as to recognize Lourdes Blanco and Luis M. Castañeda for their new scholarship published here. Many thanks to the estates of Mário de Andrade, Miguel Arroyo, Instituto Lina Bo e P. M. Bardi, Oscar Niemeyer, Clara Porset, Sergio Rodrigues, and Marta Traba for allowing the inclusion of historical texts in this book, as well as the writer and theorist Ferreira Gullar, who gave permission to publish his extraordinary poem, published for the first time in English. We would also like to express our appreciation to the Fundación Gego; the Corning Museum of Glass; and the Centro de Investigaciones de Diseño Industrial, Facultad de Arquitectura, Universidad Nacional Autónoma de México, and all of the private collectors for their generous participation in the exhibition.

Projects of the magnitude of *Moderno* are only successful with the exceptional effort of a team, which in this case was comprised of Gabriela Rangel, Director of Visual Arts and Chief Curator; Christina De León, Assistant Curator; Amanda York, Curatorial Assistant; and Nuria Mendoza, Public Programs Coordinator. Many thanks to our Development Team, including Ana Gilligan, Monica Viera, Pierre Losson, and Maria Rosa Garcia Otero for their work.

Tecla Tofano (Venezuelan, 1927–95). *Freud, Sexologia,* 1975. Ceramic, sculpted and glazed; 6 ½ x 7 ¹¹⁄₁₆ x 6 ½ in. Collection of Sagrario Berti. [Checklist no. 60]

# LINGUA FRANCA FOR THE FUTURE

## GABRIELA RANGEL

The fluid, barely inapprehensible field of what we term "design" has its own disciplinary framework with normative and pedagogic practices, institutional strategies, and networks and channels of distribution, regardless of its almost instantaneous association with architecture. These elements gradually took shape over the nineteenth century in the developed countries of the West on the basis of the processes of planning and manufacture of industrially fabricated objects. Perhaps the tenuous, hybrid, and ambiguous character of design, in tandem with its proximity to industrial production processes and services that responded to a set of dispositions, structures, and habitus, have motivated the decades-long discursive exile of design in Latin America from both museums and the academy. If there has been much discussion of the immense contribution and even the aesthetic-functional legacy of the work of architects like Oscar Niemeyer, Pedro Ramírez Vázquez, and Carlos Raúl Villanueva, the role of design (and local designers) in the historiographic narratives of Latin American modernisms has been purely incidental. Such manifest or involuntary marginalization of design has also shown the partial, incomplete orientation of the various large-scale museum revisions that have been carried out in Europe and the United States regarding the modernization projects in Latin America and their concomitant modernisms.

Indeed, design contributes a valuable, complex activity for studying and interpreting a portion of the region's creativity through functional, utilitarian, and aesthetic objects that were not necessarily conceived as works of art. With the few exceptions of Sérgio Rodrigues, Joaquim Tenreiro, Clara Porset, Lina Bo Bardi, and Michael van Beuren, there has not been an examination of the contribution of many of these designers (and artists) to the international tendencies in design in their struggle to project their *difference* or their subaltern contribution. Little is known, outside specialist circles in Brazil and Venezuela, of utopian experiments like those of the Catholic cooperative Unilabor, founded in São Paulo by the artist Geraldo de Barros and the priest João Batista Pereira dos Santos, or on the furniture company Tecoteca, founded in Caracas by the Dutch-born Venezuelan artist Cornelis Zitman and the Carbonell brothers.

It would appear that the weight of non-modern, informal elements upon our societies, combined with the heterogeneity of contexts and the historical differences among the nations making up the region, has discouraged any attempt to develop a historiographical discourse on the global importance of modern Latin American design. It is no accident that the historian Silvia Fernández singles out the multifaceted, unstable, fleeting character of design, which resists being the vehicle of stable, fixed identities recognizable to a global public eager to find exoticism in the local.[1] I wonder if this marginalization is due to design's spurious nature, or whether it reveals, rather, a conscious or unconscious reluctance to trace romantic-nationalist links with regard to artisanal and traditional practices that entailed unavoidable appropriations of, and crossings with, popular culture. One of the most problematic and interesting aspects of design in Latin America has been precisely the incorporation (and sometimes the instrumentalization) of popular elements and the use of the vernacular imagery in the fabrication of objects and furniture on abstract lines as a function of the development of modern infrastructures. It is at this point of inflection that a potent field appears, magnetized by the contradictions, struggles, and antagonisms that anticipated gaps and ruptures in modernization processes, which the designer and architect Lina Bo Bardi critically identified in industrial design used as a "regenerative force of the entire system."[2]

For the purposes of examining design from a revisionary standpoint delimited by the domestic sphere during the modernization processes in Brazil, Mexico, and Venezuela, it is important to begin by recovering an idea of Silvia Fernández, who identified the appearance of a pragmatics of design in Latin America in the projects of accelerated infrastructure that took shape at different moments of this modernization. While important designers emerged in Peru, Cuba, and Colombia, countries with fewer resources and agrarian economic structures, the apogee of design in the twentieth century was achieved in nations that were economically robust or with sudden rises in economic prosperity, such as Argentina, Brazil, Chile, Mexico, Uruguay, and Venezuela. Sooner or later, depending on the case, it was during this modernizing period driven by differing versions of local nationalisms that ambitious economic plans were elaborated through the implementation of publically oriented infrastructural programs, with the prospects of obtaining a growth that aspired to being inscribed into a universalist scheme. These ambitious initiatives, now of distant memory, also included significant contributions from distinguished design and architecture professionals and artists who emigrated from Europe and, to a lesser degree, from the United States to various regional metropolises, fleeing war or in search of better work opportunities.

Beginning in the 1940s, there began to appear a substantial increase in the production of objects commonly relegated to the field of design and intimately linked to the idea of progress that frequently underpinned the international tendencies in vogue as well as the need for technical actualization in countries like Brazil, Mexico, and Venezuela. On the other hand, the wave of massive internal migration of hundreds of thousands or even millions of work-seeking people from impoverished rural areas to cities like Mexico City, São Paulo, Rio de Janeiro, and Caracas not only radically changed the spatial configuration of those cities but also dictated the need to produce new labor markets, housing infrastructure, health and public education systems, and goods and services compatible with the constant demographic changes that these migratory movements produced. To this spectrum was added the rise of a professional middle class and a large urban proletariat enclosed in favelas or shantytowns in countries whose social structures had been highly stratified since colonial times. When Lúcio Costa, Oscar Niemeyer, Carlos Raúl Villanueva, Tomás Sanabria, Juan O'Gorman, Mario Pani, Pedro Ramírez Vázquez, and Félix Candela obtained public (and private) commissions to build houses, churches, and buildings as well as plans for important infrastructural urban projects, they needed designers to elaborate furniture, accessories, and materials for the interiors of new spaces that aimed to change the habits and mentality of citizens with the goal of adapting them to Western standards of living and consumption.

It has been estimated that the design boom in Latin America and the pedagogical institutions dedicated to that discipline that proliferated in several countries of the region between the 1950s and 1960s reached its height with the emergence of different regulatory public agendas of import policies in favor of incentives to local industrial production and the elaboration of locally inflected economic development projects of varying ideological stripes that arose in those decades. In the postwar years, which coincided chronologically with the beginning of the Cold War, design reached a clear-cut maturity that generated a theoretical-practical apparatus that crystallized in Pedro Ramírez Vázquez's

View of the Unilabor Factory, c. 1954. Photo by Geraldo de Barros. © Estate Geraldo de Barros.

rural schools, the cofounder of the Argentine Concretist movement Tomás Maldonado's pedagogical administration of the Ulm School of Design (HfG), and Lina Bo Bardi's later critical positions in her quest for the organic integration of design with popular culture and nature prompted by her experimental works made in Salvador de Bahia.[3] Recognition is owed to lesser-known contributions by important figures like Clara Porset and Miguel Arroyo, who, like their Brazilian colleagues, advocated the use of local materials and the exploration of cultural referents extracted from their contexts.[4] It is also worth mentioning Tecla Tofano's singular and pioneering gender *ars politica* in ceramics, which, according to Marta Traba, worked "against the smooth and well finished, just as later she would work against prettiness: she works on a social concept, *against* the void of the purist aesthetic."[5]

*Moderno: Design for Living in Brazil, Mexico, and Venezuela, 1940–1978* adopts an investigative line of inquiry formulated by the curatorial team of María Cecilia Loschiavo dos Santos, Ana Elena Mallet, and Jorge F. Rivas Pérez, specialists in the modern design of the countries considered in the exhibition's narrative scope, and the Visual Arts Department of the Americas Society. The word *moderno* (modern) — both in Spanish and Portuguese — has been associated with ideas of novelty and rapid development operating as a *lingua franca* that led to a path to the future.[6] The home, or in a broader sense, the domestic sphere, is the place considered in this project as a receptacle in which converged a set of ideas in dialogue with the different local contexts, their traditions, methodologies of manufacture, and local techniques and materials. The publication accompanying the *Moderno* exhibition proposes to broaden the confines of the gallery presentation through new scholarship and archival documents that aim to examine how design functioned simultaneously as a fully formed experimental discipline and a permeable channel that facilitated the adaptation and reception of the aesthetic programs of the international artistic and architectural avant-gardes in their traversals of the domestic sphere and the collective fabric. In addition, the publication displays various examples of

Danesa line by Domus, manufactured by Van Beuren, SA de CV, display at the Feria del Hogar furnishings fair, c. 1970. Courtesy of Freddy van Beuren Bernal.

the application of formal strategies and ideas of Western modernist tendencies such as rationalism, functionalism, and organic design to residential and public spaces.

Design channeled the empirical flow of the practice of Latin American architects in their struggle to develop their own vocabularies in their countries. This collaboration included the manufacture of artifacts for economic and intellectual elites and encompassed the production of more affordable — simpler, if you will — objects and products for the popular sectors, but it did not succeed in establishing a horizontal logic of production and sustainable consumption that would involve everyone equally. Nonetheless, there was important interdisciplinary collaboration among artists, architects, and designers, in which there occurred the inclusion in the creative process of women, who, in media traditionally averse to women's work, could dedicate themselves professionally to designing objects, furniture, or the quiet modeling of functional pottery or non-utilitarian ceramics that entered as a Trojan horse in the male-dominated terrain of the museum in Venezuela. From the latter, we can attest to the "lithic" force of Seka Severin de Tudja's ceramics or Cristina Merchán's masterly experiments with nooks and hollowness.[7] The reserved, discreet performance of modern design in Latin America is frequently confused with a servile obedience to international standards of taste and style. Nevertheless, this publication aims to refute this misunderstanding perpetuated by the ignorance of a productive field by means of a reflection that moves away from a set of objects that still successfully sets off reverberations of the utopian impulse of its time and of its *difference* in a multinational, deterritorialized era, without the ambition for originality possessed by works of art.

[1] Silvia Fernández, "The Origins of Design Education in Latin America from hfg in Ulm to Globalization," *Design Issues* 22, no. 1 (Winter 2005): 3–19

[2] Lina Bo Bardi, "Planajamento Ambiental 'Desenho' no impasse," *Malasartes* 2 (December–February 1976): 4–7. For the translation of this text, see Lina Bo Bardi, "Ambient Planning: 'Design' at an Impasse," in this volume's section of historical documents. Art historian Luis M. Castañeda responds to these black holes of modernization with his essay "Design's Bureaucratic Unconscious," in this volume, in which he connects various aesthetic manifestations in planning policy through design.

[3] While Maldonado encouraged the production of a canonical *doxa* to adjust design to the ideologies of reconstruction in the postwar period, separating it from Walter Gropius's Bauhaus, he also succeeded in training teams of designers and critics who advocated a materialist practice devoted to social industrial design.

[4] See Silvia Fernández, ed., *Historia del Diseño en América Latina y el Caribe* [History of Design in Latin America and the Caribbean] (Spain: Editora Blucher, 2008).

[5] Marta Traba, "Tecla Tofano, Ars Politica," in *Marta Traba, Mirar en Caracas: Crítica de Arte: [ensayos]* (Caracas: Monte Avila Editores, 1974). For the translation of this text, see Marta Traba, "Tecla Tofano: Ars Politica," in this volume's section of historical documents.

[6] Jorge F. Rivas Pérez has insisted in the ubiquitous use of the term *moderno* as a signifier of novelty.

[7] Marta Traba made a point of the importance and singularity of Seka's ceramics in a realm of formalist decorations. See "Tecla Tofano: Ars Politica" in this volume.

Alejandro Otero painting a mural on the east façade of
Quinta Perla, San Antonio de los Altos, Caracas, Venezuela,
1954. Photo by Sara Guardia de Mendoza. Courtesy of
Centro de Estudios de Archivos Audiovisuales y Artísticos
and the Mendoza Guardia Family.

# CANNIBAL HOMES: ADDITIVE MODERNITY AND DESIGN BY ABSORPTION IN BRAZIL, MEXICO, AND VENEZUELA, 1940–1979

## JORGE F. RIVAS PÉREZ

> In a feverish stillness, the intimate recesses of the domestic space become sites for history's most intricate invasions. In that displacement the border between home and world becomes confused; and, uncannily, the private and the public become part of each other, forcing upon us a vision that is as divided as it is disorienting.[1]
> —HOMI K. BHABHA

The home, by nature a private place seemingly impervious to change, has frequently proved a testing ground for modern artistic movements. Such were the cases, for example, with Gerrit Rietveld's 1924 Schröder House in Utrecht and Le Corbusier's 1928–31 Villa Savoye in Poissy, which are considered landmarks that embody the principles of De Stijl and Le Corbusier's Five Points of Architecture, respectively. The Latin American avant-garde followed this strategy. In fact, the origins of modern design in Brazil, Mexico, and Venezuela can be traced to the experiments in residential design and visual repertoires that were incubated and tested in their creators' homes. This essay identifies and analyzes certain aspects of their experiences.

## Background

The turbulent years that preceded the Second World War were the backdrop to a period of profound transformation in Latin America. It was during this time that three strikingly different countries — Brazil, Mexico, and Venezuela — each strove to position themselves as modern nations. Questions of national identity, charged ever since the border clashes that defined Latin America in the nineteenth century, were given an extra jolt by the reshuffling of European frontiers after the First World War, and the flags of nationalism were again unfurled throughout the region. Moreover, the United States's increasing interventionism, as well as the ideology of Pan-Americanism it had promoted since the 1889–90 Pan-American conference — and further enforced during the interwar period — aroused suspicion and concern in Latin America. Thus the need to reinforce national identities, particularly after the definitive rise of the United States to hemispheric predominance following the First World War, was paramount. This was also a time of momentous political change in these young nations that were open to immigration and eager to become modern and developed.

The *Industrial Design Competition for the 21 American Republics* at the Museum of Modern Art in New York in 1940 marked a design milestone for the region. For the first time, the innovative and original Latin American projects were included in a hemispheric design contest. Furthermore, thanks to the competition, local designers gained visibility in their own countries, had the chance to admire the latest design trends, and became familiar with the work of their colleagues in the Americas — the winning entries were exhibited in 1941 in the *Organic Design in Home Furnishings* show, and some designs were retailed by Bloomingdale's department store.[2]

After the Second World War, the need for new economic models for Latin America became evident. Tinged by nationalist overtones and aimed to foment autonomy, capitalism, economic growth, and to boost and educate a growing middle class, the "developmentalism" (*desarrollismo*) theory endorsed by the United States as a catalyzer of democracy, positive change, and progress was embraced by Brazil, Mexico, and Venezuela. The adoption and diffusion of modern design within these three countries is strongly linked to state-sponsored programs aimed to create modern national identities and to the industrialization programs linked to implementation and consolidation of develop-mentalist agendas in the 1950s and 1960s.

In Brazil, the ambitious goals set by president Juscelino Kubitschek in 1956, summed up by the slogan "fifty years of progress in five," fitted this developmentalist model. For his national plan, based on industrial expansion and major infrastructure construction, the sensuous curvilinear modernism promoted by such architects as Oscar Niemeyer and Lucio Costa in the late 1930s, and internationally identified with the Brazilian avant-garde, was officially embraced as the national style, creating continuity with the interwar artistic vanguards. Brazilian manufacturers turned to national talent for developing products compatible with local tastes. Designers themselves frequently became manufac-turers and ventured into the production of furniture and small household goods.

With an economy increasingly tied to the United States in the postwar years, developmentalism in Mexico became a fundamental tool to level the playing field and reassert its national identity in relation to its rich and powerful neighbor. Much as they already had during the interwar period, modern Mexican designers frequently incorporated elements from their own historical repertoires into their search for identity. The grandeur of ancient Mexican cultures and the unique character of Mexican crafts traditions — postwar Mexican design heavily relied on traditional materials and craftsmanship — were in tune with the revolutionary nationalist rhetoric promoted by the Institutional Revolutionary Party (PRI), the political organization that led Mexico for more than seven decades.

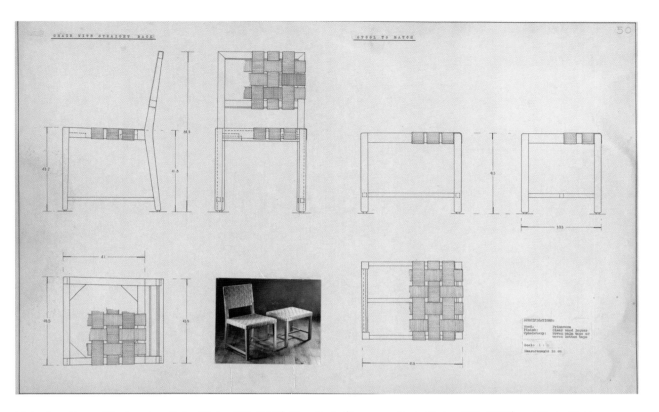

Michael van Beuren (Mexican, born United States, 1911–2004), Klaus Grabe (German, active in Mexico, 1910–2004), and Morley Webb (American, active in Mexico). *Entry Panel for MoMA Latin American Competition for Organic Design in Home Furnishings,* c. 1940. Ink and photo collage on paper; 19 ¾ x 31 ½ in. The Museum of Modern Art, New York, Gift of the designer, 2008. Digital Image © The Museum of Modern Art/Licensed by SCALA/Art Resource, NY. [checklist no. 70]

The 1940s in Venezuela were marked by political instability and a succession of short-term governments. The 1948 military junta, later followed by the dictatorial presidency of General Marcos Pérez Jiménez (1952–58), adopted developmentalism as the ideal economic model to transform Venezuela from an oil-export country into a modern autonomous industrialized nation. Although ironically aligned with the visual programs endorsed by the artistic left and financed by the country's enormous oil wealth, modern design was more the imposition of an authoritarian state (without room for dissidence) than a voluntary choice. Unlike Brazil and Mexico, which had a few but significant design experiences in the interwar years, modern design in Venezuela was mostly developed during the postwar period. It was chiefly the work of local designers and architects trained either in Europe or the United States, or of immigrants educated in their countries of origin.

Beyond sharing some temporal, visual, and programmatic coincidences, as this essay will illustrate, the adoption and development of modern design in Brazil, Mexico, and Venezuela reveal three different visions on how the developmentalist agendas were constructed, implemented, and linked to design in order to forge modern national identities as these three countries positioned themselves as modern developing nations and simultaneously connected with their own histories, traditions, and cultures to incorporate them into the new national styles. Although the downfall of the developmentalist models with the erosion of the nation-state (as well as the import substitution strategies that sustained local design) started in the late 1960s, the failing of these agendas became more overtly evident in the following decade. By the end of the 1970s — and especially after the 1979 oil crisis — global changes in the production and consumption of manufactured goods marked the end of the era of Latin American design associated with state-sponsored national industrial development.

**The Shift toward Modernity**

The development of modern narratives and visual discourses prompted a radical shift in the styles and designs associated with national identities. Whereas the 1920s had seen a reverence for historicist styles inspired by pre-Hispanic or colonial themes — steeped in symbolism linked to Latin American centennial celebrations — the following decade ushered in a distinctly different vision: modern imagery was all the rage. It was a sudden and profound change, and modernity was the clear winner in the long-running dispute between two different views on how to develop national styles. This struggle between tradition and the changing modern times was, to a great extent, brought about by the rapid change experienced in the rest of the world. It was during the frantic transformation in political and social life in the late 1930s — which saw the emergence of totalitarian regimes in Europe and the start of the Second World War — that, as art historian Patricio del Real has noted, modern architecture found a new center of gravity in Latin American culture.[3] The spread of modern styles is abundantly evident in the design of government buildings and clearly apparent in the pavilions constructed for international fairs.

This transition is obvious when the historicist architecture of the pavilions at the Iberian-American Fair in Seville in 1929 — neocolonial in the case of Brazil, Beaux-Arts for Venezuela, and neo pre-Hispanic for the Mexican pavilion — is compared to the style of the ones built for the New York World's Fair in 1939–40. Although the Brazil and Venezuela buildings in Seville were organized around central patios inspired by colonial architecture, Pedro Paulo Bernardes Vasto's exuberant façade for the Brazilian pavilion, featuring a mélange of colonial baroque architecture motifs, contrasted with the severe academic austerity of Germán de Falla's exteriors for the Venezuela building. Manuel Amábilis avoided European references for the Mexican Pavilion altogether, favoring instead the design principles and decorative motifs of the ancient Mexican monuments.[4]

In New York a decade later, conversely, all references to the past were completely expunged, and modern architecture and design emerged triumphant. There is no question that modern styles were ideally suited to the theme suggested by the organizers of the Fair — "The World of Tomorrow" — which also dovetailed very neatly with the goals of the three countries. Brazil's extraordinary pavilion, designed by Niemeyer and Costa, was based on the Swiss-French architect Le Corbusier's ideas and forms. The exuberant curves of the free-plan building raised on pilotis, with a brise-soleil protecting the front façade and a curved pedestrian ramp marking the main access, contrasted with the neighboring buildings. The pavilion was an outstanding accomplishment with which modern Brazilian architecture took its place on the world stage. The Venezuelan pavilion's bold design and futuristic style was entrusted to the American architect Gordon Bunshaft, who designed a modernist diaphanous glass and steel box crowned by a floating inclined plane featuring a painted fresco ceiling by Venezuelan artist Luis Alfredo López Méndez with the aid of Miguel Arroyo. Mexico's pavilion, on the other hand, was a far more modest affair, its modernist yet more conventional architecture the work of the Mexican architect Vicente Mendiola.

Paradoxically, the enduring effects of the Great Depression in the region favored local manufacturing. The adoption of new architectural styles led to new designs, which coincided with the proliferation of national industries — particularly furniture, ceramics, and glass — whose production replaced what had previously been imported. The outbreak of war in Europe in 1939 and the resulting sluggishness in international trade contributed to an increasingly robust local output. The boom in Latin American manufacturing and design during the postwar period was a direct result of the conditions experienced in the years between the wars. However, the worldwide postwar economic bonanza and the ambitious developmentalist policies of Latin American governments from the late 1940s until the 1970s were what really created the favorable circumstances that drove the development of design throughout the region. Design did not become a professional occupation until after the war because it was not until then that markets were sufficiently developed to support such a specialized field.

1939 New York World's Fair, Venezuela Building. Photo by the Wurts Bros. Courtesy of the Museum of the City of New York.

## The Home: A Laboratory of Modern Design

The official adoption of modern architecture and design was almost always preceded by small, isolated projects without which the subsequent widespread acceptance of these new ideas would not have been possible. The modest scale and contained costs of these early modern projects — which, almost without exception, consisted of homes built by architects for their own use — made it possible to experiment, especially if the architect was trying to adopt new forms and styles. In Brazil, the first modern rationalist house — a functionalist dwelling devoid of ornamentation — known as the Casa da rua Santa Cruz, was built in 1927 by Gregori Warchavchik, a Ukrainian architect who had studied in Rome and lived in São Paulo. Two years later, Juan O'Gorman built the Casa O'Gorman, the first reinforced concrete functionalist house with a curtain glass façade in Mexico City. In Venezuela, Manuel Mujica Millán, a Spanish-born architect who lived in Caracas, built (for himself) the Quinta las Guaycas, a modern rationalist flat-roofed house conceived as an assemblage of interlocked unadorned rectangular prisms in 1932. Some of those modern projects built in the 1920s and 1930s were so original and surprising that they were not understood, even by the local avant-garde. Perhaps one of the most emblematic cases was the Fazenda Capuava (1938) by the Brazilian architect Flávio de Carvalho, which explored the sensory aspects of architecture and design by using colored surfaces and sources of light combined with reflective metallic elements and steam devices to produce a varied range of room atmospheres and further proposed extremely novel solutions to the challenges faced by those living in the tropics by fluidly interconnecting interior and exterior spaces. It was such an advanced project that it is considered innovative to this day.

These early works were conceived as comprehensive units that included architecture, interior design, fixtures, and landscaping. They were controversial buildings, but the initial rejection of the avant-garde styles in the court of public opinion was short-lived as modern architecture and design repertoires soon became firmly established, enjoying universal acceptance and official acclaim. It is important to understand that the ideas being proposed for modern homes in Latin America were profoundly innovative because, until that time, most residential architecture was based, to one extent or another, on the design of colonial homes built around one or more interior patios, a style derived from the traditional houses with courtyards, a floor plan that can be traced back to the ancient world. Lifestyles, layouts of houses, and types of furniture had not changed much either, despite the dawn of the twentieth century. This is why the adoption of modern visual repertoires, unadorned furniture and household objects, and house design programs based on function areas in the Latin American home was a truly revolutionary step.

Infected with the same spirit of innovation and passion for modern building that took the world by storm after the Second World War, Latin America embraced modern architecture and design with boundless enthusiasm. Certain designs for residential homes in the 1940s and early 1950s were extraordinarily innovative and influential on a local level. It is interesting to see how designers and architects adapted the principles of modern architecture and design to local conditions with remarkable originality, fluidly blending architecture and design into the landscape and the specific environmental condition of each location. In many cases, the traditional materials or construction techniques of a region were combined with modern building technology. Notable examples of this process include the glass Casa de Vidro house by Lina Bo Bardi (1950–51) and the Estrada Das Canoas house by Oscar Niemeyer (1952) in Brazil, the Prieto López house (1950) by Luis Barragán in Mexico City, and the Caoma house by Carlos Raúl Villanueva (1951–52) in Caracas. The interior design and fixtures in these houses reflect that same willingness to adapt: in each case, these features are taken into account and carefully adapted to the particular conditions. Some avant-garde homes were also the site of experiments to integrate the arts in search of a total work of art (*Gesamtkunstwerk*). A timid early attempt in Venezuela of domestic *Gesamtkunstwerk* was the 1952 main door of Miguel Arroyo's house in Caracas, [checklist no. 39] a project developed with the painter Alejandro Otero. Arroyo and Otero often collaborated in this way during the 1950s. The door, based on Otero's "Ortogonales" series from the early 1950s, was conceived as an integral part of the house's façade. Projects undertaken for their friends — such as the Quinta Perla (1952–54), the house in San Antonio de los Altos that belonged to Benjamín Mendoza and Sara Guardia, a couple of young professors at the Instituto Pedagógico in Caracas — provided the perfect opportunity to experiment with new styles. In this small house on the outskirts of Caracas, Arroyo worked on the furniture and interior design, and Otero experimented with ways of blending art into the architecture of the house. He painted two large murals on the exterior façades and designed the aluminum and glass façade that encloses the living room area.[5] During that same period, Arroyo designed the sophisticated interiors for the Pampatar house belonging to the Venezuelan collector and art patron Alfredo Boulton on Margarita Island, for which Otero created his celebrated 1954 *Tablón de Pampatar*. The Quinta Perla and, to a lesser extent, Boulton's house are residential versions of the grand plans for the integration of the arts that Villanueva launched in 1952 at the Ciudad Universitaria in Caracas, an initiative that came to fruition some years later. Both Arroyo and Otero were also involved in visual art projects at the Universidad Central de Venezuela.

Mural by Alejandro Otero, Quinta Perla, San Antonio de los Altos, Caracas, Venezuela, 1954. Photo by Sara Guardia de Mendoza. Courtesy of Centro de Estudios de Archivos Audiovisuales y Artísticos and the Mendoza Guardia Family.

Interior view of Lina Bo Bardi's Casa de Vidro, São Paulo, Brazil, c. 1950s. Courtesy of Instituto Lina Bo e P. M. Bardi.

Modern houses from the late 1930s, 1940s, and 1950s were also the forerunners to the myriad multifamily developments — most of them state-sponsored projects — that were built in Latin America in the same period, many of which were extraordinarily ambitious. The construction of these large-scale buildings meant that a modern lifestyle was no longer the exclusive privilege of the cultural and economic elites — who were more in tune with international trends in contemporary art, architecture, and design — and became accessible to those with more modest financial resources. Some of the first projects of this kind took a rather timid approach to modernity, as in the case of the redevelopment of El Silencio (1941–45) by Villanueva in Caracas. The design and interiors of this property were modern, but its outer façade was executed in a neocolonial style. Many of these large urban redevelopments that included blocks of multifamily housing were inspired by Le Corbusier's designs. Some of them completely transformed large swaths of their host cities, as in the case of the Centro Urbano Presidente Alemán (1947–49), the complex designed by the architect Mario Pani in Mexico City. The development of projects of this nature reached its peak with the construction of Brasilia (1957–60), the new Brazilian capital designed by Costa and Niemeyer as part of Kubitschek's ambitious plan to transform his country into a major regional modern power.

Left: Alejandro Otero (Venezuelan, 1921–90). *Tablón de Pampatar* (Pampatar Board), 1954. Lacquer on wood; 25 ³/₈ x 1 ¹/₁₆ x 124 ¹³/₁₆ in. Colección Patricia Phelps de Cisneros. [Checklist no. 89]

Above: Alfredo Boulton, *Pampatar* (La Casa), c. 1954. Photograph of the living room of Boulton's beach house, Margarita Island, Venezuela, designed by Miguel Arroyo. Courtesy of Fundación Alberto Vollmer, Caracas. For the interior design of the house, Arroyo and Otero exercised ideas of integration of the arts (*Gesamtkunstwerk*) championed by architect Carlos Raul Villanueva in Venezuela.

The interiors of these huge multifamily complexes were usually simple and a perfect environment in which to test drive modern ideas for outfitting a home. Ever since the 1930s, designers had been working on the challenge of producing modestly priced modern furniture. In São Paulo in 1936, for example, the writer Mario de Andrade organized the first competition focused on furniture for the working class. The objective was to encourage the design of low-cost, modern furniture, but tangible progress would have to wait until the arrival of the great housing developments of the postwar period. The subject of low-cost furniture sparked a great deal of interest among designers concerned about how design would affect those with limited resources. Of all the ideas that were discussed during that period, one that stood out above all the rest was the proposal submitted by Clara Porset, the Cuban-born designer who lived in Mexico, for the Conjunto Urbano Presidente Alemán residential complex. She designed a line of modern furniture made with local materials that was "strong, comfortable, and pleasing to the eye."[6] Throughout her long career, Porset was always motivated by a desire to make modern design accessible to everyone, from her idea for "rural furniture," which she submitted with her husband, the painter Xavier Guerrero, to the *Industrial Design Competition for the 21 American Republics* at the Museum of Modern Art in 1940, to the projects she designed in the early 1960s for

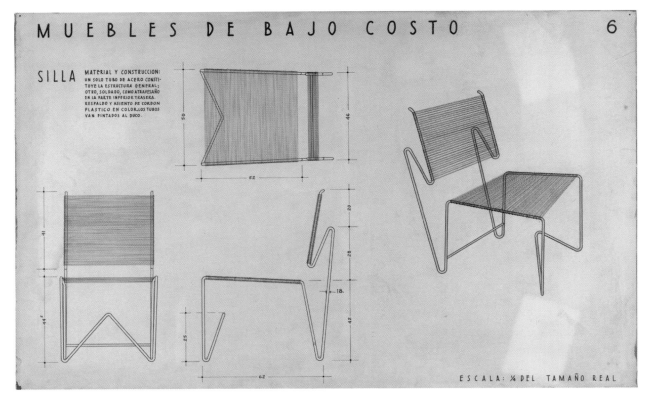

MUEBLES DE BAJO COSTO

6

SILLA

MATERIAL Y CONSTRUCCION:
UN SOLO TUBO DE ACERO CONSTI-
TUYE LA ESTRUCTURA GENERAL;
OTRO, SOLDADO, COMO ATRAVESAÑO
EN LA PARTE INFERIOR TRASERA.
RESPALDO Y ASIENTO DE CORDON
PLASTICO EN COLOR,LOS TUBOS
VAN PINTADOS AL DUCO.

ESCALA: ¼ DEL TAMAÑO REAL

Xavier Guerrero (Mexican, 1896–1974) and Clara Porset (Mexican, 1895–1981). *Entry Panel for MoMA International Competition for Low-Cost Furniture Design*, c. 1950. Ink on panel; 19 ¾ x 31 ½ in. The Museum of Modern Art, New York, Gift of the designers, 2009. Digital Image © The Museum of Modern Art/Licensed by SCALA/Art Resource, NY. [checklist no. 44]

revolutionary Cuba. A notable example is the chair made with steel rods and cotton rope that she and Guerrero presented at the *International Competition for Low-Cost Furniture Design* at the Museum of Modern Art in 1949. This combination of modern, reasonably priced materials was extremely popular among Latin American designers in the late 1940s. Miguel Arroyo and Cornelis Zitman in Venezuela [checklist no. 76] created designs of this kind, which were also very well received by designers and consumers in Brazil.

### Modern Design

In 1908, one of the great theoreticians of modern design, the Austrian architect Adolf Loos, in his provocative lecture entitled "Ornament und Verbrechen" (Ornament and Crime), denounced ornamentation as a symbol of a bygone era and accused it of damaging and retarding human evolution.[7] Loos's ideas on ornamentation and design resonated powerfully among the international modern design avant-garde and formed the basis for project methodologies that advocated the subtraction of all unnecessary elements in order to arrive at the essence of objects; in other words, to create something that included nothing superfluous. The purging process was not intended to apply solely to ornamentation; it implied a thorough review of objects that was supposed to yield a strictly rational, mechanical,

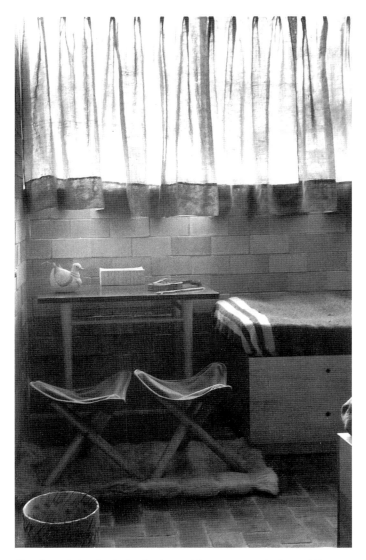

Clara Porset's interior design for the model apartment at the Centro Urbano Presidente Alemán in Mexico City, c. 1950. Centro de Investigaciones de Diseño Industrial, Facultad de Arquitectura, Universidad Nacional Autónoma de México, Mexico City.

and technical design that considered economic and hygienic factors above formal and aesthetic ones. In some cases, the objective included developing universal designs that eliminated any reference to their history, origins, or manufacturing process. Nothing captured the ultimate goal of this methodology more effectively than the famous phrase coined by the German architect (and last director of the Bauhaus) Ludwig Mies van der Rohe: "Less is more." Modern postwar design was deeply influenced by Loos and van der Rohe's ideas. Thanks to the immigration to the Unites States in the 1930s of several important Bauhaus professors who continued their teachings in American universities — most notably van der Rohe, Walter Gropius, Josef and Anni Albers, and Marcel Breuer — that particular vision of design and architecture also spread in the United States and Latin America. Numerous mid-century Latin American designers and architects were trained in American universities and technical schools, bringing back to their native countries the Bauhaus and modern avant-garde design principles.

In the catalogue for the 1952 exhibition "El arte en la vida diaria: Exposición de objetos de buen diseño hechos en México" (Art in Daily Life: An Exhibition of Well-Designed Objects Made in Mexico) — the first exhibition of modern design to be organized in Mexico — Porset, in this instance wearing her curator's hat, declared, "Design is everything, whether natural or man-made." Later in her essay she added that, "In an attempt to clarify the meaning of the term 'design' — which has not yet been firmly defined — we could say that it refers to objects we commonly use. That is, the useful form of what we come in contact with every day."[8]

"El arte en la vida diaria" was organized as part of the events associated with the 1952 8th Pan American Congress of Architects, which took place at the newly opened Mexico City University Campus, and several important American and European architects of that period, among them Frank Lloyd Wright and Richard Neutra, participated as special guests.

Undoubtedly, Porset — who had studied with and befriended Josef and Anni Albers, thus influenced by Bauhaus theories — was aware that the exhibition offered a unique opportunity to present Mexican design to the world as belonging to the international modern avant-garde.[9] The show, an extensive panoramic survey of Mexican production ranging from mass-produced industrial objects and furniture to handcrafted pieces, gave a good perspective on how international modern design repertoires were being translated and adapted to local settings. In addition, the exhibition catalogue served as a platform to define and clarify design concepts for the Mexican and Latin American contexts, by then very ambiguous.

Like Porset, designers in Mexico and Venezuela were able to have contact with modern European or American products and designers. Besides foreign training, as was the case of Miguel Arroyo, who spent two years (1946–48) in Pittsburgh at the Carnegie Institute of Technology, modern European or American design usually reached Latin America thanks to specialized literature or imported pieces.[10] For example, the Dutch-born Venezuelan designer Cornelis Zitman revealed that he was able to get his pair of much admired 1946 DCM side chairs by Charles and Ray Eames through an exchange with a Caracas dealer.[11] In other cases, a third person would mediate, such as when the Brazilian designer Geraldo de Barros declined an offer in 1950 from the Swiss artist Max Bill of a scholarship to attend the prestigious Hochschule für Gestaltung Ulm, in Germany, ceding it to his friend and colleague Alexandre Wollner on the condition that he would send copies of all the courses by mail to Brazil, and the promise to become partners in a design studio upon Wollner's return to São Paulo.[12]

## Phagocytizing Design

An overarching study of modern design as a whole in Brazil, Mexico, and Venezuela reveals the astonishing — though not initially apparent — fact that the project methodology pursued in these countries was, to a large extent, diametrically opposed to the one proposed by foreign postwar modern designers inspired by Loos and van der Rohe's theories. What we see here was, in fact, an additive process: design by absorption. In a flagrant contradiction of one of the fundamental tenets of the international modern design avant-garde, design in these three countries was frequently by nature flamboyant and affiliated with a baroque sensibility. The banishment of ornamentation, the cleansing of surfaces, and the extreme simplification of forms that was driven by rational and functional criteria were excessively arid impositions when considered in terms of Latin America's visual culture, where values are in many cases exactly the opposite. The search for a type of modern design of their own, as well as individual design styles capable of reflecting the idiosyncrasies, visual richness, and particular tastes of these three countries, would certainly have required different strategies that were relevant to the cultural and historical realities of each nation. The connection with the rich baroque artistic traditions of the region offered a promising path to achieve a different type of modernism. As Paolo Herkenhoff noted, "Brazilian modernism searched for a visual vocabulary that would be part of a national cultural project for the country. Brazil was positioning itself as a modern nation and, simultaneously, trying to recover its history. In this process, the baroque heritage was granted privilege."[13] With some differences, these postcolonial cultural strategies that produced new national identities departing from baroque legacies were also applied in Mexico and Venezuela. Design by absorption was evidently more compatible with local visual cultures, temperaments, and traditions and — as distinct from the sterility of rational modernism — could be steeped in references to histories, colors, traditions, and the sensitivities of place. Moreover, it frequently emphasized the use of handcraft manufacturing methods, a clear alternative to the industrial processes and mass production techniques that were so highly prized by foreign modern avant-gardes. But what was even more contradictory to the dogma of

Clara Porset in the Mexico City home of Architect Eduardo Yañez with Totonaca chairs of her design. Collection of Archivo Clara Porset, Centro de Investigaciones de Diseño Industrial, Facultad de Arquitectura, Universidad Nacional Autónoma de México, Mexico City.

rational modernity was the rampant use of ornamentation, albeit in modern styles, in much of Brazilian, Mexican, and Venezuelan production. Of course, there certainly were local and immigrant designers in the three countries whose products embraced the orthodox ideas of the international modern avant-garde. Porset was very clear when she asserted in 1952 that, "Every period has its own idea of beauty. In our time, our idea is based on simplicity, that is, on the elimination of the non-essential."[14] Most of the more original designs from the postwar period, however, including some of Porset's, were a departure from international canons of modernism. This evident willingness to challenge commonly accepted fundamental tenets of modern design reflects a determination to reformulate modern canons and adapt them to a different reality. Some designers stated their intention of creating a new modernity seasoned with local flavor. In a brief article published in *Cruz del Sur* magazine in 1952, Cornelis Zitman, referring to the production strategies implemented by his furniture company Tecoteca, said:

> **Its second strategy involves the simplicity and beauty of its furniture, which embodies national standards of good taste. As regards design, Tecoteca has taken the sensible approach of incorporating modern functional improvements, but has no intention of transplanting every single feature of foreign ultramodern ideas. The company has no desire to pursue a policy of mirroring forms or over-the-top originality. Tecoteca's goal is simply to produce its own kind of furniture whose functionality owes nothing to intellectual juggling acts, so that a chair is just a chair and nothing more. Tecoteca aims to produce a uniquely Venezuelan form of furniture based on critical studies of contemporary Venezuelan lifestyles, the materials involved, and the specific functions assigned to each element. Tecoteca aspires to make positive contributions to a refinement of national tastes, while steering clear of quaint traditions.[15]**

Compared to Europe or the United States, modern design certainly evolved in very different circumstances in Latin America. It was not just a matter of completely different societies, economies, markets, and wealth distribution systems. National industries — which played a huge role in the development of design — were also different, as was the range of available production technologies, to name just a couple of major factors. Handcrafts, many of which could trace their roots back to pre-Hispanic times, have always enjoyed a strong presence in Latin America, a phenomenon that has had a significant influence on local design and production. These important differences naturally affected the development and evolution of modern design but do not, in and of themselves, explain the additive nature of the methodology behind it. This idiosyncratic cultural phenomenon can be attributed to the local designers' desire to develop modern styles that were intimately linked to their place of origin and material culture, as Zitman stated, and he was by no means alone in this approach. The insistence on using local materials, for example, was a common denominator in all three countries. The Museum of Modern Art's guidelines for the Latin American section of the *Industrial Design Competition for the 21 American Republics* in 1940 — calling for an "intelligent and imaginative" use of local materials, such as bamboo, jute, and fibers from the caroá plant and the tucum palm — reflected an existing ethos.[16] As an example, ever since he began to design furniture in 1938 in Mexico, Michael van Beuren experimented with local materials, such as palm fibers, in his designs [checklist no. 66].

Unknown designer. *La Burriquita* platter, 1951. Ceramic; 10 ¼ in. diameter. Manufactured by Cerámicas Artísticas Nacionales, Antímano, Caracas, Venezuela. Private Collection, New York. [Checklist no. 81]

Unknown designer. Wineglasses, 1950. Blown glass, enameled, with cloth, each 5 ¹⁵/₁₆ x 3 ⅜ (diameter) in. Manufactured by Figadai, Rio de Janeiro, Brazil. Collection of The Corning Museum of Glass, Gift of Otto Hilbert. [Checklist no. 79]

In Brazil's case, it is easy to follow the "lineage" of the methodology involved in creation by absorption. Oswald de Andrade's 1928 "Manifiesto Antropófago" (Anthropophagous Manifesto) opened the doors to the inclusion of native elements in modern codes and created the basis for the coexistence of apparently disparate elements.[17] Although no one in Mexico or Venezuela theorized about the subject as lucidly as Andrade, it is obvious from an analysis of their respective design production that the methodologies used in those two countries were very similar to the ones used in Brazil. In the area of industrial design, the residential environment proved to be the ideal testing ground for alternatives best suited to local conditions. As Andrade stated, "Transfiguration of taboo into totem. Cannibalism"; modern Latin American houses were in fact transfiguration agents nourished by everything within reach — new and old, local and foreign, what was accepted as canonical and what was not.[18] This transfigurative "cannibalism" was an instinctive response mechanism whose roots can be found in the long history of cultural hybridization in Latin America. It was a mestizo way to assimilate elements that were by nature opposed to international modern dogma into a new, unique vision whose ultimate goal was to develop national styles and products that were compatible with local tastes.

The most direct approach in terms of additive design was often to apply decorative motifs or patterns inspired by local traditions to an object that had been designed in a modern style. This sort of cosmetic treatment was not truly innovative and was applied almost everywhere in the world, especially for high-volume products that sought to appeal to broader consumer markets. Motifs drawn from local folklore or history were frequently used in Brazil, Mexico, and Venezuela to make modern products more attractive. A far more sophisticated approach involved redesigning traditional objects and household items in a modern style. As Zitman explained so well in his *Cruz del Sur* essay, this was no

Clara Porset (Mexican, 1932–81). *Butaque,* c. 1955–56. Wood, woven cane; 28 ½ x 21 ½ x 25 ⁹⁄₁₆ in. Collection of the Familia Galvéz, Mexico City. [Checklist no. 45]

simple cosmetic job; on the contrary, redesigns were based on carefully researched reformulations of traditional products in modern styles that were compatible with new lifestyles and the places of their intended use.[19] Among the most emblematic examples of this process were *butaques*, easy chairs inspired by the ones used by pre-Hispanic Caribbean cultures. In modern interiors, traditional *butaques* were transmuted into elegant and novel versions designed by Porset and Arroyo [checklist no. 3]. The design of certain objects sometimes included a nod to the past, often echoing the styles of pre-Hispanic cultures. For example, in some of her ceramic pieces from the early 1960s, María Luisa Zuloaga de Tovar decontextualized the button-shaped appliqués used as eyes on pre-Hispanic Venezuelan figures by transforming them into decorative elements [checklist no. 62]. The pre-Hispanic flavor might also be the product of the designer's fantastic imagination, like the humanoid figures that Croatian-born Venezuelan potter Seka Severin de Tudja designed and used in many utilitarian pieces during the 1950s [checklist no. 63]. Another allusion might entail associating an object with a particular typology of the material culture of an earlier time, like the zoomorphic vessels produced in the early 1960s by José Feher, which recreated the repertoires and types found in traditional Mexican ceramics [checklist no. 23].

## Transvestite Horror

Design by absorption bears some similarity to certain forms of mid-twentieth-century modern architecture that have been identified by the Italian critic Gillo Dorfles as neo-baroque. These projects sought what he called "a more imaginative and varied approach to the art of construction" that was evocative of baroque values and experiences.[20] Dorfles singled out certain artists in whose work he identified a neo-baroque architectural "*novus ordo*" (new order) which, by extension we can apply to design.[21] Neo-baroque design's syntax relies on typical baroque mechanisms, most notably the *horror vacui* (fear of empty spaces) that has so often been used to excess in Latin America. This fear of empty spaces has in fact never been fully purged from Latin American visual culture. Though frequently cross-dressed in order to mimic modernism and become one with modernity, it has always been around, in one guise or another. The neo-baroque has used this cross-dressing as a strategy for adapting to changing times, as one of the forms of simulation that, according to the Cuban critic and writer Severo Sarduy, "connects, by grouping them into one single energy — the drive of simulation — disparate phenomena from heterogeneous, seemingly unconnected spaces."[22] The fundamental goal of the baroque approach — to overwhelm the viewer's senses — was achieved by other means in the twentieth century. The important thing, in any case, was to blur the boundaries between reality and unreality. The basic principle of the *horror vacui* remained the same: to saturate the surfaces of objects and architectural structures in order to blot out the central or axial points that helped to order their elements, thus disorienting and dazzling the viewer. Instead of figures, modernist works used the rhythm and geometrical forms of repeated abstract elements, like the surface line patterns in Miguel Arroyo's coffee table [checklist no. 7] and the Brazilian designer Joaquim Tenreiro's easy chair [checklist no. 56] to create optical effects. Other works used extremely intense saturated colors, or no color at all — pure white, when seen in searing tropical sunlight, had the same effect — to overwhelm the senses and blur the volumes of objects, transforming them into planes or floating colored surfaces as the Venezuelan glassmaker Rubén Núñez did on some of his glass designs [checklist nos. 36, 37], on which a section of an object with a saturated rich color hue seems to float as the rest of the piece visually disappears. Artists used rich textures to stimulate alternative readings of surfaces and blur the contours of objects, such as in Severin de Tudja's ceramics [checklist nos. 64, 65], and mixed different contrasting materials, like wood with distinctive grains, and unusual colors, with colored plastic laminates in complex shapes that could surprise the viewer, as the Brazilian designer José Zanine Caldas did on many of his pieces [checklist no. 74]. In some cases, the form of the objects themselves — sometimes whimsical, sometimes exaggerated, but above all a far cry from the geometric purity of the regular Platonic solids that were so characteristic of international modernity — helped to augment the effect of camouflaged baroque surfaces [checklist no. 10]. The idea was, ultimately, to design centrifugal objects — whose axes and edges are not immediately recognizable — capable of slipping the bonds of their own outlines through an eclectic repertoire of strategies focused on dazzling the senses and, for a moment, coaxing the viewer into an unreal dimension. This neo-baroque vision of modern design, which favored adding instead of subtracting — and often suggested that "more is better" — was not the exclusive province of architecture or design. In literature, for example, Sarduy claimed to have identified a neo-baroque aesthetic in the works of many Latin American writers of the same period.[23]

## Beyond the Home

The coexisting contradictions produced by hybrid postcolonial societies in many aspects of daily life in Brazilian, Mexican, and Venezuelan homes over the course of time has led to some surprising developments in the world of material culture, modern design being no exception. Perhaps that is why, as suggested by Homi K. Bhabha in the epigraph of this essay, it is precisely there, in the apparently "feverish stillness, [of] the intimate recesses of the domestic space" that the most innovative forms of modern design have been developed in these three countries. However, by the end of the 1960s, the

[1]  Homi K. Bhabha, "The World and the Home," *Social Text* 10, nos. 2/3 (1992): 141.

[2]  Eliot Noyes and Museum of Modern Art, *Organic Design in Home Furnishings* (New York: Museum of Modern Art, 1941), 39–41.

[3]  Patricio del Real, "Building a Continent: The Idea of Latin American Architecture in the Early Postwar" (PhD diss., Columbia University, 2012), 10.

[4]  Manuel Amábilis, *El pabellón de México en la Exposición Ibero-Americana de Sevilla* [The Mexican Pavilion at the Ibero-American Exhibition in Seville] (Mexico City: Talleres Gráficos de la Nación, 1929).

[5]  The house was designed by its owner, Benjamín Mendoza, with the help of the master builder, a Spaniard by the name of Cervantes. Arroyo and Otero were no doubt also involved in the project. The Quinta Perla was the first home to be built in what had originally been planned as an artist's colony in El Toronjil, a neighborhood in San Antonio de los Altos. The lot had been divided into three parts: one for the Mendoza Guardias; another for Alejandro Otero and his wife, the painter Mercedes Pardo, who were building their house there; and a third one for Miguel

Arroyo, who never managed to build the house that was designed by the architect Juan Pedro Posani. This information has been graciously provided by Emilio Mendoza Guardia and Lourdes Blanco de Arroyo.

[6]  Clara Porset, "El Centro Urbano Presidente Alemán y el espacio interior para vivir" [The Presidente Alemán Urban Center and Interior Living Space], *Arquitectura: Selección de Arquitectura, Urbanismo y Decoración*, no. 32 (1950): 117–20.

[7]  Loos first gave this lecture in Munich in 1908 and it was initially published in 1910 in the Berlin newspaper *Der Sturm: Wochenschrift für Kultur und Kunst*, Jg 1, Vol. p. 44. See Kirk Varnedoe, *Vienna 1900: Art, Architecture & Design* (New York: Museum of Modern Art, 1986), 229n33.

[8]  Instituto Nacional de Bellas Artes, Departamento de Arquitectura, *El arte en la vida diaria: Exposición de objetos de buen diseño hechos en México* [Art in Daily Life: An Exhibition of Well-Designed Objects Made in Mexico] (Mexico City: El Instituto, 1952), 13.

[9]  Oscar Salinas Flores, "La obra de una vida," in Clara Porset, Alejandro Hernández Gálvez, Ana Elena Mallet, and Oscar Salinas Flores, *El diseño de Clara Porset:*

developmentalist model started to show early signs of failure and the utopian dream route to become modern developed industrialized nations for Brazil, Mexico, and Venezuela turned out to be unclear. As elsewhere, the May 1968 events in France had important social, political, and cultural repercussions in the region, and the status quo was increasingly called into question. As a result, in design circles the gravity center for experimentation shifted spaces moving from the home to the streets and beyond. A reaction against what many avant-garde designers saw as the obsolete formulas of modern design led them to explore other directions. Since exterior space became the new arena for social change and the preferred stage for design, some projects from that period express defiant and provocative ideas often resulting in objects that subverted the way people though about them, as in the Brazilian designer Lina Bo Bardi's roadside chair *Cadeira de beira de estrada* (1967) [checklist no. 11]. Whereas in the late 1960s, the world saw space as the new frontier for design, and designers in Brazil, Mexico, and Venezuela — such as in Jorge Zalszupin, Paulo Jorge Pedreira, and Arturo Pani — experimented with man-made materials like plastics and new metal alloys [checklist nos. 40, 41, 72, 73], Bo Bardi was exploring a very different, unconventional path that led back to the ancestral roots of design. All it took were a few sturdy branches and some lengths of rope to make a chair that challenged the future; a chair that was not designed purely for the home but was created to be used out in the world, that vast territory that was waiting to be conquered by new cannibal designs inspired by whatever could nourish its development, a design that made no distinctions and was guided by a total lack of prejudice.

*inventando un México moderno* [Clara Porset's Design: Creating a Modern Mexico] (Mexico City: Museo Franz Mayer; CIDI; Difusión Cultural UNAM; Turner, 2006), 21.

10  Diego Arroyo Gil, *Miguel Arroyo* (Caracas: Editora El Nacional: Fundación Bancaribe, 2012), 39.

11  Jorge F. Rivas Pérez, *Cornelis Zitman: la década de diseño, 1947–1957* [Cornelis Zitman: The Design Decade, 1947–1957] (Caracas: Sala Trasnocho Arte Contacto, 2011), 25.

12  Ethel Leon, *Design Brasileiro: quem fez, quem faz* [Brazilian Design: Who Did, Who Does] (Rio de Janeiro: Viana & Mosley; Senac Rio, 2005), 82.

13  Paulo Herkenhoff, "Brazil: The Paradoxes of an Alternate Baroque," in Elizabeth Armstrong and Victor Zamudio-Taylor, eds., *Ultra Baroque: Aspects of Post Latin American Art* (San Diego: Museum of Contemporary Art, 2000), 150.

14  Instituto Nacional de Bellas Artes, 23.

15  "Tecoteca — como se industrializa el mueble moderno en Venezuela" [Tecoteca — the Industrialization of Modern Furniture in Venezuela],

*Cruz del Sur* 1, no. 9 (November–December 1952): center.

16  Museum of Modern Art, *Industrial Design Competition for the 21 American Republics* (New York: McKnight Kauffer, 1940).

17  Oswald de Andrade, "Manifiesto Antropófago" [Anthropophagus Manifesto], *Revista de Antropofagia* (São Paulo) 1 (May 1928): 3, 7.

18  Ibid., 7.

19  "Tecoteca," center.

20  Gillo Dorfles, *Barocco nell'architettura moderna* [The Baroque in Modern Architecture] (Milan: Libreria Editrice Politecnica Tamburini, 1951), 62.

21  Ibid., 73.

22  Severo Sarduy, *La simulación* [Simulation] (Caracas: Monte Ávila Editores, 1982), 8.

23  Severo Sarduy, "El barroco y el neobarroco" [The Baroque and the Neo-baroque], in César Fernández Moreno, ed., *América Latina en su literatura* [Latin America in Its Literature] (México: Siglo Veintiuno-UNESCO, 1971), 167–84.

# MIGUEL ARROYO AND POTTERY[1]

## LOURDES BLANCO

Miguel Arroyo (1920–2004) had a passion for pottery that embraced all crafts, for he considered each of them a link between individual creation and their multiple functions: in craftwork, design, and production. Applying much of his prodigious energy as an educator, creator, and art critic to studio craft and design, he advocated, explained, and taught that every point along the line that seems to divide the potter, weaver, enamelist, and woodworker from the distant and removed designer might be justly valued in its full dimension as part of a whole.

Ever since his years studying industrial and applied arts at the Carnegie Institute of Technology in Pittsburgh between 1946 and 1948, any type of craft—particularly pottery, enamelwork, woodwork, and weaving—caught Miguel's professional attention. It's no surprise, consequently, that he had so little time for developing his own personal creative endeavors as a potter and enamelist, activities that he practiced from 1946 to 1960.

Miguel demonstrated his passion for and faith in pottery and design in every way possible, but especially through teaching, exhibiting, and writing. In 1949, he opened the pioneering design store Gato (Cat) in the garage of a house in the La Florida neighborhood of Caracas, in partnership with the pianist and painter Alberto Brandt and Charles Sink, a young Harvard-educated American architect

Above: Entrance to the Gato store, founded by Miguel Arroyo, Alberto Brandt, and Charles Sink in La Florida, Caracas, Venezuela, 1949. Courtesy of Centro de Estudios de Archivos Audiovisuales y Artísticos and AMAC Archive.

Right: Tienda Gato logo. Courtesy of Centro de Estudios de Archivos Audiovisuales y Artísticos and AMAC Archive.

Left: Two ceramic pieces by Miguel Arroyo, 1955. Photo by Sara Guardia de Mendoza. Courtesy of Centro de Estudios de Archivos Audiovisuales y Artísticos and the Mendoza Guardia Family.

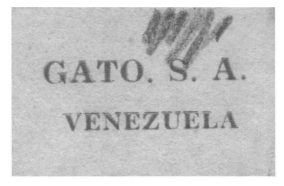

Miguel Arroyo (Venezuelan, 1920–2004). Bowl for Tienda Gato, c. 1949. Ceramic; 2 1/16 x 7 1/16 (diameter) in. Private Collection, New York. [Checklist no. 2]

working at that time in the capital.[2] At Gato, Miguel sold his ceramic wares and enamel on metal objects, books, music records, and original artworks by local artists, as well as furniture designed by him and Sink and classics by foreign designers, such as reproductions of the 1938 BKF chair (Bonet, Kurchan, and Ferrari-Hardoy). The store's overarching mission was to transform everyday life and home interiors through modern design. This objective seems to be inspired by the ideals of art historian Alexander Dorner, whose influence we can see in Miguel's review of Dorner's 1947 book *The Way beyond "Art,"*[3] for the journal *Revista Cruz del Sur* in 1952:

> [F]or Dorner, abstract art is but a stage in a process of integration that will necessarily culminate in art forms that directly address the needs of human beings. Industrial design, photography, typography, architecture, etc. . . . will be the new modes of expression that artists will resort to in order to achieve a more profound contact with reality and transform it. Static painting will no longer be necessary because the causes that brought it into being will have disappeared. The beauty of the elements that make up the houses and cities will assume its place. Then, the gap that, according to the previous argument, separates old and new modes of expression will give way to a fuller integration and a greater interaction between the two, as has occurred in the past between art and life.[4]

Dorner's conception of design as a new form of artistic expression became fundamental to Miguel's writings and teaching.

Miguel Arroyo at the potter's wheel with Tecla Tofano, 1955. Photo by Sara Guardia de Mendoza. Courtesy of Centro de Estudios de Archivos Audiovisuales y Artísticos and the Mendoza Guardia Family.

Miguel Arroyo's students: from left to right, Clarita Urdaneta, Tecla Tofano, Cristina Merchán, Ámparo de Bemporad, 1955. Photo by Sara Guardia de Mendoza. Courtesy of Centro de Estudios de Archivos Audiovisuales y Artísticos and the Mendoza Guardia Family.

From 1953 to 1956, in addition to his work as a furniture designer — Miguel's main professional activity during the early 1950s — he taught workshops in pottery and enameling on metal, as well as a course on the history of the applied arts at the Escuela de Artes Plásticas y Artes Aplicadas in Esquina del Cuño, Caracas, and, from 1957 to 1958, he gave private lessons on the same subjects for the Otepal group.[5] During those years at the Escuela de Artes Plásticas y Artes Aplicadas, Miguel under-took numerous design and exhibition projects with a colleague, the painter Alejandro Otero, by then teacher at the Escuela de Artes Plásticas y Artes Aplicadas. Their friendship grew into an influential, long-lasting informal professional partnership. As Otero noted thirty years later: "We thought that the role of the new art should be fulfilled on the street, anonymously if possible, in harmony with architec-tural structures. From there, it would pass into the interiors, until it reached small everyday objects. We imagined big teams of artists and artisans, working together from shared ideas to create a great work of social transformation."[6]

The vigorous modern studio craft movement in Venezuela — one of the most outstanding aspects of the country's mid-century creative scene — emerged to a large extent thanks to Miguel's teaching activities, which were "fraternal but demanding," as we know because of his personal notes from the period and according to his students.[7] But, as the Croatian-born Venezuelan ceramist Seka Severin de Tudja — whose exhibition *Treinta y cinco cerámicas de Seka* [Thirty-five Pottery Pieces by Seka] Arroyo installed in the interior courtyard of the Museo de Bellas Artes in 1962 — used to say, one didn't have to be Miguel's student to learn from his teachings.[8] His enthusiasm, critical eye, advice, and opportune words were all highly valued in and out of the classroom.

In a report on the activities of the workshop he directed in the Escuela de Artes Plásticas y Artes Aplicadas, Miguel defined his mission clearly: "I have tried step by step to create what might be called a philosophy of form, which takes into account aesthetic and functional factors, systems of production, and a knowledge and respect for materials."[9]

Installation view of the exhibition *Thirty-five Pottery Pieces by Seka* in the interior courtyard of the Museo de Bellas Artes, 1962. Photo by Bela Sziklay. Courtesy of Centro de Estudios de Archivos Audiovisuales y Artísticos and AMAC Archive.

When Miguel participated in the Salón Oficial in 1954 and won the Premio Nacional (Venezuelan National Prize) in the applied arts category,[10] he was aware of the difficulties studio craft faced in Venezuela in relation to workshop space, equipment, and materials. Deficiencies in these areas at the Escuela de Artes Plásticas y Artes Aplicadas, unaddressed by school officials, led him to resign from his classes three years after he began there. For this reason, together with friends and some of his former students — Tecla Tofano, Cristina Merchán, Sara Guardia de Mendoza, Benjamín Mendoza, Alejandro Otero, and Mercedes Pardo — he launched Forma Veinte (Form Twenty), a cooperative workshop located in San Antonio de Los Altos.[11] Focused on the production and promotion of studio pottery, enamelwork, and textiles, the cooperative allowed associates greater access to imported raw materials and equipment.

Seka Severin de Tudja (Venezuelan, 1923–2007). *L–13,* 1979. Ceramic; 6 ½ x 7 (diameter) in. Colección Patricia Phelps de Cisneros. [Checklist no. 65]

In a brief recollection presented to members of the cooperative in November of 1954, Arroyo outlined the ideas that drove the project:

> **Forma Veinte was born of the desire expressed by a group of friends to create a studio craft movement, artisanal in nature, that would also project itself beyond our own context and test the possibilities for developing such activities in Venezuela. . . . It would also provide insight into the forms of production that could be successfully adopted in the country. The thought was that, in the face of North America and Europe having strong serial production and manufacturing traditions, Latin American countries should seek alternative forms [of production] that could give them a competitive advantage. However, it was not absolutely certain [at that time] whether that competitiveness should be sought through the artisanal product by giving special importance to the particular product's uniqueness, or if, on the contrary, we should compete on the industrial level through serial production. This uncertainty led to an intermediate solution that would include the artisanal production. . . . Forma Veinte would demand of its members a desire for continual improvement and a production equal at least to any foreign product of high quality.**[12]

One of the most important aspects of this document is the author's proposal for how the cooperative should function: "We advocate the development of three kinds of product lines: one serially produced, another repeated in limited series, and a third consisting of unique pieces."[13] Addressing the difficult topic of methodology in production, Miguel suggested two alternatives:

Ceramics by Forma Veinte. Courtesy of Centro de Estudios de Archivos Audiovisuales y Artísticos and AMAC Archive.

We deem it impossible to determine which would be the most advantageous mode of work. This is precisely one of the experiences that Forma Veinte must undertake, that is, the practical experience of discovering through action which mode of work will be more efficient for each group member and for the cooperative itself. Nonetheless, there are two propositions to consider . . . [according to] the first, the pieces created by any of the group members and considered good for repetition, would be repeated . . . by each of the other members. This way of proceeding would oblige each member to go through an experience that might otherwise remain merely individualized.

The second proposition goes as follows: since the waste of materials that individual experiments may occasion do not matter to Forma Veinte, given that these would only lead to discoveries of other qualities in the materials that might be used advantageously, we advocate that all mechanical work (that is, cutting and hammering the metal bases and the ground preparation and application in the case of enameling) be carried out collectively by each and every group member, but that subsequent work should be carried out individually, so that each member would repeat the enamelwork that he have created and that the group has decided should be repeated.[14]

In 1955, Miguel's article *"La cerámica"* (Ceramics), published in the journal *A, hombre y expresión*, distilled these ideas, and he went further, offering a few speculations that were economic in nature:[15]

Latin Americans are, undoubtedly, at a disadvantage with respect to the production of European and North American nations. Especially that of Sweden, Norway, and Denmark, which have marvelous artisanal productions that, for reasons relating to monetary currency exchange, can be sold in our countries at quite affordable prices. . . . North America has excellent industrial production, which for the same reason and owing to the cheap prices of the mass production . . . makes the idea of competing utopian for the time being.[15]

Ceramics exhibition in the Escuela de Artes Plásticas y Artes Aplicadas, 1955. Photo by Sara Guardia de Mendoza. Courtesy of Centro de Estudios de Archivos Audiovisuales y Artísticos and the Mendoza Guardia Family.

Thus, by analyzing the different factors and difficulties of industrial production, including the cost of raw materials, currency exchange rate, demand, and competitiveness, Miguel arrived at the conclusion that, for Venezuela, the "only alternative" is "an artisanal and semi-industrial production" that can offer "great flexibility in the forms of objects produced, given that its main feature is the unique or limited edition piece."[16]

Also in 1955, the first ceramic exhibition by his students — with an astonishing array of four hundred pieces — made a huge public impact and marked a turning point in Venezuelan studio pottery.[17] The show, which succeeded in selling almost all of its pieces, allowed Miguel to showcase the high quality of the production and to present the two predominant pottery styles from that period — expressionist and concrete. At the same time, he was able to objectively analyze the real possibilities of sustaining a professional studio craft practice in modern Venezuela.[18] In other words, Miguel was forward-looking; he visualized the conditions that students would face on leaving the classroom.

In the aforementioned 1955 article, Miguel also wrote on traditional artisanal pottery — a subject that always fascinated him. He recounts a trip he made to Quíbor in western Venezuela for a project of redesigning the traditional blankets made in that place.[19] While visiting the region looking for traditional weavers willing to manufacture his designs, he also met a traditional potter who showed him:

Installation in the ceramics exhibition at the Escuela de Artes Plásticas y Artes Aplicadas, 1955. Photo by Sara Guardia de Mendoza. Courtesy of Centro de Estudios de Archivos Audiovisuales y Artísticos and the Mendoza Guardia Family.

no less than fifteen different types [of vessels] for activities related to the act of drawing water from a well, transporting it, storing it, serving it, boiling it, drinking it, etc. Almost all [the vessels] were very well designed but not well executed. The jug that appears in the illustrations is an excellent piece of design in relation to its function, the properties of the material, and the system of production. Its form allows for the containment of a good measure of water; its scale is correct in relation to the hand; the handle permits a good grip and is placed in a way that facilitates the pouring of the water. The jug's mouth is sufficiently small enough to protect the water contained but not so much so that it would prevent a cleaning brush to pass through. From its form, [we can deduct that] it is clearly a product of the potter's wheel, the [vessel's] curved profile used by the potter allows every section diameter to find support in the preceding one. . . . The only features to be lamented are the bad quality of the material used (earthenware clay) and the low temperature of the firing (approximately 650° C), which renders it too porous.[20]

Miguel admired traditional popular pottery throughout his life. Thanks to this fascination, during his tenure (1959–76) as the director of the Museo de Bellas Artes in Caracas, he acquired in the 1970s for the museum's holdings an extensive collection of traditional popular pottery amassed in the 1950s by Gediminas Orentas, a Lithuanian-born traveling photographer with a passion for traditional crafts and antiquities.[21]

Miguel's interest in ceramics had no chronological limits and went beyond the modern studio pottery to which he dedicated himself. Furthermore, his concern for preindustrial arts and crafts was a sign of his modern spirit. He demonstrated this in 1958, just before he was named director of the Museo de Bellas Artes, where he designed the gallery for the museum's Egyptian collection and undertook what Alberto Sato called "the intellectual enterprise of producing significance consciously"[22] by changing the context in which the ancient pottery pieces were exhibited. In order to do that, he brought to the Museo de Bellas Artes a long-term loan of Venezuelan pre-Hispanic art from the collection that his friend and colleague José María Cruxent, archeologist and director of the neighboring Museo de Ciencias Naturales (Museum of Natural Science), had previously displayed in an archeological context in the building on the opposite side of the museum's square. By exhibiting pre-Hispanic pottery alongside Egyptian art, Miguel wanted to create awareness for Venezuelan ancient art, by then understudied and little appreciated by the general public. A year later, Miguel and Cruxent, together with another great ally, the Rumanian-born photographer Petre Maxim, produced the book *Cerámicas venezolanas* (Venezuelan Ceramics) with a foreword by Jaime Tello.[23] This represented the first attempt to establish an affective continuity for Venezuelan pottery, from the pre-Hispanic period to modern times.

The Colombian art critic Marta Traba used to say that no one could narrate a painting better than Miguel Arroyo,[24] while the Italian-born Venezuelan graphic designer Nedo M. F. (Mion Ferrario), whose creative matrix reflects the influence of pre-Hispanic petroglyphs and art, would read Miguel's texts on pre-Hispanic art. In fact, the writings that Miguel devoted to pottery are among the most cited by scholars as well as the most beautiful.[25]

In the last decade of his life, Miguel traveled to virtually every place in Venezuela, visiting pre-Hispanic pottery collections in order to study and select the pieces that would form part of the 1999 show *El arte prehispánico de Venezuela* (The Pre-Hispanic Art of Venezuela),[26] one of his most outstanding curatorial projects at the Galería de Arte Nacional. There, he also prepared retrospective exhibitions of two of the most accomplished modern Venezuela potters, María Luisa Tovar and Seka Severin de Tudja; unfortunately, these two exhibitions were never realized. However, Miguel's last great — and also sadly unfinished — curatorial challenge was an exhibition of Venezuelan studio pottery from 1950 to 2000, focusing particularly on pottery-wheel-produced wares.[27] This last curatorial endeavor gave him the opportunity to reconsider in a new light all his previous pottery exhibitions, to study the numerous Venezuelan studio pottery collections that surged as a result of his promotion of the craft, as well as to review the work of several generations of younger potters who had followed his trail. With that exhibition, he intended to pay one last tribute to a beloved field. Unfortunately, Miguel did not live long enough to make it public but left his ideal fully articulated in an unpublished text: "It was a matter of seeing potters as designers, in both artisanal and industrial productions, which is what they have always been from prehistory times since the invention of pottery."[28]

1   Editor's note: This is an abridged version of an essay read by the author, Miguel Arroyo's widow, at the seminar "Formas de barro para la vida" [Forms of Clay for Life], which took place at the Galería de Arte Nacional in Caracas on May 3, 2006, in conjunction with the exhibition *Fuego y Arcilla. Hacedores de Formas. Homenaje a Miguel Arroyo* [Fire and Clay: Form Makers—A Tribute to Miguel Arroyo], curated by Daniel Ramírez. Another extended version will be published in an illustrated book currently in production to be published by the Archive AMAC, Centro de Estudios de Archivos Audiovisuales y Artísticos, Caracas, the first in a series dedicated to presenting and discussing different aspects of Miguel Arroyo's work and life.

2   See Lourdes Blanco de Arroyo, *"Interior Moderno: Miguel Arroyo, diseñador"* [Modern Interior: Miguel Arroyo, Designer] in *Interior Moderno. Muebles diseñados por Miguel Arroyo* [Modern Interiors: Furniture Designed by Miguel Arroyo] (Caracas: Sala Trasnocho Arte Contacto, 2005). Charles Sink came to Venezuela in the late 1940s to work in the architecture firm Carbonell y Sanabria.

3   Alexander Dorner, *The Way beyond "Art": The Work of Herbert Bayer* (New York: Wittenborn, Schultz, Inc., 1947).

4   *"Alexander Dorner: El Camino más allá del arte"* [Alexander Dorner: The Way beyond Art], trans. Miguel Arroyo, in *Revista Cruz del Sur*, no. 3 (May 1952): 53–9. The German-born Dorner had been the director of the Landesmuseum (State Museum) in Hanover before immigrating to the United States, where he became the director of the Art Museum at the Rhode Island School of Design.

5   The Otepal (a name derived from "Oteyza-Palacios") group was a private applied arts workshop in Caracas. It consisted of Amalia de Oteyza, Gonzalo Palacios Herrera and his wife, Luisa (la Nena) Zuloaga de Palacios, Antonio Peláez and María Elena Lozano de Peláez, and Sony and Clarita Requena. See María Fernanda Palacios, *Movimiento del grabado en Venezuela: una memoria* [The Print Movement in Venezuela: A Memory] (Caracas: Comisión de Estudios de Postgrado; Facultad de Humanidades y Educación;

Universidad Central de Venezuela, 2003), 57–60.

6   Alejandro Otero Rodríguez, *Alejandro Otero* (Caracas: Museo de Arte Contemporáneo de Caracas, 1985), 21.

7   Gonzalo Palacios Herrera, "Es un grato deber. . . " [It Is a Pleasant Duty. . . ]. Archive AMAC, Centro de Estudios de Archivos Audiovisuales y Artísticos, Caracas.

8   Personal communication.

9   Miguel Arroyo, "Informe acerca de las actividades del Taller de cerámica de la Escuela de Artes Plásticas y Artes Aplicadas de Caracas, del 15/01 al 15/06, de 1954" [Report on the Activities of the Ceramics Workshop at the Escuela de Artes Plásticas y Artes Aplicadas of Caracas from January 15 to June 15, 1954] submitted to Francisco Narváez, then the school's director. Manuscript transcription (1954). Archive AMAC, Centro de Estudios de Archivos Audiovisuales y Artísticos, Caracas.

10   The jury consisted of Manuel Cabré, Juan Röhl, Francisco Narváez, Carlos Otero, Alfredo Boulton, Arturo Uslar Pietri, and Gastón Diehl.

11   At that rural location, since annexed by the city of Caracas, the Mendoza-Guardia, Otero-Pardo, and Arroyo-Roo families made plans to build their homes. The land had belonged to Rafael Pardo Becerra, Mercedes Pardo's father, and the work of clearing the underbrush was undertaken by the entrepreneur and arts patron Inocente Palacios. The first home to be built belonged to Mendoza-Guardia, boasted two murals by Otero, and included a picture window created, according to some recollections, by Arroyo and Mendoza (and, according to others, by Otero, Mendoza, and a construction worker).

12   Miguel Arroyo, *"Grupo forma veinte. Informe que presenta Miguel Arroyo"* [Forma Veinte Group: Report Presented by Miguel Arroyo], Nov. 1, 1954. Manuscript transcription from a document at the Archive AMAC, Centro de Estudios de Archivos Audiovisuales y Artísticos, Caracas, 1.

13   Ibid., 2.

14   Ibid.

15 Miguel Arroyo, *"La cerámica"* [Ceramics], *Revista A: Hombre y Expresión* (Sociedad Editora "A," Caracas) (September 2, 1955): 59–66.

16 Ibid., 64.

17 See Escuela de Artes Plásticas y Artes Aplicadas, *Catálogo. XVII Exposición de trabajos de los alumnos de la Escuela de Artes Plásticas y Artes Aplicadas de Caracas* [Catalog: XVII Exhibition of Work by Students of the Escuela de Artes Plásticas y Artes Aplicadas de Caracas] (Caracas: Ministerio de Educación, Dirección de Cultura y Bellas Artes, 1955). The contributions in ceramics were made by first-year students Ámparo de Bemporad, Elvira Forero, María García, Teresa Jiménez, Fernando Maneiro, Ángela Suárez, and Clarita Urdaneta; second-year students Cristina Merchán and Tecla Tofano (de Córdova); and fourth-year students Gunda de Barazarte and Víctor Mejías. Sara Guardia de Mendoza photographed every potter who participated in the exhibition, and Arroyo included the photographs in the installation.

18 Almost at the same time, a group of important ceramists that included Miguel Arroyo, Reina Benzecri, Ámparo de Bemporad, Tecla Tofano (de Córdova), Eduardo Dorta, Elvira Forero, Carlos Guinand, Teresita Jiménez, Fernando Maneiro, Gunda Martínez B., Víctor Mejías, Cristina Merchán, and Clarita Urdaneta participated in the exhibition of the Taller Libre de Arte in Caracas as a tribute to the Guatemalan artist Carlos Mérida.

19 Through the report on Forma Veinte and other documents in Miguel's archive, we know of the designs that Miguel and Alejandro Otero made for the artisans and weavers of Quíbor. Some of the blankets and spreads are preserved in the Mendoza-Guardia family collection at San Antonio de Los Altos.

20 Arroyo, "La cerámica," 65.

21 The purchase was completed thanks to the Sociedad de Amigos del Museo de Bellas Artes de Caracas. After many years of storage and neglect, a selection from this collection, *Fuego y Arcilla. Hacedores de Formas. Homenaje a Miguel Arroyo* [Fire and Clay: Form Makers—A Tribute to Miguel Arroyo], curated by Daniel Ramírez, was exhibited in 2006 at the Galería de Arte Nacional in Caracas.

22 With Sato, Miguel engaged in an intense, written discussion on the topic of tradition in craftwork. See Alberto Sato, "Los muebles de Miguel" [The Furniture of Miguel Arroyo], in *Interior Moderno. Muebles diseñados por Miguel Arroyo* [Modern Interior; Furniture Designed by Miguel Arroyo] (Caracas: Sala Trasnocho Arte Contacto, 2005), 6.

23 Jaime Tello, *Cerámicas venezolanas* [Venezuelan Ceramics] (Caracas: Compañía Venezolana de Cerámica, 1959). The book consisted of a collection of color and black-and-white plates of pre-Hispanic and contemporary studio pottery pieces (photos by Petre Maxim) selected by Miguel Arroyo in collaboration with J. M. Cruxent with a short foreword by Jaime Tello.

24 Personal communication.

25 See Miguel Arroyo, J. M. Cruxent, and Sagrario Pérez Soto de Atencio, *El Arte Prehispánico de Venezuela* [The Pre-Hispanic Art of Venezuela] (Caracas: Fundación Eugenio Mendoza, 1971), and Miguel G. Arroyo C., *Arte Educación y Museología. Estudios y Polémicas 1948–1988* [Art, Education, and Museology: Studies and Controversies, 1948–1988], ed. Roldán Esteva Grillet with María Antonia González Arnal, Margarita Schwarck Lucca, and Douglas Monroy (Caracas: Biblioteca de la Academia Nacional de la Historia, 1989).

26 Miguel Arroyo, Lourdes Blanco, Erika Wagner, et al., *El Arte Prehispánico de Venezuela* [The Pre-Hispanic Art of Venezuela] (Caracas: Fundación Galería de Arte Nacional, 1999).

27 For that unfinished research project (working title, *La cerámica artística en Venezuela. 1940–1969*) [Venezuelan Artistic Pottery, 1940–1969], Miguel had the support of Carmen Araujo and Ernesto Guevara.

28 Manuscript. Archive AMAC, Centro de Estudios de Archivos Audiovisuales y Artísticos, Caracas.

Francisco José Serrano (Mexican, 1900–82).
Furniture by Gaston Chaussat designed for
the company El Palacio de Hierro. Edificio de
Apartamentos Jardín, Mexico City, 1931–32.
Courtesy of Archive of Civil Engineer and
Architect Francisco José Serrano.

# SOCIAL UTOPIA AND MODERN DESIGN IN LATIN AMERICA

## ANA ELENA MALLET

The ambitious goals of modernization and social change outlined in many postwar Latin American developmentalist national plans often regarded modern design and architecture among the key tools for transforming nations and societies. Inspired by ideas and concepts that had been developed in Europe during the interwar years, several entrepreneurial, design-oriented initiatives that were framed in the context of developmentalist agendas and concerned with social issues were launched in Latin America. These projects — which were, on the whole, exceptional in the region — were influenced by theories that were rooted in a socialist worldview that advocated using design as an instrument for education and social transformation. Latin American avant-garde architecture and design movements were concerned with how to implement modern ideas for middle- and lower-class housing and interior design. Such projects as the Flávio de Carvalho housing development (1936) in Alameda Lorena in São Paulo and Carlos Raúl Villanueva's Los Manolos house (1934) in Caracas are early examples of middle-class modern rationalist housing informed by European avant-garde architecture. As elsewhere, non-traditional materials, such as the industrial steel-tubing furniture that was proposed by the Dutch designer Mart Stam and some of the instructors at the Bauhaus during the Dessau period (1925–32), including Walter Gropius, Marcel Breuer, and Hannes Meyer, offered a possible alternative. For example, the French designer Gaston Chaussat,[1] who lived in Mexico, designed a set of chromed steel-tubing furniture pieces for El Palacio de Hierro, the large department store, that were highly

prized by the top Mexican architects of the period, such as Juan O'Gorman, who used them to furnish the house he designed for Diego Rivera and Frida Kahlo in San Ángel (1932), and Francisco Serrano, who placed them on the patios at the Edificio Jardín (1931) in Mexico City.[2] However, because raw materials were generally imported, in Latin America prices for modern-style metal furnishings were relatively high and out of reach for low-income clients.

These design projects were getting under way just as the Brazilian, Mexican, and Venezuelan governments were developing ambitious new approaches to infrastructure, health, education, and public housing. This essay will discuss three of the most representative projects in which design was intended as an instrument for social change in societies that both created and consumed the products in question, focusing on three furniture factories: Unilabor in Brazil, Van Beuren SA de CV (Domus) in Mexico, and Tecoteca in Venezuela. Though each was very different from the other two, they all saw modern design as a fundamental tool for social improvement and transformation. Furthermore, the visionary founders of these companies, without neglecting the business side of their enterprises, shared the common utopian dream of creating more egalitarian societies in their countries by promoting new types of entrepreneurial structures with important progressive social commitments as alternatives to traditional commercial practices and current business models.

## Background: Social Design in Europe between the Wars

The years between the two world wars ushered in a period of profound change in European social and political structures that prompted new approaches to housing. The architect Le Corbusier articulated his vision of a modern house as a "machine for living,"[3] an idea that would have worldwide repercussions. In 1929, he visited South America and gave a series of lectures in Buenos Aires that became pivotal for the introduction of his ideas on modern living in the region. In 1936, he lectured in Brazil and also became consultant for the iconic and highly influential building for the Ministry of Education and Health in Rio de Janeiro (1936–43), designed by a team directed by Lúcio Costa and Oscar Niemeyer. Le Corbusier's influence also spread to other Latin American countries, such as Mexico and Venezuela, and his legacy is evident in the work of such architects as the Mexican Juan O'Gorman and the Venezuelan Carlos Raúl Villanueva.

In the 1920s in Europe, questions of comfort, hygiene, and the utilitarian aspects of design took precedence over decorative considerations in the work of an important group of avant-garde architects and designers. The challenges raised by postwar economies and the urgent demand for social change had a huge impact on the development of new models for residential spaces. No longer viewed strictly as a middle-class asset, housing was now considered a public necessity. The mass production of well-designed, low-cost furniture and household items played a key role in plans to provide appropriate consumer goods to large segments of the population.

Germany's Weimar Republic was deeply committed to introducing social programs that would improve the lifestyle of the working class. The principles advocated by the Bauhaus, which claimed that design should be used as a tool for social progress, were in tune with those government welfare programs. Furthermore, the use of modern architecture and design to promote social change was central at the 1929 Congrès internationaux d'architecture moderne (International Conference on Modern Architecture). Delegates discussed minimum housing standards and social design, and reviewed the rural housing projects proposed by the German architect Ernst May. From 1926 to 1930, May — who at the time was the director of the Frankfurt Municipal Building Department — and his team, which included Mart Stam and Margarete Schütte-Lihotzky, designed more than ten thousand apartments and houses for middle-class and working-class tenants in Frankfurt. As part of this project, Schütte-Lihotzky, the first woman to earn a degree in architecture in Germany, transformed the traditional kitchen into a functional, standardized, hygienic space. More than 12,000 highly efficient modular kitchen units based on her ergonomically and functional standardized designs were produced. Their widespread use dramatically improved the living conditions for a considerable number of low-income and middle-class families. Thanks to the success of the program, the "Frankfurt Kitchen" became a symbol of progress in interwar Germany.[4]

These social-oriented design theories were widely applied in all areas and were very well received throughout Europe, particularly in northern countries, such as Sweden and Finland, with socialist governments, large low-income sectors, and depressed economies, and, of course, in the Soviet Union. And it was these very ideas that, about a decade later, found fertile ground in Latin American completely different social and economic contexts.

## Latin American Design, Industry, and Modernity

In addition to the opportunities that were being generated by economic growth, the developmental policies and modernizing programs introduced by the Brazilian, Mexican, and Venezuelan governments from the 1940s to the 1970s fostered ideal conditions for the creation of modern visual languages steeped in themes of national identity, while at the same time addressing the basic needs of an emerging middle class that was growing at unprecedented rates during those boom years. The three examples of mass-produced furniture design and production that will be discussed in this essay were made possible by the remarkable political, economic, and cultural conditions of that period, as well as by the intensely personal social vision of the designer-entrepreneurs involved and their grasp of the modernist movement of their times.

## Unilabor: Furniture for Everyone in Brazil

In 1952, mindful of the doctrines of Saint Thomas Aquinas on the subject of work and its important role in man's spiritual development, the Dominican priest João Baptista Pereira created a community initiative in suburban São Paulo that was designed to increase workers' self-esteem and better

The Unilabor factory with logo designed by Geraldo de Barros, c. 1954. Photo by Geraldo de Barros. © Estate Geraldo de Barros.

Above: View of the Unilabor Factory, c. 1954. Photo by Geraldo de Barros. © Estate Geraldo de Barros.

Below: The Unilabor chapel, c. 1954. Photo by Geraldo de Barros. © Estate Geraldo de Barros.

integrate them into Brazilian society. Educated in France, Brother João was familiar with the ideas of Father Louis-Joseph Lebret, who, in 1936 in Lyon, France, had founded the Économie et Humanisme association that sought a new approach to economic thinking and how to apply it in humanistic terms. An economy based on humanistic principles was the Church's alternative proposal, a third way that was neither communism nor capitalism.[5] Brother João, a devout believer in Lebret's ideology, wanted to create a cooperative economic system in which everyone involved had a seat at the table and a share of the profits.

Also in 1952, through the Museu de Arte Moderno in São Paulo, Brother João met the artist Geraldo de Barros and, in 1954, asked him to start "a business that would be the first cell of a working community."[6] The result was Unilabor, a self-managing workers' cooperative whose goal was "to transform the workforce's relationship with work by changing work's brutal, oppressive, and ultimately alienating nature."[7] De Barros, a Brazilian avant-garde concrete artist, who wanted to develop a new form of art with practical applications, imagined the vast potential that could be harnessed by getting industry and art to work together.

Recently married, he had designed the furniture for his new house, and that experience inspired him to work with Brother João's community to build a factory that would design and produce modern furniture. Designing, building, and selling modern furniture was perfectly compatible with de Barros's artistic and aesthetic interests, and was also well aligned with Brother João's philosophy of life and work. To set up Unilabor, de Barros formed a team that included the cabinetmaker Manuel Lopes da Silva and the blacksmith Antonio Thereza, both recognized master craftsmen in their fields, and set about transforming their designs into products.

Though the factory was the nucleus of the enterprise, Brother João and de Barros wanted the Unilabor experience to be about more than just work. Cultural activities were a regular part of the daily routine, encouraging spiritual development through culture and aesthetics as well as through work. Unilabor thus combined the concerns of concrete art with Christian humanist ideals, blending aesthetics with ethics in an experiment that approached design as a means to transform habits and customs in Brazilian society in the 1950s and 1960s. This totally unique initiative was inspired by an eclectic range of experiences, including the Bauhaus, Gestalt theory, concrete art ideals,[8] and the Hochschule für Gestaltung Ulm (Ulm School of Design). The latter was specially important for de Barros because, although in 1950 he had declined a scholarship offered by the Swiss artist Max Bill to study at the school in Germany in favor of his friend and business partner Alexander Wollner, he had had the opportunity to study some of the syllabus and bibliographical materials used by the students at Ulm, thanks to the notes and texts that Wollner mailed to him regularly.[9]

Geraldo de Barros (Brazilian, 1923–98). *Chaises Unilabor,* 1954. Gelatin silver print; 11 ¼ x 11 ¼ in. Courtesy of the Estate of Geraldo de Barros/Acervo Instituto Moreira Salles. [Checklist no. 21]

Unilabor's furniture designers kept an eye on the formal repertoire of modern European rationalist styles but catered faithfully to local tastes and always acknowledged Brazil's prevailing modernist style, an aesthetic that was clearly visible in the architecture of Oscar Niemeyer and the works of Brazilian concrete and neo-concrete artists. The furniture envisioned by de Barros departed from a rationalist design approach and was made with readily available local materials; its extremely lightweight, rather industrial-looking steel-rod structural frames contrasted with the warmth of the deeply grained tropical Brazilian woods and the modernist look of the plastic laminated surfaces. Structural solutions were very simple and studied to use as little steel as possible. In general, the use of materials was kept to a minimum and pieces were devoid of any type of ornamentation. However, the carefully studied use of contrast between the lines of the steel structural elements painted black set against wood planes or colored laminated plastic elements provided interesting visual rhythms with a definitely modern look [checklist no. 20].

De Barros understood the pedagogical role of design and worked with cooperative members to develop a design and production system called Padrão UL, which consisted of systematizing the production process and designing standardized modular products with interchangeable sections that could be configured according to the customer's tastes and preferences.

One of Unilabor's main goals was to benefit both the community and the ultimate user of its products by combining art, design, and craftsmanship. De Barros had been experimenting with photography, which led him to develop a truly personal language that blended light, shadow, abstraction, and contrasting planes, all of which he used to create images for the company's advertising and catalogues. De Barros's photographic experiments between 1948 and 1950, called "Fotoformas," emphasized serial elements and abstract forms and became an important source of inspiration for Unilabor furniture designs and serialization methodology.[10]

Throughout its existence (1954–67), Unilabor focused exclusively on producing household furniture. A number of commissions kept the cooperative afloat for the first four years, but the group soon realized that, in order to survive, it would have to do more than just build furniture and set about opening stores in middle-class neighborhoods in São Paulo and even Belo Horizonte, where they planned to sell their products. Although the cooperative's founding goal was to make furniture for the working classes, its prices never quite came within reach of lower-income consumers, in spite of mass production and the resulting economies of scale. The emerging middle class, however, was enthusiastic about the new opportunities offered by a modern nation and became loyal customers for Unilabor's furniture.

Unilabor came to an end in 1967 owing to financial difficulties and lack of further credit. Ironically, it was the beginning of a period of economic growth in Brazil under the military dictatorship, but also an era of political unrest, repression, and urban guerillas, a time known in Brazil as the *Anos de Chumbo* (Years of Lead). Unilabor was a unique experiment that combined reformist Christian ideology with modernist design to promote a utopian form of social change through art, craftsmanship, and manufacturing. This utopian approach to industrial design transcended traditional boundaries to become a political and social tool for transformation and progress. As the historian Mauro Claro declared, Unilabor was "a beautiful study of the relationship between aesthetic modernity and social commitment in Brazil in the 1950s."[11]

### Van Beuren: Design for Modern Mexico

Born in New York in 1911 to a well-to-do family with deep roots in the city, Michael van Beuren was always a rebel who had no use for rules or his family's customs and traditions. In 1931, he went to Europe on a cargo steamer, enrolling at the legendary Bauhaus School in Dessau for the winter

View of the Domus showroom and store on Hamburgo Street, Juárez neighborhood, Mexico City, c. 1945. Photographer unknown. Gelatin silver print. Courtesy of Jan van Beuren.

semester (1931–32) upon his arrival in Germany and later signing up for the basic architecture course taught by Josef Albers during the summer of 1932. When the Bauhaus relocated to Berlin, so did van Beuren, and he took his final classes there during the winter of 1933, the year in which the school officially closed. After his stint at the Bauhaus, he was one of a group of graduates who took private classes from Ludwig Mies van der Rohe for a few months in 1934 and 1935.

Back in New York in 1937, van Beuren met a businessman with interests in Mexico who asked him to design and build some bungalows for the Flamingos Hotel in Acapulco. After his stay in the idyllic port town, van Beuren went to Mexico City, where he hoped to practice architecture. He managed to build a couple of houses, but his plans were thwarted by his lack of a formal university degree. He did, however, find a niche in the market that had, until then, hardly been exploited: modern furniture.

He joined forces with the German designer Klaus Grabe, a former classmate from the Bauhaus, and the North American architect Morley Webb to start a small design workshop they called Grabe & Van Beuren. They set demanding standards for their workshop, where they designed and built a unique line of furniture whose extreme technical perfection and original modernist aesthetic reflected their own trainings. What set the furniture workshop apart from others was the introduction by these designers of modern furniture pieces engineered for mass production in Mexico.

In 1939, they opened the Domus store at 40 Hamburgo in the Juárez neighborhood, in order to have their own sales outlet for their products. There, they exhibited and sold their own line of furniture and also displayed imported pieces made by other modern designers, such as Russell Wright, a North American whose skillful combination of elegance and originality, as well as his commercial success, made him a role model and a guaranteed favorite with the public.[12]

Mahogany breakfast set designed by Michael van Beuren and Philip Guilmant for Van Beuren SA de CV's Danesa Line, 1957–58. Photographer unknown. Gelatin silver print. Courtesy of Freddy van Beuren Bernal.

Van Beuren and Grabe arrived at a vibrant and volatile time in Mexican history, when there was a great deal of cultural and intellectual activity, engaged mainly in self-reflection and contemplation of questions concerning national identity and the defining traits of Mexican society.[13] As foreigners, both men were in a position to view their surroundings objectively, unencumbered by local biases, and they were able to incorporate into their designs the kind of native materials — like jute and other natural fibers with symbolical links to rural and indigenous traditions — that Mexican designers could not use for fear that, in a local context, they connoted cheap or poor-quality designs. Grabe and van Beuren understood the Mexican middle-class furniture market and decided to take advantage of local conditions, including labor, materials, and vernacular forms [checklist no. 66]. Though they initially had no intention of creating nationalist designs, their aesthetic ideas ultimately contributed to the search for a national identity that dominated artistic and cultural discourse at that time.[14]

In 1941, the Museum of Modern Art in New York organized the competition *Organic Design in Home Furnishings* and, for the first time, invited Latin American designers to participate. Grabe, van Beuren, and Webb took one of the four prizes awarded to Latin America with an original chaise longue — made with primavera wood, metal, and woven rope [checklist no. 68] — that was produced by Domus, which was by then their main trademark as well as the name of their workshop.

After Grabe returned to Germany, the factory name was changed from Grabe & Van Beuren to Domus. A few years later, when Frederick van Beuren — Michael's brother — took charge of production, the firm's name was changed again, this time to Van Beuren SA de CV.[15] Michael van Beuren continued to operate in his usual shrewd fashion, with his finger on the pulse of the market, ever sensitive to its potential. A notable example of his approach can be seen in 1947 with the design of the "Miguelitos" and "San Miguelitos" lines of armchairs that were modern versions of the traditional Mexican *butaques* that were popular with virtually every designer in the country during the twentieth century.

Van Beuren applied the principles he had learned at the Bauhaus and ignored contemporary nationalist debates. A pragmatist, he relied on his own beliefs, ideals, and experience to work with local materials and local craftsmen, but giving his furniture a more universal style that helped to distinguish — and perhaps define — the tastes and interests of the new urban middle class. The "Pino" (Pine) and "Danesa" (Danish) lines that Michael van Beuren designed in 1959–60 with the British architect Philip Guilmant represented the pinnacle of his creativity and experimentation.[16] Working with pine and mahogany woods, they created a collection of modular sections that could be assembled very easily. Each piece of furniture was made with sections that were produced on the same press and were designed for easy storage. This strategy was the key to the mass-production tactics that allowed Van Beuren to sell designer furniture at very competitive prices.

By 1955, the factory had become a sort of company town, quite possibly inspired by the welfare company towns that had proliferated in the United States since the late nineteenth century. The van Beuren brothers started building houses for their employees on neighboring lots and bought a saw mill on the outskirts of Mexico City in order to control every facet of their operation in a vertical integration model similar to those adopted by large industrial corporations.

The van Beuren brothers' paternalistic entrepreneurial vision informed the relationship between the company and its workers. They thought that if their work provided them with a better lifestyle, the same privilege should apply to their employees, who provided the labor. Many of their employees therefore had their own homes, either near the factory or elsewhere in the city.

By then, the workforce had grown so much that the van Beurens allowed the workers to form their own union, with which they always kept on good terms; they would even travel with their employees to different parts of the country. The company's anniversary and Christmas parties became huge traditional celebrations that were attended by all the employees and their families. The van Beurens also encouraged social and sporting events, and the employees organized their own baseball and soccer teams, playing with the company logo on their shirts. The socializing and the company philosophy turned the Van Beuren factory employees into a sort of extended community, bonded to, and dependent on, the company. Van Beuren SA de CV stayed in business until 1971, when it was sold to the Singer Sewing Machine Company, the North American sewing machine company that, for many years, had commissioned the Van Beuren factory to produce cabinets for its machines. During its day, the factory became a successful embodiment of the utopian dreams of harmony and

Michael van Bueren with the first factory team of Domus, c. 1939. Courtesy of Ingrid van Bueren and Tiago Solis.

social justice that were so in vogue in those days. It represented a victory for design, but once it passed into other hands it fell into decline.[17]

## Tecoteca: Local Design with European Roots

Born in Leiden, the Netherlands, in 1926, Cornelis Zitman left his native land in 1947 after opposing Dutch colonial policies aimed at reconquering Indonesia and refusing to do his military service. Booking a passage to Latin America on a Swedish oil tanker, he arrived in Venezuela. His art training at the Academy of Fine Arts in The Hague and his apprenticeship in his family's construction firm helped him to land his first job in the city of Coro, where he was hired as a technical draftsman at a construction company. A few months later, he met a couple of Italian cabinetmakers — Cesare Atti and Giuseppe Verdi — with whom he made his first set of furniture for the old colonial house in Coro, where he lived with his wife, the textile designer Vera Roos.[18] Zitman was not the first operator in the field of modern furniture and lamps in Venezuela — the Taller Gunz had been started by Gego (Gertrud Goldschmidt) in 1940 in El Valle, Caracas, with the support of her husband, the businessman Ernst Gunz. However, that earlier workshop was out of business by the time Zitman arrived in Venezuela.

In 1949, the Zitman family moved to Caracas, where Cornelis began to design furniture in earnest, building his first pieces himself. Some time later, he started designing furniture for Promociones y Decoraciones Dibo — a company that would subsequently be named DecoDibo. In 1951, Zitman decided to go into business for himself and started Talleres Zitman. His most significant work during that period was a commission for the interior design and furniture for Residencias Montserrat, a residential project in Caracas designed by the North American architect Emile Vestuti for the architectural firm of Guinand & Benacerraf in 1951. Zitman's earliest modern furniture designs showed the influence of Scandinavian, Italian, and, in particular, North American designers of the period. In 1952, Talleres Zitman took on two partners, the brothers Diego and Antonio Carbonell, architect and engineer, respectively, and became Tecoteca.

Zitman was driven by a powerful social conscience and wanted his new company to be in tune with the new Venezuela, a young, rich, modern country in a state of rapid industrialization, with extensive developmental policies and plans to create social welfare programs for the entire population. All that was made possible by the vast revenues generated by the oil business and the ambitious programs implemented during the Marcos Pérez Jiménez dictatorship (1952–58), which allocated significant public funds for highways, schools, and hospitals. Most notable among these monumental projects of infrastructure was the Ciudad Universitaria in Caracas, designed by Carlos Raúl Villanueva.

The Tecoteca factory was small but extremely well organized, with separate departments handling specific tasks, thus speeding up its mass production. One of Zitman's key objectives was to keep prices affordable for the lower income sectors, so the production process was streamlined and, wherever possible, his furniture was made with local materials: cedar, laurel, mahogany, rustic woven cotton, and natural fibers like cattail. Tecoteca's furniture designs were always simple and elegant, and reflected the trends and ideas that were popular among international designers [checklist no. 77]. However, as Zitman explained in an article published in the *Cruz del Sur* magazine, he "designed furniture that he hoped would appeal to working-class and peasant families because it was affordable but also because they liked it."[19]

As can be seen from Tecoteca's first catalogue, printed in 1953, the company produced a wide range of different items, from furniture for the home — including furniture for children — to office suites and complete furnishings for large housing projects. Zitman understood that it was not enough

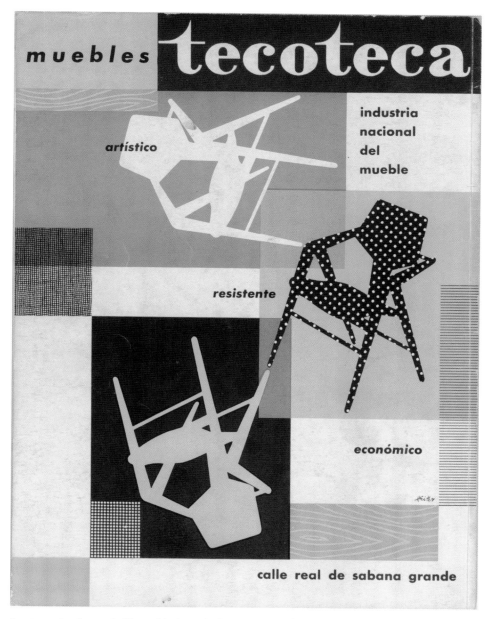

Tecoteca advertisement with graphic design by Guillermo Heiter (Venezuelan, B. Czech Republic 1915–71), published in *Revista A: Hombre y Exprésion* (Sociedad Editora "A," Caracas) (January 1954). Private Collection. [Checklist no. 86]

to produce furniture; he also needed a sales and marketing operation to distribute the company's merchandise. In 1952, therefore, he opened his first store, Tecoteca Muebles in the El Recreo shopping center in Sabana Grande, Caracas. Next came Tecoteca Este 1 in the heart of the city, and, in 1955, he opened the last and largest of his stores, Muebles Tecoteca in the Los Palos Grandes residential neighborhood. He also had agents representing the company in the rest of the country.

The stores were so successful that the investors decided to import modern furniture from Europe, especially from Scandinavia. Zitman consequently took several trips to Europe to update his range of designs with the latest trends. There was a fire at the factory in 1956, but the company survived and was able to keep supplying their customers and honoring their commitments, including one to furnish the houses in Royal Dutch Shell's camps in the Venezuelan oilfields. Zitman took on the role of

Vanity chest No. 602 and chair No. 61, 1953. Manufactured by Tecoteca.
Courtesy of Cornelis Zitman.

company president that year, and new investors were found in order to greatly expand the factory. One of Zitman's assistants in those days was the Italian architect Vittorio Garatti, with whom he would design the interiors of the stores and the newly expanded factory and create a new logo for Tecoteca in the shape of an asterisk. New lines of low-cost modular furniture, both residential and office, were designed as part of the expansion project, and a substantial number of prototypes were produced that would be used to illustrate the company's new catalogue, which unfortunately was never printed. The new lines shared standardized parts and pieces allowing a great number of possible configurations with low production costs.

In 1957, Cornelis Zitman was only 31 years old, but he was tired and in poor health, and he retired from the company. His opposition to the Marcos Pérez Jiménez dictatorship had prompted him to side with his workers and — contrary to the advice of his investors — join the general strike against the government. The enormous pressure he was under at work and the regime's retaliation had taken their toll on his health and personal life, as well as on the financial stability of the company, which at the time was feeling the effects of the political unrest in Venezuela. The economic crisis that led to the coup and the subsequent overthrow of the dictatorship by a civilian-military junta in 1958 put an end to the company's plans to expand the factory, which were already well under way. Unable to service the heavy debt they had taken on to expand the business, the partners were forced to declare bankruptcy. The factory was auctioned off, and the Tecoteca brand and assets were sold.

Zitman was both an idealist and a visionary who sought to use modern design and commercial development to create a form of welfare and promote social change in a society that was in the throes of industrial development.

Bookshelf No. 702 and chair No. 58, 1953. Manufactured by Tecoteca. Courtesy of Cornelis Zitman.

## Conclusions

The modern designers in Brazil, Mexico, and Venezuela presented as case studies based their work on formal and technical expressions of rationalist European modernism and the so-called International Style. But those repertoires were only the beginning of the local modern design movement and were more of a means than an end. Once those designers began to develop their products, they took what they had learned from Europe and adapted it to their own agendas and, most of all, to the creation of national design identities that were compatible with the societies and cultural environments that they envisioned for their countries. That much is clear from the examples discussed here. The revolutionary aspiration for social change and aesthetic renovation associated with the European avant-garde, particularly the Bauhaus and the German functional rationalist design movement at the Ulm School, were the essential pillars of all these design experiments. It is not coincidental that Michael van Beuren had studied at the Bauhaus, Cornelis Zitman was familiar with the legacy of the avant-garde in his native Holland,[20] and de Barros was aware of the pedagogical effort implemented at Ulm and interested in the principles championed by former members of the Bauhaus and their new disciples after the war. These three designer-entrepreneurs undertook the challenge of adapting these utopian ideas to the very different economic, social, and cultural conditions of their respective countries.

The three local design and modern furniture firms they started were social and entrepreneurial experiments through which they sought, in addition to creating profitable business models, to use part of the profits to offer an aesthetic and cultural education for large numbers of people to improve their daily lifestyle, transform their housing conditions, and, most of all, help eliminate the huge social barriers that have always characterized Latin American societies and entrepreneurial environments.

Although paternalistic to a differing degree, these business models diverged from the normal corporate practices in the region and incorporated a remarkable social component rarely seen in mid-century Latin American private entrepreneurship.

Geraldo de Barros and Cornelis Zitman both hoped that their employees would be the main consumers and users of the furniture they themselves produced. However, owing to the costs of production and concomitant high prices that were more accessible to the middle and upper classes and to the disconnect that existed between the simplicity of modern furniture and contemporary symbols of social mobility — which in those days were associated with historical styles and traditional materials — that particular goal was never achieved. Although Michael van Beuren's aspirations were different — since he understood the emergence of new markets created by the rise and consolidation of the local middle classes and manufactured furniture that was designed with that niche in mind — his economies of scale led to more affordable prices and, as a result, most of his employees and their social peers were able to purchase Van Beuren furniture. Unilabor, Van Beuren, and Tecoteca all understood the importance of creating flexible production systems that could be adapted to varying tastes and requirements. That is why all three factories offered "families" of furniture products based on standardized elements that could be produced in large quantities using interchangeable parts whose veneers, colors, varnishes, and upholstery could be modified to suit the customer's taste.

The management of all three factories realized that they could not sell their products through a traditional retailer, so they set about developing their own sales outlets. In addition to selling their own

\* I am grateful to Jorge Rivas Pérez for sharing his ideas and insights on how modern Latin American design was implemented in the postwar period. Some of the topics addressed in this essay try to answer questions raised during our extensive discussions on developmentalism and design.

1  The visual artist Gaston Chaussat was also the designer in charge of Studio Evolución, an innovative design, decoration, and interior design department in the El Palacio de Hierro department store, which catered to architects and the general public. Based on available information, it is believed that the studio was in operation from 1930 until the 1960s.

2  Comissioned for a lot in the Colonia Escandón by the Haghembeck family, the Jardín building was designed by Francisco Serrano in 1929.

3  Le Corbusier, Hacia una arquitectura [Toward an Architecture] (Paris: Flammarion, 1995), 73.

4  For more information on this experiment, see Juliet Kinchin and Aidan O'Connor, Counter Space: Design and the Modern Kitchen (New York: Museum of Modern Art, 2011).

5  Unilabor: desenho industrial, arte moderna e autogestão operária [Unilabor: Industrial Design, Modern Art, and Workforce Self-Management] (São Paulo: Senac, 2004), 81–96.

6  Ibid., 34.

7  Mauro Claro, "Unilabor e Geraldo de Barros: política e design para superar a alienação do trabajo" [Unilabor and Geraldo de Barros: Politics and Design to Overcome the Alienation of Work] in Zanine Caldas e Geraldo de Barros — fortes contrastes, utopias realizadas: Fábrica de Móveis Artísticos Z e Unilabor [Zanine Caldas and Geraldo de Barros — Powerful Contrasts, Utopias Achieved: Z Artistic Furniture Factory and Unilabor] (São Paulo: Artemobila, 2010).

8  While the Brazilian concrete art movement embraced the principles advocated by Theo van Doesburg (1883–1931) that were based on geometric abstraction, it was also influenced by the Bauhaus, the Ulm School, and the De Stijl group, as well as by Max Bill's theories that, though they too endorsed geometric abstraction, also included mathematical principles to arrive at the universality of forms and their relationship to nature. Brazilian concrete art eschewed lyrical or symbolic forms and was solely focused on geometric abstraction, searching for a form of total art that could influence both the visual arts and industrial manufacturing.

9  Ethel Leon, Design Brasileiro: quem fez, quem faz [Brazilian Design: Who Did, Who Does] (Rio de Janeiro: Viana & Mosley; Senac Rio, 2005), 82.

10  For de Barros, photography was an essential tool with which he could experiment with geometric nuances, shadows, and planes. In his hands, it was no longer merely an instrument for depicting reality and

designs, the Domus and Tecoteca stores sold European and North American modern furniture. The three companies created products that, although they were inspired by contemporary European and North American designs, responded to local tastes and requirements. They used wood from local sources, made seats and backrests out of palm and other natural fibers as seen in traditional Latin American furniture, introduced forms that echoed local visual repertoires, and created modern versions of traditional and indigenous furniture types.

Despite the differences in their individual visions, Geraldo de Barros and Cornelis Zitman had both trained as artists and viewed the production of their designs in terms of their art, while Michael van Beuren, who studied design and architecture, was always more interested in the production process itself. Each operation hoped to expand the impact of their transformative experiment beyond the factory walls. They were not solely concerned with creating jobs and providing social stability, housing or (in the case of Unilabor) education. While they lasted, all three initiatives were financially successful, but, like many other modernizing experiments in Latin America, they did not last long. The gap between theory and practice, realities and facts, and dreams and possibilities was apparent in all three cases. Reality eventually caught up with them all and they were ultimately undone by the vicissitudes of the processes of development in Latin America, which does not always favor every segment of the population. That said, Unilabor, Tecoteca, and Van Beuren should not be considered failures; on the contrary, though they were only in business for a few decades, these three firms blazed the trail for modern design in Latin America.

became a means to develop a new artistic language. The image shown here, which was among those he produced for Unilabor, is part of his "Fotoformas" series, in which he experimented boldly with the potential for manipulating the negative.

11  Mauro Claro, *Unilabor: desenho industrial, arte moderna e autogestão operária* [Unilabor: Industrial Design, Modern Art, and Workforce Self-Management] (São Paulo: Senac, 2004), 34.

12  Letter from Morley Webb to Michael van Beuren dated January 25, 1940. Webb, who appears to be in the United States, discusses the sort of things he is looking for to sell in the Domus store.

13  The arrival of Leon Trotsky in 1937, for example, and the resulting discussion of his ideas fired up local artists and intellectuals and stimulated intense debate about political and ideological options for Mexico and the world. In 1939, scores of artists, intellectuals, and other professionals arrived in Mexico as refugees from the Spanish Civil War, and they too stoked local passions in cultural circles. Architects, designers, and artists brought new ideas that changed the Mexican design and decoration scene, honoring local tastes and reinterpreting established styles.

14  Another notable example of this trend was the Cuban Clara Porset, who, as a foreigner, was also able to look through unbiased eyes at the local culture, understand local conditions, and work with them, inspired by indigenous forms of furniture and incorporating local wood and natural fibers into her designs.

15  Although the company changed its name, the furniture produced by Van Beuren SA de CV continued to be labeled and commercialized under the brand Domus.

16  In 1954, the British designer Philip Guilmant moved to Mexico and became part of the design team at Van Beuren SA de CV three years later.

17  To this day, the factory is called Muebles Van Beuren and sells furniture designed in historicist styles that are a far cry from those magnificent earlier lines of modern furniture.

18  Jorge Rivas Pérez, et al., *Cornelis Zitman: La década del diseño, 1947–1957* [Cornelis Zitman: The Design Decade, 1947–1957] (Venezuela: Transnocho Arte Contacto, 2011), 12. Rivas Pérez mentions that Zitman remembers that furniture as being "very simple, with straight lines and no ornamentation: a blend of strict modern Dutch aesthetics with the austerity of Venezuelan colonial furniture."

19  Cornelis Zitman, "Tecoteca — como se industrializa el mueble moderno en Venezuela" [Tecoteca — the Industrialization of Modern Furniture in Venezuela], *Cruz del Sur* 1, no. 9 (November–December 1952).

20  De Stijl, which advocated an interdisciplinary and total art approach, was an important influence in Zitman's training.

# MODERN LIFESTYLES: CLARA PORSET AND THE ART OF EXHIBITING THE MEXICAN HOME

## CHRISTINA L. DE LEÓN

> The existence of a man-made object is concrete evidence of the presence of a human intelligence operating at the time of fabrication. The underlying premise is that objects made or modified by man reflect, consciously or unconsciously, directly or indirectly, the beliefs of individuals who made, commissioned, purchased, or used them, and by extension the beliefs of the larger society to which they belonged.
> —JULES DAVID PROWN[1]

### Adopting the Machine Aesthetic

In 1932, the nascent Museum of Modern Art, directed by the innovative Alfred H. Barr, Jr., established its department of architecture, the first curatorial program of its kind at a fine arts museum. The department experienced enormous success with its inaugural exhibition *Modern Architecture: International Exhibition* (1932), curated by chairman Philip Johnson and architectural historian Henry-Russell Hitchcock. This show was followed by another groundbreaking exhibition in 1934,

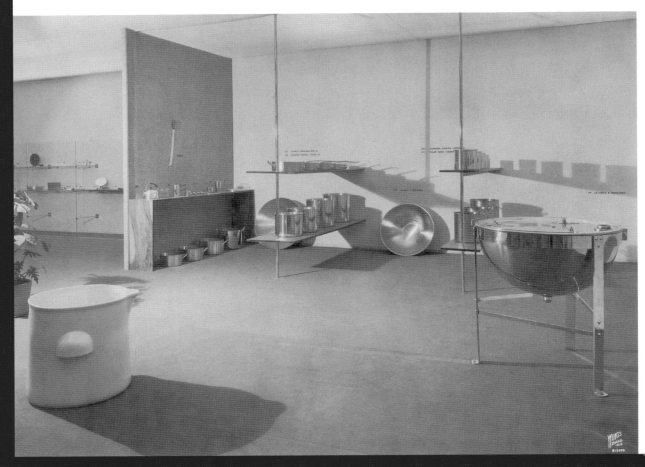

entitled *Machine Art.* Greatly influenced by the Bauhaus, the driving thesis of this exhibition was that function and beauty could be found in the machine-made "artworks" displayed, through their straightforward design and lack of ornamentation. Johnson and Barr admired the qualities of simple industrially manufactured objects that were produced with no artistic forethought. The nearly 400 objects featured in *Machine Art* were useful items made for everyday life and were distributed within the following categories: industrial units; household and office equipment; kitchenware; house furnishings and accessories; scientific instruments; and laboratory glass and porcelain. In the foreword to the exhibition's catalogue, Barr wrote:

> The beauty of machine art is in part the abstract beauty of 'straight lines and circles' made into actual tangible 'surfaces and solids' by means of tools, 'lathes and rulers and squares.' In Plato's day the tools were simple handworker's implements but today, as a result of the perfection of modern materials and the precision of modern instruments, the modern machine-made object approaches far more closely and more frequently those pure shapes the contemplation of which Plato calls the first of the 'pure pleasures'. . . .[2] Machine art, devoid as it should be of surface ornament, must depend upon the sensuous beauty of porcelain, enamel, celluloid, glass of all colors, copper, aluminum, brass and steel. . . . If, to use L. P. Jack's phrase, we are to 'end the divorce' between our industry and our culture we must assimilate the machine aesthetically as well as economically. Not only must we bind Frankenstein — but we must make him beautiful.[3]

Barr's romantic tone was used to engage interest and appeal in such objects as a heating unit, a typewriter carriage spring, a Wafflemaker, white porcelain plates, a miner's compass, a petri dish, a protractor, nest tables, cream jars, a baker's bowl, and a Dictaphone — none of which had ever

before been regarded as the focal points of beauty. The aestheticizing of these pieces was further perpetuated by the catalogue. The cover, designed by Josef Albers (previously of the Bauhaus school), included a large dramatic photograph of a self-aligning ball bearing with a simple but bold typeface underneath. The photographs were taken by Ruth Bernhard and highlighted the geometric forms of the objects through the theatric use of light and shadow.

For Johnson, *Machine Art* marked an opportunity to promote a style in the United States that he believed could substitute handicraft. In his catalogue essay "History of Machine Art," he argued that, "the craft

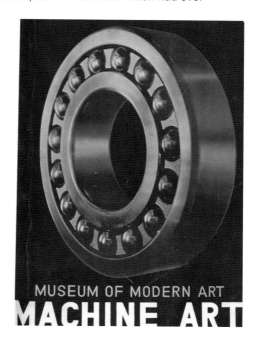

Opposite: Installation view of the exhibition *Machine Art* at the Museum of Modern Art, New York, March 5–April 29, 1934. Photographic Archive. © The Museum of Modern Art/Licensed by SCALA/Art Resource, NY.

*Machine Art*, by Philip Johnson and Alfred H. Barr Jr. (New York: Museum of Modern Art, 1934). Digital Image © The Museum of Modern Art/Licensed by SCALA/Art Resource, NY.

spirit does not fit an age geared to machine technique."[4] Johnson went on to say that in the nineteenth century, machines made "bad designs" and that well-designed objects were still created by "primitive methods."[5] Johnson stated that the United States had always been leaders in the development of machines, but its design aesthetic (with the exception of the work of Louis Comfort Tiffany) were mere European copies. Johnson was reiterating sentiments that had first come to light in 1876 at the International Exhibition of Arts, Manufacturers, and Products of the Soil and Mine, commonly known as the Centennial Exhibition and held in Philadelphia to celebrate one hundred years of independence from Great Britain. Directly influenced by the success of the 1851 Great Exhibition of the Works of Industry of All Nations (the "Crystal Palace Exhibition") in London, the Centennial declared not only its political, but industrial and artistic sovereignty from Europe. The industrial revolution marked a transition from the production of goods by hand to the use of modern machinery, and no other event had captured the global magnitude of this change than the Great Exhibition, spearheaded by Henry Cole. At the time, British industrial design was considered among the worst in Europe, and the Great Exhibition helped push Britain into the forefront of design and manufacturing. Through a virtual copycat initiative, the hope was that the Centennial Exhibition would provide a similar boost to the United States; ultimately, however, it just showed the crudeness and lack of artistic standards that perpetuated its dependency on Europe for not necessarily better made but definitively more beautifully designed goods. In the twentieth century, Johnson believed this handicap within the development of industrial design was being rectified in the same manner that architecture had done away with the nineteenth-century phase of the revivalist style and had adopted the "latest technique of building

Above: Machinery Hall, Crystal Palace Exhibition, London, 1851. Conceived by Prince Albert, the Great Exhibition was intended to showcase the "Works of the Industry of all Nations." It was housed in the purpose-built Crystal Palace, the first large-scale prefabricated ferrovitreous (iron and glass) structure, designed by the gardener and architect Joseph Paxton. The prefabricated design made the construction, and later dismantling of the building, easier and quicker. Courtesy HIP/Art Resource, NY.

Opposite: Edward McKnight Kauffer (American, 1890–1954). *Industrial Design Competition for the 21 American Republics*. In *Organic Design in Home Furnishings* (New York: Museum of Modern Art, 1941), 39. Digital Image © The Museum of Modern Art/ Licensed by SCALA/Art Resource, NY.

science."[6] After World War I, Johnson observed how designers were taking note of the potential of machines. As a student of the Bauhaus School, he believed the school at Weimar, under the direction of Walter Gropius, was a good example of how Germans had freed their industrial arts from handicraft to create the proper tools for living in a "mechanistic age."[7]

Machine Art was the vehicle for which Johnson could introduce the modern ideology constructed by the Bauhaus to U.S. consumers. Not only did the show travel extensively throughout the country but each work was identified by its name, manufacturer, designer, as well as its price, thereby blurring the distinction between museum and department store showroom. The hundreds of objects that were included in Machine Art were to be admired, coveted, and consumed. The cultural theorist Tony Bennett has credited the Great Exhibition for establishing a new system of organizing "objects for public consumption" that resulted in an institutional "ordering of the public" for "inspection."[8] This structure would have an immense effect on the ensuing evolution of museums, expositions, and department stores, whose overlapping histories and interrelationships would continue over time.[9] As Jules David Prown has stated, "Objects transmit signals which elucidate mental patterns or structures," which, in turn, can "arouse different patterns of response according to the belief systems of the perceivers' cultural matrices."[10] No one understood this power better than Barr and Johnson, who used these everyday items to stimulate a positive reaction to a modern machine aesthetic. They exercised the authority of the museum environment to not only support their institution's mission of promoting modern art, but also a modern lifestyle.

## Modernity Begins at Home

Following the success of Machine Art, MoMA established the Department of Industrial Design with Eliot Noyes as its first director, who continued the museum's agenda to support innovative and useful design for everyday life. In 1940, he spearheaded a new initiative called the "Industrial Design Competition for 21 American Republics."[11] The competition projected the ideals fostered by President Franklin Delano Roosevelt's Good Neighbor Policy (1933), which encouraged social and economic exchange with Latin America. It also came just one year after the New York World's Fair, which, with World War II looming, had been used as a platform to nurture better North and South relations, as well as interdependence. The Good Neighbor Policy coupled with the end of the Depression and the advent of war were all factors that contributed to the desire for cultural exchange, economic progress, and modern living — a sentiment echoed in the 1939 World's Fair's motto: "Building the World of Tomorrow." After the Great Exhibition, world fairs had begun to take place regularly in cities throughout Europe and North and South America, as well as in Asia and Oceania. And as it had been with the Great Exhibition, modernization became an overarching theme that promoted a utopian ideal that promised the eventual alleviation of collective social problems.[12]

The competition instructions were distinct for designers from Latin America, declaring that, "The competition is interested particularly in bringing out suggestions on the part of these designers as to how their own local materials and method of construction might be applied in the making of furniture for contemporary American requirements."[13] This was in stark contrast to how U.S. competitors were asked to create designs for middle-income homes that had "a contemporary expression and will reflect today's social, economic, technological, and aesthetic tendencies and possibilities."[14] Noyes understood that, during the current social climate, modernization had to begin with the home, and designers were encouraged to create lighting and fabric designs, as well as furniture for the living room, dining room, bedroom, and patio. All the winners were included in the 1941 MoMA exhibition *Organic Design in Home Furnishings*. Noyes wrote in the exhibition's catalogue:

**We are not as modern as we think. In private, at home, most of us still live in the clutter of inheritance from the nineteenth century. Much of this out-of-date and rigidified furniture is no longer in tune with today's esthetic requirements, and is certainly far from suitable for our needs. Through inertia, modern mass manufacture has simply seized upon and lifelessly repeated many weary old styles that are often neither beautiful nor practical.**

**Obviously the forms of our furniture should be determined by our way of life. Instead, for the most part, we have had to adapt ourselves uncomfortably and unreasonably to what has happened to be manufactured. For several years the Museum of Modern Art has been studying this problem in order to foster a collaboration between designer, manufacturer, and merchant, to fill this strange gap in the convenience of modern existence.[15]**

Noyes excluded the consumer in the list of "collaborators" in this new "modern existence" MoMA was helping to shape. Nevertheless, he diligently informed the public that, unbeknownst to them, they had been living an inconvenient life, tormented by the ghosts of bad nineteenth-century design. Moreover, the clutter of home life — or perhaps, life in general — was a problem that the museum was working to ameliorate through modern design, because a modern home equated to an orderly existence.

The catalogue also highlighted not only the U.S. winners (among them Eero Saarinen and Charles Eames), but also the honorable mentions, which totaled nearly thirty designers; however, only the five Latin American winners were included at the very end of the publication in a separate section. One can only assume that at the time MoMA believed this gesture to be "neighborly" enough. Under the guise of American unity, it is obvious that the competition was really intended to promote U.S. designers and manufacturing. With the rising threat of Nazi Germany and the fear of falling back into the grip of the Depression, the country had to ensure its continued economic growth occurred responsibly by creating consumer products at reasonable prices. Although the project had some success in the select production and sale of these new modern furnishings, ultimately World War II prevented the wide distribution that had been desired.

One Latin American winner was Clara Porset from Mexico, who submitted her design for low-cost rural furniture made with pine, ixtle, and jute under the name of her husband, Xavier Guerrero, an accomplished Mexican painter and muralist. Porset was a Cuban-born designer who had studied at Columbia University, the Paris École des Beaux Arts, and with Josef Albers at Black Mountain College in North Carolina. She was also an active writer on modern design and contributed to the monthly Cuban periodical *Social,* founded by the illustrator Conrado Walter Massaguer, which covered literature, art, sports, theater, and contemporary society. Before Porset's political exile to New York in 1935 and permanent move to Mexico in 1936, she had great success working as an interior and furniture designer for both private and public projects in Cuba. She was also an active educator, presenting lectures on the principles of modern design and serving as the director of the Escuela Técnica Industrial Fundación Rosalía Abreu, a technical school for women. Despite Porset's burgeoning career, the economic and social crises that plagued Cuba under President Gerardo Machado's repressive government followed by the military coup led by Fulgencio Batista drove her to leave Cuba. Nevertheless, Porset took full advantage of the MoMA competition, which not only brought her back to New York, but also exposed her to the commercial enterprise of design manufacturing and distribution in the United States. Porset understood MoMA's campaign for a modern lifestyle. She was heavily influenced by the Bauhaus, and her experience in the United States would affect her as she worked to educate the Mexican public on modern living.

## Art in the Daily Life

In 1951, one hundred years after the Great Exhibition, Porset inaugurated *El arte en la vida diaria. Exposición de objetos de buen diseño hechos en México* (Art in the Daily Life: An Exhibition of Well-Designed Objects Made in Mexico) at the Palacio de Bellas Artes in Mexico City. Oscar Salinas Flores, who has written extensively on Porset, believes *Art in the Daily Life* was inspired in part by the Great

Installation view of *Art in the Daily Life* at the Universidad Nacional Autónoma de México, 1952. Archivo Clara Porset, Centro de Investigaciones de Diseño Industrial, Facultad de Arquitectura, Universidad Nacional Autónoma de México, Mexico City.

Exhibition.[16] Because of the emergence of factories in the first half of the nineteenth century, the industrial revolution had grown to such unchecked heights that there was a widespread fear that artisanal craft might eventually be phased out. By showing the evolution and accomplishment of material culture, the Great Exhibition had aimed to educate the public on how art and science could be fused to create the most industrious and aesthetically pleasing products for use.[17] Nevertheless, there was an obvious aesthetic difference between objects produced by hand and those made by machine, which, in Great Britain, had triggered an impetus to fuse hand artistry with industrial production. Clearly, for Porset, the Great Exhibition presented a fascinating model for how the cultural display of everyday commodities could be used to promote nationalist ideals, as well as form the public's taste and consumption.

In Mexico during the 1950s, a large percentage of manufactured goods were still made by hand, and even though the machine-made industry was steadily growing, it was also marred by poor design. Up until the early part of the twentieth century, Mexico had focused most of its exportation on primary products, while importing much of its industrial goods, which made its manufacturing industry late to develop.[18] Nevertheless, World War II severely affected the export production of countries that were devoting all of their industrial strength into the war effort, a situation that presented a favorable economic climate for Mexico to begin to expand its own industry.[19] The government began to offer fiscal incentives and loans, as well as commercial protection, to support a national industrial movement that would satisfy its local market. Public stimuli also included the infrastructure development of roads and bridges, in addition to economic stability that involved balanced public finances, stable inflation, and accessible prices that permitted fast growth.

The 1940s and 1950s were particularly fortuitous decades for Porset to be in Mexico, as the country was just beginning to develop design styles all its own. Although Porset's ideas were shaped by Bauhaus principles, she did not take these ideologies to the extremes of *Machine Art.* Porset understood the significant relationship between culture and commodity, and she adapted to the Mexican aesthetic that was deeply rooted in Pre-Columbian and folk art. With Guerrero, Porset traveled extensively throughout Mexico and was aware of the

HAY DISEÑO EN TODO...

...en una NUBE

...en una SILLA

18

handcraft work that characterized each region. After the Mexican Revolution, popular art traditions became powerful symbols of national identity; however, Porset was concerned that these practices would eventually begin to die out owing to the rapid industrialization occurring in the country. She began to advocate that industrial manufacturers work closely with craftsmen to create useful objects that were beautiful, appropriately designed for the environment (meaning space and climate), and marked with a touch of "personality."[20] This hybrid approach was in stark contrast with that of Johnson, who believed modernity came with the absolute adoption of the machine aesthetic and the abandonment of superfluous ornamentation and archaic production methods that marked artisanal craft. Porset knew industrialization was important to the growth of the country, but the need to preserve an artistic patrimony was also essential, and she believed that ultimately the two could flourish side by side. This is the ideology at the heart of her exhibition *Art in the Daily Life.* Just as Barr had done with *Machine Art,* Porset wanted Mexicans to open their eyes to the natural beauty that surrounded them. In the exhibition catalogue for *Art in the Daily Life,* a double-page spread of images with text reads: "THERE IS DESIGN IN EVERYTHING. . . in a cloud. . . in a rock. . . in the sea. . . in the sand. . . in a chair. . .

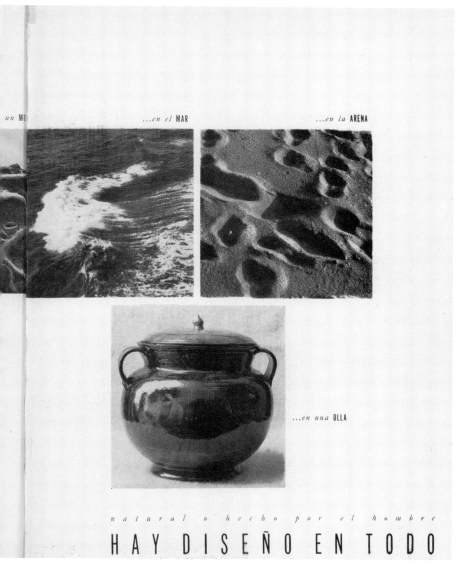

*El arte en la vida diaria: exposición de objetos de buen diseño hechos en México* [Art in the Daily Life: An Exhibition of Well-Designed Objects Made in Mexico]. Exh. Cat., text by Clara Porset and others (Mexico City: Instituto Nacional de Bellas Artes, Departamento de Arquitectura, 1952.) Art & Architecture Collection, The Miriam and Ira D. Wallach Division of Art, Prints and Photographs, The New York Public Library, Astor, Lenox, and Tilden Foundations. Courtesy of Biblioteca y Hemeroteca Nacionales de México. [Checklist no. 82]

in a pot. . . [whether] natural or made by man THERE IS DESIGN IN EVERYTHING."[21] Barr invoked a similar imagery in his foreword to *Machine Art* when he wrote: "The beauty of machine art in so far as it is a mere byproduct of function may seem a meagre and even a trivial kind of beauty. But this is not necessarily so. The beauty of all natural objects is also a byproduct — the helix of a snail's shell (and a steel coil), the graduated feathering of a bird's wing (and the leaves of a laminated spring), the rabbit's footprints in the snow (and the track of non-skid tires), the elegance of fruit (and of incandescent bulbs)."[22]

Through *Machine Art* and *Organic Design in Home Furnishings*, Porset learned the influential power an institution could have on both the public and the manufacturing industry; nevertheless, she established a distinct framework for *Art in the Daily Life* that fit the reality of the Mexican material world. In the post–World War II era, Mexico was profiting from both a stable economy and a government that had embraced a developmentalist agenda, yet Mexico still did not have the advanced industrial technology that had emerged in the United States or Europe. However, the growing middle class sought to live at the same level as their neighbors to the north, which helped to drive local consumption for both industrial products and decorative goods.[23] It was a climate that boded well for

Installation view of *Art in the Daily Life* at the Universidad Nacional Autónoma de México, 1952. Archivo Clara Porset, Centro de Investigaciones de Diseño Industrial, Facultad de Arquitectura, Universidad Nacional Autónoma de México, Mexico City.

the fusion method that Porset championed. In *Art in the Daily Life,* Porset presented examples of serial production, handcraft, and decorative art in a complementary manner that created an attractive viewpoint for the common person — all while keeping a strong emphasis on accessible prices. Of the project Porset wrote, "We hope that this Exhibition will encourage the manufacture of functionally efficient household products imbued with educational aesthetic values that will contribute to a higher standard of living."[24] Although it was a long and difficult journey, with the support of Enrique Yáñez, Fernando Gamboa, and Carlos Chavez from the Instituto Nacional de Bellas Artes, she opened the *Art in the Daily Life* in 1951 at the Palacio de Bellas Artes in Mexico City. The exhibition was shown again the following year at the inauguration of the new Humanities building at the Universidad Nacional

Installation view of *Art in the Daily Life* at the Universidad Nacional Autónoma de México, 1952. Archivo Clara Porset, Centro de Investigaciones de Diseño Industrial, Facultad de Arquitectura, Universidad Nacional Autónoma de México, Mexico City.

Autónoma de México, which coincided with the 8th Pan-American Conference on Architecture. Among the attendees were the great teachers of the Bauhaus, including Gropius, Albers, Hannes Meyer, Marcel Breuer, Mies Van der Rohe, and Herbert Bayer, as well as the prominent architect Frank Lloyd Wright. As the sole woman among so many powerful men, Porset's perseverance is undeniable. This initiative was a significant endeavor that not only merged handcraft with manufactured goods, but elevated them to a status that merited museum display. Just as Henry Cole, Alfred Barr, Philip Johnson, and Eliot Noyes had done before, Porset introduced Mexicans to the potential of modernity.

### Creating a Stage for Taste and Consumption

Porset took full advantage of the opportunity the museum offered as a platform for drama and stagecraft, and she skillfully used photography as a means to create an environment that would produce her desired objectives. She invited the photographer Lola Álvarez Bravo to make a series of photomontages that demonstrated the evolution of Mexican industry that were then sold in stores as decorative pieces.[25] The images included portraits of artisans, craftsmen, and factory workers, as well as modern homes and new contemporary architectural projects in Mexico City designed by Mario Pani and Enrique de Moral. These images helped portray a Mexico that had a reverence for the past as a means to move forward into a modern future. Moreover, it helped stress the equal importance of architecture alongside interior and furniture design. It was fitting that Porset chose Álvarez Bravo since the photographer had experience capturing documentary images of everyday Mexican life in

Installation view of *Art in the Daily Life* at the Universidad Nacional Autónoma de México, 1952. Archivo Clara Porset, Centro de Investigaciones de Diseño Industrial, Facultad de Arquitectura, Universidad Nacional Autónoma de México, Mexico City.

Installation view of *Art in the Daily Life* at the Universidad Nacional Autónoma de México, 1952. Archivo Clara Porset, Centro de Investigaciones de Diseño Industrial, Facultad de Arquitectura, Universidad Nacional Autónoma de México, Mexico City.

both cities and rural villages. In the mid-1930s, Bravo had been the chief photographer for *El Maestro Rural* (The Rural Teacher), a magazine published by the Ministry of Education with the purpose of disseminating the cultural and educational initiatives sponsored by the government. She was a firsthand witness to the changes occurring throughout the country and understood the task at hand in portraying the history and evolution of Mexican industry. The photomontages Bravo produced for *Art in the Daily Life* in some cases hung from the ceilings in mural-like form or were used as backdrops for a number of dioramas constructed for visitors to use as a reference to the potential ways modern furnishings and decorative objects could be incorporated into their homes. In one instance, for the display of metal office furniture, a mural-sized photomontage depicting machinery and factories with a family in the foreground looking out at a sea of productivity symbolized the industrial modernization of Mexico, as well as economic stability for the nuclear family. Adjacent to this environment was a large, idyllic photograph of a beach with waves crashing on the sand, which was used as the background for the display of outdoor lounge furniture that was accessorized with a live palm tree. The pieces in the exhibition were presented in an accessible manner to the viewer and organized to be both admired and inspected. For example, with the textiles Porset included samples on display boards to showcase the patterns and she also had them hung all together on various poles perpendicular to a wall of windows to mimic how such fabrics would look as drapes in a home.

Reflecting the influence of *Machine Art* and *Organic Design in Home Furnishings*, the show comprised hundreds of objects, such as stoves, metal kitchen cabinets, stainless-steel pots and pans, in addition to textiles, dining room sets, outdoor furniture, and living room pieces. Products made by large industrial companies successfully coexisted with limited and one-of-a-kind works made by smaller artist workshops. The participating designers were also diverse and included native Mexicans along with émigrés from Europe and the United States. However, Porset understood that a purely modern and minimalist aesthetic would not work for the Mexican market and she astutely mixed pared-down pieces with traditional craft and contemporary designs, which had a higher level of adornment. Moreover, these works were to be viewed not only as functional objects for daily life, but as fine works of art. She expanded upon this idea in a 1952 article written for the magazine *Espacio* about *Art in the Daily Life*:

> We have drawn particular attention to the artistic quality of useful forms and, in so doing, have tried to debunk the old idea — which is fortunately on the wane — that there are hierarchies in the arts that can be used to designate those that have an artistic function as "minor arts," and those that do not as "major arts."
>
> That idea denies that all forms of art are simply art, which can just as well be found in a ceramic plate as in a painting. Almost eight hundred objects have therefore been designated as Fine Arts, with no question of hierarchy or

---

\* I would like to thank Gabriela Rangel for giving me the opportunity and encouragement to write this text and Jorge Rivas for his generous research guidance.

1  Jules David Prown, "Mind in Matter: An Introduction to Material Culture Theory and Method," *Winterthur Portfolio* 17, no. 1 (Spring 1982): 1–2.

2  Barr began his foreword with a quote by Plato: "By beauty of shapes I do not mean, as most people would suppose, the beauty of living figures or of pictures, but, to make my point clear, I mean straight lines and circles and shapes, plain or solid, made from them by lathe, ruler and square. These are not, like other things, beautiful relatively, but always and absolutely." Plato: *Philebus* 51 c in Alfred Barr, *Machine Art* (New York: Museum of Modern Art, 1934), n.p.

3  Alfred Barr, foreword to *Machine Art*, n.p.

4  Philip Johnson, "History of Machine Art," in *Machine Art*, n.p.

5  Ibid.

6  Ibid.

7  Ibid.

8  Tony Bennett, *The Birth of the Museum: History, Theory, Politics* (London: Routledge, 1995), 61.

9  Ibid.

10  Prown, "Mind in Matter," 6.

11  Puerto Rico, Guyana, and Belize were not included as part of the eligible countries because they were colonies of the United States and Great Britain.

12  Bennett, *The Birth of the Museum*, 82.

13  Museum of Modern Art, *Industrial Design Competition for the 21 American Republics* (New York: Museum of Modern Art, 1940), n.p.

14  Ibid.

15  Eliot Noyes and Museum of Modern Art, *Organic Design in Home Furnishings* (New York: Museum of Modern Art, 1941), 4.

16  Oscar Salinas Flores, *Clara Porset: una vida inquieta, una obra sin igual* [Clara Porset: A Restless Life, A Work Unequaled] (México: Universidad Nacional Autónoma de México, Facultad de Arquitectura, 2001), 39.

17  Bennett, *The Birth of the Museum*, 82.

distinction, simply because they are considered well-designed objects made in Mexico, to be used at the ranch or in the kitchen. We would like to see this trend contribute to the revival of the Mexican people's fine custom of handling beauty in all the objects they use.[26]

At its core, *Art in the Daily Life* was a public exercise in the cultivation of taste, consumption, and private collecting. The scholar James Clifford has observed that, in an effort to make the world our own, we strive to surround ourselves with pleasing and appropriate things, but our inability to have it all teaches us to exercise an aesthetic judgment in order to create what we believe to be the best collections.[27] Porset wanted the public to realize that living well and comfortably was not just for the upper class, but could be achieved by all economic groups. The key was through a restrained collection of things that were at once beautiful, useful, and suitable for one's environment. It was a difficult balance to achieve, and it is precisely this lesson that Porset wished to teach. The cultural theorist Jean Baudrillard stated that, "our everyday objects are in fact objects of a passion — the passion for private property, emotional investment in which every bit as intense as investment in the 'human' passions. Indeed, the everyday passion for private property is often stronger than all the others, and sometimes even reigns supreme, all other passions being absent."[28] Porset understood this inherent desire to possess things, but she also acknowledged the need to educate the public on responsible consumption. It is safe to say that sometimes these attempts were failures and at others times they succeeded in a spectacular way that struck a true balance between natural and man-made beauty.

[18] Manuel Álvarez Fuentes and Dina Comisarenco Mirkin, "México. Diseño industrial" [Mexico: Industrial Design] in *Historia del diseño en América Latina y el Caribe: industrialización y comunicación visual para la autonomía* [History of Design in Latin America and the Caribbean: Industrialization and Visual Communication for Autonomy], ed. Silvia Fernandez and Gui Bonsiepe (São Paulo: Editora Blücher, 2008), 173.

[19] Ibid.

[20] Ana Elena Mallet, "El arte en la vida diaria. Exposición de objetos de buen diseño hechos en México" [Art in the Daily Life: An Exhibition of Well-Designed Objects Made in Mexico, 1952], in *El diseño de Clara Porset: inventando un México moderno* [Clara Porset's Design: Creating a Modern Mexico] (Mexico City: Museo Franz Mayer; CIDI; Difusión Cultural UNAM; Turner, 2006), 48.

[21] Instituto Nacional de Bellas Artes, Departamento de Arquitectura, *El arte en la vida diaria: Exposición de objetos de buen diseño hechos en México* [Art in the Daily Life: An Exhibition of Well-Designed Objects Made in Mexico] (Mexico City: El Instituto, 1952), 18-19.

[22] Barr, foreword to *Machine Age,* n.p.

[23] Salinas Flores, *Clara Porset,* 40.

[24] Clara Porset, "El Arte en la vida diaria," [Art in the Daily Life], *Espacio. Revista integral de rquitectura y artes plasticas* (August 1952): n.p.

[25] Mallet, "El arte en la vida diaria," 54.

[26] Porset, "El arte en la vida diaria," n.p.

[27] James Clifford, *The Predicament of Culture: Twentieth-century Ethnography, Literature, and Art* (Cambridge, MA: Harvard University Press, 1988), 218.

[28] See Jean Baudrillard, *The System of Objects,* trans. James Benedict, 1, http://web.mit.edu/allanmc/www/baudrillard.collecting.pdf (accessed, October 30, 2014).

Interior view of Gregori Warchavchik's Modernist House
at Santa Cruz Street, São Paulo, Brazil, built 1927–1928.
Courtesy the Gregori Warchavchik Collection.

# MODERN BRAZILIAN DESIGN

## MARIA CECILIA LOSCHIAVO DOS SANTOS

> In our tradition, the family home is a living entity, delineated by meanings, from both inside and out. Besides its physical architecture, the features in the mind and in the plans of architects and contractors, the house also has a symbolic architecture, that of the mind of its dwellers.
> —JOSÉ DE SOUZA MARTINS[1]

Brazilian cultural life during the period covered by this exhibition (from the 1940s to the 1970s) demonstrates a wide scope, corresponding to transformations that impacted architecture, design, the habitat and the configuration of the domestic interior, and the daily life of Brazilians. In this context, there are various questions — the presence of handcrafts and the work of craftsmen in the production of furniture, the replacement of the crafts-based production by industrial manufacturing, the verticalization of urban areas in the 1950s, the boom of architecture, the relevance of architects to the modernization process of furniture design in Brazil, design in wood and other materials — that lead to reflection and debate on Brazilian design. There is also the presence of signature furniture conceived by designers, explaining the basic design ideas, ideals, and processes.

This text is an overview of certain decisive landmarks, inflection points indicating themes and paths of the institutionalization process of design and the evolution of the domestic interior. Because of the complexity, it is important to establish a chronological framework to situate the historical matrices and delineate the practice of design in Brazil, insofar as it concerns aspects of furnishings, life, and domesticity.

The analytical paths that aid in understanding the processes and dynamics encompass the following themes: modernism, modernity, modernities, national identity of house and furniture, city/country relationships, authorial design/vernacular design, the dwellings of traditional native populations based on the legacies of their ancestors — these are some of the categories that offer perspectives on design and the Brazilian house. The chosen themes do not exhaust the study of design during the period from the 1940s to the 1970s but cause reflection that goes beyond the scope of the present study.[2]

## Art, Culture, and Society within the Formative Period of National Design

In order to understand Brazilian design in the 1940s, it is necessary to review the efforts at modernization undertaken by a generation of pioneers from the 1920s and 1930s, composed of designers, architects, and artists who voiced the ideas of European vanguards. This earlier period witnessed the acceptance in Brazil of international design in the production of furnishings for the home.

John Graz, Theodor Heuberger, and Gregori Warchavchik were among the European-born professional designers active in Rio de Janeiro and São Paulo. Graz, who designed furniture by creating environments still linked to the Bauhaus concept of total design, began his career in Brazil in São Paulo, in 1920, and later declared: "I have introduced in Brazil these cubistic furniture, with metal and a diversity of noble materials."[3] His work, together with his wife, Regina Gomide, was commissioned for a variety of houses, and they oversaw all the details and components of their interior designs.

In 1929, construction of the residence at Rua Itápolis in São Paulo gave rise to the *Exposição de uma Casa Moderna* (Exhibition of a Modern Home, 1930), organized by the Ukrainian-born architect Gregori Warchavchik (1896–1972). This first example in Brazil of the integration of furnishing and architecture, which Le Corbusier visited the year it was built, created an extremely modern environment with harmony of forms from carpets to lighting to furniture.

Commenting on this exhibition, the writer and critic Mário de Andrade reacted critically to the eclectic furnishings and the spirit that dominated the arrangement of interior spaces. With subtle humor, he rebuffed, for example, the Louis XV chairs: "If I owned a modernist house (logically, outfitted entirely modernistically like this house on exhibit), among the modern living room furniture I would place a Louis XV chair. Let's picture it: what's the sensation it causes? The only legitimate one currently as regards a Louis XV chair: the sensation of an art object. A Louis XV chair isn't a chair, it's an art object and, as such, can decorate our life. I'm not to blame if people in. . . [the eighteenth century] sat around on art objects instead of sitting in chairs, but it should be remembered that the dukes and duchesses back then were art objects themselves."[4]

There was, then, a clear mismatch between the modern building and its furnishings, but the intellectual and artistic elite subscribed to modern concepts that, in combination with possibilities coming from new construction materials, gradually contributed to changing this picture.

The 1930s were an exceptional moment, an axis and catalyst for Brazilian culture. As sociologist Antonio Candido stated, there occurred "the expansion of literary and artistic practices gradually transforming into the pattern of an age that which was considered a manifestation of small vanguard groups."[5] During that period, the emergence of modern architecture in the country constituted a fundamental factor in the renewal of design and the production of furniture. That renovation brought new demands in terms of furniture design, setting, and interior design.

A cornerstone of modernist architecture in Rio de Janeiro and Brazil was the construction of the new site of the Ministry of Education and Health, the Palácio Gustavo Capanema, which brought developments in modern design of furniture, lighting, landscape design, and other components in addition to expressing a new visuality in the field of interior design.

In 1938, the German cultural animator Theodor Heuberger (1898–1987) inaugurated the "A Forma Decorativa S.A – Casa e Jardim" (House and Garden), a store that fostered modern design, especially projects with links to the Bauhaus. According to Heuberger, "Casa e Jardim had everything that was needed for a house: from tableware to glasses, pottery, metal, furniture and even artwork."[6] In São Paulo, this studio was run by the Moravian-American architect, curator, critic, and designer Bernard Rudofsky. The cultural milieu was still in the process of modernization and innovation, and the styles available in the marketplace bespoke their ties to past forms, but the experiences cited point to the possibilities of transformation, and, little by little, furnishings, interiors, and houses adopted the patterns of modern architecture.

During the 1940s, the Second World War spread a sense of crisis and instability. Artists, architects, and designers of diverse origins fled Europe and arrived in Brazil to occupy its territory culturally. The myth of the Americas as a promised land was an essential element in the imagination and hopes of those professionals. Three exceptional professionals were leading forces in Brazilian design during that decade: Joaquim Tenreiro, Lina Bo Bardi, and Bernard Rudofsky.

## Wood, Modernity, and Tradition: Joaquim Tenreiro

The Portuguese-born designer Joaquim Tenreiro (1906–92) achieved an extensive artistic production — in design, watercolors, painting, and sculpture — and enchanted the Brazilian public with his delicate command of line. But it was through furniture design that he established his closest tie with Brazilian culture. He collaborated with the renowned Rio cabinetmakers Leandro Martins and Laubisch, Hirth & Company Ltd., where he worked as draftsman of sketches and floor plans and produced eclectic furnishings in different styles and periods for homes of the bourgeoisie of the nation's capital.

His broad knowledge of types of wood and artisanal techniques and their application, as well as his command of the development of styles in the history of furnishings, imbued great consistency and firmness to Tenreiro's work. His esteem for artisans and workmanship was a family heritage, of which he stated, "Back in Portugal I learned woodworking perfectly with my father, who was a first-class artisan of furniture, of everything."[7] In the provincial regions of Europe, men capable of inventing and producing objects were absolutely essential to daily life. Tenreiro absorbed the belief in the dignity and importance of craftsmanship in the totality of his production.

Regarding the craft of furniture, Tenreiro felt that "Industries were not equipped to produce furniture industrially, but because it has older roots: it came to industry through artisanship. In my view, one of the greatest mistakes of industry is not to make a strictly industrial piece of furniture with appropriate materials and machinery. That means not doing either one thing or the other; there is neither artisanship nor industry in the true sense of the word. Industrialization, instead of producing high-quality furniture for the masses, ends up contributing to large-scale production of inferior articles."[8]

Joaquim Tenreiro (Brazilian, 1906–92). Three-legged chair, c. 1947. Wood; 27 ½ x 22 x 24 in. Courtesy of Zesty Meyers and Evan Snyderman, R & Company, New York. [Checklist no. 56]

In 1942, a signal moment in his career occurred when he planned the first modern pieces of furniture, manufactured in limited number, commissioned by Oscar Niemeyer for a home he designed for Francisco Inácio Peixoto in Cataguases, Minas Gerais. Tenreiro happily recalled this moment: "When the client came to see the plan, his eyes grew wide and he said, 'That's what I wanted.' That began my history of modern furniture."[9]

Tenreiro's pieces for the Minas Gerais residence had a great impact on the history of Brazilian furnishings because he implemented his own principles that design should be in a dialogue with the building's architecture and the local climate, appear consistent, and not adopt the language of Art Deco in vogue among designers at the time. It should be mentioned that the client, Peixoto, belonged to the artistic elite of the city of Cataguases, which was notable for advocating the ideals of modernity through cinema with the work of Brazilian filmmaker Humberto Mauro (1897–83), literature (*Revista Verde*), architecture, and design.

In 1947, Tenreiro opened his first store on Rua Barata Ribeiro in Rio de Janeiro, later moving to Praça General Osório in Ipanema. This store, Langenbach & Tenreiro, was an important center for the commercialization and publicizing of modern furniture, along with unornamented pieces and accessories for enhancing the domestic setting. His commercial activity furthered Tenreiro's integration into the artistic and cultural milieu of Rio, and he received a request from theater actor and director José

Silveira Sampaio to create the stage sets for the play *Da necessidade de ser polígamo* (On the Need to Be a Polygamist). It was in this way that an icon of his production came about: the three-legged chair. The mixture of woods of varying tones — Brazilian walnut, pau-marfim (*Balfourodendron riedelianum*), jacaranda, purpleheart, and mahogany — created interesting chromatic effects and brought much attention to this sculptural stage prop. These qualities were highlighted by the critic Mário Pedrosa, who noted that, "there is Tenreiro's spectacular chair, of perfect craftsmanship, beautiful, but which doesn't make us feel like sitting in it, so we can continue to admire it for itself."[10]

Tenreiro's output was extensive. Familiarity and a sublime love of wood led him to develop a significant and diverse number of pieces that renewed not only furniture design but instituted new ways of relating to the interior space of a house, new ways of residing, of living the daily life in the Brazilian home and its environment.

Today, his inspired creations are celebrated worldwide for their use of materials and elements of our culture, for their formal precision, creativity, and charm that the conceptualization of his works always challenged: "archisculptures, sculptpaintings, paintcultures," as the professor, diplomat and philologist Antônio Houaiss (1915–99) said; or as Pedrosa so aptly defined, "an art of repose."[11] Viva Master Joaquim Tenreiro!

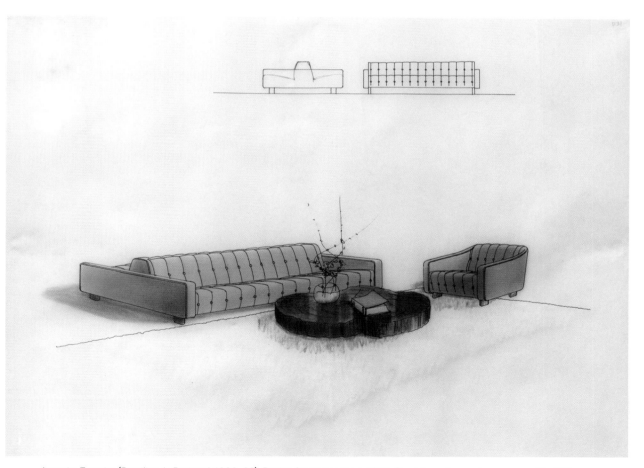

Joaquim Tenreiro (Brazilian, b. Portugal, 1906–92). Design for an interior, c. 1945. Graphite and gouache on paper; 10 x 13 in. Courtesy of Zesty Meyers and Evan Snyderman, R & Company, New York. [Checklist no. 55]

### Bernard Rudofsky: Organic Design and the MoMA Competition

Also noteworthy in the 1940s was the victory in 1941 of the Moravian-born architect, curator, critic, and designer Bernard Rudofsky (1905–1988) in the *Industrial Design for Latin America* competition sponsored by the Museum of Modern Art in New York. The resulting exhibition, entitled *Organic Design in Home Furnishings,* featured furniture design that used native materials. Rudofsky submitted a design of an armchair of tubular metal with seat and back lined with fabrics made from natural Brazilian fibers: jute, caroa, and hemp. This prize was the first international recognition accorded Rudofsky, who, despite his brief stay in Brazil, left an expressive contribution to modernist architecture (notably the João Arnstein and Frontini residences — both from 1940 — in São Paulo), product design, and graphic design, with the creation of expressive labels for the Brazilian market. The MoMA competition gave Rudofsky the opportunity to experiment with a unique combination of materials during this period of design modernization in Brazil.

Architect Bernardo Figueiredo's living room in Rio de Janeiro, Brazil, c. 1960s. Courtesy of Angela Figueiredo.

## Seeking to Understand Brazil: Lina Bardi

In the same period, seminal contributions were made by the talented architect Achillina Adriana Giuseppina Bo — Lina Bo, who, after her marriage to Pietro Maria Bardi (1900–99), assumed the name Lina Bo Bardi (1914–92). The Italian couple settled in Brazil in 1946, bringing with them an extensive professional, cultural, and political background. Their arrival represents a significant moment in the history of Brazilian culture, architecture, and design, as both acted on several fronts, engaging in theoretical and practical positions that engendered a watershed in twentieth-century Brazilian culture.

Lina's furniture stands at a remove from the work of her Portuguese contemporary Joaquim Tenreiro. The use of solid wood and the slender "toothpick legs," characteristic of the latter's output, are not found in her work. She preferred the use of glued veneer, favoring pieces with a reduced number of components. Lina's furnishings are supported by ample critical discussion, the fruit of her notable intellectual maturity.

The magazine *Habitat,* which she cofounded with her husband in 1950, is the extraordinary manifestation of the critical breadth of Lina's thought and of her engagement with Brazilian themes. Its

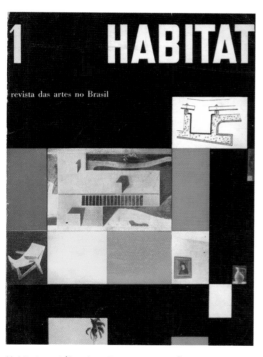

*Habitat*, no. 1 (October–December, 1950). Edited by Lina Bo and Pietro Maria Bardi. Courtesy of Zesty Meyers and Evan Snyderman, R & Company, New York. [Checklist no. 83]

powerful graphic design and the presentation of editorial objectives expresses the following ideas: "The imaginative beauty of a forest, of a wattle-and-daub hut, of a Marajó pot, a Baroque church, [the Baroque sculptor] Aleijadinho, the goldsmiths of Bahia, the Manueline furniture makers of Recife, the disciples of the French mission, the architects of the theater at Manaus and those of the Ministry of Education and Health in Rio, the backlands painters and the artists of renown, ceramists, the basket weavers of the coast, *gameleiros,*[12] indigenous peoples, Africans, the descendants of conquerors, emigrants, all those who have contributed, continue to contribute and participate in some form in art in Brazil, will have their activities recorded in *Habitat* with the zeal of one cognizant of that which is most characteristic of the country."[13]

In 1947, Lina designed the folding chair of leather and wood for the auditorium of the initial installation of the Museu de Arte de São Paulo. That same year, the couple founded the Fábrica de Móveis Pau Brasil in partnership with Giancarlo Palanti. From then on, countless projects of their authorship or coauthorship were realized, always prioritizing the accommodation of the piece to local conditions and to its public. The furniture was simple and unadorned, without upholstery of any kind, their seats and backrests using canvas, leather, and calico from the Casas Pernambucanas stores. In a statement to the author, Lina emphasized her goals: "to create a chain of industrial design, of objects. I also occupied myself with jewelry made from Brazilian materials. The tendency was to create a movement in that field, which offered nothing, while Brazilian architecture already existed and was extremely important."[14]

In addition to design and production of furnishings, Lina's sensitivity and acute observation of manifestations of popular culture resulted in a lucid militancy evident on various fronts: teaching, studies, critical debate, curatorship of exhibitions, stage design, and editorial activity in the realm of design and architecture, as well as architectural plans. In all these activities, she was always motivated by a strong democratic spirit, cognizant of the central relationship between artistic-cultural creation and social justice, an aspect often ignored in the design field.

Among Lina's extensive work dedicated to popular culture and themes of the Brazilian Northeast is an emblematic piece that demonstrates her provocative vision: the *Cadeira de beira de estrada* (Roadside Chair) of 1967. A purposeful object, it makes use of three tree branches forming a triangle, tied with liana in its upper part and base. Horizontally, it features binding with a shorter branch, which serves as a support for the body. A simple, rudimentary piece but an integral part of the repertoire of survival and a way of life, it was designed to recapture the manner of sitting practiced by

Lina Bo Bardi (Brazilian, 1914–92). *Cadeira de beira de estrada* [Roadside Chair], 1967. Wood, rope, iron nails; 77 ⁹⁄₁₆ x 35 ⁷⁄₁₆ x 24 ⁷⁄₁₆ in. Instituto Lina Bo e P. M. Bardi, São Paulo, Brazil. [Checklist no. 11]

the backwoodsmen and the indigenous populations. It used natural materials at a time when (un)
sustainability and the throwaway culture were not yet dominant trends in the design universe. In
this sense, the Roadside Chair anticipated the awareness of these themes and demonstrates the
richness of the material culture and the dignity and modesty of the Brazilian people.

The Roadside Chair further raises the question regarding the act of sitting and the "art of repose."
What is this repose if not a reflexive attitude that leads us to a reassessment of the vital experience of
the seated human body itself, the essential material for design? Ultimately, this chair can be considered as a manifesto of anti-design, in the currently accepted meaning of the term, and as a manifesto
in favor of the imaginative beauty of simple and popular things; as Lina stated, "the people always hold
freedom as a value and in general represent the strength of a country, but not as folklore, and in Brazil
they are marginalized."[15]

In 2014, as we celebrate the centennial of the birth of that unique personage in Brazilian architecture and design, we can observe the great interest and admiration her work arouses in everyone,
echoing the words of anthropologist Darcy Ribeiro. He defined the crucial role of Lina in the Brazilian
cultural scene: "Lina wanted Brazil to have industry springing from abilities in the hands of the people,
from the original vision of the people. We could reinvent tableware, plates, shirts, shoes. There was
an entire possibility of remaking the world, the world of consumption as something that resonated in
our heart. Lina was a person who helped us to think along those lines — prosperity for all, beauty that
was attainable, achievable."[16]

**Consolidation, Industrialization, and Assimilation of the Modern: The Fifties and Sixties**
The 1950s, the so-called golden years, constitute a unique and singular moment in Brazilian history, a
time of the establishment of an industrial policy to incentivize manufacturing. Adopting the slogan
"Fifty Years of Development in Five," the administration of President Juscelino Kubitschek (1956–61)
inaugurated the construction in Brasília of the new capital of the country, the project of Lúcio Costa
(1902–98) and Oscar Niemeyer (1907–2012). The experience of building Brasília had a powerful effect
on the imagination of the Brazilian people, and the city's construction has since been recognized as
part of the cultural patrimony of humanity.

In 1950, the first TV channel in Latin America, TV Tupi, began its broadcasts in Brazil, extolling the
virtues of modernization, industrialization, and the reconfiguration of interior domestic space. Furniture
introduced new patterns, settings, and comfort. Part of the production was artisanal but gradually
became mechanized, creating an opening for a professional role for designers.

The principles of modernization launched in previous decades were already absorbed, and the
emerging industrial base brought conditions for total incorporation of the modern into the process of
industrialization of furniture design, which definitively transformed the home, the configuration of
interior space, and Brazilians' way of life.

During that period, the design of furnishings was enriched through the talents of José Zanine
Caldas (1919–2001), the creator of the Fábrica de Móveis Z, who displayed a deep concern with
industrialization and modular components; Sérgio Rodrigues (1927–2014), the Rio architect who in
1955 founded the Oca firm, where he developed an extensive line of furniture; the Brazilian artist,
photographer, and designer Geraldo de Barros (1923–98), who, first with Unilabor and later with
Hobjeto Indústria de Móveis, was excited by the possibilities of industrialization of Brazilian furniture;
and the Polish-Brazilian architect and designer Jorge Zalszupin (b. 1922), whose firm L'Atelier worked

Jose Zanine Caldas (Brazilian, 1918–2001). Plant stand, c. 1949. Wood, plastic, laminate; 13 x 21 x 18 in. Courtesy of Zesty Meyers and Evan Snyderman, R & Company, New York. [Checklist no. 74]

with wood and plastics. The companies Branco & Preto and Mobília Contemporânea, under the leadership of Michel Arnoult (1922–2005), are also worth noting among the several initiatives that participated in this highly significant moment in the history of Brazilian furniture design.

This wealth of experiences presented conflicts of positions and of techniques; mass production made possible the emergence of retail in design and thus different approaches to the consumer market proliferated, including the impact of specialized media dedicated to design and architecture. One thing is definite: the 1950s afforded a strategic and privileged point of view for assessing design and the Brazilian home. From a certain lag in forming a national character in the area of furnishings, the country moved on to industrial production. A developmental mindset came into play.

The close dialogue between art and design took on specific shape through the interfaces between design and groups of concretist and neoconcretist artists emerging in São Paulo and Rio de Janeiro starting in 1950. The rationality of art intertwines with the plan for a new society, offering developments in the field of furnishings.

The possibility of industrializing furniture manufacture and bringing design to broad segments of the population was a fervent desire of the Bahian Zanine. While Warchavchik and Graz accompanied the European vanguards, and Lina plunged into the popular that afforded her the major references for furniture design, Zanine was highly attuned to the possibilities the industry offered; but his contribution goes beyond the system of production. He was concerned with the consumer, the acceptance of his products, and their distribution and usage in the home.

His relationship to wood and the technical research into that material show a lengthy involvement, nurtured by unconditional support from architects and professors of architecture in Brazil. Zanine was unanimously praised by Luis Inácio Romeiro de Anhaia Mello, Lúcio Costa, Alcides da Rocha Miranda, Oscar Niemeyer, and Oswaldo Bratke, to cite some of the professionals with whom he collaborated. Zanine moved easily through all the domains of wood: he designed types and algorithms of wood, publicity placards, mockups, furniture, and houses, and ultimately worked with the remains from the appalling deforestation of the Brazilian rainforest.

Zanine's production of furnishings began precisely at mid-century, when he installed his Fábrica de Móveis Z in São José dos Campos in the state of São Paulo. One of the major characteristics of Zanine, Pontes & Companhia was the use of plywood. He produced a set of pieces industrially, applying modular principles to achieve maximum utilization of the layers of veneer, thus opening the possibility of affecting the modern discourse of furniture design.

In this period, he designed an extensive line of pieces with seventy types: desks, wardrobes, beds, chairs, armoires, and tables. He took pride in these creations and emphasized, "I had everything for a home, and it was extremely cheap. I managed to reduce the price of furnishings by 70 to 80 percent in relation to what was done with ordinary wood. At that time, the factory had 150 employees, because it sold a lot."[17]

The work of the aforementioned designers allowed manifesto-pieces that synthesized the concerns and foundations they adopted. What distinguished Zanine's work was the repertory of basic furniture, with organically inspired design, necessary for the functionality of the home's interior, an attempt to popularize design.

Amebalike forms, the boomerangs, verging on the abstractionism of Joan Miró and Alexander Calder or the sculptures of Jean Arp, in vogue at that time, were dominant forms in these pieces. The color and asymmetry were also an innovative element, for until then surfaces were practically neutral, sober, and symmetrical. The new discoveries, the use of plastics, the multifunctionality and energy of Zanine's pieces definitively consolidated the role of design in domestic interiors.

Distinct approaches to materials and forms circulated in the modern-furniture market: the classical-modern of Joaquim Tenreiro, with jacaranda, rattan, and toothpick legs; the cut-out veneers of José Zanine Caldas; and hardwoods with the vigorous forms of Sérgio Rodrigues.

Rodrigues's work displayed uniqueness. In addition to the upper class that always sought in furnishing and in domestic decoration icons to demonstrate their status, Sérgio identified an emerging young intellectual middle class, with greater power of choice in domestic accouterments as a way of expressing their values, tastes, and lifestyles, and exuding a certain informality that came onto the scene as the 1960s began.

At the start of the decade this informality set the style. Brazilian culture was becoming a kind of grand laboratory for experimentation and innovation. Furniture also reflected the dissonance of the trending musical style: the bossa nova. Rodrigues's work fitted into this context, and one of the most representative pieces of this new aesthetic plan was the *Poltrona Mole* (Soft Armchair). Its unique features won prizes, in addition to occupying a place of prominence in collections of the world's major museums, such as the Museum of Modern Art.

The Soft Armchair was not an armchair — it was a sofa! This is the metaphor for the emergence of Sérgio's most important work, which appeared in 1957 as the result of a commission from the photographer Otto Stupakoff, who approached him, saying, "'Sérgio, come up with a spread-out sofa fit for a sultan, for the corner of my studio.' I [Rodrigues] caught the ball on my chest, but where was the head to send it into the net?"[18]

This armchair manifests Sérgio's enthusiasm for researching and finding solutions to satisfy his clients' demands but also challenges well-established reigning patterns: to the slim and elegant toothpick legs the Soft Armchair counterpoised the strength and thickness of Brazilian jacaranda in an era when the mantra of sustainability was as yet unheard of.

The Soft Armchair expressed this daily posture of the designer, pursuing the new habits of sitting, especially the informality of Rio, the atmosphere of relaxation produced by loose cushions tossed onto the structure, thus altering the very concept of seating. This was the emergence of patterns inspired by the hippie movement. The Soft Armchair anticipated the trend of production of overstuffed furniture, such as the Sacco Chair by Gatti, Paolini and Teodoro produced by Zanotta in Milan (1970). It also corresponded to the desire to conceive a piece that expressed the Brazilian identity: the quest for nationalism in furniture.

Experimentalism, informality, and nationalism were basic trends in Brazilian design of the 1960s and 1970s, but what processes were at work to bring them about?

Above and opposite: Sérgio Rodrigues (Brazilian, 1927–2014). *Mole* armchair, 1957. Wood, leather; 32 ½ x 40 x 29 in. Manufactured by Oca. Courtesy of Zesty Meyers and Evan Snyderman, R & Company, New York. [Checklist no. 50]

The 1960s were a time of cultural and political agitation in Brazil, but on March 31, 1964, the military took power in a coup. Subsequently, the country endured a somber period. All the vitality of the transforming and vanguardist experiments of the previous years went into a long hiatus. The country plunged into paralyzing authoritarianism, violence, and censorship. Creative and intellectual activities were limited. In this framework of repression and coercion, the private space of the home occupied a preponderant role, but the pleasure of domestic intimacy was threatened by orders and decrees of every type.

### The 1970s: Design During the Miracle

The Brazilian cultural and artistic reality in the 1970s was under the dominion of military power. The slogan "Brazil: love it or leave it" was pervasive. Attempts at resisting the regime were uncoordinated; this was a period of dissolution and exhaustion.

A complex of social, political, and economic factors — especially a new linkage of Brazilian capitalism with the world market and integration with industrial production of the time — exerted influence over the professional practice and the production of design.

This was the era of the "Brazilian Miracle," marked by the prevalence of competent discourse in technical areas, for both private and public enterprises, new market demands, and intense state interference in Brazilian cultural life. Two paradigmatic design experiments merit attention: one in the area of textiles, the other in furniture design.

Arte Nativa Aplicada (Brazilian, f. 1976). Upholstery fabric with pre-Columbian figures, c. 1970s. Cotton; 63 x 53 in. Manufactured by Arte Nativa Aplicada. Private Collection. [Checklist no. 9]

In the first case, natural fibers, graphic art, earth colors, body art, geometric motifs, basketry, feather art, and various indigenous objects were transposed and reinvented as fabric prints for decoration by Arte Nativa Aplicada (Applied Native Art), whose activities began in São Paulo in 1976. A rich chromatic variation applied to textiles made of natural fibers: cotton, silk, and wool in several collections of fabrics for decoration, home accessories, bedspreads, blankets, cushion cases, place-mats, and towels. The team of designers, coordinated by Maria Henriqueta Gomes, included recent graduates of schools of design, such as Circe Bernardes, João de Souza Leite, and Manuel Guglielmo.

1   José de Souza Martins, "Nossa Casa, nossa mãe," *O Estado de S. Paulo* (São Paulo), April 25, 2011.

2   I would like to express my gratitude to the interest of the Americas Society in Brazilian themes and for the opportunity to disseminate knowledge of Brazil, its designs, and its designers. As this essay was nearing completion, Brazilian design lost Sérgio Rodrigues. From our earliest conversations in 1979, when he generously shared chapters of his history of design, furniture, and the Brazilian house, Sérgio became a mentor and guide to many researchers and students of design in Brazil. I am grateful and miss him.

3   John Graz, interview by Maria Cecilia Loschiavo dos Santos, São Paulo, 1979.

4   Mário de Andrade, "Exposição duma casa modernista (considerações)" [Exhibition of a Modernist House: Considerations], *Diário Nacional* (São Paulo), April 5, 1930. Republicado em Depoimentos n.2. Centro de Estudos Brasileiros, GFAU, São Paulo, 1966.

5   Paulo Duarte, *Mário de Andrade por ele mesmo* [Mário de Andrade By Himself] (São Paulo: Hucitec, 1977), XII–XV.

6   Theodor Heuberger, interview by Maria Cecilia Loschiavo dos Santos, São Paulo, 1980.

7   Joaquim Tenreiro, interview by Maria Cecilia Loschiavo dos Santos, Rio de Janeiro, 1979.

8   Ibid.

9   Ibid.

10   Mário Pedrosa, "O Salão Moderno III" [The Modern Show III], *Jornal do Brasil,* November 25, 1961.

A mature and surprising experiment because of the anthropological aspect of the project, it promoted the reencounter of the metropolitan dweller with the magic of the Indian's house, village, land, and life.

The second notable design experiment during the "Brazilian Miracle" was the search for continuity between Oscar Niemeyer's architecture and the elements that it complemented, bringing to the market an exceptional contribution of furniture design. Brazil owes much to his sensitivity, talent, refinement, and nobility of character. The poet, writer, and journalist Ferreira Gullar defined the architect's greatest legacy: "Oscar teaches us that beauty is weightless."[19] This lightness can also be seen in his furnishings.

It was a direct intervention of architecture into the planning and industrial production of furniture, and Niemeyer explained how it came about: "The problem that I encountered in the equipment of buildings is that often the furniture, the internal arrangement completely works against the architecture. The architecture anticipates spaces that must remain free among groups of furniture, and at times the pieces are placed improperly, the spaces are lost, and the architecture suffers."[20]

At the end of the 1970s, the policy of gradual easing of tensions created openings for cultural and artistic production and for design. Emotions and surprises would accompany the new decade.

## Final Notes

The exhibition *Moderno: Design for Living in Brazil, Mexico, and Venezuela, 1940–1978* makes possible a critical reassessment of furniture design and interior design of the Brazilian home during that period.

There are certain chronological and thematic axes that accompany the development of design and modernist identity of furnishings during the period: design in the 1940s was influenced by the postwar diaspora, as well as the conceptualizations and hopes of Brazil; design in the 1950s marked the golden age of industrialization; design in the 1960s signified a cultural effervescence, a popular emergence interrupted by the dictatorship; design in the 1970s reflected the work and grace of the "Brazilian Miracle."

The work of the artists cited possesses great vitality and there persist in it some of the aspects already mentioned: the presence of wood and the culture in modern furniture strongly tied to architecture. One particularity must be emphasized: in the modern period, while the woman's role in the domestic sphere is a significant theme, the history of modern Brazilian design is eminently masculine, with the single exception of the masterly work of Lina Bardi.

[11] Maria Cecilia Loschiavo dos Santos, "Tradição e Modernidade no Móvel Brasileiro. Visões da Utopia na Obra de Carrera, Tenreiro, Zanine e Sérgio Rodrigues" [Tradition and Modernity: Visions of Utopia in the work of Carrera, Tenreiro, Zanine and Sérgio Rodrigues] (PhD diss., University of São Paulo, 1993), 232.

[12] *Gameleiro* is a term applied to those who made receptacles or containers from hollowed-out tree trunks or other suitable sources of wood (translator's note).

[13] *Habitat*, no. 1 (1950).

[14] Lina Bardi, interview by Maria Cecilia Loschiavo dos Santos, Pompéia Factory, São Paulo, 1979.

[15] Lina Bardi, interview by Carolina Lefévre, School of Architecture and Urbanism of the University of São Paulo, São Paulo, October 1991.

[16] Darcy Ribeiro, *Tempos de Grossura: o Design no Impasse* (São Paulo: Instituto Lina Bo e P.M. Bardi, 1994), back cover.

[17] José Zanine Caldas, interview by Maria Cecilia Loschiavo dos Santos, Rio de Janeiro, November 30, 1992.

[18] Sergio Rodrigues, "A Dura Estória, Paixão e Vida do Sofá que Era Mole" [A Hard Story, Passion and Life of a Sofa that was Soft] ,*Revista Senhor,* Rio de Janeiro, 1962, n.p. (manuscript).

[19] See Ferreira Gullar, "Lição de Arquitetura," a poem dedicated to Oscar Niemeyer published in this volume.

[20] Oscar Niemeyer, interview by Maria Cecilia Loschiavo dos Santos, Rio de Janeiro, September 1979.

# DESIGN'S BUREAUCRATIC UNCONSCIOUS

## LUIS M. CASTAÑEDA

Cildo Meireles's (1948–) *Insertions into Ideological Circuits: The Banknote Project* is among the most emblematic works of conceptual art produced in the last century. At the *Information* show at the Museum of Modern Art in New York (1970), Meireles exhibited banknotes suspended from circulation. These were to be subsequently returned into circulation with stamped inscriptions that denounced the murderous acts of Brazil's military regime and its perceived collusion with "Yankee" interests.

A significant but generally overlooked part of this critique involves the role that design plays in the ideological circuits under scrutiny. Among the bills that Meireles modified were the new *cruzeiros* produced by the graphic designer Aloísio Magalhães (1927–82) as part of an official commission in 1966, two years after the beginning of military rule in Brazil. Magalhães reinforced the desired state of perpetual mobility of his bills by creating their distinctive moiré surface. He achieved this effect, with a debt to the language of optical art, by printing overlapping reticular patterns just slightly out of alignment with each other on their surface.

Meireles counteracted the form and function of these bills: his gesture interrupted their circuit of exchange, a self-perpetuating process driven by capitalism's most basic logic. Also suspended was the imbrication between design practices and acts of state authority that the production and circulation of the bills represented. This aspect of the *Insertions* provides a glimpse into a fundamental dimension of official design in Brazil and most of the Americas, which may be described as its "bureaucratic unconscious." Because its prominence rose alongside that of state administrations (primarily but not exclusively developmentalist ones), by midcentury the underlying ideological imperatives that official design served were often inseparable from those of these state formations. This conditioned not only the production and consumption of these works but was also fundamentally bound up with their formal language: the textures, forms, and materials of modern design were often tantamount to the very physical incarnation of the modern states being consolidated at this time.

Cildo Meireles (Brazilian, b. 1948). *Insertions into Ideological Circuits: The Banknote Project,* 1970. Tate Modern.

Although the relationship among these domains remained fluid, the "golden age" of modern design (1950–70) in the Americas saw the division between the practice of design and those of architecture and the visual arts become gradually more explicit. This shift was concomitant with the emergence of schools like the Escola Superior do Desenho Industrial do Rio de Janeiro, which Magalhães helped establish in 1962. Like several of its peer institutions in Latin America, this school was modeled closely on the Hochschule für Gestaltung Ulm, founded in 1953 by Max Bill, Otl Aicher, and Inge Aicher-Scholl. The subsequent exchange between Europe and the Americas was reciprocal. While Bill's trajectory would become closely tied to concretist and neoconcretist experimentation in Brazil, the Argentinian-born designer Tomás Maldonado would eventually become a key figure in the Ulm experience.

This shift also entailed the division between the private and public dimensions of design. In its public, official dimension, design interventions operated on a variety of scales and temporalities in the Americas: from the production of banknotes to the conformation of significant elements of new cities; from ephemeral propaganda events to permanent monuments. This is the unconscious dimension of design that Meireles disrupts. He reminds us that, in order for them to work, the relationships between the components of ideological circuits have to be collectively taken for granted. What, after all, could be more mindlessly circulated than a banknote, an object not only never meant to be looked at for too long but actually engineered to endure the constant motion driven by its own exchange?

Meireles's "insertion" denaturalizes the link between bills and capitalism as well as the connection between the signature form of Magalhães's bills and the stamp of authority of the state that they bear. With a similar aim, this essay examines three interrelated episodes in which official design strove to actualize the fantasies of control of its sponsoring states but also bore witness to the limitations of such illusions. In each of these cases, design operated as a powerful currency for the exercise of state authority.

## Alchemy at the Plateau

By the time he produced the new *cruzeiros,* Aloíso Magalhães was already well established as a designer of governmental and corporate commissions. Among his lesser-known early works, those that first opened doors to this kind of success, was the appropriately titled book *Doorway to Brasilia,* which he produced in collaboration with U.S.-born designer Eugene Feldman. In more ways than one, the book, published in the United States in Portuguese, French, and English in 1959, before the new capital was finished, represented Magalhães's entry into the realm of official design he would occupy for the rest of his career.[1]

The book's textual component is conventionally official: it features a poetic foreword by John Dos Passos, short aphorisms by President Juscelino Kubitschek (who sponsored the construction of the new capital), and equally aphoristic statements by Lúcio Costa and Oscar Niemeyer, the architects responsible for Brasília's planning and construction. However, in its attempt to encapsulate the alchemical dimensions of the building of the spectacular new city, the book is visually unconventional. In its large-scale plates, the contours of recently built structures, like Niemeyer's presidential Palácio da Alvorada (Palace of Dawn), meld together with the ethereal surfaces of clouds, sky, and earth that surround them. The building's various architectural components are portrayed in a stark, metallic gray, the same tone of the clouds. In another of the book's large-format prints, Niemeyer's Congresso Nacional (National Congress Building) appears as a collection of purely geometrical volumes — the building's half domes are colored in a stark gray, the office towers in between are a combination of white and orange, and an almost black background, that of the vast sky of the *planalto,* defines them

by opposition. More explicitly than the promotional photographs of Brasília's construction — such as Marcel Gautherot's — these plates push the formal principles of Niemeyer's architecture to their radical conclusion: the slender monumentality of the new buildings achieves its heroic dimension when it becomes one with the emptiness of its surrounding environment.

The sublime effect of these images was a result of their experimental printing method, which, Magalhães and Feldman asserted, "has a potential limited only by the boundaries of the imagination and the creative talents of the artists who choose to use and develop it." Feldman and Magalhães used photosensitized aluminum plates printed directly onto the bookplates from negatives. In several cases, like the one of Niemeyer's Congress, a single illustration in the book was the result of several printing stages. This created an eerie effect, as the accretion of layers of geometric building blocks became almost palpable from the book's surface. The new capital city, the book's coauthors claimed, was "chosen as subject matter" not because of its official status but "because of the mood it suggests — a frontier city with strong graphic shapes and a vitality that is both timely and timeless."[2] The "doorway" to the city they produced was thus rooted firmly on its graphic support and almost architectural in its construction, and its implied expansiveness extended well beyond the precious surface of the book's pages.

### Kinetic Magic
Abstraction of the kind found in Feldman and Magalhães's prints enjoyed a long life as part of official design's *lingua franca* in the Americas (South, Central, and North) perhaps nowhere more clearly than at the Venezuelan national pavilion exhibited at Expo '67, the World's Fair organized in Montreal. The

Aloísio Magalhães (Brazilian, 1927–82) and Eugene Feldman (American, 1921–75), plates from *Doorway to Brasilia* (New York: Wittenborn, 1959).

architect Juan Pedro Posani wrote that, upon first receiving this commission, Carlos Raúl Villanueva (1900–75), the architect with the closest links to political power in twentieth-century Venezuela and Posani's longtime collaborator, "[began] to imagine the ambiance of the Expo, cluttered, exhibitionist, typical of these kinds of international exhibitions since 1851. . . . [He also began] to wonder how a building of a small country can situate itself reasonably in an international competition of this kind. . . . The folkloric solution. . . [he] immediately rejected. . . . For pagodas, we have the nationalist Chinese."[3]

The formal solution thus turned elsewhere. The pavilion consisted of three large cubes of aluminum, not photosensitized this time but burnished. Nonetheless, these were painted in primary colors similar to those that Feldman and Magalhães achieved in their experimental attempt to represent the unfinished Brasília. Inside one of these volumes was a *Penetrable* by the Venezuelan artist Jesús Rafael Soto (1923–2005), which consisted of a series of thin plastic tubes suspended from a metal frame hanging from the ceiling. Soto's cube of pure color, at once virtual and intensely material, invited not only visual appreciation but also an immersive interaction. Soto's *Penetrable* thus approximated the

Carlos Raúl Villanueva's Venezuela Pavilion, Expo '67, Montreal. Photo by Juan Pedro Posani, from *Expo 67: Villanueva, Soto* (Caracas, 1967).

notion of a "non-object" articulated in 1959 by the Brazilian-born art critic Ferreira Gullar in relation to neo-concretism.[4] Soto's "non-object" was closely related to this experimental episode on account of its participatory dimension and departure from the rigid geometries of concrete art, the earlier trend that — as imported to the Americas by Bill, imagined by Maldonado and his collaborators, and encountered en route between the old and new worlds by Soto and his Venezuelan peers — probed the boundaries between design's surfaces and objects, and those of the visual arts. Owing to the literal and metaphorical transparency of its formal language, which disclosed its grounding in the abstract geometry of the virtual cube, the *Penetrable* could simultaneously provide the kind of "pure appearance" and intensely material presence that Gullar also perceived in the experiments of Lygia Pape and Hélio Oiticica.

Like most "non-objects," Soto's cube had an explicit political dimension, though one perhaps not aligned with Pape or Oiticica's emancipatory efforts. Posani argued that the Venezuela pavilion was the architectural expression of tensions between Villanueva's design team and the pressures imposed

Jesús Rafael Soto (Venezuelan, 1923–2005). *Penetrable.* At the Venezuela Pavilion, Expo '67, Montreal. Photo by Juan Pedro Posani, from *Expo 67: Villanueva, Soto* (Caracas, 1967).

upon it by the "mysterious apparatuses of the bureaucracy" that commissioned it. These apparatuses, he claimed, did not object to the geometric abstraction of the structure's envelope, but the tripartite curatorial project they set forth conflicted with Villanueva's plans. The bureaucracy wanted one cube to include "an audio-visual program" that represented "what Venezuela is like today"; another to feature an *au naturel* representation of "the landscape, the jungle, etc.," or "the pre-human natural environment" of the country as it may have appeared before the state civilized it; and a third cube to contain a café, a fitting response to the dictum, so common at world's fairs, of "tell me how you eat, and I will tell you who you are."[5]

Posani's point about the often tense relationship between the aims of architects, artists, and designers in the context of these commissions is well taken. But, just like the boundaries between real and virtual space in the pavilion, in this case the ideological boundary that divided the mysterious bureaucracy from the team of architects was also fluid. The Expo '67 pavilion was, after all, only one of the multiple official commissions that Villanueva realized over the course of several decades in close collaboration with Posani. Throughout their careers, these architects worked almost exclusively as public employees under the direct sponsorship and oversight of state authorities. Many of their projects — most famously, perhaps, the campus of the Universidad Central de Venezuela in Caracas — had employed geometric abstraction, optical art, and kinetic art as their formal languages of choice.[6] The participatory dimension of these spaces, often understood as an emancipatory aspect that distanced them from the hard expressions of authority of the state that commissioned them, frequently supplemented the public dimension of state authority; it provided a "soft" public interface apparently open and inhabitable within what may have otherwise been inaccessible or even intangible spaces of authority.

In the case of the curatorial program of the Expo '67 pavilion, Soto's *Penetrable* more directly embodied the space of operation of what Fernando Coronil described as Venezuela's "magical state": it replaced the room initially planned by the "apparatuses of the bureaucracy" to showcase this state's relationship to the vast geographies and resources of Venezuelan national space under its custody.[7] Soto's artwork was conversant not only with a long tradition of interactive displays at world's fairs but also with a use of abstraction similar to the one exemplified by Magalhães and Feldman's *Doorway to Brasília*. Like the sublime plates of that book, Soto's kinetic artwork brought into being the realm where states work their magic over the territories that they control. To put it differently, the *Penetrable*'s space of altered, heightened perception represented the alchemical ground where empty plateaus become new capitals and mysterious bureaucracies stage their illusions of control.

## Image Travels

Nowhere was this kind of space given an urban dimension more clearly than at the 1968 Summer Olympics in Mexico City. Lance Wyman (1937–) and Eduardo Terrazas (1936–) were responsible for creating a "total design" campaign in the city, one comprising urban sculptures, painted pavements, and urban graphics with a common origin: Wyman's logo of radiating patterns that merged the word "Mexico," the number "68," and the five Olympic rings.[8] This campaign was only one component of the Cultural Olympiad — a wide-ranging initiative of cultural events undertaken alongside the athletic competitions.

In its attempt to create a unified brand image for the events across diverse media, the campaign (without which Otl Aicher's graphics for the Munich 1972 Olympics are hard to imagine) was grounded

Lance Wyman (American, b. 1937). Postage stamps for Mexico '68 Olympics. Courtesy of Lance Wyman.

in the culture of design that evolved in the United States during the mid-twentieth century. Aligned in its logic of production with the Ulm experiments but more intimately bound up with corporate capitalist culture, this was the context that Terrazas and Wyman encountered at the New York office of designer George Nelson, where they met a few years before the Olympics.[9]

These designers were only two members of a large team commissioned by the Mexican Olympic Committee, an institution headed by the architect Pedro Ramírez Vázquez (1919–2013), the most politically connected of twentieth-century Mexico and a prominent champion of the discipline of industrial design. The committee was directly under the authority of the single-party government of Mexico, then led by the Institutional Revolutionary Party (PRI), with whose presidential circle Ramírez Vázquez had longstanding and intimate ties. As is well known, the urban space thus envisioned was the theater of the PRI-governed state's megalomaniacal ambitions and of widespread manifestations of dissent against it, some of them expressed through an appropriation of Wyman's graphic language.[10] However, while it was rooted firmly in the fabric of the Olympic city, this graphic initiative also traveled far and wide.

Two postage stamps designed by Wyman, engineered for mobility and exchange like Magalhães's bills, illustrate how these travels worked. The radiating lines that extend from the Pyramid of the Sun in Teotihuacán on one stamp and those surrounding the Estadio Olímpico Universitario (University Olympic Stadium) at the University City of UNAM in Mexico City on another communicate across a series of specific events and places. They refer to the spatial connection established by the travels of the Olympic torch between the pre-Hispanic site and the modernist building between October 11 and 12, 1968. The night of October 11, the torch, carried by Enriqueta Basilio (1948–), the first female runner to undertake such a task in Olympic history, was spectacularly received at Teotihuacán after having traveled across Western Europe, the Atlantic, and much of Mexico on its way from Olympia, Greece, to Mexico City.

The following day — not by coincidence Columbus Day — the torch reached the UNAM Olympic stadium for the inauguration of the Olympics. A modernist building completed as part of the ambitious University City south of the Mexican capital, the stadium was mimetically connected to the volcanic topography of the region. Specifically, its form and construction method sought to refer its visitors to the pre-Hispanic eruption of the Xitle volcano, responsible for the vast lava bed where the University

City rises.[11] In Alberto Isaac's *Olimpíada en México,* the official film for Mexico '68, these events transcended the site-specificity of architecture or their ephemerality. The film portrayed virtually every stage of the travels of the torch in its fully epic dimension, especially its triumphant arrival at the stadium grandstands.[12]

## Coda: A Global Footprint

The displacement of the Olympic torch across time, space, and media so succinctly conveyed by Wyman's graphics encapsulates the political ambitions of the Mexico '68 design campaign as a whole. Its aim, simply put, was to harness design's persuasive powers in order to create, at a time of the PRI-led regime's increasingly tenuous legitimacy, a spectacle of state might on domestic and international fronts. While exceptional owing to its magnitude and the range of media it deployed, the operative logic underlying this spectacle was well ensconced in Mexican design culture and defined the majority of official design projects in the Americas during the mid-twentieth century.

In Mexico, few projects anticipated Mexico '68's territorial ambitions so clearly as the prefabricated rural schools that Ramírez Vázquez patented in 1959, shortly after he became the head of the Comité Administrador del Programa Federal de Construcción de Escuelas (CAPFCE), the federal school construction program of Mexico.[13] These schools, which included living quarters for rural

Pedro Ramírez Vázquez and Rafael Mijares, Aula Casa Rural, 1960. Archivo Ramírez Vázquez, Mexico City.

Pedro Ramírez Vázquez and Rafael Mijares, Aula Casa Rural, 1960. Archivo Ramírez Vázquez, Mexico City.

teachers, were basic frames of steel elements that, in theory, could be assembled with relative ease and at low cost. These frames could be combined with diverse infill materials depending on their regional availability. The final assembly of each of these units would reflect the local conditions of its production, but the prefabricated frame also functioned as a radical equalizer of building cultures across Mexico. Ramírez Vázquez would attempt a similar synthesis of universally modern design principles and culturally specific execution through his *Equipal* chair (1964) [checklist no. 49], which used materials like chrome-plated steel and leather but adopted the format of a "traditional," folkloric chair found throughout Mexico and bore a name derived from the Nahuatl language. Like the prefabricated schools, this chair was meant to be produced *en masse,* in this case becoming the official chair for diplomatic and government spaces in the decades after its introduction.

The designer Ernesto Gómez-Gallardo (1917–2012) produced the interiors of Ramírez Vázquez's prefabricated schools, which were envisioned as functionalist to the extreme: the entire service core of each building (wiring, pipes, and other functional components) was enclosed within one structural wall, freeing up space for teaching and living. In a staged photograph of an interior of the school prototype exhibited at the 1960 Milan Triennale, where it was awarded the Grand Prize, its propaganda dimension becomes explicit: a heroic rural teacher sits on a metal desk with built-in cabinets and a lamp holder. Surrounding him are the daily tools of his task: a library of key texts articulating Mexican national identity, images of Father Miguel Hidalgo and the heroes of the Mexican Revolution, and custom-designed slide projectors and screens.

Pedro Ramírez Vázquez and Rafael Mijares, Aula Casa Rural as built in India, late 1960s. Archivo Ramírez Vázquez, Mexico City.

¹ See Felipe Taborda and João de Souza Leite, *A herança do olhar: o design de Aloísio Magalhães* [The Heritage of Looking: The Design of Aloísio Magalhães] (Rio de Janeiro: SENAC Rio, 2003).

² Aloísio Magalhães and Eugene Feldman, *Doorway to Brasilia* (New York: G. Wittenborn, 1959).

³ Juan Pedro Posani, "Un Cubo, Dos Cubos, Tres Cubos" [One Cube, Two Cubes, Three Cubes], in *Expo 67: Villanueva, Soto* (Caracas, 1967), 59.

⁴ Ferreira Gullar, "Teoria do Não-Objeto" [Theory of the Non-Object], *Jornal do Brasil: Suplemento Dominical,* December 20–21, 1959.

⁵ Posani, "Un Cubo, Dos Cibos, Tres Cubos," 60.

⁶ See Alberto Lovera and Leopoldo Martínez Olavarría, *Desarrollo Urbano, Vivienda y Estado* [Urban Development, Housing and the State] (Caracas: Fondo Editorial ALEMO, 1996), and Viviana d'Auria, "Caracas Cultural (Be) longings," in *Latin American Modern Architectures: Ambiguous Territories,* ed. Patricio del Real and Helen Gyger (New York: Routledge, 2012), 115–34.

⁷ See Fernando Coronil, *The Magical State: Nature, Money and Modernity in Venezuela* (Chicago: University of Chicago Press, 1997).

Built in multiple locations across Mexico, especially in areas where the state, historically based in Mexico City, had very minimal representation, these schools were explicitly envisioned as both concrete avatars of its presence and as spaces for its civilizing "magic" to operate. Their radically functionalist form was literally and figuratively an extension of the Mexican state's apparatus for cultural production. This apparatus, specifically CAPFCE, was not only the patron of Ramírez Vázquez's most famous building, the Museo Nacional de Antropología (National Museum of Anthropology), inaugurated in 1964 in Mexico City, it was also a sponsor of the Cultural Olympiad.

The design of the schools gave form to the territorial ambitions of the design campaigns of most developmentalist states in the Americas, and, eventually, did so not just in theory. Not long after it was introduced in Mexico, the prototype, already modern from its inception, became fully Latin American. After UNESCO adopted it as its standard for school construction in 1966 through CONESCAL, its school-building agency, Mexico's prefabricated schools were built throughout the continent, from the tropics to the Andes, and even as far beyond the continent's boundaries as rural India.

Arguably, the construction system for the schools traveled more fluidly than Wyman's spectacular postage stamps, Magalhães's banknotes, or the custom-made components of Villanueva's pavilion at Montreal. While the temporary events and monumental new cities of the Americas were certainly influential in global design culture, perhaps the most fundamental contribution was that of these comparatively laconic prefabricated structures. Their radical design, emblematic in the most basic way of its sponsoring the state's cultural and territorial ambitions, remained active long after the prototype was introduced; its ideological circuits continued to operate, mostly undisturbed, as the prototype gradually became part of the building vernacular of the majority of the developing world.

[8] George F. Flaherty, "Responsive Eyes: Urban Logistics and Kinetic Environments for the 1968 Mexico City Olympics," *Journal of the Society of Architectural Historians* 73, no. 3 (September 2014): 372–97.

[9] Luis M. Castañeda, "Choreographing the Metropolis: Networks of Circulation and Power in Olympic Mexico," *Journal of Design History* 25, no. 3 (2012): 290–91.

[10] See Eduardo Terrazas, "Creation of Environment: Mexico 68," in *Arts of the Environment,* ed. György Kepes (New York: George Braziller, 1972).

[11] Alberto Kalach, "Architecture and Place: The Stadium of University City," in *Modernity and the Architecture of Mexico,* ed. Edward R. Burian, trans. José Carlos Fernández and Edward R. Burian (Austin: University of Texas Press, 1997), 110.

[12] Alberto Isaac, *Olimpíada en México* (1969).

[13] CAPFCE, *Ecole Rurale avec Maison pour l'Instituteur* [Rural School with a House for the Teacher] (Mexico City: Secretaría de Educación Pública, 1960), 8–9.

# PLATES

**MICHAEL VAN BEUREN** (MEXICAN, B. UNITED STATES, 1911–2004),
**KLAUS GRABE** (GERMAN, ACTIVE IN MEXICO, 1910–2004), and
**MORLEY WEBB** (AMERICAN, ACTIVE IN MEXICO)
*Alacrán* **(Scorpion) chaise,** c. 1940
Primavera wood, fabric straps; 28 x 57 x 25 ½ in.
Manufactured by Van Beuren SA de CV for Domus
Private Collection, Mexico City
[Checklist no. 68]

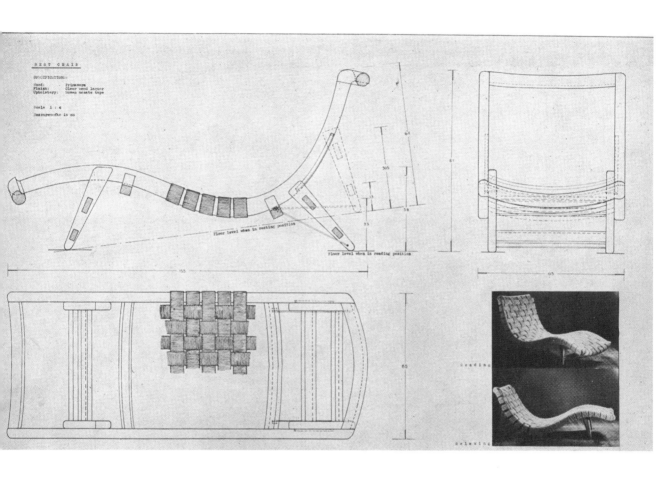

**MICHAEL VAN BEUREN** (MEXICAN, B. UNITED STATES, 1911–2004),
**KLAUS GRABE** (GERMAN, ACTIVE IN MEXICO, 1910–2004), AND
**MORLEY WEBB** (UNITED STATES, ACTIVE IN MEXICO)
*Entry Panel for MoMA Latin American Competition for
Organic Design in Home Furnishings,* c. 1940
Ink and photo collage on paper; 19 13/16 x 31 1/2 in.
The Museum of Modern Art, New York. Gift of the designers, 2008.
Digital Image © The Museum of Modern Art/Licensed by SCALA/Art
Resource, NY
[Checklist no. 69]

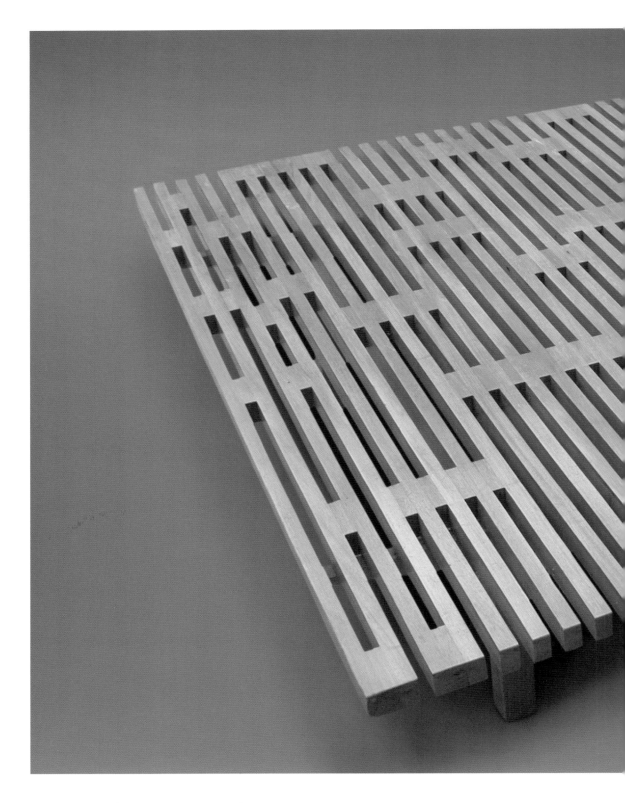

**MIGUEL ARROYO** (VENEZUELAN, 1920–2004)
**Mendoza coffee table,** 1956
Wood; 14 x 47 ¹⁄₁₆ x 44 ½ in.
Manufactured by Pedro Santana, Carpintería Colectiva
Emilio Mendoza Guardia Collection
[Checklist no. 7]

GEGO (GERTRUDE GOLDSCHMIDT, VENEZUELAN, B. GERMANY, 1912–94)
**Chair,** c. 1948
Wood; 36 x 16 ⅝ x 15 in.
Private Collection
[Checklist no. 25]

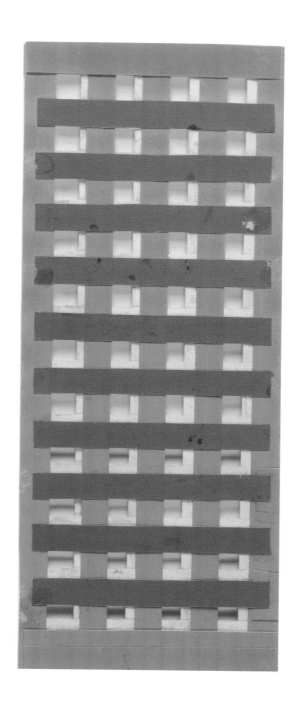

**ALEJANDRO OTERO** (VENEZUELAN, 1921–90) AND **MIGUEL ARROYO**
(VENEZUELAN, 1920–2004)
**Model for the door of Miguel Arroyo's house,** 1953
Colored paper on board; 10 ¼ x 4 ⅛ in.
Collection of Manuel Vegas Chumaceiro
[Checklist no. 38]

**MIGUEL ARROYO** (VENEZUELAN, 1920–2004)
**Pampatar butaca prototype,** 1953
Mahogany and cedar, painted; 33 ⅞ x 31 ⅞ x 24 ⁷⁄₁₆ in.
Manufactured by Pedro Santana, Carpintería Colectiva
Collection of Claudio Mendoza
[Checklist no. 3]

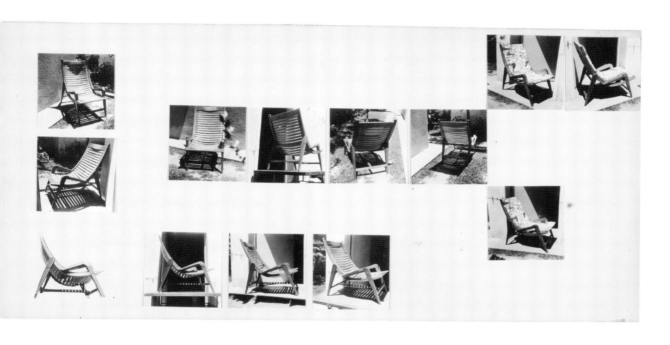

**MIGUEL ARROYO** (VENEZUELAN, 1920–2004)
**Design panel for the Pampatar butaca,** 1953
Photography on board; 18 ½ x 8 ½ in.
Private Collection
[Checklist no. 4]

**DONALD SHOEMAKER** (AMERICAN, ACTIVE IN MEXICO, 1912–98)
**Coffee table,** c. 1960
Wood, leather; 15 x 45 ½ x 21 ½ in.
Manufactured by Señal, S.A.
Private Collection, Mexico City
[Checklist no. 53]

**MICHAEL VAN BEUREN** (MEXICAN, B. UNITED STATES, 1911–2004)
**Chair and desk,** c. 1940

Pine, palm; desk: 29 ½ x 47 ¼ x 19 ⁵⁄₁₆ in.; chair: 31 ½ x 18 ½ x 17 ⁵⁄₁₆ in.

Manufactured by Van Beuren SA de CV for Domus

Collection of Jan van Beuren

[Checklist no. 66]

**CORNELIS ZITMAN** (VENEZUELAN, B. THE NETHERLANDS 1926)
*Chair No. 58,* c. 1952
Steel rod, laminated wood; 29 ½ x 18 ⅞ x 20 ⅞ in.
Manufactured by Tecoteca, C.A.
Private Collection, New York
[Checklist no. 77]

**GERALDO DE BARROS** (BRAZILIAN, 1923–98)
**Telephone bench,** c. 1960s
Enameled steel, wood, vinyl upholstery;
17 ³⁄₈ x 36 ⁵⁄₁₆ x 15 ⁹⁄₁₆ in.
Manufactured by Unilabor
Collection of Mauro Claro
[Checklist no. 20]

**PAULO WERNECK** (BRAZILIAN, 1907–1987)
*Side tables,* c. 1950s
Wood, ceramic mosaic;
10 x 16 x 20 in. each
Courtesy of Gaspar Saldanha
[Checklist no. 71]

**GENARO ÁLVAREZ** (MEXICAN, ACTIVE 20TH CENTURY)
**Coffee table,** c. 1960
Wood, metal, glass mosaic;
14 ³⁄₁₆ x 48 x 9 ¹⁄₁₆ in.
Guillermo Martínez-Cesar /Urbanity Mobiliario, Mexico City
[Checklist no. 1]

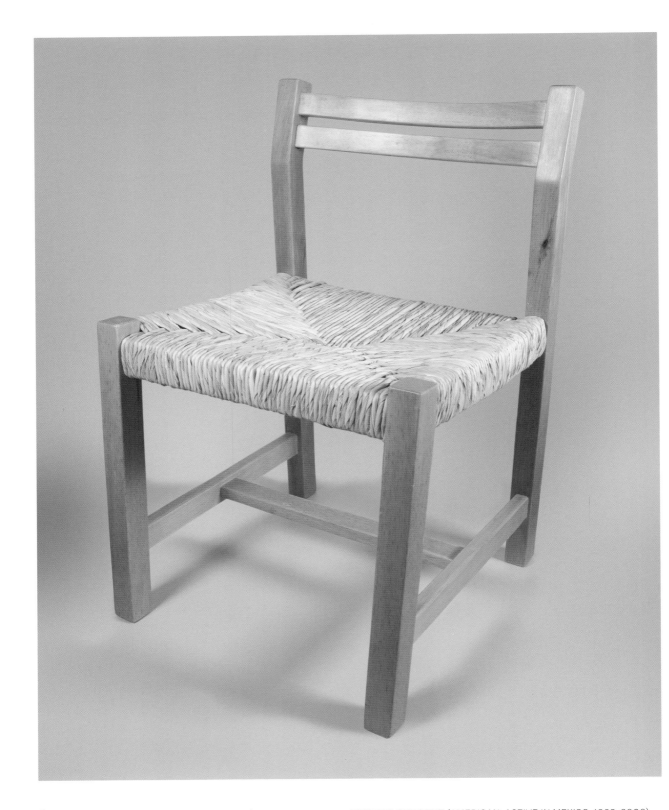

ÓSCAR HAGERMAN (MEXICAN, B. SPAIN 1936)
*Silla Arrullo* (Lullaby Chair), 1963
Pine, tule or palm; 27 ⅜ x 18 ⅛ x 20 1/16 in.
Collection of the designer
[Checklist no. 26]

CYNTHIA SARGENT (AMERICAN, ACTIVE IN MEXICO, 1922–2006)
*Scarlatti* rug, c. 1969
Wool and mohair on cotton, hand dyed and hooked; 80 x 129 in.
Riggs-Sargent Family Collection
[Checklist no. 51]

121

**PEDRO RAMÍREZ VÁZQUEZ** (MEXICAN, 1919–2013)
**Equipal armchair,** c. 1964
Leather, chromed steel; 31 x 27 x 25 in.
Collection of the Archivo Diseño y Arquitectura, Mexico City
[Checklist no. 49]

**WILLIAM SPRATLING** (AMERICAN, ACTIVE IN MEXICO, 1900–1967)
**Pitcher,** c. 1940
Silver; 8 ¼ x 8 x 7 ½ in.
Marc Navarro Gallery
[Checklist no. 54]

**LOS CASTILLO** (MEXICAN, F. 1934)

**Jar with a mockingbird,** date unknown

Silver, copper, brass, green stone; 10 ⅝ x 5 ⅞ x 3 ½ in.

Collection of Juan Rafael Coronel Rivera

[Checklist no. 30]

**LOS CASTILLO** (MEXICAN, F. 1934)

**Jar with a parrot handle,** c. 1950

Silver-plated metal, brass, abalone shell; 9 3/16 x 5 15/16 x 7 1/16 in.

Guillermo Martínez-Cesar/Urbanity Mobiliario, Mexico City

[Checklist no. 28]

**ARTURO PANI** (MEXICAN, 1915–81)
**Bar cart,** c. 1970
Enameled steel, glass, glass mirror, brass; 29 ⅛ x 18 ⅛ x 30 ¹¹⁄₁₆ in.
Private Collection, Mexico City
[Checklist no. 41]

LOS CASTILLO (MEXICAN, F. 1934)
**_Metales casados_ (married metal) tray with geometric designs,** c. 1960
Silver, copper, brass; 11 9/16 x 13 9/16 x 13/16 in.
Private Collection
[Checklist no. 29]

**JOSÉ CARLOS BORNANCINI** (BRAZILIAN, 1923–2008) AND
**NELSON IVAN PETZOLD** (BRAZILIAN, B. 1931)
**Picnic flatware set,** 1973
Stainless steel; 1 x 1½ x 8 in.
Manufactured by Hércules S.A., Brazil
Collection of Claudio Farias
[Checklist no. 17]

**ALEJANDRO OTERO** (VENEZUELAN, 1921-90)
**Bowl,** 1958-60
Enamel on copper; 2 ¾ x 6 ⅛ (diameter) in.
Private Collection, New York
[Checklist no. 39]

**MARIO SEGUSO** (B. ITALY 1929, ACTIVE IN BRAZIL)
**Bottle with stopper,** 1978
Mold-blown glass; 6 ½ x 5 ³⁄₁₆ (diameter) in.
Manufactured by Ca D'Oro Ltda., Rio de Janeiro, Brazil
Collection of The Corning Museum of Glass,
Gift of Ca D'Oro Ltda.
[Checklist no. 52]

**RUBÉN NÚÑEZ** (VENEZUELAN, 1930–2012)
**Bottle-shaped vase,** 1958
Blown glass; 12 ¹³⁄₁₆ in. tall
Collection of The Corning Museum of Glass,
Gift of Rubén Núñez
[Checklist no. 36]

**RUBÉN NÚÑEZ** (VENEZUELAN, 1930–2012)
**Vase,** 1958
Glass; 11 x 10 ⅝ (diameter) in.
Colección Mercantil, Caracas
[Checklist no. 37]

**ODILÓN ÁVALOS** (MEXICAN, 1881–1957)
**Table lamp,** c. 1950s
Blue glass, iron; 27 9/16 x 15 ¾ (diameter) in.
Manufactured by Gran Fábrica de Vidrio de Odilón Ávalos
Private Collection, Mexico City
[Checklist no. 10]

**JORGE ZALSZUPIN** (BRAZILIAN, B. POLAND 1922)
**PAULO JORGE PEDREIRA** (BRAZILIAN)
**Eva ice bucket,** 1976
Plastic; 6 $^{11}/_{16}$ x 7 $^{7}/_{8}$ (diameter) in.
Manufactured by Hevea, Brazil
Collection of Claudio Farias
[Checklist no. 73]

134

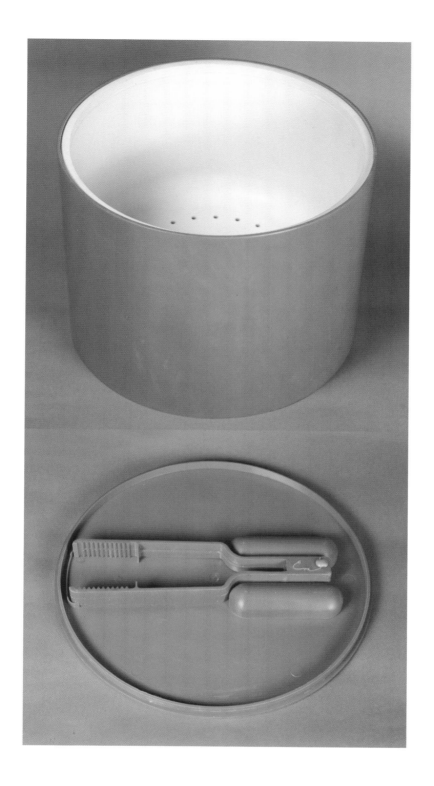

**JORGE ZALSZUPIN** (BRAZILIAN, B. POLAND 1922)
**Putskit wall-mounted organizer, No. 15515,** c. 1970–79
Plastic, mirror; 17 ½ x 4 ½ x 26 ½ in.
Manufactured by L'Atelier, São Paulo, Brazil
Courtesy of Zesty Meyers and Evan Snyderman, R & Company, New York
[Checklist no. 72]

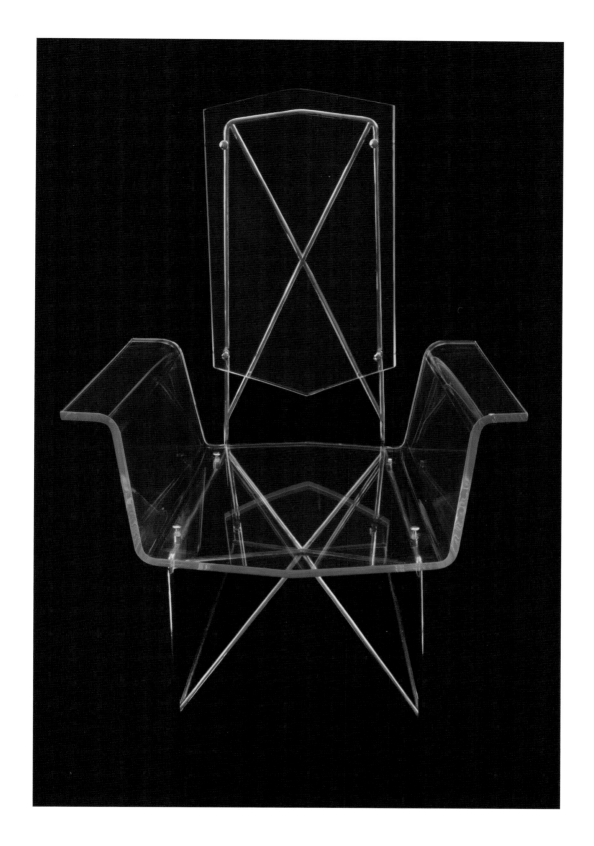

**ARTURO PANI** (MEXICAN, 1915–81)

**Chair,** c. 1970

Methacrylate, chrome-plated steel; 41 ¾ x 27 ¹⁵⁄₁₆ x 20 ¹⁄₁₆ in.

Private Collection, Mexico City

[Checklist no. 40]

**SEKA SEVERIN DE TUDJA** (VENEZUELAN, B. YUGOSLAVIA,
NOW CROATIA 1923–2007)
*E–4,* 1974
Ceramic; 10 ¼ x 11 ⅞ (diameter) in.
Colección Patricia Phelps de Cisneros
[checklist no. 64]

**CRISTINA MERCHÁN** (VENEZUELAN, 1927–87)
**Bowl,** 1957
Ceramic; 2 ⅝ x 6 ⅝ (diameter) in.
Private Collection, New York
[Checklist no. 34]

**TECLA TOFANO** (VENEZUELAN, B. ITALY 1927–95)

**Pitcher,** 1963

Earthenware with gray and white slip, gas fired;

8 ¼ x 6 ⁵⁄₁₆ x 7 ½ in.

Private Collection

[Checklist no. 59]

**JOSÉ FEHER** (MEXICAN, B. HUNGARY 1902–88)
**Zoomorphic pitcher,** c. 1960
Ceramic; 11 7/16 x 10 5/8 x 6 5/16 in.
Manufactured by Cerámica Artística de Texcoco
Collection of Daniel and Pablo Feher
[Checklist no. 23]

**MARÍA LUISA ZULOAGA DE TOVAR** (VENEZUELAN, 1902–92)
**Vase decorated with Pre-Hispanic motifs,** 1968
Glazed earthenware; 6 ⅝ x 8 ⁷⁄₁₆ in.
Private Collection, New York
[Checklist no. 62]

**SEKA SEVERIN DE TUDJA** (VENEZUELAN, B. YUGOSLAVIA,
NOW CROATIA 1923-2007)
**Dish,** c. 1950s
Ceramic; ½ x 10 ¾ (diameter) in.
Private Collection, New York
[Checklist no. 63]

**ROBERTO BURLE MARX** (BRAZILIAN, 1909–94)
**Bowl,** c. 1970
Glazed ceramic; 5 ½ x 4 ⁵⁄₁₆ x 3 ¹¹⁄₁₆ in.
Collection of Jacques Leenhardt
[Checklist no. 18]

**ROBERTO BURLE MARX** (BRAZILIAN, 1909–94)
**Plate,** c. 1970
Glazed ceramic; 7 ⅞ in. diameter
Collection of Jacques Leenhardt
[Checklist no. 19]

**MIGUEL PINEDA** (MEXICAN, B. 1940)
**Plate,** c. 1960
Enamel on copper; 10 ⅝ x 10 ¹³⁄₁₆ x 1 in.
Galería Julio de la Torre, Mexico City
[Checklist no. 42]

**ALDEMIR MARTINS** (BRAZILIAN, 1922–2006)
*Cangaceiro* **dish,** c. 1966
Melamine; 7 ⅞ x 7 ⅞ in.
Manufactured by Goyana Melcrome
Private Collection
[Checklist no. 31]

**FÉLIX TISSOT** (AMERICAN, B. FRANCE 1909–D. MEXICO 1989)

**Platter,** c. 1950

Glazed ceramic; ½ x 15 x 11 in.

Manufactured by Cerámica de Taxco, S.A.

Private Collection, New York

[Checklist no. 57]

**FÉLIX TISSOT** (AMERICAN, B. FRANCE 1909–D. MEXICO 1989)
**Vase,** c. 1960
Ceramic, hand-painted and fired at a high temperature;
11 7/16 x 13 3/8 in.
Manufactured by Cerámica de Taxco, S.A.
Collection of Ione Tissot
[Checklist no. 58]

**GOTTFRIED** (GERMAN, ACTIVE IN VENEZUELA, B. 1929) AND
**THEKLA ZIELKE** (GERMAN, ACTIVE IN VENEZUELA, B. 1928)
**Decanter and tumbler set,** c. 1960
Ceramic; decanter: 6 ⅞ x 4 ¹⁵⁄₁₆ x 4 ¹⁵⁄₁₆ in.;
tumblers: 1 ¾ x 2 (diameter) in.
Manufactued by Gotek, Colonia Tovar
Private Collection, New York
[Checklist no. 75]

**UNIDENTIFIED DESIGNER** (MEXICO)
**Pitcher and glasses,** c. 1970
Glass, metal; pitcher: 10 ⅝ x 6 ½ x 4 ⁵⁄₁₆ in.;
glasses: 7 ½, 2 ¹⁵⁄₁₆ (diameter) in.
Manufactured by Vidrio de Texcoco
Private Collection, Mexico City
[Checklist no. 80]

**CRISTINA MERCHÁN** (VENEZUELAN, 1927–87)
**Tea set,** 1961
Ceramic, wood; dimensions variable
Colección Mercantil, Caracas
[Checklist no. 33]

**CRISTINA MERCHÁN** (VENEZUELAN, 1927–87)
**Elongated ovoid with relief,** 1976
Stoneware with olive green glaze; 8 ¹¹⁄₁₆ x 5 ⅛ (diameter) in.
Private Collection
[Checklist no. 35]

**TECLA TOFANO** (VENEZUELAN, B. ITALY, 1927–95)
**Bottle with phallic stopper,** early 1970s
Glazed ceramic; 5 ½ x 10 ⁷⁄₁₆ x 10 ⁵⁄₈ in.
Colección Mercantil, Caracas
[Checklist no. 61]

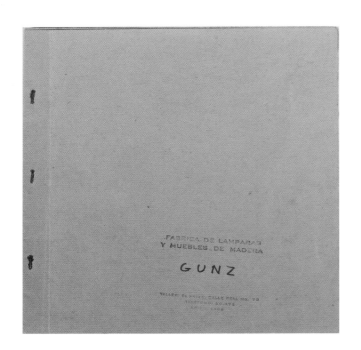

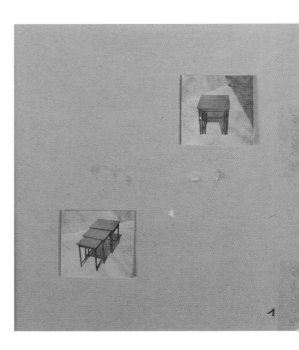

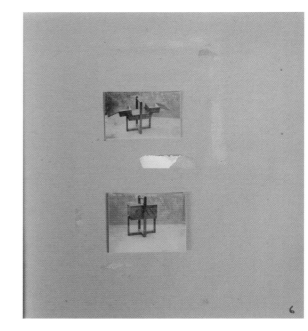

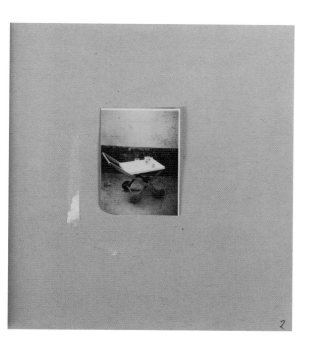

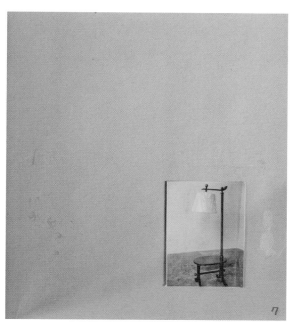

GEGO (GERTRUDE GOLDSCHMIDT, VENEZUELAN, B. GERMANY 1912–94)
**Gunz Lamp and Furniture Factory catalogue maquette,**
c. 1943
Booklet; 6 ⅝ x 6 ⅝ in.
Collection of the Fundación Gego Archive
[Checklist no. 24]

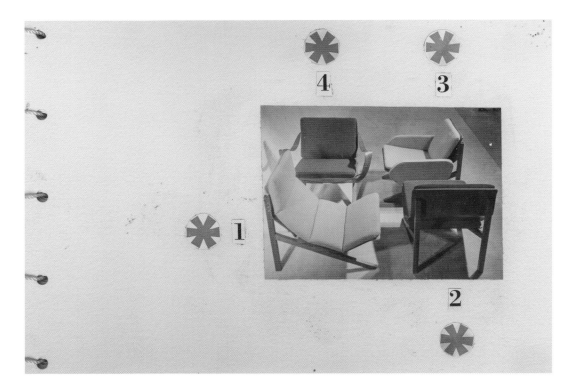

**CORNELIS ZITMAN** (VENEZUELAN, B. THE NETHERLANDS 1926)
**Maquette for Tecoteca catalogue,** 1957
with logo design **VITTORIO GARATTI** (ITALIAN, ACTIVE IN VENEZUELA, B. 1927)
7 x 10 x 1¼ in.
Collection of Cornelis Zitman, Caracas
[Checklist no. 78]

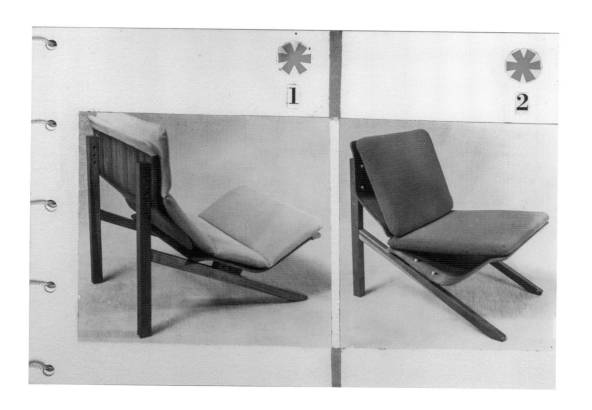

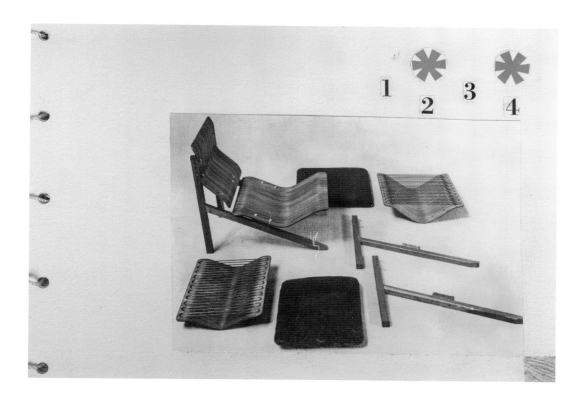

159

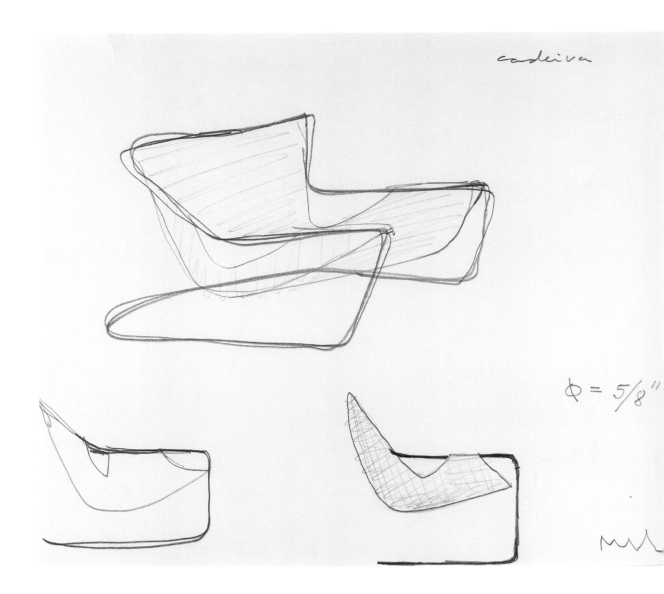

**PAULO MENDES DA ROCHA** (BRAZILIAN, B. 1928)
**Study for the Paulistano armchair,** date unknown (chair
designed 1957)
Graphite on paper; 13 ¾ x 12 ⅝ in.
Private Collection
[Checklist no. 32]

**CORNELIS ZITMAN** (VENEZUELAN, B. THE NETHERLANDS 1926)
**Model for a chair,** 1950
Enameled steel wire, cotton cord; 3 ⅜ x 2 x 2 ⅛ in.
Collection of Cornelis Zitman, Caracas
[Checklist no. 76]

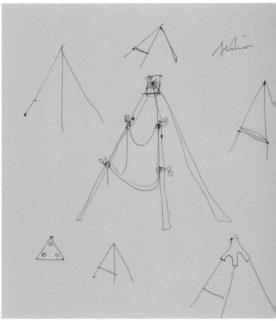

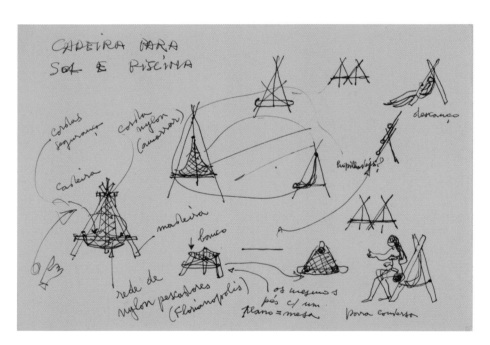

**LINA BO BARDI** (BRAZILIAN, B. ITALY, 1914–92)

Top left:

**Drawing for the *Beira de Estrada Chair,*** 1967

Felt tip pen on paper; 4 x 5 ⅞ in.

Collection of Instituto Lina Bo e P. M. Bardi

[Checklist no. 13]

Top right:

**Drawing for the *Beira de Estrada Chair,*** 1967

Ballpoint pen on paper; 7 ¾ x 7 ⁵⁄₁₆ in.

Collection of Instituto Lina Bo e P. M. Bardi

[Checklist no. 16]

Above:

**Drawing for the *Beira de Estrada Chair,*** 1967

Felt tip pen on paper; 6 x 8 ⁷⁄₁₆ in.

Collection of Instituto Lina Bo e P. M. Bardi

[Checklist no. 14]

Opposite:

**Drawing for the *Beira de Estrada Chair,*** 1967

Felt tip pen on paper; 9 ¾ x 6 ⅛ in.

Collection of Instituto Lina Bo e P. M. Bardi

[Checklist no. 15]

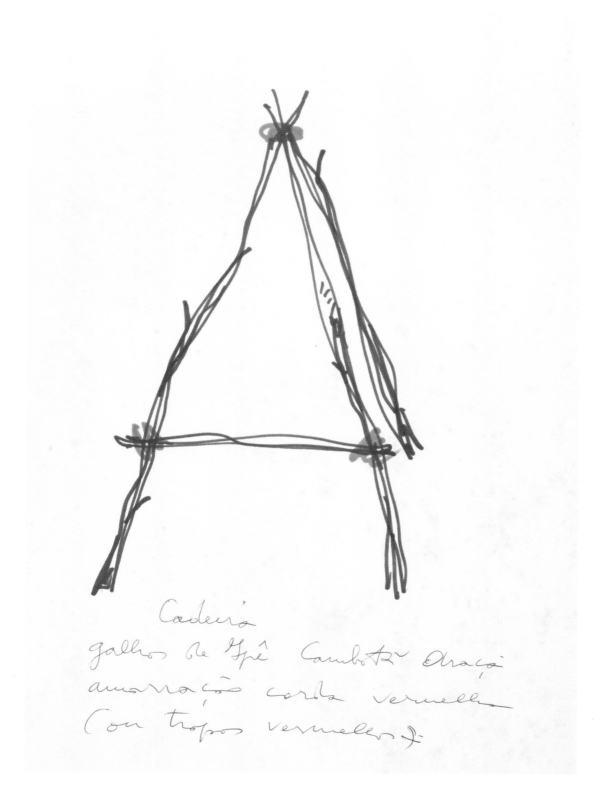

Cadeira
galhos de Ipê Cambotã Oração
amarração corda vermelha
(com trapos vermelhos)

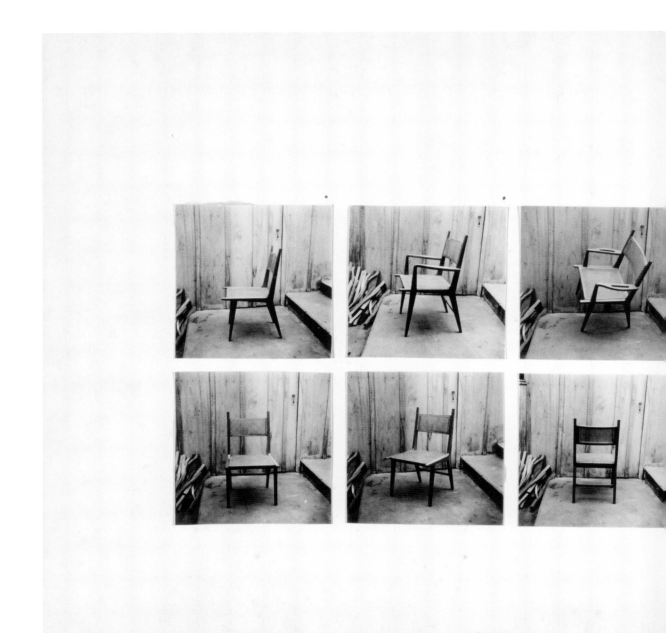

**MIGUEL ARROYO** (VENEZUELAN, 1920–2004)
**Design panel for the Pampatar dining armchair,** 1953
Photography on board; 18 ½ x 8 ½ in.
Private Collection
[Checklist no. 5]

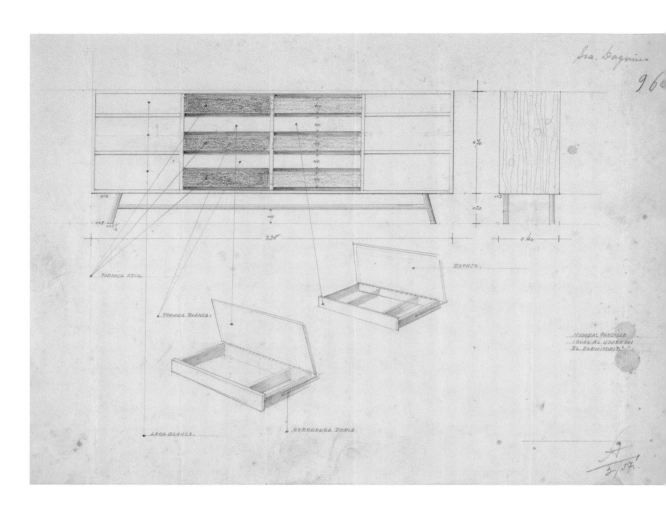

**MIGUEL ARROYO** (VENEZUELAN, 1920–2004)
**Design for Mrs. Dagnino's vanity chest,** 1957
Pencil and crayon on notebook paper; 12 x 18 ⅛ in.
Private Collection
[Checklist no. 8]

**MIGUEL ARROYO** (VENEZUELAN, 1920–2004)
**Study for Inocente and Josefina Palacios
dining room, Quinta Caurimare, Caracas,** 1955
Pencil on Lana Docelles paper; 19 ⅞ x 25 ¹³⁄₁₆ in.
Private Collection
[Checklist no. 6]

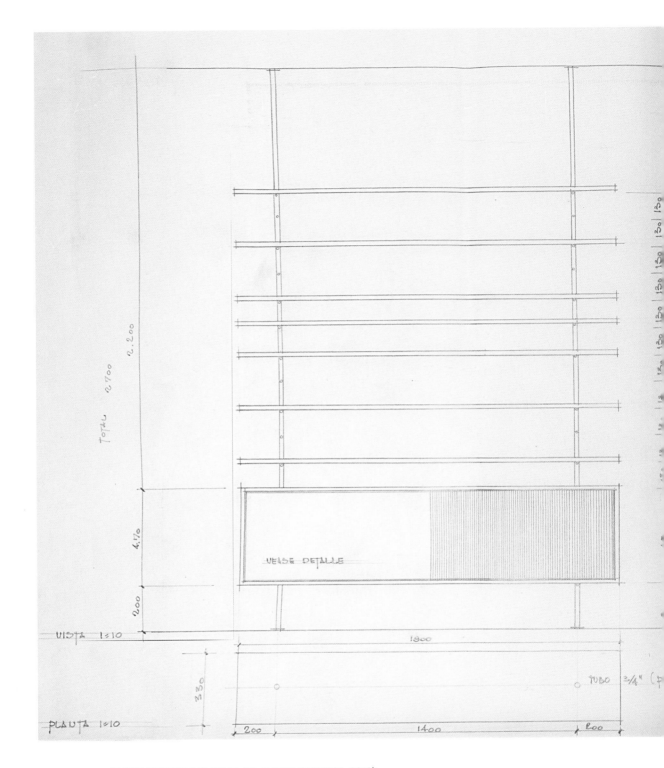

**KLAUS HEUFER** (VENEZUELAN, B. GERMANY 1923–2013)
**Design for a bookshelf for Joh Johannson's
apartment in Caracas,** c. 1960s
Graphite on tracing paper; 14 3/16 x 26 3/8 in.
Private Collection, New York
[Checklist no. 27]

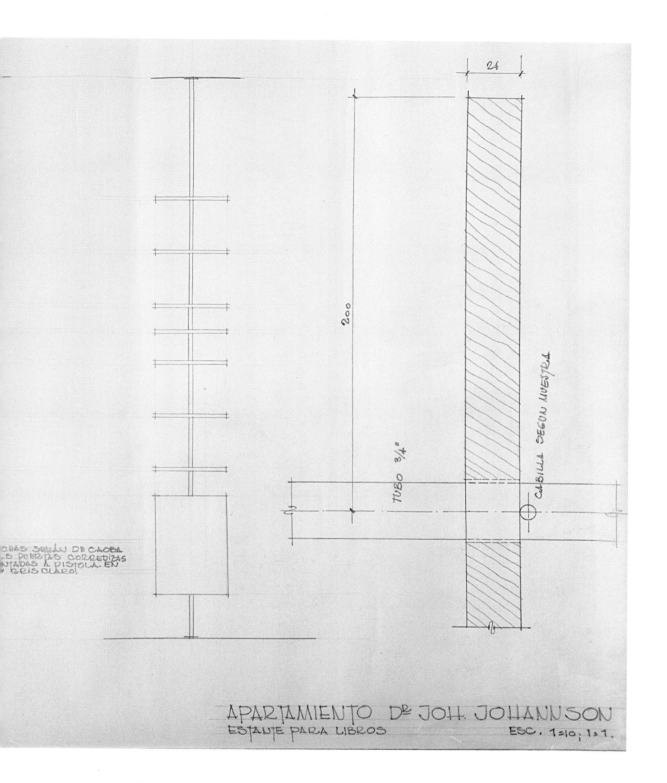

24

200

TUBO 3/4"

CABILLA SEGUN MUESTRA

...CHAS SERÁN DE CAOBA
...O PUERTAS CORREDIZAS
...NTADAS A PISTOLA. EN
... GRIS CLARO.

APARTAMIENTO Dº JOH. JOHANNSON

ESTANTE PARA LIBROS            ESC. 1=10; 1:1.

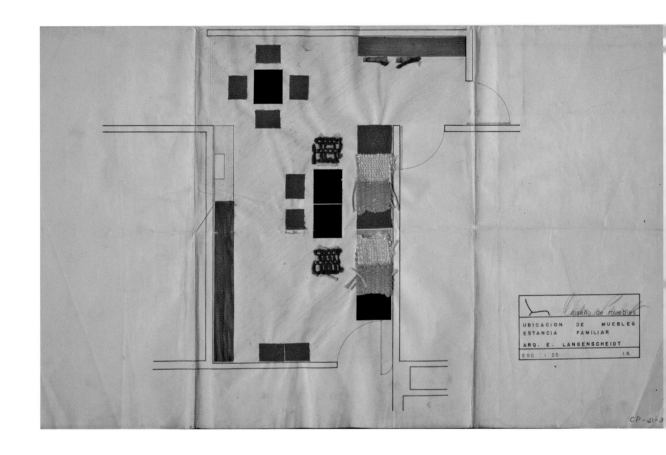

CLARA PORSET (MEXICAN, B. CUBA, 1895–1981)
**Interior for Arq. Enrique Langenscheidt,** c. 1950
Ink on paper and fabric samples;
14 9/16 x 24 in.
Archivo Clara Porset, Centro de Investigaciones de
Diseño Industrial, Facultad de Arquitectura, Universidad
Nacional Autónoma de México, Mexico City
[Checklist no. 43]

SALA

CLARA PORSET (MEXICAN, B. CUBA, 1895–1981)
**Interior design for a living room,** c. 1960
Graphite and color pencil on paper;
8 ⅞ x 11 ¹³⁄₁₆ in.
Archivo Clara Porset, Centro de Investigaciones de Diseño
Industrial, Facultad de Arquitectura, Universidad Nacional
Autónoma de México, Mexico City
[Checklist no. 46]

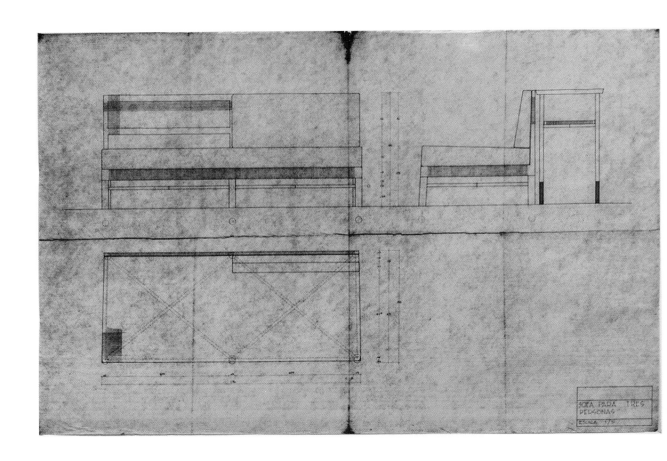

**CLARA PORSET** (MEXICAN, B. CUBA, 1895–1981)

**Three-seat sofa,** c. 1950

Heliographic print;

35 x 24 in.

Private Collection, Mexico City

[Checklist no. 47]

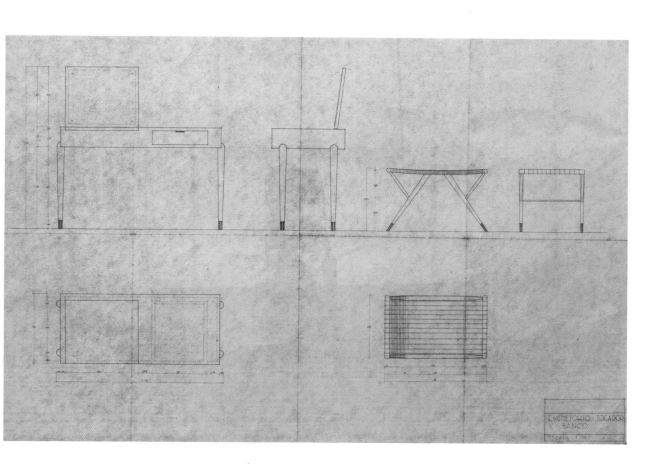

**CLARA PORSET** (MEXICAN, B. CUBA, 1895–1981)
**Writing desk vanity,** c. 1950
Heliographic print;
35 x 24 in.
Private Collection, Mexico City
[Checklist no. 48]

**An installation image of *Moderno* at Americas Society, 2015.**

[Checklist nos. 22, 50, 53, 64, 65, 88]

# HISTORICAL TEXTS

Gregori Warchavchik's Modernist House on Santa Cruz Street, São Paulo, Brazil, built 1927–1928.
Courtesy of the Gregori Warchavchik Collection.

# EXHIBITION OF A MODERNIST HOUSE
## (considerations)

### MÁRIO DE ANDRADE*

One of the things that most distinguishes Architecture from the other Fine Arts (if it is recognized as one of the Fine Arts, which is debatable) is its liberation of individualism. We speak of Dante's *Inferno,* of Velázquez's *Nymphs,* of Myron's *Discus Thrower.* And even when we speak of *The Lusíadas* or *The Night Watch,* the creator of these works is acting on the complexity of our appreciation of things, not only as an integral part but as a part primarily and absolutely fundamental, one even enhanced by them. And when we listen to music or look at a pretty painting, we reflexively ask, "Whose is it?"

Now, with true Architecture that generally doesn't happen. No one thinks to ask who did the sublime St. Peter's apse, and it borders on pretentiousness to speak the names of the Florentine architects in public. And, if we carefully examine our complex appreciation, we realize that indubitably for the totality of an architectural work, the name of its creator adds almost nothing. It will add only subsequently as a curiosity, a *carioca* itch for erudition or appetite for idle chatter.

But the same thing doesn't happen when Architecture betrays its principles and totally turns into a disinterested Fine Art. "Bernini's colonnade," "Garnier's Opera House," and "the Eiffel Tower" are clichés of artistic discourse. Many modernists may beg to differ, seeing me attack the Eiffel Tower, but if that bold effort from the 1889 Universal Exhibition could have useful consequences for

Engineering, it was and always will be an architectural falsification. The paths that have been given it are not its own, and other architectural devices would fill them better.

These observations are, with some rare exceptions, inarguably true. Now, if no one thinks about the Gothic or Italian Renaissance architects when seeing their admirable works, it is because Architecture departs greatly from creative individuality. It departs from creative imagination itself, not only because of the immediately practical ends that must be met but also the most primordial importance that, in its broadest conception, bears historical determinism.

Currently, we are still talking about "the houses of the engineer Warchavchik," the way we speak of the neo-Gothic house of Engineer So-and-so, merely because Gregori Warchavchik was the first and almost only one to build modernist houses in São Paulo. But let three more engineers begin constructing houses of that type here, and the name of Warchavchik will vanish. He will always be highly honored in our architectural history, of course, but that's a fine point. To the world and to us, Warchavchik's houses will be just houses. . . by no one: Architecture.

Something else interesting has happened that will clarify still further what I am stating: if an ordinary engineer were to build a house similar to those of [Francisco de Paula] Ramos de Azevedo or Mr. Dácio de Moraes, everyone would know him to be a plagiarist. That was just what was said *sub rosa,* and, be it noted, incorrectly about our Teatro Municipal for having adopted the three-part division of Garnier's Opera House. So, if anyone wishes houses in the style of Warchavchik, no one will call him a plagiarist. He is a modernist architect. He is making Architecture.

All of this proves, I believe, that the current era is succeeding in that rare thing that happens with isolated civilizations or with fundamental mutations in a civilization: attaining an architecture with its own style.

If I owned a modernist house (furnished, obviously, completely modernistically like the house on exhibit), among the modern pieces of furniture in the living room I would place a Louis XV chair. Picture that in your head: what sensation would it cause? The only admissible one in the presence of a Louis XV chair: the sensation of an art object. A Louis XV chair isn't a chair — it's an art object and as such can decorate our lives. I'm not to blame if people in those days sat around on art objects instead of sitting in chairs, but it must be remembered that dukes and duchesses were themselves art objects back then.

But, of course, I would decorate my living room with a *legitimate* Louis XV chair and not with a "false" one. The false might be well made and pretty, but it's false, and life is more than just beauty. The false may possess a lot of exterior glitter, but that's vanity, a despicable thing. It doesn't possess that proud and interior reason for being that legitimates a past. Between an admirable fake da Vinci and a mediocre legitimate Ettore Tito, only the nouveau riche of all external and internal riches prefer the fake.

Now, modernist architecture does not belie or destroy any of the "true" styles of architecture that history enumerates. But if we imagine Amiens [Cathedral] next to the Parthenon, naturally, the two styles *hurlent d'être ensemble* [screaming/howling at being together]. The same way that a modernist house, like those of Gregori Warchavchik, screams next to the bungalows, neocolonial dwellings, puddings, marmalades, and syrups seen out there.

There is a difference: next to each other, the Parthenon and Amiens [Cathedral] both scream. The Parthenon screams and Amiens screams. A Warchavchik house next to a neocolonial, whether Spanish or Portuguese, screams alone. The bungalow doesn't scream. It is quite calm in its discombobulated unconsciousness, in its devout and Boeotian ignorance. We are the ones who feel ashamed for it, the same way that any well-born person, facing the braggadocio of the nouveau riche, the machinations of an arriviste, suffers instead of laughing.

Reducing this sensation of ours of shame to language a bit more technical, we perceive that the case is always the same issue of the "false." The neocolonial, the bungalow, the neo-Florentine are "false," as much as a cultured pearl, an object of Flosel, or the blameless Raphael in a São Paulo collection. They lack that proud force of legitimacy that justifies and enhances even their defects. I am not interested in the fact that they are, in the infinite majority of cases, heinous falsifications. It's not the concept of the distorting falsification of architectural principles that worries me now, it's the notion of the *faux,* of that which is made to deceive, of extratemporaneous acts. A woman prefers a real diamond to a fake one. We prefer a canvas by the *douanier* Rousseau to the fake ones of his that are showing up, or a Stravinsky piece to one by his numerous imitators. A Warchavchik house screams next to the others, screams proudly because it is legitimate. It is as much a force of nature as the existence of Alexander or a storm. A storm on stage can be theatrically admirable but will never be horrifying. And that is why the destiny of theater will never be to imitate nature (man included) but to transport it, as do Chaplin, Shakespeare, and the *Bumba-meu-Boi.*[1] I use "theater" in the more general sense to include cinematography.

Now, Architecture also has a destiny, which does not consist of being pretty but of adequately sheltering not a body but a human being, with a body and a soul as well. Florentine souls were well sheltered during the Renaissance. And the Greeks and the Chinese. And the mixed-race and *emboabas*[2] of eighteenth-century Ouro Preto, who had never ceased to contemplate building a São Francisco in Gothic or Manueline style. We too, if present-day souls, have to shelter our souls in the present-day houses that are called "modernist." Everything else is lack of shelter, disrespect for itself, and only serves to deceive. It is the "false."

---

\* Editor's note: This text was originally published in Portuguese as "Esposição duma casa modernista (considerações)," *Diário Nacional*, São Paulo, Brazil, April 5, 1930. Reproduced in *Depoimentos*, N. 2 (São Paulo: Centro de Estudos Brasileiros/GFAU, 1966).

[1] The *Bumba-meu-Boi* is a folkloric dance of the Brazilian Northeast.

[2] *Emboabas* was the designation applied in the colonial period to those who went to present-day Minas Gerais in search of gold (translator's note).

# NORTH AMERICAN INTERIORS: CONTEMPORARY EXAMPLES

## CLARA PORSET*

It is interesting to note how little the United States appears to understand about the functionality of interiors — in spite of having created their fantastic skyscrapers, which are the epitome of functional architecture.

New York City may be home to more atrocities than anywhere else in terms of contemporary interiors, which are generally referred to as being modernist in style.

Inspired by the decorations presented at the 1925 Exhibition in Paris — regrettably, the worst of them—they exude vulgar ostentation and unseemly gaudiness.

They are devoid of sobriety and sincere simplicity.

They consist of an assortment of furniture and objects that have little in common with each other.

The furniture is chosen on an individual basis, as it was in the past, for purely decorative reasons—and is as baroque as any Louis XV piece.

Gold and silver, black for dramatic effect, a profusion of drapes and cushions, improbable lamps, provincial theater decorations, and so on. This describes most of the interiors, referred to as modern, that are for sale in New York.

A restaurant in New York designed by John Vassos.

One is surprised by this evident lack of understanding, while on the other side of the Atlantic one sees more and more of the artistic rationalism of Le Corbusier, J. J. P. Oud, and Gropius. The only explanation would seem to be that America is an extremely young country that still demands royal-style luxury with over-stuffed furniture and plenty of bright, colorful cushions. These interiors reflect the country's childish spirit and its craving for magnificent, complicated surroundings that create a barrier between an American's working life and his home, which is seen as a place of refuge and the antithesis of the former.

The preceding comments, of course, reflect the impression made by what one sees everywhere, but do not apply to the work produced by a select minority that is as good here as it is anywhere. The furniture mentioned above is mass produced and undoubtedly sets the standard for contemporary North American interiors.

There are, however, several artists among that select minority who are sensitive to the new aesthetic and skillful interpreters of their inspiration.

One of them is the Greek-American John Vassos, the creator of the interiors illustrated here—including views of a penthouse and a restaurant—that show how well he has understood the essential characteristics involved in these projects.

The balanced composition of vertical and horizontal elements, with smooth surfaces and a soft and cleverly arranged color scheme, transform these interiors into a restful place that contributes to a person's wellbeing; that is, the sort of environment that is so often sought after and so infrequently achieved.

The back side of the corner divan is used as a convenient bookshelf. New York penthouse designed by John Vassos.

*  Editor's note: This text was originally published in Spanish as "Interiores norteamericanos. Los de ahora," *Social* (Havana, Cuba) 16, no. 8 (August 1931).

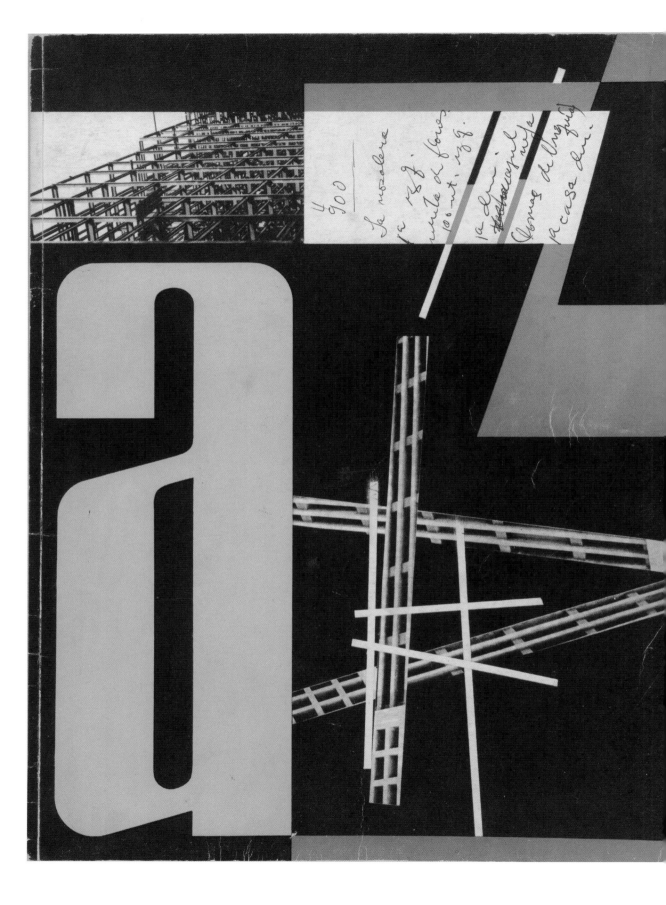

184

# MODERN FURNITURE FOR A COLONIAL HOUSE

## MIGUEL ARROYO*

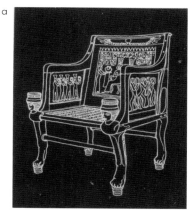

a

About six months ago, Mr. Alfredo Boulton asked me to design the furniture for a house he had acquired in Pampatar (on the Isla de Margarita). The house faces the beach and is designed in a style that could be described as "colonial." He wanted modern furniture that would be compatible with the style of the house; he also wanted me to use materials that were commonly used in Venezuela until the beginning of the century — such as wicker, marble, and so on — that would be perfectly suited to the climate of the region.

b

This text and the accompanying illustrations describe the various problems I encountered over the course of this assignment and the general considerations I took into account before I started working on the design. I have presented the different points in the same order in which they arose during the process of design and manufacture.

### the requirements

c

### general requirements
a) Keep in mind, while designing the furniture, that the climate is warm (hot during the day and cool at night).
b) Preferably use local Venezuelan materials.
c) Create a modern style that does not clash with the colonial style of the house.
d) The furniture should be light, easy to clean and move, and so on.
e) Create a bright, uncomplicated environment.
f) Owing to the corrosive effect of the salty air, avoid the use of metals as much as possible.

a    egyptian chair. approximately 1400 BC.
b    french chair. louis XV style. eighteenth century.
c    english chair. Adam style. eighteenth century.
d    carlos mollino chair. italy.
e    charles eames chair. USA.

d

e

f

## specific requirements

### Dining Room–Living Room
The dining room–living room space is thirteen meters long by five meters, fifty centimeters wide. There are to be three tables and twelve chairs in the dining room section, and six chairs, two tables, a sofa or divan, and a cabinet for books, a record player, and records in the living room area.

### Dining Room
The three tables are to be arranged in a "U" shape to accommodate twelve people, who will sit on the outside of the "U," leaving the inside for table service.

The seats and backs of the chairs are to be made of wicker (a very suitable material for the climate), and the tabletops are to be made of Venezuelan marble (Mr. Boulton has already picked out some beautiful green marble slabs from a quarry in Margarita).

GUESTS

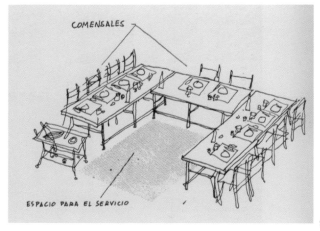

FOOD SERVICE AREA

g

f g   dining room.

h   floor plan of the living room – dining room.

## The Style

Before starting to work on the design of the furniture, we thought it would be helpful to review the styles that have been used in similar architectural environments, so that we might see how well they blended with particular buildings and lifestyles. Essentially, we were seeking a *spiritual* affinity with colonial furniture, so of course we wanted to look at examples of that style to see how close we might be able to come. Unfortunately, we had very little information at our disposal other than vague memories of furniture we remembered having seen when we were children, and the pieces displayed at the Museo de Arte Colonial (Museum of Colonial Art) and the house where Simón Bolívar was born. We therefore studied the furniture at the museum and were able to determine that those pieces shared a number of more or less constant features, as follows:

a)  A heavy, simple look (the wood used was six or more centimeters thick).
b)  Scale: Generally speaking, large in terms of the human body.
c)  Materials: Wooden frames; leather seats and backs; cloth and cotton upholstery was usually used on furniture that was neither indigenous to Venezuela nor made in Spain.
d)  The use of lathe-turned pieces and ornamental carving.
e)  A preference for the use of curves, either as an ornamental feature or as part of the frame.
f)  Evidence of craftsman-like skill and technique.

BEACH ACCESS

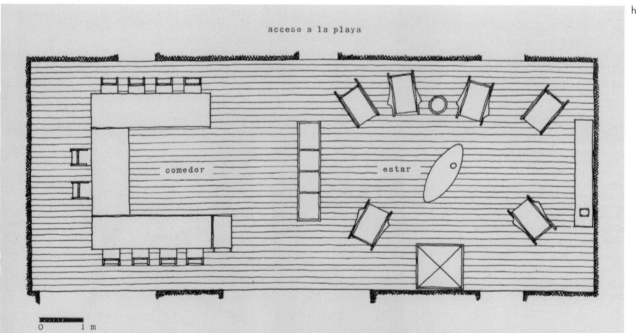

acceso a la playa

comedor

estar

DINING ROOM

LIVING ROOM

But none of these features was found to be common to every piece of furniture reviewed; there were different features that were common among designs other than the Spanish or indigenous models, such as Chippendale and other styles whose finely wrought, intricate curves are dramatically different from the rustic grace and simplicity of the *ture* [a small X-shaped Venezuelan chair of pre-Hispanic origins].

Our research thus yielded more questions than answers because the furniture we reviewed reflected both the architectural style and the lifestyle of its particular period; it would therefore have been absurd to use its features as the basis for the designs we envisioned. It seemed to us, for example, that Chippendale chairs — whose refined style was perfectly suited to our ancestors' slightly, or decidedly, stiff social customs — were incompatible with the size of the rooms and the thickness of the walls and columns and were, in fact, out of place in the spacious, spare interior of a colonial house.

The second style-related problem we encountered was as follows: It occurred to us that people have had to sit, eat, rest, and so on since time immemorial; over time, they have developed ways of doing those things, and those ways are universal. There must therefore be a corresponding universality attached to the solutions that spawned the objects that are used to perform each of the abovementioned functions. So, if these solutions are universal, how does one go about making a distinctly local kind of furniture that is totally different from any other furniture?

This line of questioning prompted us to take a close look at different styles of furniture from earlier periods, and we concluded that the differences between one style and another were not structural but ornamental. It is the ornamentation that gives, for example, seventeenth-century French furniture its own unique style and distinguishes it from furniture made in other countries, even when produced during the same period.

The three chairs shown in Figures a, b, and c illustrate this point about the ornamentation. Note that the design is essentially the same; the arrangement of structural elements is based on the same logic, but the ornamental elements are what give each chair its own unique character: The carved heads and figures on the Egyptian chair, the plant motifs on the French chair, and the grooved legs on the English chair.

None of the above, however, *totally* negates the local character of contemporary furniture: it merely suggests that the differences are more subtle and therefore more difficult to perceive. These days we cannot — and should not — rely on the ornamentation as a guide but should instead look at the origin of the furniture if we really want to understand what we might describe as its local character.

To illustrate the "subtleties" mentioned above, let us consider the examples of Italian and North American furniture (see Figures d and e). Both schools — if we might call them that — are influenced by the same principles of functionality and adaptability that apply in contemporary manufacturing. There are, however, fundamental differences between these two styles of furniture. Italian manufacturers tend to blend machine production with handcraft techniques that, on the whole, lead to finer, more sensitive designs than the North American alternative. Most Italian furniture has more parts and a wider range of curves and thicknesses than the models produced in the United States, which are more likely to be machine manufactured. The combination of handcraft technique and machine production is what gives Italian furniture its own unique flavor, because it includes the

j          photographs by m. arroyo.

i    dining room: chair without arms.
j k  dining room: chair with arms. the seat and back
     are made of wicker.
l n  living room chair. the seat and back are made of
     white cord.
m    colonial *butaque* chair.

k

finest aspects of Italian tradition, which eschews the obvious in favor of greater subtlety. So, what are the differences in the example we were discussing above? One of the things that struck us as odd at the Museo de Arte Colonial was the eclectic range of styles in use during the colonial period. It occurred to us that a possible explanation might be that style was thought to have a potential for shock value even when, in some cases, it meant sacrificing the physical comfort of the user.

n

l

m

living room chair. wooden slats, shaped to accommodate the human body, are mounted on the curved frame. the spaces between the slats provide ventilation.

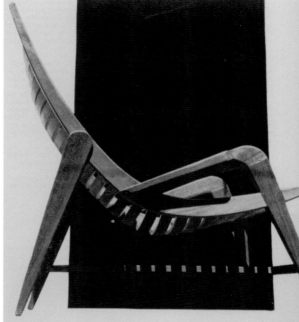

photograph by m. a

furniture in the architectural environment.
there is a vertical composition by alejandro otero mounted on the
back wall, and a mobile sculpture by [alexander] calder hanging from
the ceiling. A colonial cupboard stands against the wall on the right.
the juxtaposition of contrasting elements — some modern, some old —
is invigorating and creates a sense and scale of the period.

There are three clearly defined environments there. One of them is intimidating and represented by the office or study, where the size of the furniture, and even its color, seem to conspire to make humans feel small. Another one — the room on the left for example — is what we might describe as "court-like," in which the French and English furniture, Venetian mirrors, and curved lines of the gold-painted chairs, tables, lamps, etc., convey a mood of frivolity that prompts thoughts of ladies and gentlemen sitting in "elegant" though occasionally uncomfortable positions.

The third environment, which could be described as "organic," consists of indigenous or creole furniture, such as the *ture,* the *butaque* chair [a colonial low chair with inclined seat and back derived from pre-Hispanic types], the *baqueta* chair [a traditional cowhide], the *coriana* chair [from Coro, Venezuela], and the *tinajero* [a piece of furniture in which a family's drinking water is kept in an earthenware jar]. These are all examples of very straightforward designs; furniture of this kind was not intended to "beautify" but to make life more comfortable. That is why it was almost never found in living rooms but was used in a home's more intimate spaces and rooms — the closest thing to an organic environment — where a family would retire to rest after sitting stiffly in their Chippendale chairs during a social gathering. In these family rooms, they might even drink directly from the ladle hanging on the *tinajero,* which should really only ever be used to draw water from the jar.

The unpretentious functionality of creole and indigenous furniture is the quality we have sought to emulate in our designs.

It would be remiss of us not to mention Pedro Santana, the excellent craftsman from the Canary Islands who assisted us at every turn with his advice and his fine craftsmanship.


**Dining Room Tables**
Capacity: Twelve people sitting on one of the sides. These tables involved the following problems:

a)  They could not be more than eighty centimeters wide because the food servers were to approach from the front and because that was the maximum width of the available marble slabs.
b)  The legs were to be narrow, so as not to interfere with the guests' movements, and were to be compatible with the chair design; they also had to be strong enough to support approximately 200 kilos (the weight of the marble top and the downward pressure exerted by the guests).
c)  The crossbeams were to be arranged so that they were not in the way of the guests' legs or the arms or legs of the chairs; this requirement was complicated by the fact that the tables were just eighty centimeters wide.
d)  The tables had to be easy to dismantle (to facilitate transportation, cleaning, moving from one place to another, etc.).

## A Solution

It was agreed that each guest would be allotted a space measuring seventy by eighty centimeters. Two of the tables would be two meters, eighty centimeters long (each to accommodate four people), and the third table would be two meters, ten centimeters long; this third one could not be as long as the others because it was to be placed across the width of the room (see floor plan, Figure h).

The table arrangement should clearly indicate that guests were to be seated on just one side. This requirement — together with the fact that, if the crossbeams were centered, they would inevitably get in the way of the guests' legs — led to the decision that the table should be asymmetrical. Furthermore, since meals were to be served from the inside of the "U" shape, the table legs on that side should not in any way hamper the servers as they did their job. Once all these factors were considered and the weight of the marble tabletop was factored in, a design was created (see Figure f). As can be seen, the front table legs lean back at the same angle as the rear legs of the chairs, but the rear table legs are straight and vertical, an arrangement that does a better job of supporting the weight of the marble top, and interferes minimally with the food server's movements. The table legs, which are designed as separate parts, are attached to the tabletop and held in place with dowels. The legs are held together by a frame that hooks onto the rear legs; this frame also functions as a crossbeam, which ensures stability in the event that the table is accidentally bumped from the side.

## Dining Room Chairs

The frames are very light and made of wood; the wicker seats and backs are screwed onto the frames. The seats and backs are designed as separate parts so that they can be easily removed and repaired — since wicker deteriorates fairly quickly — which in turn makes the chair stronger. The arms of the armchairs are designed with carved openings (see Figure j) to ventilate the user's arm. The upper surface is concave, the better to accommodate the user's elbow and forearm. The dining room chairs are narrower than the armchairs and do not have arms.

## Living Room Chairs

Two different styles of chair were designed for the living room. One of them (see Figures l and n) has a curved frame — whose size and shape are reminiscent of the old *butaque* chairs (see Figure m) — and a seat and back made of white cord. The spaces between the cords allow air to circulate easily and keep the user's body cool. The other model (see Figures o, p, q, and r) also has a curved frame, but has wooden slats that have been shaped to accommodate the human body. The spaces between the slats provide ventilation even when a cushion is used. The upper surfaces of the arms are concave and have openings carved in them, like the dining room chairs. This model, like the one shown in Figures l and n, can be used with or without a cushion.

o

## Bench

Instead of a divan or sofa, there was to be a bench that could be used in various ways. One alternative was to position the bench as a divider — that was more psychological than physical — between the dining room area and the living room. The bench could also be used as a table or as a place to rest or read, since both end sections could be raised and used as a backrest that could be positioned at three different angles. The surface of the bench is perforated with multiple tiny holes as a ventilation aid and is exactly twice the size of the cushions on the chairs. When these cushions are not in use, they can be placed on the bench. The legs are designed as a separate unit that is attached to the upper part of the bench; this unit is made of vertical and horizontal pieces that, to some extent, echo a negative version of the horizontals and verticals created by the panels of the doors and windows (see Figure q).

q

THE TWO END SECTIONS CAN BE RAISED
LAS DOS SECCIONES EXTREMAS SE LEVANTAN

r

GREEN MARBLE
MARMOL VERDE

ESTRUCTURA DE MADERA
WOODEN FRAME

s

o p   bedroom chair. the seat and back are made of wicker. note the elegant lines and the cross that holds the legs together.
q   bench.
r   living room coffee table.
s   cabinet for books, records, record player, etc.

194

the dining room as seen from the living room. the simplicity and refreshing sparseness of the furniture translates the colonial spirit into a contemporary language.

**Living Room Coffee Table**
It consists of a frame (see the sketch in Figure r) that is designed to support the elliptical green marble top. Its elliptical shape is reminiscent of the old marble tables, many of which are still in use, but the legs are different and it is only 32 centimeters high.

**Cabinet for Books, Records, Record Player, etc.**
The compartments for the record player, speaker, and amplifier are perforated in order to create good acoustics and to avoid overheating. There are no doorknobs, since the perforations can be used to open the doors. The speaker box is designed as a stand-alone unit that can be taken out of the cabinet and placed anywhere (see Figure s).

**Bedroom Chair**
Wicker seat and back mounted on a wooden frame. Like the dining room chairs, the seat and back are designed as separate, removable parts (see Figures o and p).

\*  Editor's note: This text was originally published in Spanish as "Muebles modernos para una casa colonial," *Revista A: Hombre y Expresión* (Sociedad Editora "A," Caracas, Venezuela) (January 1954). The translation maintains the original images and layout. [checklist no. 86]

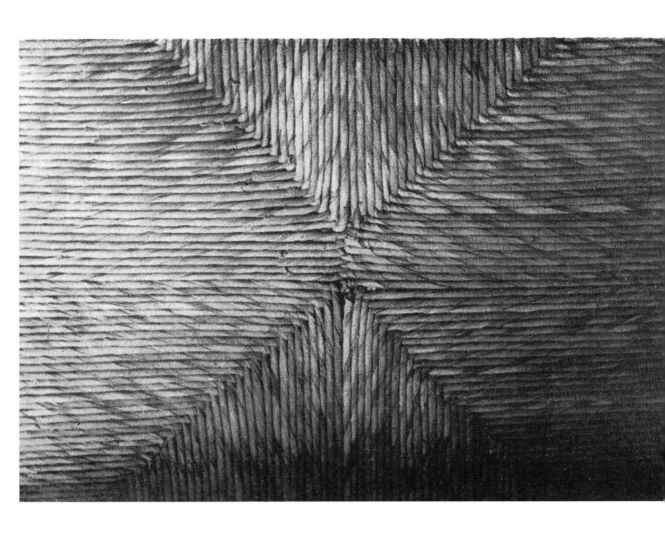

# LIVING DESIGN
## In Search of Our Own Kind of Furniture

### CLARA PORSET*

When we embrace the living organic order that contemporary design trends encourages us to accept, it becomes immediately apparent that, when synthesized, the influences exerted on the form by its physical and cultural environment and its artistic heritage will inevitably produce different formal expressions. We must therefore answer yes to the question we posed in the previous article, which asked if the different conditions and lifestyles of the regions in which objects are produced would naturally lead to different designs. We believe that this phenomenon is becoming increasingly apparent in many of the products that we use every day and that it is even more evident in furniture design.

Guided by their own innate wisdom, people use cool, light materials like tule, reeds, grasses, or palm fibers.

*Equipal* chairs from the coastal region of Michoacán, made of flexible wooden strips and goat hide.

Furniture design — like architectural design — involves a particularly acute sensitivity to a region's climate, natural materials, level of technical development, and evolution in terms of its social structure, aesthetics, and customs.

Climate has a considerable bearing on the choice of materials. In the hotter parts of Mexico, the most popular kinds of furniture — models of design rationality — are mainly made with cool, lightweight materials, such as reeds, grasses, tule, bamboo, and open-weave canvas. Pig, deer, and cowhides are also used; though not ideal for extremely hot conditions because they are nonporous and therefore block the flow of air, these hides always manage to stay cooler than the body sitting on them. Hides are abundant and easily accessible in these parts of the country and are therefore widely used. Guided by their innate wisdom, [in hot regions] local people have long used these hides, but we have recently been introducing palm, sisal, and ixtle fibers — which are cool to the touch, long lasting, and have extremely interesting texture qualities — as alternatives to the wool, cotton, and plastic that we have traditionally used to cover wooden or metal frames, which are usually filled with plastic foam, horsehair, or cotton, and that are especially designed for temperate or cold regions.

But the materials are not the only things affected by the climate. It also influences the shape of the furniture, especially of chairs, which must be designed to accommodate the human anatomy. In warmer regions, people want easy, airy chairs, on which they can lounge almost horizontally, taking refuge from the intense heat in comfortable positions that are conducive to physical and mental relaxation in torrid, enervating environments. In cooler regions, on the other hand, people prefer to be hunched up in chairs that make them sit almost erect and protect them from the flow of cold air. This explains why *butaque* chairs and hammocks are so popular in warmer areas: they are so perfectly suited to the hot climate.

Technique, as we have mentioned before, also has a powerful influence on form. This is even more obvious now when we look at our local furniture production, which is both handmade and manufactured.

These two furniture production methods have not been operating side-by-side for very long, because although industrial manufacturing in this country began in the late nineteenth century, it did not really hit its stride until after 1925. Until then, furniture was handmade in traditional styles, which is to say that most of it was authentic and beautiful. Mexican artisans have a long tradition of skill and creativity that they revere and want to preserve. Their artistic ability is strong enough to have withstood the devastating forces of national marketing and the indiscriminate demand of unsophisticated tourists.

Manufactured furniture accounted for about 20 percent of total production until 1948, when manufacturing increased after imports were almost totally banned. The total value of furniture imports in 1947 was $9,940,000, but the figure dropped to $240,000 in 1949.

Today, handmade furniture accounts for 70 percent of the total furniture market, and manufactured products make up the remaining 30 percent. That same ratio also applies to quality. We simply cannot describe manufactured furniture in the same terms we would use to describe what is made by hand. The blend of function and beauty that one consistently encounters in handmade furniture is only rarely found in the manufactured equivalent. Until now, most manufacturers have either been unaware of how art and industry should work together or — worse — they have stubbornly refused to listen to any explanation. There are a few manufacturers, however, though they are in the minority, who are beginning to accept the concept of blending art and industry that the others reject. These are not philanthropists; they are well-informed people who realize that the demand for well-designed, well-built furniture is constantly increasing and that these features are good selling points. In other words, they have understood that manufacturing well-designed furniture is good business.

In the current situation, in which there are two production methods operating side-by-side and a majority of manufacturers who are unwilling to produce the kind of furniture that is in demand among sophisticated consumers, the Mexican furniture designer is burdened with a heavy responsibility. On the one hand, he must address the two discrete sets of challenges involved in handmade furniture and manufactured furniture. On the other, the inertia of many manufacturers frustrates the designer's legitimate desire to adapt his designs to the pace and requirements of economic development that is driving industrial production to ever higher levels. Manufacturing can also make his designs more meaningful by producing them as a solution to the essential needs of large numbers of people, instead of limiting them to a small group of privileged consumers as inevitably happens in the case of a handmade product.

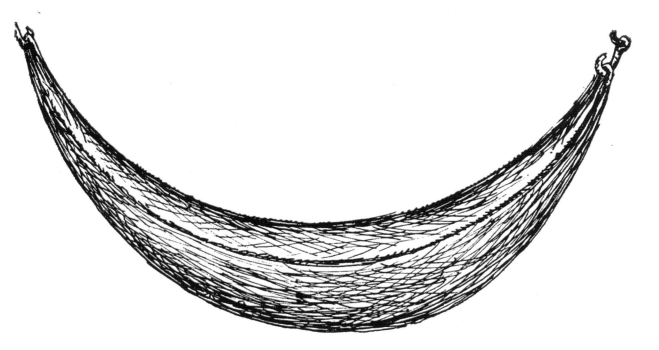

But climate also affects the shape of furniture and, in warmer regions people want easy, airy alternatives, on which they can lounge almost horizontally, as in a hammock.

In the situation mentioned above, those who design furniture to be manufactured exclusively by industrial means risk their own financial prospects, and some Spartan spirited types do just that. A little under a year ago, [1952] the architect Ernesto Gómez Gallardo designed a school chair that won first prize at the competition for this kind of furniture sponsored by the Ciudad Universitaria (University City). It was a well-designed, lightweight, easy-to-move, comfortable, attractive chair, designed to be made of laminated, shaped wood that was attached to an iron frame with aluminum hardware. It was a typical industrial design to be mass-produced by electronic machinery at low cost and was thus ideally suited to general school use.

The architect Carlos Cortés Gómez also produced an excellent industrial design for an easy chair, to be assembled with individual parts, including padding and metal supports. The various elements could be manufactured separately and simultaneously, using different techniques, all of which would make it easy to mass produce.

I, too — the writer of this essay — have recently designed various kinds of chairs that would be partly manufactured and partly made by hand. They were designed with both techniques in mind, to be produced at the same time. The shaped, laminated wooden seats and backrests were to be manufactured by electronic machinery, and the solid wooden frames were to be hand carved with the kind of sensitivity that only a skilled craftsman could provide.

The architect Ernesto Gómez Gallardo's light,
easy-to-move school chair was designed to be
industrially manufactured.

But so far only a few of the architect Gómez Gallardo's school chairs have been produced, to fill a special order from the Ciudad Universitaria that awarded them a prize. The other designs mentioned above have either had to be produced manually, a process that involves a thousand steps, or they are still just ideas on paper. As an encouraging thought, we should remember that Alvar Aalto's famous pieces of furniture made of laminated wood were finally built twenty years after they were originally designed.

Whether handmade or industrially manufactured, good quality furniture is still only available to the wealthier classes. Those with the fewest resources — in other words, most Mexicans — are forced to live in the sort of sparsely furnished spaces that Bernal Díaz del Castillo mentioned in his descriptions of Montezuma's palace, which, of course, was the height of fashion for the elite at the time. Blue collar workers and employees — who are only marginally better off than those on the bottom rung of the economic ladder — have to furnish their homes with whatever they can find at the market: manufactured furniture of abysmal quality and even worse taste, if that were possible, and at prices out of all proportion to their worth. People in these demographic groups seem to sense that the only furniture in their price range is utterly devoid of quality and therefore attempt to compensate for it by buying as many pieces as they can afford, thus adding another layer of ugliness to their homes, which are already unattractive in every possible way.

There is as yet, in official circles — that is, among those who are responsible for these things — no awareness that low-cost furniture is an important factor in the national economy.

A few years ago, the Mexican Department of Pensions set out to build 1,080 fully furnished apartments in the multifamily "Presidente Miguel Alemán" housing project in Coyoacán. The furnishings were designed to be compatible with the size of the apartments and the average needs of future tenants. It was, to our knowledge, the only initiative of this nature to have been attempted in Mexico, but unfortunately it failed for the same reasons that similar projects had failed in other countries. The tenants could not be forced to buy the furniture that had been designed expressly for their new homes, and no attempt was made to take well-intended, reasonable steps to encourage them to do so by educating them about new design ideas and helping them to bring a measure of culture into their new living spaces. And so, though the families that moved into the housing project in Coyoacán could have had furniture, dishes, and fabrics that were ideally suited to the size and architectural style of their new apartments, most of them preferred to bring with them all their old, bad household items, to which they were inextricably attached. In other cases, they brought new, bad items whose ostentatious appearance disguised their poverty, or so they thought. And of course, in both cases, what the families brought was totally incompatible with the size and style of their new homes. Mexico thus squandered its first opportunity to find a comprehensive solution to the problem of low-cost living.

There is no point in mentioning the flood of pseudo-modern furniture that has overwhelmed our country, other than in passing and to note a fact that is relevant to our current situation. These pieces are, by and large, copies of the worst furniture produced in the United States for purely commercial reasons; these products corrupt both the idea and the public's appreciation of design.

Butaque chair from the Isthmus of Tehuantepec, made of mahogany and cowhide.

Evolution of the Spanish *"butaque* chair." Designed by Clara Porset.

There is, however, every reason to consider another factor among those that influence the form of furniture, which is the lingering echo of our artistic heritage — Mexico's vast artistic tradition. This is something that we have barely been aware of for a long period of time and have only recently begun to pay attention to.

As the reverberations of the past grow stronger, they demand attention and continuity. The grandest periods of ancient Mexican culture encourage us to develop their ideas and express them in the present and the future. In other words, these cultural traditions are an inheritance that, like all inherited wealth, should be increased rather than kept in storage, passively intact.

We can already see the results of this approach in contemporary art that views our past culture as a source of ideas waiting to be re-expressed. It is common knowledge what our great Mexican painters have achieved by reinterpreting pre-Hispanic, indigenous art, for which they naturally feel a greater affinity than they do for Hispanic art, which is, after all, foreign and was imposed on us as part of our conquest and colonization.

And, albeit on a smaller scale, the same acknowledgement of the influence that art can sometimes have over the course of time can be seen in today's more sophisticated types of furniture. Chairs reflect this process more than any other type of furniture

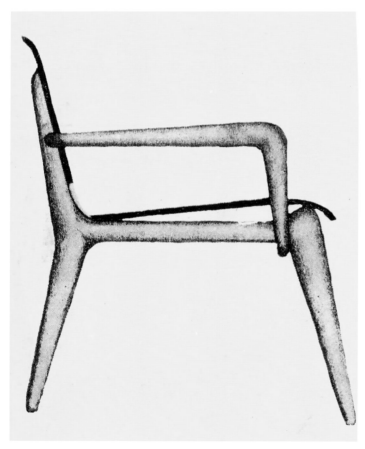

Clara Porset has recently designed a line of chairs that include some skillfully handmade parts and others that are manufactured, all of which can be produced at the same time.

The architect Carlos Cortés Gómez designed an easy
chair that could easily be mass produced.

because their evolving sizes and shape are most intimately involved with the general public's changing circumstances. More than any other type of furniture, chairs must be precisely designed to accommodate the average anatomy of the residents of a particular region. They are made with local materials and must be compatible with the population's level of economic and technical development and with their cultural customs. The chair is always a regional piece of furniture and is the most representative of its period.

Some of the chairs that we are designing these days reveal the influence of the two underlying sources of our Mexican culture: the Indian and the Spanish influences that have, for centuries, kept their distance from each other but which are now converging and blending together. The indigenous *icpalli* chair and the *butaque* chair that the Spanish introduced represent these two influences in furniture design.

We have mainly worked on the development of the *butaque,* which has been the most popular of all our designs. This is no doubt because, although it was originally imported, the *butaque* has become so much a part of Mexican life that it is no longer considered foreign. The same is true of the Windsor chair that was originally English but is now the most sought after chair in the United States, both in its original form and in the versions that have evolved since it was first imported.

Type of chair used by the Spanish, whose design was similar to the *butaque.*

*Icpalli* — from before the time of Cortés.

Tipo de silla usado por los españoles, de principios constructivos parecidos a los del butaque.

Icpalli" p

remin

We do not believe it is an exaggeration to say that we are in the process of developing our own kind of furniture. We are on the same path that was taken by architecture, whose evolution in this sense is more advanced than ours, but we do not know when our furniture will find its own particular form of expression or what that form of expression will ultimately be like. Architecture has blazed the trail for us and has done so by zigzagging back and forth in search of its own identity.

Does this mean that we do not have a style of our own, will never have one, and shouldn't want to have one? A style is, after all, the language of a period; it is something that develops naturally and gradually, only taking on an identifiable shape after the period in question has ended and a new one has begun. Style is a "post mortem" idea that should only concern those who live after it has taken shape, not those who helped to create it.

But we do think that, at the very least, we can look forward to the power and international acclaim that Mexican design will enjoy in the future if it reflects Mexican life and its peerless artistic heritage.

*ICPALLI* — Royal chair or throne used in Mexico before the time of Cortés.

*BUTAQUE* — Mexican popular version of the Castilian word *butaca.*

Easy chair designed by Clara Porset, reminiscent of the *icpalli* chair used before the time of Cortés.

*Equipal,* sacred chair from Nayarit, made with reeds.

ara Porset

precortesiano.

Equipal sagrado de Nayarit, en carrizo.

\* Editor's note: This text was originally published in Spanish as "Diseño viviente," *Espacio. Revista integral de arquitectura y artes plasticas* (July 1953). The translation maintains the original images and layout.

Lina Bo Bardi (Brazilian, 1914–92). *Museo de Arte de Sao Paulo,* 1957–1968. Pen on paper. Courtesy of Instituto Lina Bo e P. M. Bardi, São Paulo, Brazil.

# IN SOUTH AMERICA: AFTER LE CORBUSIER, WHAT IS HAPPENING?

### LINA BO BARDI*

With the assurance of one who is rich, handsome, and well educated, Mr. [C.] Ray Smith, associate editor (Feature and Interior Design) of the important American magazine *Progressive Architecture*,[1] presents a panorama of the architecture of South America.

He interviews several architects of renown and other younger ones, making a "balance" and drawing conclusions after the discovery of a "New Wave" — which is purported to be the triumph of the Corbusian theme — and paternalistically advises South American architects not to copy the "industrialized international" architecture of developed countries but to find inspiration in the huts of Indians, the "ranchitos," and the "favelas" of the poor, as befits the underdeveloped architects who work in an equally underdeveloped continent.

Overcoming the "disorganization," the lack of technical preparation, and the "sociological" velleities, young Latin American architects, firmly situated in their own generation, can become aware of the true problem of current architecture — "how to provide vast quantities of inexpensive housing, in terms of an artistic form similar to a jewelry store." Such a new direction will lead both continents, North and South America, to a more intimate architectural understanding.

Based on an error (we do not wish to consider it bad faith), the author of the survey, with veiled disdain for the summarily dismissed Corbusian "plastic-formalistic" positions, makes explicit his conviction that the true architecture is the North American, based on industrial mass production, to which young

South American architects "still" lack access because of the underdevelopment of their countries and of themselves.

The relocation to North America of Gropius and Mies van der Rohe put an end to the inventiveness of [George] Grosz and the violence of Kurt Weill — who became the composer of saccharine tunes for the movies — and convinced Brecht and Adorno that the mass media were formidable instruments in the hands of monopolistic capitalism. Moreover, according to these thinkers, in order for the "mechanism" to be put to good use in a more just and humane society, it was necessary to base it on humanistic values, exactly those that engendered Le Corbusier's "plastic" architecture — which is not plastic but it has become comfortable to so define it nowadays, deliberately forgetting the socio-political revolutionary values of the movement that was rationalism.

The rationalist poetics is not exhausted; its revolutionary and political content was purposely surpassed by that which historically may be classified as a return to the positions that rationalism itself had left behind with its affirmations of constructive honesty and social equality.

With the exception of the great Frank Lloyd Wright (who belongs to the Anglo-Saxon movement of the nineteenth century), from Ruskin to Morris (with the still politically undefined impact of the pioneers sung by Whitman), and of Antonio Gaudí, so Spanish (or rather, Catalonian) as to have no serious international followers, the new "organic" architecture of the second half of the twentieth century (as well as the "brutalisms," the "actions," the "spontaneisms," and all the movements viewed as reactions to the shoe-boxes of rationalist architecture) need to be defined today by what they represent: movements that, accompanying the process of cultural revision of a large part of Western culture, define as progress outmoded situations that emerge draped in new meanings to defend old positions.

To the mass media, accepted as a phenomenon of nature rather than analyzed in the light of its socio-historical causes, one must add Mass Architecture, the expression of the "construction industry," which also cannot be studied critically by means of idealistic historicism, formal criticism, or linguistics without considering its true determinate basis: the socio-historical dimension.

This does not mean rejecting the computer and valuing the mechanical era over the electronic but placing the computer in its true historical perspective, considering it merely as a means of achieving the new mass culture and consequently the new architecture on a vast scale.

That Le Corbusier, welcomed by underdeveloped South America while ignored or mocked in developed countries, has exercised great influence here is important as a positive criticism of the possibilities of the cultural vision of South America. The fact of his teaching having assumed different aspects is related to factors of cultural formation, and the consequent judging of values must be made on a strict critical basis that takes such factors into account. It is irrefutable that the technical-folkloric position espoused by the North American interviewer is linked to a paternalistic view of South America and is the reflection of its economic, political, and social instability, its cultural doubts, and, above all, its lack of economic, political, and social freedom.

The New Wave, *la Nueva Ola,* is an attempt by the younger generation to move away from the idealization of an era that "disassembles and reassembles man," like Galy Gay, the porter in Bertolt Brecht's play *Man Equals Man.* The New Wave can be considered not as the triumph of Corbusianism but as the search for a path out of inhuman industrial monopoly. What the American writer failed to appreciate was the danger of innate "folklore" in this attempt, which does not take into sufficient account the heritage of a great movement, soon dismissed, whose development, when taken in its true dimension, could at least provide the means for arriving at a new architecture. An architecture that through rationalistic instruments would record the experiments of the "non-perfectionism" and the structuring of "interlocking cells."

An architecture of the new electronic era and of true mass civilization, in which man, rationally responsible for great technological conquests whose process we already see in action, be it as "owner" rather than succubus of events judged "ineluctable," fatalistically endured and recorded.

Architecture is at an impasse. After Le Corbusier, after the North American "block style," after the Wright-Gaudiesque trends, what is the path? In Europe and Japan the search has begun for atomic expression in architecture. In South America, social problems have affected this search. A great legacy cannot be forgotten: the rationalist legacy.

---

\* Editor's note: This text was originally published in Portuguese as "Na América do Sul: após Le Corbusier, o que está acontecendo," *Mirante das Artes* 1 (January–February 1967): 10–11.

1 Ray Smith, "In South America: After Corbu," in *Progressive Architecture* (September 1966): 140–55.

Lina Bo Bardi sitting in the *Cadeira de beira de estrada* [Roadside Chair], 1967. Gelatin silver print, 6½ x 8½ in. Instituto Lina Bo e P. M. Bardi, São Paulo, Brazil. [checklist no. 12]

# AMBIENT PLANNING: "DESIGN" AT AN IMPASSE

## LINA BO BARDI*

An analysis of the resolutions of the Architecture Congress, its betrayal of the constructive principles of the Modern Movement with its proposal to socially objectify the practice of art, architecture, and industrial design. The acrylics that replaced Mies van der Rohe, industrial design at the service of consumption, technocracy as simulacrum of the rational equating of issues relating to the human environment. And more: the situation in Brazil confronted with these questions, their contradictions, particularities, and anthropological richness.

At home, money was tight. He was forced to do engravings and drawings. I remember the Easter eggs in particular. Round, they twirled and squeaked like doors. He sold them in an artisanal boutique on Neglinnaja Street. Ten to fifteen kopeks each. Since then I have an endless hatred of the watercolors of the Ladies, the Russian style, and the "artisanal."

—VLADIMIR MAJAKOVSKIJ

These considerations may be deemed "obvious" or "outmoded." The answer is: there are judgments that define as "obvious" and "outmoded" anything that directly impinges on well-established caste interests. The timid conclusions of the 12th World Congress of Architects in Madrid (May 1975), dedicated to ideas and technology in architecture, are the demonstration of fear of the "obvious" and the "already outmoded"; in this case, the obvious and outmoded is the position of the architect vis-à-vis the collectivity. In the specific field of architecture, the most flagrant betrayal of the principles that informed the entire Modern Movement, interrupted by the Second World War and afterward abandoned as outmoded.

In the avalanche-cancer of disorientation, everything is encompassed and disappears into total obsolescence, in a rapid aging and loss of meaning, in a "complete loss of metaphor." Thus "Savage" architecture pulverizes Gaudí, the "acrylics" and "metals" pulverize Pevsner and Arp. To individualize the true values of Mies van der Rohe's pavilion at the Barcelona Exposition of 1929, a highly precise historical operation is necessary, the original significance of the architecture of Le Corbusier is swallowed, and Frank Lloyd Wright is saved only through the goodwill of several critics. But Fallingwater is on the path to total loss of the violence of its originative communication.

Art isn't all that innocent: the great attempt to make Industrial Design the regenerative force of an entire society failed and was transformed into the most horrifying denunciation of a system. The consciousness-raising of over a quarter of the world's population that believed in unlimited progress has already begun. The demystifying of design as weapon of a system, the anthropological search in the field of the arts as opposed to the aesthetic search, which informed all the development of Western artistic culture from antiquity to the vanguards, is under way in a lucid debate that excludes any return to romantic-artisanal situations, to the vision of Ruskin and Morris; a reexamination of the recent history of "doing" in the arts. Not a block refusal but a careful process of revision. The effort against technological hegemony, which in the West follows the "technological inferiority complex" in the field of the arts, collides with the structure of a system: the problem is fundamentally politico-economic. Regeneration through art, the Bauhaus credo, proved to be merely utopian, the cultural or tranquilizing error of the consciousness of those who didn't need it, and the metatheses of the uncontrollable mass proliferation aggregated the basic conquests of the Modern Movement, transforming its great fundamental idea — Planning — into the utopian error of the technological intelligentsia, which with its failure exhausted "rationality," counterposed to "emotionality," in a fetishism of abstract models that viewed the world of numbers and the world of men as equals.

If the problem is basically politico-economic, the task of the "activist" in the field of design is, despite everything, fundamental. It's what Brecht called "the ability to say no." The artist's freedom was always "individual," but true freedom can only be collective. A freedom aware of social responsibility, which knocks down the frontiers of aesthetics, the concentration camp of Western civilization; a freedom linked to the limitations and the great conquests of Scientific Practice (Scientific Practice, not technology fallen into technocracy). To the romantic suicide of "nonplanning," the reaction to failed technocracy, it is urgent to counterpose the grand task of Ambient Planning, from urbanism and architecture to industrial design and other cultural manifestations. A reintegration, a simplified unification of the components of the culture.

What is the situation in a country of capitalist-dependency structure, where the national democratic-bourgeois revolution failed to process itself, which enters industrialization with the remnants of national-oligarchic structures?

Brazil came late to Western-style industrialization, bearing elements from prehistory and from Africa, rich in popular vigor. All the contradictions of the great Western ambiguity are evident either contemporarily or in the short term in its process of modernization, with violent characteristics of a bankrupt situation. A process that in the industrialized nations took centuries takes only a few years here. Abrupt, unplanned, structurally imported industrialization leads the country to experience an uncontrollable natural event, not a manmade process. The sinister signs of land speculation, lack of planning in popular housing, speculative proliferation in industrial design: gadgets, objects for the most part superfluous, influence the cultural ethos of the country, creating extremely serious obstacles and rendering impossible the development of a truly autochthonous culture. Collective consciousness-raising is necessary; any digression is a crime at present — deculturation is under way. If the economist and the sociologist can diagnose with detachment, the artist must act, linked to both the active populace and the intellectual.

A reexamination of the country's recent history is imperative. A balance sheet of "popular" Brazilian civilization is called for, even if poor by standards of high culture. This balance sheet is not that of Folklore, always paternalistically fostered by higher culture; it is that "seen from the other side," of participation. It is Aleijadinho[1] and Brazilian culture prior to the French Mission. It is the Northeasterner of leather and empty tin cans, it is the inhabitant of the "Vilas," it is the Black and the Indian, it is a mass that innovates, that brings a dry, hard, difficult-to-digest contribution.

Such urgency, the inability to wait any longer, is the real basis of the Brazilian artist's work, a reality that needs no artificial stimuli, a cultural abundance within reach, a unique anthropological richness marked by tragic and fundamental historical events. Brazil has industrialized, and the new reality must be accepted in order to be studied. The "return" to extinct social bodies is impossible, the creation of artisanal centers, the return to artisanship as antidote to an industrialization alien to the cultural principles of the country is wrong. Because artisanship as social body has never existed in Brazil; what exists is a sparse domestic pre-artisanship, what existed was a weak immigration of Iberian or Italian artisans and, in the nineteenth century, manufacture. Never artisanship.

The cultural rise of Brazilian pre-artisanship could have been achieved before the country went down the path of dependent capitalism, when a democratic-bourgeois revolution was still possible. In this case, the cultural options in the field of Industrial Design could have been different, closer to the country's real needs (even if poor, much poorer than the cultural options of China and Finland).

It is necessary to begin again, starting with a new reality, but today one thing is quite clear and definite: those who concern themselves with the needs of a highly limited portion of society, the authors of the quiet note-taking of the facts, those who raise no scandals, with certainty are on the other side.

---

* Editor's note: This text was originally published in Portuguese as "Planajamento Ambiental 'Desenho' no impasse," *Malasartes,* n. 2 (December-February 1976): 4–7. The original essay was acompanied by images with captions written by Bo Bardi.

[1] Aleijadinho ("little crippled one") was the popular nickname given to Antônio Francisco Lisboa (1738?–1814), considered the greatest sculptor of Brazil's colonial period.

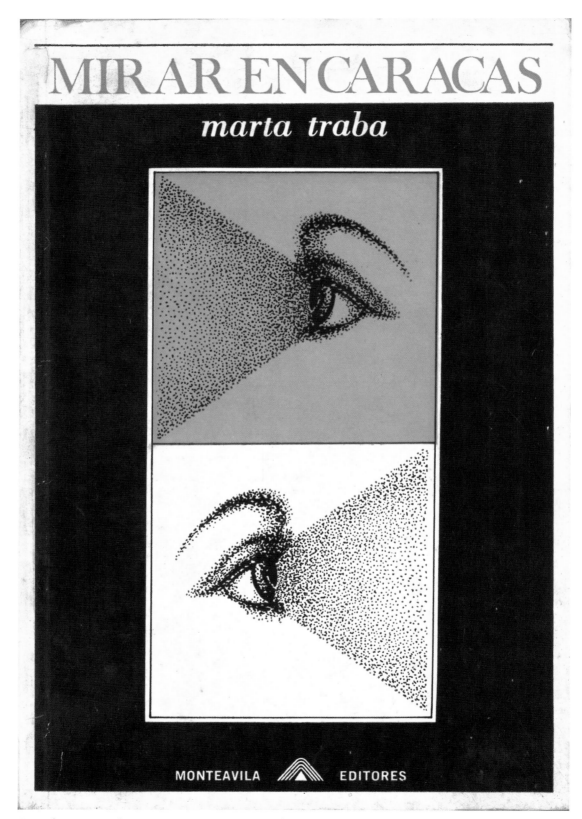

Cover for Marta Traba's *Mirar en Caracas: Crítica de Arte: [ensayos]*. Caracas: Monte Avila Editores, 1974.

# TECLA TOFANO: ARS POLITICA

## MARTA TRABA*

Over the last few months, the ceramist Tecla Tofano has prepared the ingredients for her exhibition entitled *Lo que comen los que comen* (What People Who Eat Eat). The clarification is valid because not everyone eats, regardless of whether or not they live in Caracas going out of their minds on the freeways and getting crushed in the supermarkets. And even less do they eat the succulent dishes that Tecla elaborated, based on the orgiastic ads vomited up by the magazines of the consumer society, as if it involved a horn of plenty. But, in cooking a ceramic banquet, she has definitively clarified her work's intention, its underlying, semi-hidden, and now openly explicit intention. It goes beyond the "bitch of a world" or the tender world she has described throughout her work from 1964 until now [1974]. It goes toward the political definition that declares that the world is always divided in two — between the haves and the have-nots, the eaters and the non-eaters — and proclaims that she is on the side of the have-nots and the non-eaters, not just in order to piously accompany them, but to harass those who have and eat while forgetting about the rest. That's what I believe to be more than obvious in the present exhibition; I believe that, over the past nine years, she has developed an *ars politica* with a clarity and a decisiveness that go far beyond her often-remarked expressive vehemence and the explosive Naples-Caracas combination that generates it.

For me, the difficulty in approaching Tecla's work and explaining it in light of this construction of an *ars politica* is rooted in the ceramicist's own personality, which interferes with the analysis of her works. In the first place, she is *too much* of a human being; in the second, she is a complex human being. With respect to the first reason, she is capable of expressing herself simultaneously through drawing, literature, and ceramics, namely, through three completely different systems of communication, and in no way attempting to complement what she says in one language with what she says in another, but, rather, forcing the three to form themselves into effective vehicles for everything she wants to say.

Faced with this alternative, the public has chosen the activity of hers that appears most permanent or at least most professional — ceramics — while attempting to put the others to the side, not because they lack interest or are not on the level of the ceramics, but because they are unable to hear three voices that are saying three different things at once. Thus, Tecla's triple production has remained amputated as it were, and, despite the fact that she nurtures tales and drawings with the same maternal ferocity that overprotects less pretty and less brilliant children, she is identified as a ceramist. For the same reason, I will only speak of her as a ceramist. However, I am not forgetting her dozens of unpublished pages and her piles of drawings in order to reconstruct the complex human being behind her *ars politica.* Nor do I want to accept, as the new critics do so frequently, that the notion of the author is a myth and that it is Tecla's ceramics — to allude to only this one of her languages — that think and decide for her.

It is important for me to start with what she has said, since her work is constantly accompanied by an anxious explanation of motives and situations she prefers to debate in public. "The results of my work are dictated by a great need to say things, to speak with everyone, to speak about everything and not knowing how," she wrote in 1964. Her almost ingenuous sincerity and the determination with which she works appear simultaneously in this declaration. But at the same time that she wanted to *say everything* — which meant that she was thoroughly entangled — she began to clear things up: "For me, what is smooth and well-finished are like letters addressed to close and dear friends where the paper is left blank and placed in a blank envelope." So despite her confession of ignorance, she knew very well what she didn't like, thereby opening that path — characteristic for her — of *choosing through rejections.* She worked *against* the smooth and well finished, just as later she would work against prettiness: she works on a social concept, *against* the void of the purist aesthetic. She decided not to send blank letters, and her writing was an urge to fill, to say, to penetrate. She sincerely adopted Rimbaud's *"Je est un autre."* But, in order *to be the other,* to present something charged, not empty facts, she resolved to be herself with uncommon intensity, in such a way that throughout her construction of the *ars politica,* she and her expression became reinforced, so that what comes through in the form of an artwork is truly effective *for the other.*

In 1967, she gave the definitive coup de grace to vessels in order to devote herself to modeling. Why? Let us listen to her explanations: a pot is "clear and open"; the object, filled with nooks, labyrinths, meanderings, has an *internal mystery* that needs to be unraveled. As always, she decided in favor of difficulty against facility, the richer against the less rich, the heaviest against the most weightless. There is something tremendous in the concept of weight, richness, and difficulty. I mean that, for the ceramist Bernard Leach, for example (who in that decade passed with his ceramics through Caracas, where he applied the criterion of "truth and beauty"), both truth and beauty dwell in the simple. However, Tecla has an organic, tribal concept of truth and beauty, and refuses the cultured path of synthesis and stripping down. For the truth and beauty of Tecla's work do not exist *in themselves,* they do not pursue their own reference but exist with reference to the world in which they are produced. Because of this, "if it's baroque, not easy on the eye, shocking in some instances, it's because what I'm trying to say *isn't pretty.*" In other words, life isn't *pretty,* anything but. She said this in 1969, fully immersed in what Perán Erminy termed in 1969 "an orgiastic display."

At this stage of her work, nothing resembled her point of departure.

At her debut, she emerged along with an exceptional group of ceramists: Cristina Ziells, María Luisa de Tovar, Eduardo Gregorio, and later Reyna Herrera. I am leaving Seka [Severin de Tudja] out of this group, because her formidable, almost lithic units are set apart from the rest, where refinement and Leach's "beauty and truth" predominate, in a display of good taste digested immediately by the dominant culture.

Tecla is profoundly receptive with regard to the demands of this dominant culture: to the same clear extent she detects them, she rejects them as well. In 1958, when she began to distinguish herself and was still marching in step with the platoon, she was already starting to give evidence of her position of mistrust, reserve, and distance from the dominant culture. Her pottery remained docile but it looked crude next to her colleagues'. The inside and outside graphite give it a bas-relief texture, but she hastened to declare that the texture is not a decoration superimposed on the form, but an attempt at a *new form* over what was achieved with the potter's wheel. She worked with few glazes, muted ranges of color, which she would never abandon, and local clays.

From that moment, she attracted the attention of the critics, and, at the same time, and needless to say, because of her direct language and aggressiveness, the reviews were scared of her. She was fortunate to have been constantly accompanied by Perán Erminy and Roberto Guevara. The former not only understood her but praised her with as much intelligence as comprehension. The latter maintained a "hand-to-hand" combat with her, which began with a skirmish in which Tecla displayed her particular intolerance to all criticism, which stemmed from her certainty that she was doing things as best she could, and he would follow her from afar like an inevitable event (or catastrophe), with a good will that was truly moving. In 1959, those who most clearly saw the originality of her work were Perán Eminy, who remarked that, "what is most important about her experiment is her refusal of decorativeness and all sensationalist superficiality," and Sergio Antillano, who spoke of a "vitality" rarely achieved in ceramics. Later, in 1964, Juan Calzadilla noted for the first time the relationship between Tecla's new ceramics and a craft tradition "completely ignored by previous ceramists."Régulo Pérez marked the division: "She has left behind perfect forms, refinement, and good taste in order to enrich herself with the brutality and exuberance of the reality that surrounds her and which has made her vibrate and in the end define her authentic, rich, imaginative personality, filled with grace and good humor." I became acquainted with her work at that time and can attest, partly, to my own observations, which often coincide with those of her major critics.

This means that I have known Tecla's work for ten years. I follow it when I can, I believe in it, and I think it makes up one of the moist important artistic events of the continent: of that continental expression laboriously built up by the will of a few in order to achieve an identity.

Although in 1964 Tecla was still making vessels, she turned and, with much timidity, modeled "odd things" on the lids of the vessels; she was still far removed from "high-culture" Venezuelan ceramics. Some vessels of that period are so powerful that functional language, mediated by the object's use and destiny, no longer fits them in the slightest. I would point out that with them, the culminating moment is produced in which the object is its own reference, and that, by virtue of this, they have so much aesthetically communicative power, something that would not occur later when the modeled objects incessantly seeking greater *thematic expansion* and the aesthetic is entwined with the ethical. Calzadilla, as always, was clear- and farsighted in noting the relationship between the ceramics of that moment and the craft tradition. I did not perceive this until quite some time later, when she devoted herself fully to modeling. In the dark, dramatic vessels of 1964, I read, on the contrary, a grave, arrogant writing that broke bonds and stipulated ethical demands on the language of ceramics: it was here that there began for me, at this point of testing, severity, and rigor, her declaration of an *ars politica*.

But in 1964 as well, Tecla had her first exhibition of modelings at the Museo de Bellas Artes. In the catalogue, Tecla wrote breathless texts that were confessions, struggles, outbursts, fights with the word, mistrust and love for the public, ill humor, benevolence: "I busted out"; "I ask myself, why do I come out with these strange things?"; "Ignorance has also helped me"; "I don't know how to answer myself." And immediately after: "I wish somebody knew how to do it for me" (something she would never have allowed had it been possible). Confusion increased: she called them ceramics, statuettes, sculptures, signs, totemic figures, little pyramids. All of it was inscribed in another dimension distinct from the marvelous ceremonial vessels; it was much more formal and, strangely, animated and picturesque, with a bad taste and verbal richness that were only insinuated and would later become elements of her expressive system.

However, her rupture with the dominant art did not become explicit until the 1964 group show at the Museo de Bellas Artes. Tecla's works collided outright with the *beau monde* of ceramics and Venezuelan enamels, which, on the contrary, accompanied perfectly, in a restrained, aristocratic procession, the beautiful works of the invited ceramists Hamuda, Leach, and Francine de Pierre. The visual scandal of Tecla's pieces acted as a kind of detonator: I felt then and still feel now, while looking over the photographic material of that exhibition, that the collision was not due to the confrontation of one formal concept with another, but to a formal concept with an increasingly commanding expressive urgency that was well on the way to exploding its own framework.

What did she say? She rejected "study," "technical perfection," and possible influences, accepting only that everything could somehow be digested and "vomited out." Her laminated jars, which formed part of her large exhibition of eighty pieces that same year in the Museo de Bellas Artes, alternated with free forms, arbitrary models, and the broadest opening to all the possibilities offered by skilled work in clay, manipulated with as much mastery as respect for the experience of the material. "I'm someone who lives transformations and because of that I perceive consequences, not abrupt changes"— a violent text typical of Tecla Tofano. In addition, she reinforced the state of alertness with regard to her own movements, dealing out blows left and right, to those who wanted to reclassify her and bring her to order again.

Her faithful Perán Erminy followed her amid the chaos: "All this orgiastic parade of protuberances and tumultuous profiles is completely lacking in functional application. But it has an impressive intensity of presence and a heavy emotional charge."

In 1968, abruptly, she herself put herself in order. The first exhibition of modeled pieces with a single theme was called *Habitat y habitantes:* the *ars politica* was being unveiled, and Tecla's finger, hand, arm, and body, artisanally surrendered to the challenge of clay, were aimed at men — for the moment, any man and any situation. Tecla gave in to her formidable descriptive fantasy, to her powerful imagination entering and leaving the field of the real without the slightest problem of transportation or location. She touched on everything: literature and poetry, love and poverty: her indiscriminate totalization was once again present. In this terrible global world, *poetry and the memory of the imaginary* served her, surprisingly, as guides. Colorful and excessive, this world suffered from a defect that through hypostasis became a virtue: its lack of self-critique, its self-gratification, and indulgently requited love changed by means of the pieces into a furious love. Roberto Guevara surrendered at the end of a review and recommended, "letting oneself be transported through these exalted realities filled with a vital impulse, a crude poetry." This was a wise recommendation and should be taken literally in order to follow Tecla on a path that, as an idea, is increasingly imperative, and as a language for the transmission of this idea, increasingly frenetic.

*De la silla a la cápsula* [From Chair to Capsule], in 1969, in the [Sala] Mendoza: the commentaries became harsher. Tecla attacked: "what I'm trying to say isn't pretty." "On the evidence, prettiness is the petty bourgeoisie's basic aesthetic category"[1] retorted the inevitable Anonymous. The situations were defined: evidently, the petty bourgeoisie was looking for the "prettiness" Tecla had referred to scornfully, but Tecla's pieces dialectically and aggressively attacked on two fronts at once: "prettiness" was understood as a demand of groups who were, or pretended to be, "distinguished," and *lo cursi* (corniness), which, simultaneously, also in a paradoxical and all-absorbing movement, was treated as a matter *to be judged* and a matter *to be welcomed:* such was the case with *Las cuatro gracias en una silla* [The Four Graces in a Chair], where the piece may be decoded according to three movements: either as a language that exposes the vulnerable expedients of kitsch; as a language that aligns itself with *lo cursi* as an expression of the popular and the spontaneous affinities of the masses; or as an attack on the petty bourgeois and his routine porcelains or knickknacks. And also — why not? — as a private diversion of Tecla's own making: a labyrinthine chair and therefore filled with mysterious meanderings.

In contrast, in 1970's "cans," seven pieces in which people fight to get out of prison-like spaces, the hands scratch, gesticulate in the air, freeing themselves from the box, can, prison, where they struggle, her critical project is made clear, not just through her concentration on one theme, but through her *expository decision.*

Free, delirious poetry surrenders its influence and makes way for a clear polemical spirit, which does not accept excessive digressions. Roberto Guevara pointed out this change, moving from reticent praise in 1970: "too many crude flowers like lumps of earth" to the interest with which he greets 1971's *La cama y sus posibilidades* [The Bed and Its Possibilities] at Galería "Viva Mexico!" along with *Los acesorios* [Accessories] at Galería Banap. *La cama. . .* was greeted as a "strong and clear" ceramic; about the second, it was emphasized that Tecla "fixes the limits of reality disdained for their apparent banality." Perán Erminy, who, in 1970, pointed out that, "the gratuitousness and disharmony. . . add an imperfection that gives the work even more life," did not stint in his enthusiasm: "They are more personal, more original, freer, more baroque, more ingenious, more humorous, more rigorous, more expressive, more arbitrary, more beautiful, uglier, more gratuitous, more spontaneous, more shocking, etc., etc., than ever."

Without a doubt, *La cama y sus posibilidades* is Tecla Tofano's definition of principles of her *ars politica.*

She persists in her constants and emphasizes them as true instruments of meaning: one of them is that of showing *from the beginning,* already present in the *habitat,* which began in the cave, and in the cycle *De la silla a la cápsula.* A cyclical will which is at once ingenuous, pedagogical, and preoccupied by the same totalizing urge to say "everything," to go back over the process from the beginning and retell it; which constitutes, on the other hand, one of the characteristics that typify children's as well as primitive art. But the difference is that Tecla, as opposed to children and primitives, conveys a vision of the world penetrated by a critical spirit; it does not involve simple traversals, but traversals where situations are denounced and corrected. For example, when she speaks, in the "accessories," of "a joke that makes demands," she hastens to demonstrate in this way her solidarity with scorned things and humble objects; she is performing the same amending action as Van Gogh painting old shoes. Obviously, she is making *social art* to the extent that she solidly inscribes her artistic project in the real life of the community. It is through her critical spirit that her second constant, the *baroque quality and disharmony of her forms,* comes to be controlled for the first time and submitted to strict vigilance, without losing withal their qualities of excess, but, on the contrary, endowing them with a meaning that goes beyond mere ornament. In this way, her baroque quality, which was an incidental ornament and always judged as such, as delirium, nonsense, absence of restraint, and not infrequently crudeness and lack of elegance, assumes in the bed its true character as a key element in a system of signifiers: it consists of unhinging form, disfiguring it, depriving it of all balance and harmonic articulation. She pursues a deformed articulation, an exacerbation of the grotesque. She approaches, in a deliberate manner, popular ceramics, the solid awkwardness with which the latter recurrently seeks to describe situations and things through clay: nothing to do with artisanal ceramics, where the artisan repeats, in an anti-creative, repetitive, and progressively degraded process, forms preserved by the demand of the bourgeoisie and not by tradition. Caustic humor and a corrosive gaze tinge the system of significations: in the accessories, even more than in the bed, firing lines are formed against the consumer society, its fashions, its caprices, its atrocities, its waste.

Tecla Tofano now defines herself without any timidity: the modeling has liquidated the turn, prettiness has been replaced by ugliness, deliberation has swept away innocence, the political has supplanted the poetic. The new galleries where she exhibits are called Aztlán, "Viva Mexico!"; [they are] popular, relaxed, anti-commercial, eliminating a public from the society pages that doesn't go under the bridges. Thus, the end result is the direct confrontation of *Lo que comen los que comen,* a frontal attack on the orgy of meals taken as the symbol of a minority class for which consumer society has been organized: expansion of the grotesque to achieve an ambience, a table set with the banquet of ceramics, rigid and daubed guests, made of cloth, seated at the banquet, cumulative collages piling up the gastronomical bacchanal of the magazines.

In this coming to consciousness, Tecla has not lost an ounce of her humor, imagination, and powerful and uncanny creative force; she has simply aimed them well, as if her time adrift has ended once and for all. Her extraordinary *ars politica,* which expresses the aspirations and misfortunes of the nation's majority, alien to the dominant art, has enabled her to display to the maximum, reverently, all her inventive force and her rough and tender originality.

---

\* Editor's note: This text was originally published in Spanish as "Tecla Tofano, Ars Politica," in *Marta Traba, Mirar en Caracas: Crítica de Arte: [ensayos]* (Caracas: Monte Avila Editores, 1974).

1 *Semana* (June 1969): 19–20.

# LESSON IN ARCHITECTURE— FOR OSCAR NIEMEYER

**FERREIRA GULLAR**

(1975)

On the planet's shoulder
(in Caracas)
Oscar placed
forever
a bird a flower
(he didn't build our homes
of stone:
he worked with wings).

In the heart of suffering Algeria
he brought to earth one afternoon
a starship
lovely
as life even now can be.

(with his futuristic lines
Oscar teaches us
the dream is for us all).

He teaches us to dream
even when we're dealing
with hard stuff, hard textures:
the iron the cement the hunger
of human architecture.

He teaches us to live
in that which he transforms:
in the sugar of stone
the dream of an egg
the clay of dawn
flakes of snowy weather
the whiteness of an egg.
—Oscar teaches us
that beauty weighs light as a feather.

Photograph of architectural model of the Museum of Modern Art of Caracas, designed by Oscar Niemeyer in 1955.

No ombro do planeta
(em Caracas)
Oscar depositou
para sempre
uma ave uma flor
(ele não fez de pedra
nossas casas:
faz de asa).

No coração de Argel sofrida
fez aterrissar uma tarde
uma nave estelar
e linda
como ainda há de ser a vida.

(com seu traço futuro
Oscar nos ensina
que o sonho é popular).

Nos ensina a sonhar
mesmo se lidamos
com a matéria dura:
o ferro o cimento a fome
de humana arquitetura.

Nos ensina a viver
no que ele transfigura:
no açúcar da pedra
no sonho do ovo
na argila da aurora
na pluma da neve
na alvura do ovo.
—Oscar nos ensina
que a beleza é leve.

Oscar Niemeyer (Brazilian, 1907–2012), Interior design for unbuilt apartment buildings in Salvador da Bahia, Brazil, 1983–1984; Ink on paper, Collection of Biblioteca da Faculdade de Arquitetura e Urbanismo da Universidade de São Paulo. Courtesy of Fundação Oscar Niemeyer.

living room

# INTERVIEW WITH OSCAR NIEMEYER

## MARIA CECILIA LOSCHIAVO DOS SANTOS

### RIO DE JANEIRO, SEPTEMBER 1979

Oscar Niemeyer (1907–2012), the renowned Brazilian architect, has gone down in the history of modern world architecture owing to his seminal works. He also left a legacy for the history of furniture design, and this previously unpublished interview affords a quick exposure to his ideas and objectives relating to the furniture design he conceived.[1]

**MCLDS:** I'd like you to talk about your experiences in furnishing the buildings you designed.

**ON:** The problem I found in furnishing the buildings is that often the furniture and the interior layout completely undermined the architecture. Architecture foresees the spaces that must remain free, among groups of furniture, and sometimes the furniture is placed in such an improper way that the spaces are lost and the architecture is harmed. Therefore we always try to specify the location of the furnishings, but even so, even respecting the placement of the furniture, at times the furniture isn't in agreement with the architecture and the atmosphere lacks the unity we would like. Because of all that, I began designing furniture; of course there are good designers in Brazil, but when we're not lucky enough to find those decorators our projects suffer. So later I began studying with my daughter [Anna Maria Niemeyer] some pieces of furniture and my idea was to take advantage of the type of laminated wood that was used in Swedish chairs and make furniture with larger surfaces. And so we made chairs, armchairs, we made tables, we made a rocking chair, a lounge chair, a *marquesa*.[2] They're pleasant pieces to make and are quite functional; we look for the form we desire. It's something even a bit linked to architecture. And we have been manufacturing this furniture without any great commercial interest but have sold a lot and they've even been placed overseas. In Baubigny, France, they were used at the headquarters of the French Communist Party. But we like to use them in combination with other furniture and other architects, so there's a variation, but all of them bound to the principle that a piece of furniture is a complement to the architecture and must be up-to-date and modern, like the architecture itself.

**MCLDS:** When did you begin the production of furniture with Anna Maria?

**ON:** That business of dates is tough for me. I think I began something like two years ago, maybe. But the work is more hers than mine. I advise, design one or another piece with her.

**MCLDS:** In the case of Brasília, when you planned the buildings, what were the criteria adopted to find furniture compatible with the spirit of the architecture you were doing?

**ON:** In those days there was no time to think about designing furniture. We used ordinary furniture that was available on the market. Selecting, seeking the piece that best adapted to the architecture, the simplest piece, comfortable, such as the palace demanded. But our concern with furnishings was not to use too much furniture, few pieces, leaving open space between them, which is architectural space and is part of the architecture.

**MCLDS:** Who were the principal designers from whom you solicited furniture?

**ON:** Sérgio Rodrigues.

**MCLDS:** Why Sérgio Rodrigues?

**ON:** Because he's intelligent, designs well, and has types of furniture that are beautiful. Not that he's the only one, but he's the one who worked most closely with us.

**MCLDS:** What is the accommodation that must exist between the furniture and the interior?

**ON:** It depends on the type of building. In a residence, for example, the furnishings should accompany the lifestyle of the man of today, they're simpler, less austere. Older furniture adapted to a different attitude. Today things have changed a great deal and furnishings go along with that different lifestyle, people's way of being nowadays.

**MCLDS:** What about the tendencies toward extremely rational lines such as those espoused by Bauhaus — how do they look in a piece of furniture?

**ON:** I don't have the slightest interest in Bauhaus. Le Corbusier himself says that Bauhaus was a paradise of the mediocre, because the people of Bauhaus established a set of rules that their adepts followed and thought was the only solution possible. We believe that in both architecture and furnishings the tendency is to return to the older criterion, to do the thing with imagination and fantasy, because only in that way were the great monuments of architecture of the past done.

**MCLDS:** Do you believe in the existence of a relationship between politics and furniture design?

**ON:** That's asking for too much speculation. It's done when the guy says that a building represents a political sense. Not so. I, for example, did the Palaces in Brasília, and in the Palace of the Planalto I made a pulpit facing the Square of the Three Powers, and it was never used the way I would have liked. Never, from the pulpit of the Palace of the Planalto, did the people hear what we would have liked them to hear. So, it's the people and the governments that give architecture the character that emerges. For example, you see there in Italy, in Moscow the Kremlin was built by the czars and today it's the Communist Party that uses the building as its very well pleases, so there's no such thing as that business of political style in architecture, much less in furniture.

**MCLDS:** How do you view the problem of obsolescence in furniture?

**ON:** In the past, furniture was more elaborate, more artisanal, something very well done, very well thought out, and today it's competition. But there are also very well crafted and resistant pieces. There are others that are made that way to be sold like everything is made today.

**MCLDS:** It's the law of capitalism.

**ON:** It's competition, which is something different. Take the early old chairs, they were made with love, more care, more time for making them. Today, things made in series are quite different.

**MCLDS:** How do you characterize your production? Still artisanal?

**ON:** No, because the firm that makes the furniture is a well organized firm and acts using the best technique possible. They're Japanese there from São Paulo, Tendo Brasileira. They adapted to making the type of furniture we like, laminated wood, and they're very well made.

**MCLDS:** Of current production, based on what you recall of Brazilian furniture, who are the great designers, if we can apply the term to any of those professionals?

**ON:** I don't know if there are any great designers, but I do know that Sérgio Rodrigues designs furniture very well. He's a very good decorator, he did the furnishing for residences very well, there are many others around the country that I can't recall at the moment, I don't want to pass along wrong information. Sérgio Bernardes also makes interesting pieces.

**MCLDS:** I'd also like to find out about the consumption of furniture designed by you. You spoke of the exporting of your pieces. Can you elaborate?

**ON:** My furniture has been exported to France. It's being used in the Baubigny Center, as well as in the headquarters of the French Communist Party. But for me the subject of furniture is something parallel to my work and to which I devote little time. I'm talking about it solely out of consideration for you.

**MCLDS:** Thank you, but I'd like to know whether you don't see a very intimate relationship between furniture and the building.

**ON:** Yes, I do, greatly. I think that when they don't coincide, when there isn't unity, the architecture is harmed.

**MCLDS:** Do you agree with me that in Brazil this relationship isn't always honored?

**ON:** Sometimes it isn't honored, and a very large number of pieces are put in. Look at the Japanese house, which is the best possible. It showed great moderation in furnishing. Few rooms and few pieces of furniture. The house was simple. I think the Japanese house is a good example of interior furnishing. It's the most beautiful house that I'm acquainted with. But the issue of the number of pieces in a building is so complicated! For example, look at the reforms that we made in the congress, where we used carpets to specify the spots where the furniture should go, and it was only on the carpets that the pieces are placed. That was done with the idea of reserving the space between groups of furniture that constitutes part of the architecture. It's this free space that I'm talking about. For example, in every era a palace has demanded very little furniture. For it to be more imposing it has to have protected spaces and not be covered in furnishings. In my opinion, furnishings must remain in the setting and locations planned by the architect.

**MCLDS:** And what about Brazilian popular furniture?

**ON:** I'm not an expert on furniture. I've seen it but don't remember, and as I told you, I'm not very curious about it. But obviously good furniture, simple pieces, more refined furniture exists. Furniture nowadays is much better than in the past.

**MCLDS:** And what about the use of the hammock?

**ON:** I find hammocks very pretty, I value highly a hammock on the veranda, but sometimes people want to give a Brazilian air and think that stringing a hammock is the answer. I consider that complete nonsense.

**MCLDS:** Do you see any sense in looking for Brazilian character in furniture?

**ON:** I think it's good to create. I even think the mixture of modern furniture and old furniture, when done in moderation, is very pretty too. I think a decorator with good taste can use hammocks, old-fashioned furniture, but with modern pieces predominating, which is what balances well with today's architecture.

[1] The author wants to thank the Foundation for Support of Research of the State of São Paulo (FAPESP) for providing a grant that allowed her to conduct a series of interviews and conversations with the principal Brazilian designers for a master's thesis presented to the Department of Philosophy, Letters, and Human Sciences of the University of São Paulo (FFLCH) in 1985.

[2] A *marquesa* is a type of backless sofa with a cane seat (translator's note).

Living room with Sergio Rodrigues furniture photographed for the Oca catalogue.
Courtesy of Instituto Sergio Rodrigues

# INTERVIEW WITH SÉRGIO RODRIGUES

## MARIA CECILIA LOSCHIAVO DOS SANTOS

### RIO DE JANEIRO, 1979

Sérgio Rodrigues (1927–2014) was one of the architects and designers who together with other professionals like Oscar Niemeyer, José Zanine Caldas, Joaquim Tenreiro, Geraldo de Barros, and Lina Bo Bardi made Brazilian furniture design recognized and appreciated throughout the world.

Rodrigues gained a place in world design history with the Soft Armchair (*Poltrona Mole*) and other pieces that distinguished the twentieth-century Brazilian home.

I confess that I never met a designer with as copious and impassioned an oeuvre, possessor of a rich, complex biography and production and an integral devotion to wood and furniture. I reproduce here excerpts from the interview, based on unpublished originals recorded in 1979, in which Sérgio Rodrigues retrospectively examines aspects of his career, affording us a rapid glimpse into his world. The interview starts by dealing with aspects of the beginning of his career and closes with our final conversation, which took place in June 2014 in his atelier in the Botafogo district of Rio de Janeiro. Long conversations, meetings, telephone chats in which emerged aspects of the history and details of his adventures. On September 3, 2014, I said farewell to this great designer and friend, in a funeral ceremony at the Caju crematorium, enraptured by the celestial music of soft guitars played by nuns of the Order of Grace and Mercy. Thanks to FAPESP — the Foundation for Support of Research of the State of São Paulo — I carried out a series of interviews and conversations with the principal Brazilian designers for the master's thesis presented to the FFLCH — the School of Philosophy, Letters, and Human Sciences of the University of São Paulo — in 1985.[1]

**MCLDS:** Let's talk about the beginning of your career.

**SR:** I can't forgo saying what my grandmother in that period told me: "Sérgio, whatever you need, I'll provide the money for you." I said I was really going to need it because I want to open a firm with the people from São Paulo. And she asked me, "How much do you need?" I said 200 *contos*.[2] That was a huge amount of money, it was real money. "But what is it you're going to do?" [his grandmother asked] "I'm going to start a furniture business." "What? You're going to sell furniture? What nonsense is this? You studied Architecture, what nonsense. What a shame!" Then we opened the first one, which was a boutique. Boutique, in the sense of treatment, all carpeted, which wasn't common. The store was decorated with special finishing touches of paint, the first matte black paint there, which was one of the many talents of Carlo Hauner.[3] I was there for contingent contributions. Then we sent for the furnishings from São Paulo to be brought to Curitiba. They were pieces from Artesanal.

**MCLDS:** What was the store called?

**SR:** With their enthusiasm for their undertaking, with my passion I didn't even think about a name and used Paranaense Artisanal Furniture, a total lack of inspiration. I could have exploited my name, I could have arranged a Brazilian name the way I wanted to. I supplied the money and he supplied the furniture. After six months I had only sold one piece, a sofa there in Curitiba. The store was packed, with the governor's wife and her whole family visiting it, which was a point of interest in Curitiba, but no one was buying a thing. Everyone asked questions, but I wasn't selling anything.

**MCLDS:** Why?

**SR:** Because I was selling furniture in Curitiba, which was the land of classical furnishings. So when families were going to buy furniture in Curitiba, they would buy bedroom sets, groups of furniture, everything was bought in Curitiba. The large furniture firms, the traditional factories were in Curitiba, it was no Laubisch Hirth, or a Leandro Martins, but it was a good finishing. They weren't colonial pieces, they were all furnishings of style: Louis XV, Louis XVI, all those Louises, not even any Maries, it was only based on the Louises. To give you an idea of my business sense, I'm going to tell you about the single piece I sold. I received all the pieces and the price list was supposed to arrive from São Paulo, but it didn't come. And a person showed up who was interested in a certain type of sofa. "What a beautiful sofa, I want it." So I said I would call São Paulo, because the number wasn't written correctly, or it was missing from that page. I phoned São Paulo, which was kind of complicated to do, and the guy there was Italian, who was my partner, informed me that the price was 13–13 or 3? And I looked at the sofa and thought 13 contos was a lot of money for a sofa, so I sold for 3 contos a sofa that was 13. You're thinking I went to claim the money and say I had made a mistake and apologize? I didn't, and for the first time I dropped a bundle because I was too embarrassed to tell the guy I'd made a mistake. That was the first and only purchase made in Curitiba. So I packed up all the furniture and shipped it back to Artesanal. In the six months they were in the showroom, some of the pieces ended up damaged. I kept some of them and opened a smaller firm in Curitiba and made use of those pieces; others were sold for less than I had paid. It was a total loss and practically all of the 200 contos my grandmother gave me disappeared.

**MCLDS:** What was your experience like with Carlo Hauner in São Paulo?

**SR:** Carlo called me to São Paulo. I rented a house in Itaim, near the factory, on Arnaldo Street. It was the Artesanal Furniture Factory. Now, if I'm not mistaken, it's Urussui Street, where Forma is. Because Forma was the store on Barão de Itapetininga and still had something of Artesanal Furniture. When Martin Eisler and Ernesto Wolf became partners with Carlo Hauner, Carlo opened another store on Augusta Street that came to be called Forma. It was in the high part, on the same side as L'Atelier. I started in January 1954, making 10 contos, admiring the work of Carlo Hauner. His wife, Franca Hauner, wove spectacular fabrics and a large part of the pieces were done with fabrics she made. Then there was Martin Eisler with his toothpick-leg furniture, and I experienced great professional shocks with him, because he was very European. Carlo Hauner had nothing to do with Brazil and loved everything new, everything that was arriving on the scene. Lina Bo herself, with her drawings, I saw that it was stuff in Italian magazines of the time, but that it was catching on. I saw it up close and saw the architect herself up close. I had one or two encounters with Lina and would stand beside her, sort of stunned. Lina used to wear bangs, does she still wear bangs? I started to make my things. I showed them to Martin and he said: "Sérgio, don't try to make that thingamajig, don't." I even did architectural work with him in Atibaia. We talked a lot then and I didn't like the things he did, I liked Carlo's better. So one day I said: "I have a drawing I'd like to show you." And he replied, "With this here you're not going to be able to design furniture, with this you're not going to get anywhere." I was really put out, but I said to myself, It's the master talking, and who am I? I got discouraged but continued working there. I had contacts with Warchavchik and we had incredible chats. He had done the Paulistano Club, and I would talk with him a lot. I found him very interesting, because he was much older than me, and after a few meetings I had exhausted the topics of furniture and ambience. At that time he wasn't designing furniture. He was doing architecture, and his architecture was already absorbing something of the Brazilian, so that it was a half-hybrid architecture, not a classical Brazilian thing. From my conversations, I consider both Lina Bo and Warchavchik gods in that sense. I stayed in São Paulo for only a year and left at the end of that time.

**MCLDS:** When did you return to Rio de Janeiro?

**SR:** I arrived here in Rio at the beginning of 1955, my only possession was an old Volkswagen worth 150 contos. I stayed at my ex-father-in-law's place and he offered me a drawing board. I sat down and began to scribble. I had an idea and went to see Professor James, who had a school for decoration. Then I told my ex-father-in-law that I was going to open a store and that it would be called — I scribbled a few names, it had to be a Brazilian name, had to say something related to architecture and interiors, had to be a short name... I thought and thought, and out popped Oca. With three letters, it's the perfect name. It's the dwelling of Indians and surely it's Indian architecture, and to me a house without equipment isn't architecture. In my view, only a functioning house is architecture. So Oca would be the architecture that Lúcio Costa defined as: "indigenous dwelling, structurally pure, in which utensils and equipment, the implements and personal accessories are joined to and integrate with the formal support in service of life. The simple choice of name defines the meaning of the work accomplished by Sérgio Rodrigues and his group." There you see the spirit of the thing, to make something Brazilian. I was dazzled and my wife's then brother-in-law told me: "I want to be your partner." Partner in what? It would be a furniture laboratory, with art linked to everything artisanal, research into things Brazilian, along with architecture. The store's inauguration was on May 10, 1955. It was something! Modern furnishings. Lina Bo's chairs hadn't appeared here yet. And I hauled furniture on top of my head, on top of the car, and trying to attend everyone. I started designing furniture, little things. The store had everything, fabrics, Dominici lamps. In 1956 Otto Stupakoff showed up and took an interest in it all. He brought a portfolio of exceptional photographs.[4] We also had in the store an art gallery, and the exhibitions were overseen by Jaime Mauricio. Tenreiro also did them. It was a fashion that came from São Paulo, from Hauner and the people who came and did things too. It was in my interest, because the gallery attracted people. He showed me the photos and I said, "Organize this and I'll do an exhibition." And he asked, "You're going to put on a photo exhibition here in Brazil?" At the inauguration there was my grandmother, my sister, and my mother. The next day, a page in the *Correio da Manhã:* Photographer at the Oca gallery. At that time Oscar [Niemeyer] was beginning to design Brasília, doing the Catetinho.[5] To build Brasília they planned a small palace there of wood, and he came to see me. It was the first time I had spoken with him. He entered the store with three or four other people. He spoke with me and wasn't very open, he was rather dry and I was overly deferential: "I want to take some of these pieces for the Catetinho." He selected half a dozen pieces and looking at the display asked, "What's that over there?" I said it was the work of Otto Stupakoff, and he said, "Have him come see me and I'll give him four pages in the *Revista Módulo.*" That's how Sérgio became a promoter of photography, in an art gallery, with the backing of Oscar Niemeyer.

**MCLDS:** How was it that you conceived of the Soft Armchair? How did it all start?

**SR:** In those days I did some work for Mario Simonsen's office. Otto established himself here and, looking like a kid, asked me to design a large sofa for his studio. It turned out to be expensive, he couldn't pay, and I got worried, irritated, because I really wanted to do it for Otto. I stored everything, and as I already had the idea for the exhibition *Furniture as Art Object*, and in order not to have only the sofa I ordered an armchair made too. And I said, I'm going to do it either in leather or mesh, it'll be with real thick hammock cloth. That was a weave that Lili Correa de Araujo carried, a gray fabric of which we had used a remnant. Otto photographed the armchair. We took the chair and two more pieces to the end of the beach at Leblon and placed them close to the sea, on top of that hard sand, like the sand at Santos. We put them there, set up the camera, and just when we were ready to take the photo a wave came and it was all captured by Otto. My despair at seeing the water rise over the furniture! It wet the edge, but didn't soak the piece, so we rearranged and took the photo. It would be the photo for the catalogue of the *Furniture as Art Object* exhibition. Then I took everything to Oca and my partner said, "What's this business?" and I said, "It's going to be in the show window." The partners said never, and I said "It's my life, I believed in that piece and I've been thinking about something like it all my life, and I want it to be just so and that's how it's going to be." As far as art was concerned I was the responsible party and the others shut up and said, "We'll see." Then came the launching, and the faces the partners made about the Soft Armchair and the Soft Sofa were as horrible as could be. Close friends said it was pretty, it's something new. "Look here, Sérgio, this doesn't go with my other furniture, maybe for a house in the country." One joker said, "This would do for a dog's bed, but only an expensive dog." And to top everything, the armchair stayed in the display window for a year without a single sale. The first concept of the Soft Armchair, with thick legs, came from the sofa designed for Otto Stupakoff. I already had those elements in mind, thick legs etc., to show a lot of wood. After it won a prize, in 1961, everybody started buying, foreign magazines published articles about it, and it became a success.

**MCLDS:** What about Brasília? How did your participation in designing the furnishings for the public buildings come about?

**SR:** In Brasília, in the Itamaraty Palace, I did the minister's story. [Joaquim] Tenreiro did the Banquet Room. Bernardo Figueiredo, along with Jorge Souza Hue, did the ambience. I also did furnishings for the Palace of the Dawn, in 1968. When Oscar called me to Brasília, before the inauguration in 1957, I went to the UN to see what was new for palaces and such. In 1961 Darcy Ribeiro got in touch, praised me, and said, "I want you to make the chairs for the Auditório Dois Candangos, which was planned by Alcides da Rocha Miranda.[6] It's 250 chairs to manufacture and set up. You have two weeks to make and assemble." That was a very serious business. Every time I talk about it I get very emotional and tears fall. Then Darcy Ribeiro appeared the day before Good Friday and asked, "How are things going there? Do you have a chair assembled?" He commented, "That's good, how pretty! The chair is wonderful, spectacular, you're a genius." I knew it did no good to be a genius if the chairs weren't ready. If Jango Goulart came, if he showed up, there were just those iron skewers and such. And me wondering how it could be solved. I saw the leather part, the seat part, the fasteners, and we put everything on the stage and there were thousands of small parts. And I thought, Workers are welding the ceiling and they're not going to understand it, how's it going to be? Then Darcy said, "Let's call the people at the university." And I said it was the day before Good Friday and no one would be there. Darcy said, "I'm going to attach banners to the sides of the university's three buses saying HELP THE AUDITÓRIO DOIS CANDANGOS." He had the banners painted and the next day the buses arrived packed with students by the thousands! All those people arrived, but what now? I said, "We're going to set up an assembly line." We told the women: "You put in the fasteners," and some fit and others didn't — naturally, the thing hadn't been done in series, hadn't been studied with precision. Hand-crafted leather is like that; people pulled, one strong guy helped, helped till his hands gave out! Well, the auditorium was inaugurated with only two chairs missing. We stayed up all night, you have no idea! Everybody working and enthusiastic, and in the end everything was assembled, minus the two chairs. Two people stood there as if they were assistants. Really something impressive, and a general clamor, everyone hugging, a great sense of unity. Darcy was possessed.

**MCLDS:** Sérgio, how good to be here again, on Conde de Irajá Street! You received me in this place a long time ago, many memories and conversations!

**SR:** That's right, girl, but things are different now. Rio has changed a lot, now we have good restaurants, like São Paulo. Look at the one next door. If everything works out I'm going to the exhibition in New York. If you want the Soft from the office here, you can take it, it's yours. I found out you're with those young people from Brasília who interviewed me.

Editor's notes:

[1] The author wants to thank the Foundation for Support of Research of the State of São Paulo (FAPESP) for providing a grant that allowed her to conduct a series of interviews and conversations with the principal Brazilian designers for a master's thesis presented to the Department of Philosophy, Letters, and human Sciences of the University of São Paulo (FFLCh) in 1985.

[2] *Conto* means 1,000 escudo, the currency of Portugal from 1911 until the introduction of the euro in 1999.

[3] Carlo Hauner was an Italian-born Brazilian designer who opened the furniture firm Forma in São Paulo.

[4] Otto Stupakoff was a pioneer of fashion photography in Brazil with an international career that included important works of photo journalism.

[5] A frame building, the Catetinho, or "little Catete," was the first structure in the new capital and served as on-site headquarters for the planners (translator's note).

[6] Darcy Ribeiro was a Brazilian anthropologist and political scientist who worked in topics of education and culture. He served as Ministry of Education under the João Goulart government.

# DESIGNERS
# BIOGRAPHIES

## AMANDA YORK

## GENARO ÁLVAREZ (MEXICAN, ACTIVE 20TH CENTURY)

Genaro Álvarez's mosaics are expressive designs applied to floors, murals, furniture, lamps, and trays. His designs incorporating natural rocks, semiprecious stones, and glass were constructed by hand through his workshop, Genaro Álvarez Studio, in Mexico City. Collectors and institutions in the United States embraced Alvarez's work. He completed several murals in Chicago, including a large composition titled *The Spirit of Public Housing* at the Chicago Housing Authority. [Checklist no. 1]

Miguel Arroyo in the ceramics studio at the Escuela de Artes Plásticas y Aplicadas (School of Fine and Applied Arts), Caracas, 1955. Photo by Sara Guardia de Mendoza. Courtesy of Centro de Estudios de Archivos Audiovisuales y Artísticos and the Mendoza Guardia Family.

## MIGUEL ARROYO (VENEZUELAN, 1920–2004)

During his prolific career, Miguel Arroyo was a designer, painter, sculptor, potter, educator, museum director, curator, and art critic. After studying at the Academia de Bellas Artes in Caracas, he assisted Luis Alfredo López Méndez with the production of a painted plafond for the Venezuelan pavilion at the 1939–40 World's Fair in New York City. Returning to Venezuela, he taught drawing and art history at the Liceo Aplicación de Caracas (1944–46), before continuing his studies at the Carnegie Institute of Technology in Pittsburgh (1946–48). Arroyo served as the head of the Escuela de Artes Plásticas y Aplicadas (School of Fine and Applied Arts) in Caracas from 1953 to 1956 and mentored a group of potters, including Maria Luisa Zuloaga de Tovar, Seka Severin de Tudja, Cristina Merchán, Reyna Herrera, and Tecla Tofano, and founded the artist cooperative Forma Veinte (Form Twenty) in 1954. Exhibitions he organized promoted their work, thus elevating the status of the medium from craft to fine art. His pottery group earned the National Prize for Applied Arts at the XV Salón Oficial (1954). Arroyo was pivotal to the organization of the *Venezuelan Pottery* exhibition held in 1963 at the Museum of Contemporary Crafts in New York City. He later joined the staffs of the Facultad de Arquitectura y Urbanismo (Faculty of Architecture and Urbanism) (1957–59), the school of architecture at the Universidad Simón Bolívar in Caracas (1975–78), and the school of arts at the Universidad Central de Venezuela (1978–84). Arroyo's extensive work as a museum director and curator distinguished him as the father of the modern Venezuelan museum. In 1959, Arroyo he was appointed director of the Museo de Bellas Artes (Caracas), a position he held until 1975. Administratively, he organized the museum's staff and departments, created the registration department, systematized conservation, began collections of drawings, prints, graphic design, and photography, and promoted international loans of works. In 1949, Arroyo established Tienda Gato, a small store that brought modern design objects and furniture, books, music records, and contemporary art to Venezuelan audiences. Arroyo designed furniture and interiors, particularly between 1948 and 1959, and his work in this field is distinguished by his fusion of local materials with modern forms, which could be installed harmoniously in typical eighteenth-century colonial architecture. For his design for the photographer and writer Alfredo Boulton's home in Pampatar, Venezuela, Arroyo situated his furniture alongside a mobile by Alexander Calder and an abstract geometric painting by Alexander Otero, with whom he frequently worked on design projects in the 1950s. [Checklist nos. 2–8, 38]

## ODILÓN AVALOS (MEXICAN, 1881–1957)

Odilón Avalos was born to a family of glassmakers in Puebla, Mexico, where the technique of blowing glass was introduced by Spaniards in the sixteenth century. He relocated to Guadalajara in 1903 (during a period of economic and industrial development) and introduced blown-glass techniques to the area. Avalos established a workshop in the Analco neighborhood, where he experimented with materials and taught his craft. His designs are diverse, spanning from abstract, bulbous forms to others that are whimsical and representational, such as vessels resembling cacti or cartoonish faces. In 1954, he was honored with *El Premio Jalisco* (The Jalisco Award) by the state of Jalisco for his cultural and economic contributions. Upon his death, the company was passed on first to Avalos's son, then his grandson. [Checklist no. 10]

## LINA BO BARDI (BRAZILIAN, B. ITALY, 1914–92)

Italian-born Lina Bo Bardi moved to Brazil after a visit in 1946, when she met such prominent architects as Oscar Niemeyer (1907–2012) and Roberto Burle Marx. Life in postwar Italy was made difficult for Bardi and her husband, Pietro Maria Bardi, both participants in the Italian resistance. Her career was multidisciplinary, with roles as a writer and editor, designer, architect, curator, and educator. While still in Italy, she served as editor of *Domus* magazine, wrote for *Stile* and *Rima,* founded the architecture periodical *A Cultura della Vita,* and — once in Brazil — cofounded with her husband the periodical *Habitat* [checklist nos. 84, 85]. She is most widely known for her architectural endeavors, including her own residence (1951), known as the Casa de Vidro (Glass House), and the Museu de Arte de São Paulo (1968), for which her husband was appointed the founding director in 1947. The museum's inventive Brutalist structure is characterized by unadorned concrete and expanses of glass that carried over into the interior, while paintings appear to levitate on panels of glass installed in the middle of the main gallery. She designed the museum as a hub for wide-ranging activities in an attempt to remove the barriers between art and everyday life, an aim that defined much of her career. In 1959, she converted an abandoned sugar mill in Bahia into a craft museum, the Solar do Unhão, and a 1963 installation there titled *Civilização do Nordeste* (Civilization of the Northeast) designed by Bardi mimicked a street market with shelves and stalls of materials. Later projects include the Centro de Lazer Fábrica da Pompéia (Pompéia Factory Leisure Centre) (1986), which housed arts and crafts workshops, a theater, restaurant, library, gallery, sport areas, and multipurpose public spaces, and the Teatro Oficina (1991), a variable space composed of repurposed materials that dissolved the distinctions between actor and audience, stage and backstage. In 1948, she founded the Studio de Arte e Arquitetura Palma with Giancarlo Palanti (1906–77) to design economical furniture of pressed wood or plastic manufactured by Pau Brasil Ltda., the fabrication studio they opened, and through which they furnished the Museu de Arte de São Paulo's first headquarters. In the 1950s, Bardi began designing metal-framed furniture with upholstered seats and backs. Later designs, such as her 1967 *Cadeira de beira de estrada* (Roadside Chair), embody an unfussy aesthetic with simplicity of design and reduction and rawness of material. [Checklist nos. 11–16]

## JOSÉ CARLOS BORNANCINI (BRAZILIAN, 1923–2008) AND
## NELSON IVAN PETZOLD (BRAZILIAN, B. 1931)

A diverse range of industrial design projects characterizes José Carlos Bornancini's and Nelson Ivan Petzold's longtime collaboration. The pair strove to improve the functionality of everyday products by designing mass-produced household items customized for a Brazilian market. Divergent educational backgrounds perhaps enhanced their interdisciplinary projects. Bornancini trained as a civil engineer, while Petzold studied architecture. Both men studied at the University of Rio Grande do Sul, and graduated in 1946 and 1949, respectively. Their over two hundred products include items such as scissors with a pliable handle for use in both hands and a thermos with an internal mechanism to avoid spilling. The utensils that composed Bornancini and Petzold's culinary sets for picnicking conveniently click together when not in use. The designers also astutely reimagined preexisting industrial products and operations. For example, the Wallig company produced their stove design, which was 15 cm shorter than the international standard to better suit the average height of Brazilian women. The pair also worked with a failing accordion manufacturer, saving the business by using its existing facilities to shift factory production: rather than accordions, they began using the equipment and materials like composite wood to make modular cabinetry. Thus, the company was able to remain in business while simultaneously introducing modern kitchens to Brazil. [Checklist no. 17]

Home of Roberto Burle Marx in Rio de Janeiro, Brazil, c. 1955. Photo by Marcel Gautherot. Courtesy of Instituto Moreira Salles.

## ROBERTO BURLE MARX
## (BRAZILIAN, 1909–94)

Roberto Burle Marx is credited with establishing a Brazilian style of garden design, featuring indigenous fauna — sometimes in flowing biomorphic arrangements — a sharp contrast to the rigid compositions of formal European gardens. Initially trained as a painter, he saw landscape design as an extension of his diverse artistic practice, which included sculpture, mosaics, and murals in addition to household objects, such as jewelry, ceramics, and glass vessels. From 1928 to 1930, he studied painting in Berlin, where his experience of the Dahlem Botanical Garden proved pivotal; there he observed the respectful treatment of plants native to Brazil and was later motivated to elevate their status in his home country, where European species were often given preferential treatment in landscape designs. Upon his return to Brazil, Burle Marx studied painting, architecture, and landscape design at the Escola Nacional de Belas Artes in Rio. He became acquainted with the architect Lúcio Costa, and the two completed the first of many collaborations, a private residence named the Schwartz house in 1932. They later worked together with the architect Oscar Niemeyer on the plans for Brasília, Brazil's new capital, which was established in 1960. He is most widely known for his 1970 design of the geometric patterned walkways for Copacabana Beach, and his landscape designs can be found today throughout Brazil, as well as Argentina, Chile, Venezuela, France, South Africa, and the United States, among other countries. An early environmentalist, he was outspoken on ecological issues over the course of his career. Burle Marx settled in a house on the edge of Rio in 1948, and, for the remainder of his life, it served as his home and studio. His legacy includes the nearly three thousand gardens he designed as well as the fifty plant species that now bear his name. [Checklist nos. 18, 19]

## GERALDO DE BARROS (BRAZILIAN, 1923–98)

Initially a painter and photographer, Geraldo de Barros promoted experimental photography in Brazil by founding a photography laboratory at the Museu de Arte de São Paulo (1949), where he developed an exhibition of his work titled *Fotoformas* the following year. In 1951, de Barros traveled to Paris to study lithography at the École Nationale Supérieure des Beaux-Arts. Afterward, he studied briefly at the Hochschule für Gestaltung Ulm (Ulm School of Design) in Germany with the institution's founders, Otl Aicher and Max Bill. The two teachers offered a scholarship from de Barros to study at Ulm for a longer period of time, but de Barros decided to return to his family in Brazil and ceded his position at the school to Alexandre Wollner, his future business partner. Upon returning to Brazil in 1952, he — along with six other artists — established Grupo Ruptura, which also exhibited at Museu de Arte de São Paulo. His photographic interests are evident in the experimental method he employed when documenting his later furniture. In 1954, he shifted his focus to champion the possibilities for industrial design in Brazil by founding the furniture design and production company Unilabor, a São Paulo Christian workers' collective. Espousing utopian collectivism throughout its thirteen-year lifespan, the company's primarily wood-and-metal furniture was the product of group decision-making. At the same time, de Barros founded Forminform, Brazil's first design firm, in 1958 with Wollner, Ruben Martins, and Walter Macedo. De Barros also designed for the company Hobjeto Indústria e Comércio de Móveis S.A., which he cofounded with Antonio Bioni in 1964, and they opened a storefront for its affordable furniture in 1966. Despite the success of these ventures, de Barros decided to dedicate himself more fully to painting and photography soon thereafter. [Checklist nos. 20, 21]

## FELIPE DERFLINGHER (MEXICAN, 1931-2013)

Felipe Derflingher championed glassmaking in Mexico by organizing exhibitions of glass (and religious art) in Mexico City, directing the stained glass school Kaleidoscopio, and calling for glassworkers to unite to share ideas and boost academic interest in their craft. He referred to Mexico as "the magic land of colored glass" and stated that color is engrained in Mexican culture. Derflingher's works are characterized by his experimental approach to materials, including the fusion of basalts to make genuine obsidian, which he combined with silver. He also produced "caged glass" works, the form of which is dictated by a metal armature with cutouts filled with molten recycled glass. His works are produced in Cuernavaca by Feders, a company owned by his family and established in 1890 that today spans five generations of Derflinghers. [Checklist no. 22]

## JOSÉ FEHER (MEXICAN, B. HUNGARY, 1902–88)

José Feher (born József Fehér) studied at the Academy of Fine Arts in Budapest (1924–28), after which he traveled to Italy, briefly worked for the French painter André Lhote, and exhibited his paintings in the Salon d'Automne in Paris, where he settled. He fled the Nazi invasion in 1940 for Mexico, where he continued painting and began making ceramics, eventually settling in the state of Texcoco. He quickly became acquainted with fellow artist émigrés José and Kati Horna, Emerico "Chiki" Weisz, and Leonora Carrington. Later, he met Cynthia Sargent and Wendell Riggs, who sold Feher's ceramics at their Bazaar Sábado in Mexico City. While he became best known for his ceramics, which were characterized by the incorporation of pre-Columbian imagery, Feher was trained as a painter, and his paintings were included in exhibitions in Mexico City, such as an exhibition of Hungarian painters (1945) at the Palacio de Bellas Artes (Mexico City) and shows at the Galería de Arte Mexicano (1952 and 1960) and the Palacio de Bellas Artes (1970). The painter Rufino Tamayo, who shared similar artistic ideologies, wrote the introduction to the catalogue of his 1952 solo exhibition. In 1964, Mexico's Instituto Nacional de Antropología e Historia commissioned Feher to make reproductions of early Mexican pottery, a field in which he continued to specialize. Shortly before his death, the exhibition *José Feher: Pintor, Escultor, Dibujante, Ceramista* (José Feher: Painter, Sculptor, Cartoonist, Ceramist) premiered at the Museo de Monterrey in 1985. [Checklist no. 23]

Logo of the Gunz wooden lamp and furniture factory, c. 1942. Courtesy of Fundación Gego

## GEGO (VENEZUELAN, B. GERMANY, 1912–94)

Born as Gertrude Goldschmidt, the designer, architect, and artist Gego is considered one of the most important Latin American postwar artists. Gego studied architecture and engineering at the Technische Hochschule (Institute of Technology) in Stuttgart with the architect Paul Bonatz, graduating in 1938. As a member of a Jewish family, it was crucial that she escape Germany, and she fled to Venezuela by way of England in 1939. Gego was hired as an architect at a firm and soon married the exiled German businessman Ernst Gunz. Together, they founded Taller Gunz (1940–44), a design firm specialized in wooden furniture and lamp designs. In 1952, Gego and her husband separated, and she became a Venezuelan citizen. She moved with her new partner, Gerd Leufert (a graphic designer, artist, and teacher), to the coastal town of Tarma, Venezuela, in 1953, where she practiced drawing and watercolor painting. Her paintings were shown for the first time in XV Salón Oficial Anual de Arte Venezolano (Official Annual Venezuelan Art Salon) in 1954. The following year, she returned to Germany to install her first international exhibition at the Galerie Wolfgang Gurlitt in Munich. In 1956, she relocated to Caracas from Tarma and made her first three-dimensional artwork. Gego began teaching in 1958 at the Universidad Central de Venezuela with a watercolors course. From 1971 to 1977, she taught at the Instituto de Diseño Fundación Neumann INCE (Institute of Design — Foundation Neumann INCE) in Caracas. Gego spent part of 1960 conducting research for her academic courses in New York City, and her work was acquired by the Museum of Modern Art and the New York Public Library. The Museo de Bellas Artes (Caracas) hosted a solo exhibition of her drawings the following year. Gego traveled for workshops and courses in 1963, attending the University of

California–Berkeley, the Tamarind Lithography Workshop (Los Angeles), and the Pratt Institute (New York); she returned to the Tamarind Lithography Workshop as an artist fellow in 1966. Soon after she was awarded the National Prize in Drawing at the XXIX Salón Oficial Anual de Arte Venezolano in 1968, she began her most widely known environmental work, *Reticulária.* These works, for which Gego assembled stainless steel wires in triangular netlike arrangements filling entire rooms, were first shown in 1969 at the Museo de Bellas Artes and the Center for Inter-American Relations (now the Americas Society). In 1979, Gego was awarded the Premio Nacional de Artes Plásticas de Venezuela (National Award for Applied Arts). She remained artistically active in Caracas, with frequent international exhibitions and museum acquisitions, until her death. [Checklist nos. 24, 25]

## KLAUS GRABE (B. GERMANY 1910, ACTIVE IN MEXICO, D. UNITED STATES 2004)

Klaus Grabe met Michael van Beuren while the two were studying at the Bauhaus in the early 1930s. In 1938, Grabe moved to Mexico City, where he and van Beuren established Domus, a furniture design firm with a workshop nearby in Naucalpan. The two collaborated on an early successful and popular design for the company, the *Alacrán* chaise, a submission to the Museum of Modern Art's (New York) 1940 competition *Organic Design in Home Furnishings*. Grabe left Domus and returned to Europe at the beginning of the Second World War to serve in the German army. [Checklist nos. 68–70]

John Hay Whitney, President of Museum of Modern Art's Board of Trustees, and Ira A. Hirschmann, Vice President of Bloomingdale's, congratulate Xavier Guerrero on winning the museum's Latin American Industrial Design Competition on June 19, 1941. Fellow winners from left to right: Bernardo Rudofsky, São Paulo, Brazil; Julio Villalobos, Buenos Aires, Argentina; Alfredo Fresnedo, Montevideo, Uruguay. Sponsored in conjunction with the Museum of Modern Art's exhibition *Organic Design in Home Furnishings* (September 24–November 9, 1941). Digital Image © The Museum of Modern Art/Licensed by SCALA/Art Resource, NY.

## XAVIER GUERRERO (MEXICAN, 1896–1974)

Although primarily known as a muralist associated with Diego Rivera, David Alfaro Siqueiros, and José Clemente Orozco, Xavier Guerrero achieved great success in collaboration with his wife, Clara Porset, on furniture designs. After learning house and sign painting from his father, Guerrero moved in 1912 to Guadalajara, where he began his first murals. Upon moving to Mexico City in 1919, he met many fellow artists and assisted in the production of murals by Roberto Montenegro and Rivera. He was a founding member of the Marxist Syndicate of Revolutionary Painters, Sculptors, and Engravers of Mexico (1922). Through this organization, he cofounded the progressive magazine *El Machete* in 1924 with Siqueiros, which was markedly different from other publications because of its emphasis on imagery over text. Management of the publication was transferred to Mexico's Communist Party later that year, and the publication continued until 1938 with its format vastly altered. He participated in the Museum of Modern Art's (New York) 1940 competition *Organic Design in Home Furnishings* with Porset. The couple also collaborated on an entry for MoMA's *International Competition for Low-Cost Furniture Design* (1950). [Checklist no. 44]

## ÓSCAR HAGERMAN (MEXICAN, B. SPAIN 1936)

Born in Spain of Swedish descent, the designer and architect Oscar Hagerman arrived in Mexico at the age of 17 by way of Havana, Cuba. Like many designers of the period in Mexico, Hagerman was greatly inspired by local materials, but his career differs from the others in that he designed for the rural and poor, rather than appropriating their aesthetics for a larger market. Hagerman studied architecture at the Universidad Nacional Autónoma de México (UNAM, National Autonomous University of Mexico) and he put his studies to use by designing homes, schools, and furniture with the indigenous and underprivileged communities of Mexico in mind. In the 1960s, Hagerman began work with the Cooperativa de Carpinteros Don Emiliano (Don Emiliano Carpenters Cooperative) in Ciudad Nezahualcóyotl on the outskirts of Mexico City. His process became collaborative and participatory, and he constructed children's furniture and the *Arrullo* (Lullaby) chair with the Cooperativa. He stretched his reach further into rural Mexico, where he observed traditional construction practices, and proposed ways to thoughtfully and respectively integrate modern technology and materials, incorporating local materials, forms, uses, and scales. Hagerman makes minimal interventions, and his designs consist mainly of subtle improvements, such as gentle alterations for increased comfort. Hagerman taught at the Universidad Iberoamericana, Universidad Autónoma de San Luis Potosí, and UNAM. [Checklist no. 26]

## KLAUS HEUFER (VENEZUELAN, B. GERMANY, 1923–2013)

During the postwar reconstruction era of the Marshall Plan, Klaus Heufer studied architecture at the Technische Universität Carolo–Wilhelmina zu Braunschweig (Technical University, Braunschweig, Germany, 1945–50) under Friedrich Wilhelm Kraemer, for whom he also worked. The university architectural curriculum was based on the International Style, characterized by modern materials, open and unornamented spaces, and multipurpose structures. These themes had a deep impact on Heufer, and, when he immigrated to Venezuela in 1952 on the invitation of the architect Luis Malaussena to assist with the design of the Salón Venezuela del Círculo Militar (Venezuela's Military Circle Hall, 1956) and the Hotel Maracay (1955), he spread these ideas in his new country. In 1958, Heufer cofounded the firm Arquitectos Asociados (Architectural Associates) with Francisco Pimentel. Despite their short-lived collaboration (the two parted in 1960), they designed several buildings in Caracas: La Sede Centro del Banco Nacional de Descuento (The Headquarters of the National Bank de Descuendo, 1960), the Edificio Santa María (1959), Hotel Caracas (1960), and the Liveca Laboratories (1958). Throughout his career, Heufer grew increasingly interested in domestic projects. Inspired by his adopted country, he began formulating a "tropical" modern architecture, which collapsed the boundaries between local and international styles as well as interior and exterior spaces, reinforcing connections between the garden, terrace, and house. In 2014, *Arqueología de la modernidad* (Archeology of Modernity), a comprehensive exhibition devoted to his work and legacy, was organized at the Centro Cultural del B.O.D. in Caracas. [Checklist no. 27]

## LOS CASTILLO (MEXICAN, F. 1939)

The silversmithing collective Los Castillo was founded by Antonio Castillo Terán (1917–2000), who moved to Taxco, Mexico, from Toluca in 1933. He was among the first apprentices in William Spratling's workshop, where each of his brothers and Los Castillo cofounders (Jorge, Miguel, and Justo) later worked. The American artist Margot van Voorhies Carr toured Spratling's atelier in 1937, where she met Antonio, and the two soon married. The Castillo brothers founded their own workshop in 1939, and Carr contributed to the company's designs for the remainder of their marriage. (The couple divorced, and she established her own company, Margot de Taxco, in 1948.) The brothers experimented with materials while simultaneously reviving ancient techniques, and they become known for the skillful execution of married metals — precise solders fusing silver, copper, or brass so that these different elements appear to form a single sheet — and inlays of unusual materials, such as abalone shells. Like Spratling, the brothers established an apprenticeship program, and their business grew rapidly; in the postwar years Los Castillo employed roughly 300 craftsmen. Two Taxco and two Mexico City storefronts were opened, and a school was founded for the apprentices' children. Since Antonio's death, Los Castillo has continued to operate under the leadership of his daughter Emilia Castillo. [Checklist nos. 28–30]

Los Castillo Plateros." 4 15/16 x 6 7/8 in. Spratling-Taxco Collection, The Latin American Library, Tulane University.

The Los Castillo store. 4 15/16 x 6 7/8 in. Spratling-Taxco Collection, The Latin American Library, Tulane University.

## ALDEMIR MARTINS (BRAZILIAN, 1922–2006)

Aldemir Martins was active throughout his career as a painter and sculptor, but it is his illustrations that are most recognized, and his drawings frequently accompanied the writings of such Brazilian authors as Rachel de Queiroz and Franklin Távora. Despite moving to São Paulo in 1946, his childhood in the northeastern Brazilian state of Ceará colors much of his works, as is evidenced in his recurring use of *cangaceiros* (bandits), animals, and cacti. [Checklist no. 31]

## PAULO MENDES DA ROCHA (BRAZILIAN, B. 1928)

Having earned a degree in architecture from Universidade Presbiteriana Mackenzie (Mackenzie Presbyterian University) College of Architecture in São Paulo in 1954, Paulo Mendes da Rocha opened an office the following year. Ever since, his career has mostly been dedicated to the São Paulo school of Brutalist public and private architecture. At just thirty years old, Mendes da Rocha completed an early masterpiece, São Paulo's Paulistano Athletic Club (1958), a commission that he was awarded through a competition; his design earned the 1961 São Paulo Biennial Grand Prize. The Athletic Club characteristically fused architecture and furniture, and he designed the *Paulistano* chair (1957) [Checklist no. 32] to furnish the Club's living room. The chair consists of a 17-foot-long bent steel rod looped with a single weld and topped by a single sheet of leather or canvas to form a combined seat and back — a design both simple and extraordinary [checklist no. 33]. Other significant projects include the Museu Brasileiro de Escultura (Brazilian Museum of Sculpture, 1986), the revitalization of São Paulo's Patriarch Plaza and Viaduct do Cha (completed 2002), and extensive renovations of the Pinacoteca do Estado de São Paulo (1993), the city's oldest art museum. In addition to his prolific architectural career, Mendes da Rocha taught architecture at the University of São Paulo, joining the faculty in 1959. The Mies van der Rohe Prize for Latin American Architecture (2000) and the Pritzker Architecture Prize (2006) have recognized his notable contributions to the field. [Checklist no. 32]

Cristina Merchán. Photo by Fina Gómez Revenga.

### CRISTINA MERCHÁN (VENEZUELAN, D. FRANCE, 1927–1987)

Initially a painter, Cristina Merchán became a potter. In 1951, she earned a degree from the Universidad de Guadalajara (Mexico), where she had accompanied her spouse, painter and cartoonist Manuel Antonio Salvatierra. Afterward, she studied low-fire pottery at the Escuela de Artes Plásticas y Aplicadas (School of Fine and Applied Arts) in Caracas (1954–57) with Miguel Arroyo, alongside the potters Tecla Tofano and Reyna Herrera. During these years, she participated in the cooperative Forma Veinte (Form Twenty), and her work was included in the Salón Oficial Anual de Arte Venezolano (Official Annual Venezuelan Art Salon); in 1957, she earned the Premio Nacional de Artes Aplicadas (National Award for Applied Arts). Merchán received grants from the Fundación Eugenio Mendoza that enabled her to travel to Barcelona to study high-fire stoneware with Francesc Albors and José Llorens Artigas at the Conservatorio Municipal de Artes Suntuarias "Massana" (Municipal School of Luxury Arts) from 1958 to 1961. In 1958, she began dividing her time between Barcelona, Paris, and Caracas and continued to show in group exhibitions at the Sala Mendoza (a *Kunsthalle* run by the Fundación Mendoza in Caracas) in 1959 and 1960. Her first one-person exhibition of her high-fire pottery was held at the Museo de Bellas Artes (Caracas) in 1963, followed by a solo exhibition at the Sala Mendoza in 1964, where she presented works from her *Los Bichos* (Bugs) series of fantastical animals. This exhibition marked a pivotal moment, as Merchán transitioned from the tradition of utilitarian ceramics, and became more interested in the medium as sculpture. Her work was shown internationally throughout her lifetime, including solo exhibitions at the Museo de Bellas Artes (1969), Henriette Gomès gallery in Paris (1973, 1976, and 1977), and at the Museu de Cerámica in Barcelona (1980). Her later works consisted mainly of ovoid vases, glazed and fired at high temperatures. Merchán is distinguished by her glazes of subtle tonal variations that are laid over surfaces alternately smooth, textured, or incised with simplistic geometric patterns. Her personal collection of works is now housed at the Musée des Arts Décoratifs, the Louvre, Paris. [Checklist nos. 33–35]

Rubén Núñez, Paris, 1951.

Advertisement for Cristalería Araya, C.A. in Caracas.

## RUBÉN NÚÑEZ (VENEZUELAN, 1930–2012)

Rubén Núñez began studying at the Escuela de Artes Plásticas y Artes Aplicadas (School of Fine and Applied Arts) in Caracas in 1945, where he focused on drawing and printmaking. He traveled to Paris in 1949. There, he joined fellow Venezuelan artists (including Alejandro Otero) and participated in the founding of the avant-garde group Los Disidentes (The Dissidents), which launched a short-lived magazine opposed to the antiquated visions of arts organizations in Venezuela and in favor of abstraction. In Paris, Núñez studied the history and technology of film, painted Op compositions of black dots that appeared to vibrate on a white background, and created kinetic sculptures inspired, in part, by Alexander Calder. Núñez's interest in kinetic art led him to study the technology of glass (whose appearance can be manipulated by light) in Murano, Italy, from 1955 to 1959. His crystal-and-glass works earned him the 1959 Premio Nacional de Artes Aplicadas (National Award for Applied Arts). Upon his return to Venezuela, he founded the Taller Araya in Caracas, a glass workshop where he produced most of his works until the 1990s. In 1962, he ventured into industrial design, producing a glass bottle design for Ron Añejo Pampero Especial; known as the "caneca," the bottle is still in production. In 1969, Núñez began learning how to create three-dimensional holograms. He visited universities and museums of science and technology to understand the field better, and between 1972 and 1974, he continued his studies at the University of London and the Science Museum. Taking up the medium as an art form, he studied further at the Institut d'Optique in Paris and the School of Holography in New York. He combined his extensive knowledge of glass, crystals, and lasers to create works he termed as "holokinetic," and established himself as a pioneer in this artistic field. These works were displayed in a solo exhibition at the Museum of Holography, New York, in 1978. Núñez eventually returned to Venezuela and founded the Fundación Espacio-Luz (Space-Light Foundation) to continue the promotion of holographic art. [Checklist nos. 36, 37]

## ALEJANDRO OTERO (VENEZUELAN, 1921–90)

After studying painting at the Escuela de Artes Plásticas y Artes Aplicadas (School of Fine and Applied Arts) in Caracas from 1939 to 1944, Alejandro Otero went to Paris in 1945 on scholarships from the French government and Venezuela's Ministry of Education. His work had previously been inspired by Paul Cezanne's landscapes, but his style quickly shifted to abstraction when he studied the work of Piet Mondrian and Pablo Picasso in Paris. His *Cafeteras* (Coffeepots, 1946–47) series was exhibited at the Museo de Bellas Artes, the Taller Libre de Arte, and the Instituto Pedagógico (all Caracas, 1949), shows that marked the arrival of Geometric Abstraction in Venezuela. Otero was among the founding members of Los Disidentes (The Dissidents, 1950), a group of Venezuelan avant-garde artists who launched a magazine from Paris aimed at transforming the conservative nature of art making, display, and reception in their home country, and promoting the adoption of abstraction. In the early 1950s, the architect Carlos Raúl Villanueva was in the process of designing the Proyecto de Integración de las Artes (Integration of the Arts Project) of the Ciudad Universitaria de Caracas and invited Otero to contribute the design of four murals and a stained glass window. During those years, he collaborated with Miguel Arroyo on numerous design projects and also became a member of the Forma Veinte (Form Twenty) cooperative, which was dedicated to the practice of pottery and enamelwork. During the second half of the decade, Otero and his wife, the painter Mercedes Pardo, produced a small series of utilitarian enamel objects that they sold to supplement their income. After teaching briefly at the Escuela de Artes Plásticas y Artes Aplicadas (1954–56), Otero attained several milestones: he represented Venezuela at the 1956 Venice Biennale (and again in 1982); he was awarded the Premio Nacional de Pintura Venezuela (National Venezuelan Award in Painting) in 1958; he received honorable mention at the 1959 São Paulo Biennial; and he earned the 1964 Premio Nacional de Artes Aplicadas de Venezuela (National Award for Applied Arts). He began to sculpt, and a grant from the John Simon Guggenheim Memorial Foundation provided Otero the opportunity to be a visiting artist at the Massachusetts Institute of Technology (1971–72), where he researched the interaction between his kinetic sculptures and the natural environment. An example of the product of his study is the large sculpture *Delta Solar* (1976) installed outside the National Air and Space Museum in Washington, DC, which was donated by the Venezuelan government on the occasion of the United States Bicentennial. Otero embraced new technologies throughout his career, as is evident in his 1987 residency at the Centro de Investigaciones IBM de Venezuela, where he experimented with computer-aided design. In 1991, he was posthumously represented at the São Paulo Biennial, where he received honorable mention. His contribution to art was recognized in Venezuela, where he is considered a pioneer of modern art, as well as Latin America at large. Otero was commissioned to complete a number of public art projects and wrote pivotal texts that contributed to the canon of abstraction; with the writer Miguel Otero Silva and critic Marta Traba he polemicized about abstraction and the autonomy of art. After his death, the Museo de Arte La Rinconada was renamed the Fundación Museo de Artes Visuales Alejandro Otero by presidential decree. [Checklist nos. 39, 40, 89]

### ARTURO PANI (MEXICAN, 1915–81)

The Mexican-born designer Arturo Pani lived in Belgium, Milan, and Paris from 1919 to 1935 owing to his father's diplomatic career. While in Paris, Pani studied at the École des Beaux Arts with his older brother, Mario Pani (1911–93), the future renowned modernist architect and editor of *Arquitectura México* magazine. They returned to Mexico City, where each began to work in his respective field. Arturo designed furniture and interiors for the lobby and several other rooms of Mario's Hotel Reforma (1936), and the project as a whole was seen as the beginning of a new era of cosmopolitanism in Mexico City. He later worked as a senior designer for the decorating firm De la Pena, Lascurain y Compania, before founding Arturo Pani S.A., which continued functioning into the 1970s. Pani became known as the preeminent designer for Mexico City's elite. His style is known as the Acapulco Look and is distinguished by the elaborate use of gilt iron, glass, and mirrors. [Checklist nos. 40, 41]

### MIGUEL PINEDA (MEXICAN, B. 1940)

Miguel Pineda grew up in the town of Tlalplan, just south of Mexico City, where he had the good fortune to have the renowned American enamelist Maggie Howe as a neighbor. Pineda apprenticed under Howe from 1958 to 1960, when she moved to Cuernavaca. He later attended Mexico City's Academia de San Carlos art school, but cut his formal studies short to establish his own studio in the city. The silversmithing firm Los Castillo was an early client, and he soon joined the ranks of respected local artisans at the city's Bazaar Sábado. The subject matter of his works demonstrates a lifelong interest in pre-Columbian and folk imagery. He received prestigious religious commissions, including the 36 doors to the modern Basilica of Our Lady of Guadalupe (1976) in Mexico City, and his depiction of the Virgin of Guadalupe is on permanent display in the Vatican's chapel of San Lorenzo. [Checklist no. 42]

## CLARA PORSET (MEXICAN, B. CUBA, 1895–1981)

Clara Porset's prolific designs strike a balance between Latin American material culture, modern aesthetics, comfort, and affordability. Born to a wealthy Cuban family, Porset had the opportunity to travel widely, accumulating a broad range of artistic and political influences. She studied at the Manhattanville Academy, New York (1914–18), attended technical courses in architecture and design in Cuba, then completed her art degree in 1925 at Columbia University. Porset traveled to Europe in the late 1920s and met Bauhaus teachers Walter Gropius and Hans Emil "Hannes" Meyer, with whom she remained in contact for many years. From 1928 to 1931, she studied architecture and furniture design in the Paris studio of the designer and architect Henri Rapin and attended classes at the École des Beaux Arts, the Sorbonne, and the Louvre. In 1932, she returned to Cuba, and shortly after presented a lecture titled "La decoración interior contemporánea su adaptación al Tropic" (Contemporary Interior Decoration: Its Adaptation to the Tropics), demonstrating the nascent interests that defined her career. She worked professionally as a designer in Cuba during this time, but returned to her studies in the summer of 1934 under former Bauhaus instructors Josef and Anni Albers at Black Mountain College, North Carolina. She was briefly artistic director of the Escuela Técnica para Mujeres (Technical School for Women) in Cuba, but, owing to her political outspokenness, was forced to leave Cuba in 1935. She moved to Mexico, married the painter Xavier Guerrero, and, through their partnership, was introduced to the folk arts as well as the prominent artists of the country, which influenced her career. The couple collaborated on a proposal for the Museum of Modern Art's (New York) 1940 competition *Organic Design in Home Furnishings.* This was the first time Latin American designers were included in the museum's call for proposals; however, despite this expanded inclusivity, Guerrero was given sole credit for the design in the accompanying publication. Porset's furniture updated vernacular Mexican materials (such as woven agave fibers) and forms (the colonial *butaque* chair). In 1952, Porset curated the exhibition *El arte en la vida diaria: exposición de objetos de buen diseño hechos en México* (Art in the Daily Life: An Exhibition of Well-Designed Objects Made in Mexico) at the Instituto Nacional de Bellas Artes (Mexico City), which featured both handcrafted and mass-produced objects [checklist no. 83]. This expansive exhibition included many artists and designers, some of whom are on display in *Moderno,* such as Odilón Avalos, José Feher, Los Castillo, Cynthia Sargent, William Spratling, and Michael van Beuren. Porset was able to return to post-revolutionary Cuba in 1959, and Fidel Castro commissioned her to design the furniture for the school of Camilo Cienfuegos, an institution symbolic of the new society envisioned by revolutionaries. She also created furniture for a number of other universities before her return to Mexico in 1963, after her plans to establish a new design school in Cuba went unrealized. In 1969, designer Horacio Durán founded an industrial design program at the Escuela Nacional de Arquitectura (now part of Universidad Nacional Autónoma de México) and invited Porset to give a seminar. She continued teaching for the remainder of her life. The Instituto Nacional de Bellas Artes recognized Porset as a pioneer of Mexican modern design by awarding her a Gold Medal in 1971. Her achievements remain celebrated, in part, through a scholarship awarded annually. [Checklist nos. 44–48]

## PEDRO RAMÍREZ VÁZQUEZ (MEXICAN, 1919–2013)

Pedro Ramirez Vázquez was one of Mexico's premier architects; he designed government buildings, sports stadiums, museums, and religious buildings alike. He earned a degree in architecture from the Escuela Nacional de Arquitectura (Mexico City) in 1943. Among his first projects was a large-scale initiative to design cost-effective prefabricated structures to be used for rural schools and teachers' housing. In the next two decades, 35,000 frames were fabricated for these buildings and finished with local materials to integrate these structures with a variety of sites. Ramírez Vázquez's work was soon known internationally, and he designed Mexico's pavilions for the 1958, 1962, and 1964 World's Fairs; in 1960, his rural schools design was awarded the Grand Prix at the Milan Triennial. Throughout his life he held several positions in Mexico's government, and he led the organization committee for the 1968 Olympic games in Mexico City. Ramírez Vázquez designed Mexico City's expansive Museo Nacional de Antropología (1964), which greatly impacted the study of anthropology and ethnography in Mexico. The modernist structure incorporated elements of pre-Columbian architecture with its imposing scale and use of unrefined materials. Similarly, his *equipal* chair (ca. 1964) is an updated version of a Nahuatl design. In Ramírez Vázquez's adaptation, the traditionally used wood and plant fibers have been substituted for crisscrossing stainless steel rods. A design suitable for mass production, the chair became the official chair used in Mexican government spaces for several decades. In 1966, construction was completed on the architect's design for Estadio Azteca, a stadium still in use by Mexico's soccer team. He designed the Basilica of Our Lady of Guadalupe (1976), Mexico's most popular pilgrimage site. [Checklist no. 49]

## SÉRGIO RODRIGUES (BRAZILIAN, 1927–2014)

Sérgio Rodrigues graduated from the Faculdade de Arquitectura da Universidade do Brasil (Architecture College of Brazil University) in 1951. His ingenious furniture designs were initially unappreciated in Brazil, which led him to form is own company in 1955. He titled the Rio de Janeiro–based company Oca, after indigenous dwellings that prioritized function and simplicity, a title that communicated Rodrigues's concerns of establishing a distinctly Brazilian design aesthetic free from European influences. While the majority of his designs used materials sparingly, he is best known for his lush *Mole* furniture series, characterized by overstuffed leather cascading over a turned jacaranda frame — a daring disregard for the spindled legs and spare forms of midcentury design. The unstructured materials encourage the user to adopt a relaxed posture, and the original model was designed for the photographer Otto Stupakoff to relax in his studio. The *Mole* couch and chair premiered in a 1958 exhibition at Rodrigues's store titled *Móveis como Objeto de Arte* (Furniture as Objects of Art). Although the *Mole*'s form is atypical of Rodrigues's practice, the utilization of raw materials, such as wood, leather, and cane, shares much in common with the designer's larger oeuvre. The chair was awarded first place in the 1961 Italian *Concorso Internazionale del Mobile* (International Furniture Competition). Starting in 1957, Rodrigues furnished architect Oscar Niemeyer's buildings in the newly established capital city of Brasília. Rodrigues's later designs were made available to Brazil's middle class through Rodrigues's 1963 *Meia-Pataca* line, which could be manufactured in large quantities. Rodrigues left Oca in 1968 in order to shift focus onto architecture. [Checklist no. 50]

ynthia Sargent models fabric she designed
nd printed with Wendell Riggs in the early 1950s
the Riggs-Sargent showroom, San Angel
strict, Mexico City.

he Riggs-Sargent showroom, 41 Amberes
t., Mexico City. The couple hired Guerrero Native
mericans to paint the storefront. A *Scarlatti* rug
angs on the far wall.

worker hooks a rug by hand. Courtesy the
iggs-Sargent Family.

ll photos courtesy the Riggs-Sargent Family.

## CYNTHIA SARGENT (AMERICAN, ACTIVE IN MEXICO, 1922–2006)

A wide range of influences converge in Cynthia Sargent's textile designs. She learned piano from an early age, then studied dance at Bennington College (Vermont) and Mills College (California), and traveled to Haiti with the choreographer and dancer Maya Deren. She studied painting with Josef Albers at Black Mountain College (North Carolina), and block printing with Adja Yunkers at the New School for Social Research (New York). She continued her studies in New York at Columbia University under the professorship of Robert Motherwell and Meyer Schapiro. Sargent briefly owned a publishing company before establishing herself as a designer. Her creative and business partner was the artist Wendell Riggs, her second husband, whom she married in 1950. The pair initially lived and worked together in Woodstock, New York, and, in 1951, settled in Mexico City. Their home, which included their workshop, in addition to an art gallery, bookstore, and theater, became a catalyst for the local art community. José Feher's ceramics were shown in their gallery, and Clara Porset became a client. Sargent and Riggs continued working on hand-painted and block-printed designs before expanding fabric production to large mural panels, then evolved to designing hooked rugs incorporating the vibrant colors of Mexico. In 1958, they erected a new factory and residence in Desierto de Leones to house their growing operations and, in 1960, opened a Mexico City showroom and established Bazaar Sábado, a fair featuring local handicrafts that is still active today. Riggs died in 1963, and Sargent struggled to balance her creative role with the managerial responsibilities of running a studio, factory, and store — aspects of the business that Riggs had previously overseen. She expanded the business, however, and opened a new showroom in 1964 and began selling rugs through outlets in Toronto, Los Angeles, Boston, New York, Scottsdale, and Palm Beach, Florida. The rhythmic, geometric *Scarlatti* rug (1969) of this time is part of a larger series inspired by the classical music she listened to while working. In order to focus solely on her designs, in 1970, she sold her factory to the workers, who paid her salary as sole designer, and the company was renamed Tamacani. A later rift between Sargent and the company resulted in her being shorted royalty fees while her designs were altered. Despite these hardships, she continued to design textiles throughout the 1970s, as well as paint, draw, weave, and write until her death. [Checklist no. 51]

## MARIO SEGUSO (BRAZILIAN, B. ITALY 1929)

Born in Italy to a long lineage of Murano glassmakers, Mario Seguso studied glass engraving at Venice's Regio Instituto d' Arte. In 1949, he founded an engraving workshop, which he ran until 1954. Later that year, an invitation from the São Paulo–based company Cristais Prado S.A. prompted Seguso to move to Brazil. He worked with the company until 1956, when he established his own glass design and fabrication workshop. He partnered with fellow Italians Vittorio Ferro and Piero Toso to found Cristaleria Artística Cá d'Oro in 1965 in the town of Poços de Caldas, Brazil. The factory also housed Seguso's experimental laboratory, the Oficina de Fogo e Arte (Fire and Art Workshop), where he worked to develop new techniques. This, combined with the geographical separation from the European traditions of his early training and immersion in Brazilian culture, led to Seguso's later distinctive colorful style. The restrained palette and refined form of the untitled bottle with stopper (1978) in this exhibition marks it as transitional, situated between Seguso's training in Italy and his mature experimental works. [Checklist no. 52]

Donald Shoemaker, 1978. Courtesy of Stanley Shoemaker.

## DONALD SHOEMAKER (AMERICAN, ACTIVE IN MEXICO, 1912–90)

The Nebraska-born painter Donald Shoemaker arrived in Mexico in 1947 with the intention of attending a summer art school seminar; however, he remained in Mexico and established a permanent residence with his wife in the small city of Morelia in 1951. There, he founded the company Señal, and their operations involved every aspect of furniture manufacture, including harvesting the hardwood, curing the raw materials, design, and painstaking carving and assembly. The extremely dense local woods were not compatible with modern machinery, so most work was done by hand and with the strategic use of modern tools. Shoemaker's designs were produced in small quantities and sold in Chicago, Los Angeles, Houston, and throughout Mexico. Shoemaker and his family abruptly returned to the United States in 1955, but they went back to Mexico in the 1960s and re-established operations as Señal, S.A. The company later produced a commercial line of colonial-style furniture from softwoods, such as pine and cedar, for hotels and government offices. After Shoemaker passed away, his son George handled operations (later renaming the now-dissolved company Arrendadora Shoemaker), until his own death, in the early 2000s. [Checklist no. 53]

## WILLIAM SPRATLING (AMERICAN, ACTIVE IN MEXICO, 1900–67)

Born in Sonyea, New York, William Spratling revived the tradition of silversmithing in the town of Taxco, Mexico, with his designs featuring pre-Columbian motifs. Spratling studied architecture at Auburn University, Alabama, and, in 1922, began teaching architecture at Tulane University, New Orleans. In 1926, he went to Mexico on a commission for drawings from *Architectural Forum,* and, until 1928, he spent summers teaching at the Universidad Nacional Autónoma de México (National Autonomous University, Mexico City). Spratling became acquainted with many artists in Mexico City, and he promoted the work of Diego Rivera and participated in the organization of the traveling exhibition *Mexican*

The "Big Four" silver designers: Héctor Aguilar, Antonio Pineda, William Spratling, and Antonio Castillo, undated. Photo by Juan Guzmán. 3 x 5 in. Spratling-Taxco Collection, The Latin American Library, Tulane University.

*Arts* (1930), which premiered at the Metropolitan Museum of Art, New York. He resigned from Tulane in 1928 and began to live fulltime in Mexico in 1929, mainly to focus on writing his second book about the culture of Taxco, titled *Little Mexico* (1932). (His first book, *Sherwood Anderson and Other Famous Creoles,* was cowritten with William Faulkner in 1926.) Spratling purchased a house in Taxco, where, in 1931, he opened La Aduana, a shop to sell the furniture, handwoven textiles, and objects in tin, copper, and silver that he designed. By 1933, his silver designs became his primary focus, and, in 1935, he moved to a larger shop named Taller de la Delicias (Workshop of Delights) after the street on which it was located, later renamed Spratling y Artesanos. In part through an apprenticeship program, Spratling's workshop grew rapidly from his first employed silversmith, Artemio Navarrete, to one hundred artisans by 1937, and three hundred by 1940. The decline of the production of European goods during the Second World War opened possibilities for selling luxury goods in the United States, and the workshop began using equipment to speed production and send products to Neiman Marcus, Macy's, and Saks Fifth Avenue. This boom was unfortunately short-lived; Spratling sold shares but he lost control of the business, and the company soon became bankrupt. Spratling was approached by the chairman of the Arts and Crafts Board of the U.S. Department of the Interior and the governor of Alaska, and, looking for new opportunieis, he conducted extensive research, but the promised funding was never delivered; however, this new environment was influential, and Spratling incorporated stones from Alaska (jade, jasper, and quartz) into his works. In 1951, he founded William Spratling SA de CV at his ranch outside Taxco, where he continued production through an apprenticeship program. The people of Taxco honored Spratling in 1953 by naming a street after him as well as giving him the title of *Hijo predilecto* (Favored Son). In 1967, Spratling died in a car crash. The Museo William Spratling was later founded to house his collection of pre-Columbian art. [Checklist no. 54]

## JOAQUIM TENREIRO (BRAZILIAN, B. PORTUGAL, 1906–1992)

A pioneer of Brazilian modern furniture, Joaquim Tenreiro is regarded for his rigorous craftsmanship and early appreciation of indigenous Brazilian materials, such as jacaranda and imbuia woods. Born into a family of Portuguese woodworkers, he immigrated to Rio de Janeiro in 1929 after two earlier trips to Brazil (1909–12 and 1925–27). Tenreiro, who had previously studied drawing, cofounded the group of painters known as Núcleo Bernardelli in 1931, before working for various furniture manufacturers (Laubisch & Hirth, 1933–36; Leandro Martins, 1936–40; and Francisco Gomes, 1940–1942). His first opportunity to fully explore his ideas about Brazilian materials and forms came when the Brazilian architect Oscar Niemeyer (1907–2012) invited Tenreiro to furnish his Francisco Inácio Peixoto Residence (1942–43) in Cataguases, Minas Gerais. Subsequently, in 1943 Tenreiro established a workshop dedicated to the frugal use of materials and the introduction of more humble elements, such as split cane chair seats and backs (typical of Portuguese furniture), in a modern context. Tenreiro first displayed his iconic curvilinear three-legged chair of contrasting Brazilian woods — imbuia (walnut), purple heart, rosewood, ivory, and cabreuva — in a Copacabana storefront he opened in 1947. His designs demonstrate his investment in objects made for a Brazilian market, as they feature materials suitable for Brazil's tropical climate with glass-topped tables, wicker, and Brazilian hardwoods in addition to dimensions modified to better accommodate the typical Brazilian stature, such as lowered tabletops. Tenreiro closed his furniture store in 1968 to focus on creating art, primarily sculpture, for his many remaining years. [Checklist no. 55, 56]

### FÉLIX TISSOT (AMERICAN, B. FRANCE 1909, D. MEXICO 1989)

French-born Félix Tissot arrived in Taxco, Mexico, in 1956 by way of Leona Valley, California. He sought to establish a new ceramics studio, which he did in partnership with Anthony Castillo of the Los Castillo silversmithing workshop, and together they created a limited number of pieces. Tissot became aware of the craftsmanship of the Nuhautl people, who lived near Taxco, and he imported bisqueware for them to ornament with indigenous designs for the *Fantasia* line of ceramics, for which he is best known. No two patterns are identical, but the line is unified by its subdued color palette and near-monochromatic use of blue, pink, or yellow. The verso of each piece is marked with Tissot's signature alongside the initials of the painter, sander, and glazier. [Checklist nos. 57, 58]

Tecla Tofano turning a piece in the ceramics workshop at the Escuela de Artes Plásticas y Artes Aplicadas (School of Fine and Applied Arts), Caracas, 1955. Photo by Sara Guardia de Mendoza. Courtesy of Centro de Estudios de Archivos Audiovisuales y Artísticos and the Mendoza Guardia Family.

### TECLA TOFANO (VENEZUELAN, B. ITALY, 1927–95)

Tecla Tofano studied ceramics and enamel with Miguel Arroyo at the Escuela de Artes Plásticas y Aplicadas (School of Fine and Applied Arts (Caracas) alongside fellow students Cristina Merchán and Reyna Herrera. A member of the cooperative Forma Veinte (Form Twenty), her works garnered wide acclaim, and she became known for her controversial, political, and feminist imagery. Tofano was awarded the National Prize for Applied Arts in XIX Official Venezuelan Art Salon (1958) and the gold and silver medals at the *International Exhibition of Contemporary Ceramics* (in Prague in 1961 and Buenos Aires in 1962). Two distinct phases characterize her oeuvre: from 1955 to 1963, Tofano worked in a more traditional vein, creating utilitarian objects with incised and textured surfaces; thereafter, she became unconcerned with her work's usefulness, instead creating uniquely expressive sculptures from clay. Tofano's ceramics are charged with emotion, sexuality, and humor. She created series of works for display in exhibitions, such as *Los accesorios* (The Accessories, 1970) — featuring handbags, shoes, and other feminine items — and *Lo que comen los que comen* (What People Who Eat Eat, 1973), a feast of ceramic food complete with table, chairs, and diners. She was part of the faculty of the school of architecture and urbanism at the Universidad Central de Venezuela (1959–80). Tofano also wrote extensively as a columnist for the *El Nacional* newspaper in addition to several books, including *Quién inventó la silla* (Who Invented the Chair, 1968), *Yo misma me presento* (I Presented Myself, 1973), and *Ni con el pétalo de una rosa* (Not with Rose Petals, 1975). From 1977 until 1987, Tofano refrained from exhibiting her work and focused instead on her writing and feminist activism undertaken through the women's collective *Miércoles*. Her work returned to the public realm in 1987 and 1989, when she exhibited her drawings. [Checklist nos. 59–61]

## MARIA LUISA ZULOAGA DE TOVAR (VENEZUELAN, 1902–92)

Maria Luisa Tovar studied painting with the Catalan artist (then based in Caracas) Ángel Cabré i Magriñá alongside her sister, the painter Elvira Elisa Zuloaga, through private classes arranged by their father in 1916. Finding that she preferred sculpture to painting, she began studies in 1936 at the newly reopened and updated Escuela de Artes Plásticas y Aplicadas (School of Fine and Applied Arts) in Caracas. There she studied in the nascent ceramics program directed by João Gonçalves, as well as sculpture under Ernesto Maragall. Tovar traveled to New York in 1939 to study in a workshop established by sculptor Alexander Archipenko, where she continued her studies in ceramics. Returning to Caracas in 1941, she constructed a workshop that housed a brick kiln, only the second in the country. In 1946, she earned the National Prize for Applied Arts at the VII Salón Oficial Anual de Arte Venezolano (Official Annual Venezuelan Art Salon) as well subsequent awards in 1960 and 1961. Throughout her career, Tovar had an interest in Venezuelan vernacular traditions, which manifested itself in the form of abstract patterns recalling pre-Columbian motifs or religious imagery, such as angels or the Virgin and Child. For example, from 1949 until her death, Tovar displayed a glazed ceramic crèche in her home on which she added new figures every year. Aside from explorations with folk imagery, Tovar experimented with materials and familiarized herself with iridescent glazes that gave a metallic appearance to her ceramics. She also used her kiln to form glass plates, which she decorated with the imprint of leaves and plants. In 1962, she earned the gold medal at the *International Exhibition of Contemporary Ceramics* in Prague and in 1965 the silver medal at the *Exposition Internationale, les émaux dans la céramique actuelle* (Current Ceramic Enamels) at the Musée Ariana (The Swiss Museum of Ceramics and Glass) in Geneva. Her work was featured in solo exhibitions at the Sala Mendoza (Caracas) in 1968 and 1979, and again in another one-person exhibition at the Museo de Arte Contemporáneo de Caracas in 1986. [Checklist no. 62]

Seka in her studio, 1980. Photos by José Sigala. Courtesy Daniel and Marina Tudja.

## SEKA SEVERIN DE TUDJA (VENEZUELAN, B. YUGOSLAVIA, NOW CROATIA, 1923–2007)

Seka (as she was publicly known) studied sculpture at the Academy of Fine Arts in Zagreb with Frano Krsinic and Krsto Hegedusic (1942–45) before moving to Paris on a scholarship from the French government from 1946 until 1948. There, she continued her studies in sculpture as well as drawing at the Grande Chaumière academy before earning a degree from the Sorbonne (1948) in art history and archaeology. While in Paris, Seka experimented with materials and processes and made animations with wax-sculpted figurines; her work in a ceramic button workshop led to a more technical understanding of the medium. In 1952, she moved to Caracas, where she continued making utilitarian objects while testing variations in heat and firing times in her newly acquired large kiln. Her work at this time remained varied, however; she presented a ceramic bas-relief mural at the 1955 XVI Salón Oficial Anual de Arte Venezolano (Official Annual Venezuelan Art Salon), the latter earning the National Prize for Applied Arts. She was also awarded with gold medals at the *Exposition Internationale, les émaux dans la céramique actuelle* (Current Ceramic Enamels) at the Musée Ariana (The Swiss Museum of Ceramics and Glass) in Geneva (1965) and the exhibition *Form und Qualität* (Form and Quality) in Munich, Germany (1967); as well as distinguished with diplomas in the *International Exhibition of Ceramics* at the Victoria and Albert Museum in London (1972) and the World Triennial of Fine Ceramics in Zagreb, Yugoslavia (1984). Her first solo exhibition *Treinta y cinco cerámicas de Seka* (Thirty-Five Ceramics by Seka) was organized by Miguel Arroyo in 1962 at the Museo de Bellas Artes (Museum of Fine Arts, Caracas). From this moment, Seka began to garner international attention and represented Venezuela in exhibitions abroad. This show was followed by two major retrospective in Caracas at the Museo de Arte Contemporáneo (1982) and at the Centro Cultural Consulado (1993). Her early Venezuelan works incorporate pre-Columbian-inspired figures, whereas later works rejected ornamentation in favor of featuring process, medium, and concerns of form, texture, and color. After 1972, Seka explored the possibilities of ovoid forms with a completely solid exterior, further bridging the divide between ceramics and sculpture. She molded the clay by hand, forming coils that she stacked and smoothed, then fired the works multiple times at low temperatures with several applications of glaze to create various colors and textures often achieved by crazing. The coded titles of these works, such as *E-4* (1974) and *L-13* (1979), reflect her unique and highly technical process. Seka's work was shown internationally in numerous group exhibitions staged during her lifetime. [Checklist nos. 63–65]

Domus label used 1938–44.

## MICHAEL VAN BEUREN (MEXICAN, B. UNITED STATES, 1911–2004)

Born in New York, an adventurous seventeen-year-old van Beuren traveled to Europe via a merchant ship. He began studying at the Bauhaus in Dessau in 1931, moved with the school to Berlin the following year, and continued training under Mies van der Rohe after the Bauhaus's closure by the Nazis in 1933. He soon returned to the United States and studied architecture at New York University (1934–36). In 1936, he traveled to Acapulco for what was planned to be a brief period of work but decided to remain in the country and moved to Mexico City. Because Van Beuren's architecture degree was incomplete, his opportunities to work in that field were limited. He shifted his professional focus and founded Domus, a line of handcrafted furniture, with Klaus Grabe in 1938. They soon opened a storefront to sell their designs, which were alternately fabricated in their factory or by craftsmen in local workshops. The business and public relations aspects of Domus were managed by American émigré Morley Webb, and the three men submitted a design together for the 1940 competition, exhibition, and publication *Organic Design in Home Furnishings* organized by the Museum of

Bottom: Domus bookshelf and chair, c. 1949, Gelatin silver print; 8 ¼ x 10 in. Collection of Jan van Beuren. [Checklist no. 67]

Modern Art (New York). Domus gained a reputation in the United States through the success of their design, the *Alacrán* chaise, which won an award and was produced and sold by Bloomingdale's. Grabe returned to Germany after the onset of the Second World War, leaving the company to van Beuren, who established Van Beuren, SA de CV, an umbrella for various companies, including the pre-existing Domus line and the new and widely popular Calpini and Decapól brands. This larger company established the first assembly line construction in Mexico, where van Beuren produced his designs as well as those of other designers, such as Clara Porset. Van Beuren's designs were informed by his Bauhaus training, but it was fused with an appreciation of folk art and the use of regional materials. Simplicity of design and low production costs made the furniture more affordable for the Mexican consumer, and van Beuren's company continued to be a leader in the Mexican furniture market through the 1960s. He valued the factory workers' quality of life as well, and prioritized fair pay and recreational activities for his numerous employees. Van Beuren sold his company to the Singer Sewing Machine Company in 1973 and opened a particleboard factory in 1975, but continued to make furniture for his family and friends until he retired to Cuernavaca. [Checklist nos. 66–70]

## MORLEY WEBB (AMERICAN, ACTIVE IN MEXICO, 20TH CENTURY)

The architect Morley Webb joined designers Klaus Grabe and Michael van Beuren's Mexican company Domus in the late 1930s. He served as the company's business and public relations manager, and his name was included on Domus's award-winning submission for the Museum of Modern Art's (New York) 1940 design competition *Organic Design in Home Furnishings*. He remained with the company, then Van Beuren, SA de CV, until it was sold to the Singer Sewing Machine Company in 1973. [Checklist nos. 68–70]

Mosaic mural designed by Paulo Werneck for Hotel Nacional in Brasília, 1958. Courtesy of Gaspar Saldanha.

## PAULO WERNECK (BRAZILIAN, 1907–87)

Paulo Werneck was a self-taught designer and illustrator. He is best known for over two hundred mosaic murals executed from 1942 through the late 1970s. Interestingly, Werneck attended primary school in Rio de Janeiro with two of his most frequent professional collaborators, the renowned Brazilian architects Oscar Niemeyer (1907–2012) and Marcelo Roberto (1908–64). In 1927, Werneck began illustrating periodicals and children's books, and the following year opened an office with Roberto, where Werneck continued to design for print. The two also collaborated on designs for the interiors of public spaces, such as soccer and

Paulo Werneck with long-time assistant Germinal Bueno, in his atelier in Rio de Janeiro, 1945. Courtesy of Gaspar Saldanha.

Advertisement for *Eva* Ice Bucket, c. 1976.

tennis clubs. Roberto later formed MMM Roberto with his brothers, Milton and Maurício, and through this firm he designed the Instituto de Resseguros do Brasil (Reinsurance Institute of Brazil, 1942) for which Werneck created six murals in the building's roof garden. Werneck soon covered the sweeping exterior of Niemeyer's Igreja São Francisco de Assis (Church of Saint Francis of Assis, finished in 1944) in Belo Horizonte with his first abstract public mural. He also contributed murals to the architectural projects of Affonso Eduardo Reidy, Marcelo Campelo, and Firmino Fernandes Saldanha, among others. In 1960, Werneck began an ongoing partnership with the Banco do Brasil and by 1980 had installed roughly one hundred mosaics in bank branches throughout the country. New and nontraditional materials, such as wood, polyester, glass, and Formica, figure in his mosaics, sometimes also assembled with tools of Werneck's invention. In the last years of his life, Werneck returned to drawing and painting. [Checklist no. 71]

## JORGE ZALSZUPIN (BRAZILIAN, B. POLAND 1922)

Born Jerzy Zalszupin, he fled Nazi-occupied Poland for Romania, where he studied architecture. Zalszupin participated in the postwar effort to build houses in France, then, in 1949, went to Rio de Janeiro for three months, where he learned Portuguese. There he made contact with fellow Polish architect Lucjan Korngold, who invited Zalszupin to join his firm in São Paulo, where he worked for two years. Zalszupin founded his own architectural firm, Escritório Técnico Prumo, in 1958. Though he was originally solely an architect, his clients returned to him with requests to furnish their homes, as they found the premade furniture of the time unsuitable for his modern designs. This led to the formation of L'Atelier in 1959, with the aim of producing furniture and design interiors, as well as of continuing Zalszupin's architectural projects. L'Atelier's products were often commissioned, then subsequently made in multiples for sale in the company's showroom. L'Atelier later transitioned mostly to the design and mass-produced fabrication of office furniture and household objects, and the simple design and synthetic materials allowed for assembly-line fabrication. The company's 1968 *Hille* chair is an early example of the use of plastics in furniture and household objects, especially in Brazil, where the equipment to inject plastic into molds was rare at the time, and, consequently, L'Atelier was uncontested in this area. L'Atelier was sold in 1970 to the Forsa Corporation, which also owned iron fittings manufacturer Laminação Brasil, plastics company Hevia, and computer manufacturer Labo, and Zalszupin, as the corporation's newly appointed product and research development director, was able to experiment with resources from all

Advertisement for *Putskit,* c. 1970.

of Forsa's sectors. Utilitarian objects, such as Zalszupin's *Putskit* wall mounted organizer and *Eva* ice bucket (both manufactured from 1970 to 1979), further embraced new advancements in plastics technology and were fabricated in bright colors that appealed to the Brazilian consumer. These and other designs raised the status of plastic (previously considered to be of low quality) to being suitable for well-designed, versatile, and affordable objects. His working method was to develop prototypes, which he then presented to the public for feedback. Thus, L'Atelier's products were influenced by the people of Brazil, illustrating Zalszupin's interest in a fundamentally local design aesthetic, his collaborative design process, and his acute business acumen. Forsa's team disbanded in the late 1980s, and Zalszupin has since focused on architecture and painting. [Checklist nos. 72, 73]

## JOSÉ ZANINE CALDAS (BRAZILIAN, 1918–2001)

José Zanine Caldas was a self-taught architect, designer, and fabricator, distinguished by his extraordinary woodworking abilities. He also worked as a model-maker, landscape designer, ceramist, and sculptor. After starting an architectural model workshop in Rio de Janeiro at the age of twenty, he later aided the projects of the designer Joaquim Tenreiro and architects Lúcio Costa and Oscar Niemeyer,

Home of architect Clóvis Felipe Olga with furniture from Móveis Z, 1950. Photo by Hans Gunter Flieg. Courtesy of Instituto Moreira Salles.

among others. With Sebastião Pontes, he cofounded the furniture company Móveis Z (1948–61), whose furniture featured efficient and cost-saving measures such as utilizing compressed and laminated wood (hitherto seen only as a construction material) in designs that could be assembled and disassembled without the need for specialized labor. In the 1950s, Caldas served as secretary of the Brazilian Communist Party, and, with the implementation of a military dictatorship in 1964, was stripped of most civil rights and forced to take refuge in the town of Nova Viçosa, Bahia. During this exile, he created furniture with reclaimed or partially burned wood from the Brazilian rainforests. The incorporation of salvaged fallen timber and the embracing of each piece's unique organic form transformed Caldas's aesthetic from a mass-produced to a highly individualized one. Caldas regained his public persona in 1982, when he founded both the Fundação Centro de Desenvolvimento das Aplicações das Madeiras do Brasil (Foundation Center for the Development of Applications of Brazilian Wood) and the Escola do Fazer (The Making School). Later recognition came with a 1989 exhibition of his architectural and design work at the Musée du Louvre. He taught in Paris and Lausanne before he returned to Brazil, where he designed houses and inns. His furniture was exhibited in 1999 at the IV Bienal de Arquitectura de São Paulo (São Paulo Architecture Biennial). [Checklist no. 74]

## GOTTFRIED AND THEKLA ZIELKE (B. GERMANY 1929 AND 1928, ACTIVE IN VENEZUELA)

The potters Gottfried and Thekla Zielke met at technical school in Germany and started a personal and professional collaboration. After graduating college, Thekla designed pottery for two years at a German factory before immigrating to Sweden, where she apprenticed for three years in a ceramics workshop. While Thekla studied ceramics design, Gottfried learned the technical aspects of the craft, with an emphasis on enamel. After attaining his bachelor's degree, Gottfried apprenticed for three years in two ceramics workshops, where he gained further knowledge of ceramics technique, theory, and chemistry. This led to later scientific studies of the medium, such as organic chemistry, mineralogy, and geology. After being hired to open Azulejos Corona, a tile factory in Bogotá in 1952, Gottfried relocated to Colombia and was asked three years later to open another factory for the Vencerámica company in La Victoria, Venezuela. After Gottfried and Thekla were married in Italy in 1955, she too moved to Venezuela. Unhappy with managing the factory, the couple established a quieter life in Colonia Tovar (an isolated mountain village founded in the nineteenth century near Caracas by Bavarian immigrants). They constructed a modest house on a friend's land with the intention of establishing a small ceramics studio, where they completed their first pieces in 1959. Thekla used a wheel to form the clay, while Gottfried spearheaded the technical aspects of production, such as clay selection, glazes, and firing lengths and temperatures. The remote village, without a road to draw visitors, left them free to experiment with artistic forms. They won the National Prize for Applied Arts at the 1961 Salón Oficial Anual de Arte Venezolano (Official Annual Venezuelan Art Salon), which brought attention to their practice. After a road was completed from Caracas to Colonia Tovar in 1967, the couple began to produce utilitarian objects to sell to tourists. Increased production led them to implement a partially mechanized process. Also in 1967, they won an award at the Salón Arturo Michelena and were invited to become members of the World Craft Council, which led to more awards and recognition. In Colonia Tovar, the Zielkes partnered with other craftspeople to form a trade school for the town's youth so they could learn skills such as ceramics, forging, and blacksmithing. Their project evolved into a thriving school for woodworking and the manufacture of musical instruments. [Checklist no. 75]

ornelis Zitman, c. 1948.

luebles Tecoteca store, Los Palos Grandes, Caracas,
1957. Interior design by Cornelis Zitman and Vittorio
aratti. Courtesy of Cornelis Zitman.

## CORNELIS ZITMAN (VENEZUELAN, B. THE NETHERLANDS 1926)

Cornelis Zitman was born into a Dutch family of artists and construction workers, two threads that have influenced his long career. He started his formal education early; in 1939, he enrolled in a drawing class at the university in his hometown of Leiden and transferred to the Royal Academy of Art, The Hague, two years later to study painting. He fled the Netherlands in 1947 to avoid compulsory military service and traveled to Aruba via a tanker. Zitman's artistic training was soon put to use as a draftsman for a construction company in Coro, Venezuela, and, in 1949, he moved to Caracas, where he designed furniture, building some himself. Between 1949 and 1951, Zitman designed furniture for Promociones y Decoraciones Dibo in Caracas, while continuing painting and taking up sculpture. In 1951, he was awarded the National Prize for Sculpture at the XII Salón Oficial Anual de Arte Venezolano (Official Annual Venezuelan Art Salon). That same year, he also founded the small factory Talleres Zitman, which grew to include two additional partners in 1952 and became Tecoteca. The company created affordable modern furniture, often out of local woods, fabrics, and natural fibers. Tecoteca quickly became well known and successful, and three stores were opened in Caracas between 1952 and 1955, the year he began teaching fine arts courses at the Universidad Central de Venezuela (Caracas). He retired from Tecoteca in 1957, and the company collapsed under economic and political hardships the following year. Zitman's departure from Tecoteca marked a turning point in his career, and he began to devote himself to his artistic practice. In 1958, Zitman relocated to the island of Grenada to focus on painting but soon shifted his energies to bronze casting. He returned to Venezuela in 1965 to rejoin the faculty of the university, a position he held until 1970. His figurative bronze sculptures were well received — in 1967, he was awarded the Premio Julio Morales Lara for the XXV Salón Arturo Michelena at the Galería de Arte Nacional (Caracas) and, in 1976, the Premio Henrique Otero Vizcarrondo for the Salón Nacional de las Artes Plásticas (National Salon of Fine Arts) at the Museo de Bellas Artes (Caracas). He was also featured in solo exhibitions in Caracas at the Museo de Bellas Artes (1968), the Sala Mendoza (1968), and the Museo de Arte Contemporáneo de Caracas. Zitman represented Venezuela at the XIX International Biennial of São Paulo in 1987, where his life-size figurative sculptures were arranged to approximate a Venezuelan neighborhood; the grouping was subsequently shown at the Museo de Bellas Artes. Additionally, Zitman's work has been shown in France, Switzerland, the Netherlands, the United States, and Japan. [Checklist no. 75–78]

# SELECTED BIBLIOGRAPHY

Aguilera, Carmen, et al. *El mueble mexicano: historia, evolución e influencias.* Mexico City: Fomento Cultural Banamex, 1985.

Barbieri, Nelly. *El movimiento cerámico en Venezuela.* Caracas: CONAC, 1998.

Barros, Geraldo, Reinhold Misselbeck, and Marcos A. Gonçalves. *Geraldo De Barros, 1923–1998: Fotoformas.* Munich: Prestel, 1999.

Bayeux, Glória. *O móvel da casa brasileira.* São Paulo: Museu da Casa Brasileira, 1997.

Bermúdez, Jorge R. *Clara Porset: diseño y cultura.* Havana: Editorial Letras Cubanas, 2005.

Blanco, Lourdes, et al. *Interior moderno: muebles diseñados por Miguel Arroyo: exposición homenaje.* Exh. cat. Caracas: Sala Trasnocho Arte Contacto, 2005.

Blanco, Lourdes, and Jorge F. Rivas Pérez. *Cornelis Zitman: la década de diseño, 1947–1957.* Exh. cat. Caracas: Sala Trasnocho Arte Contacto, 2011.

Brillembourg, Carlos. *Latin American Architecture, 1929–1960: Contemporary Reflections.* New York: Monacelli Press, 2004.

Cals, Soraia, et al. *Sérgio Rodrigues.* Rio de Janeiro: Icatu, 2000.

——. *Tenreiro.* Rio de Janeiro: Bolsa de Arte do Rio de Janeiro, 1998.

Canti, Tilde. *O móvel no Brasil origens, evolução e características.* Rio de Janeiro: Cândido Guinle de Paula Machado, 1980.

Centro Cultural Consolidado. *La cerámica de Seka, 1960–1993.* Exh. cat., Caracas, 1993.

Claro, Mauro. *Unilabor: desenho industrial, arte moderna e autogestão operária.* São Paulo: Editora Senac, 2004.

Comas, Carlos Eduardo, and Miquel Adrià. *La casa latinoamericana moderna: 20 paradigmas de mediados del siglo XX.* Mexico City: Editorial Gustavo Gili, 2003.

Comisarenco Mirkin, Dina. *Diseno industrial mexicano e internacional: Memoria y futuro.* Mexico City: Editorial Trillas, 2006.

Comisarenco Mirkin, Dina, et al. *Vida y diseño en Mexico: Siglo XX.* Mexico City: Fomento Cultural Banamex, 2007.

Coronil, Fernando. *The Magical State: Nature, Money, and Modernity in Venezuela.* Chicago: University of Chicago Press, 1997.

Costa, Lúcio. *Notas sobre a evolução do mobiliário luso-brasileiro.* 3 vols. Rio de Janeiro: Revista do Serviço do Patrimônio Histórico e Artístico Nacional, 1939.

Dantas, Thereza Christina Ferreira. *O mobiliário infantojuvenil: da casa paulista da década de 1950 e suas relações com o espaço físico da criança.* São Paulo: Alameda, 2014.

Del Real, Patricio, and Helen Gyger. *Latin American Modern Architectures: Ambiguous Territories.* New York: Routledge, 2013.

Departamento de Arquitectura del Instituto Nacional de Bellas Artes. *El arte en la vida diaria. Exposición de objetos de buen diseño hechos en México.* Exh. cat., Mexico City, 1952.

iccionario biográfico de las artes visuales en
enezuela. 2 vols. Caracas: Fundación Galería de Arte
acional, 2005.

arias, Claudio Lamas de. "Panorama e cronologia
o desenvolvimento do design de produto no
io de Janeiro (1901–2000)." PhD diss., University of
ão Paulo, 2012. http://www.teses.usp.br/teses/
isponiveis/16/16134/tde-15062012-164739/.

ernández, Miguel Angel. *El vidrio en México.* Mexico
ity: Centro de Arte Vitro, 1990.

ernández, Silvia, and Gui Bonsiepe. *Historia del
iseño en América Latina y el Caribe: industrialización
comunicación visual para la autonomía.* São Paulo:
ditora Blücher, 2008.

erraz, Geraldo. *Warchavchik e a introdução da nova
rquitetura no Brasil: 1925 a 1940.* São Paulo: MASP,
965.

uevara, Ernesto. *La intensidad contenida de la forma,
ristina Merchán en la colección Mercantil.* Exh. cat.
aracas: Fundación Mercantil, 2006.

ullar, Ferreira. "Teoria do Não-Objeto" [Theory of the
on-Object], *Jornal do Brasil: Suplemento Dominical,*
ecember 20–21, 1959.

istituto Nacional de Bellas Artes. *Diseño en México.
rospectiva y restrospectiva.* Exh. cat., Mexico City,
975.

———. *El objeto cotidiano en México.* Exh. cat., Mexico
ity, 1969.

*The Journal of Decorative and Propaganda Arts*
(Wolfson Foundation of Decorative and Propaganda
Arts, Miami), vol. 21 (1995), Brazil Theme Issue.

*The Journal of Decorative and Propaganda Arts*
(Wolfson Foundation of Decorative and Propaganda
Arts, Miami), vol. 26 (2010), Mexico Theme Issue.

Katzman, Israel. *La arquitectura contemporánea
mexicana; precedentes y desarrollo.* Mexico City:
Instituto Nacional de Antropología e Historia, 1964.

Kaufmann, Edgar. *Prize Designs for Modern
Furniture from the International Competition for
Low-Cost Furniture Design.* Exh. cat. New York:
Museum of Modern Art, 1950.

Krispin, Karl. *Alemania y Venezuela: 20 testimonios.*
Caracas: Fundación para la Cultura Urbana, 2005.

Leon, Ethel. *Design Brasileiro: Quem Fez, Quem Faz.*
Rio de Janeiro: Viana & Mosley; Editora Senac, 2005.

———. *Memórias do design brasileiro.* São Paulo: Editora
Senac, 2009.

Lima, Zeuler. *Lina Bo Bardi.* New Haven, CT: Yale
University Press, 2013.

Loschiavo dos Santos, Maria Cecilia. *Jorge Zalszupin:
design moderno no Brasil.* São Paulo: Editora Olhares,
2014.

———. *Móvel moderno no Brasil.* São Paulo: Studio
Nobel, 1995.

——. *Sérgio Rodrigues: redescobrindo o Brasil pelo móvel. Retrospectiva 1954/1991.* Museu de Arte Moderna do Rio de Janeiro, 1991.

——. "Tradição e modernidade no móvel brasileiro. visões da utopia na obra de Carrera, Tenreiro, Zanine e Sérgio Rodrigues." PhD diss., University of São Paulo, 1993.

Mallet, Ana Elena. *La Bauhaus y el México Moderno. El diseño de van Beuren.* Mexico City: Arquine, 2014.

Mari, Marcelo, et al. *Mobiliário moderno: das pequenas fábricas ao projeto da UnB.* Brasília: Editora Universidade de Brasília, 2014.

Melo, Alexandre Penedo Barbosa de. "Móveis Artísticos Z (1948–1961): o moderno autodidata e seus recortes sinuosos." Master's thesis, University of São Paulo, 2005.

Milan Acayaba, Marlene. *Branco e Preto: uma história de design brasileiro nos anos 50.* São Paulo: Instituto Lina Bo e P. M. Bardi, 1994.

Moraes, Dijon De. *Análise do design brasileiro entre mimese e mestiçagem.* São Paulo: Edgard Blucher, 2006.

Musée des Arts Décoratifs. *Cristina Merchán: céramiste vénézuélienne, 1926–1987.* Exh. cat., Paris, 1991.

Museu de Arte de São Paulo. *O Design no Brasil: história e realidade: exposição inaugural do Centro de Lazer, SESC, Fábrica Pompéia.* Exh. cat., São Paulo Assis Chateaubriand, 1982.

Novais, Fernando Antonio, and Nicolau Sevcenko. *História da vida privada no Brasil: República: da Belle Époque à era do radio.* vol. 3. São Paulo: Companhia das Letras, 1998.

Noyes, Eliot. *Organic Design in Home Furnishings.* Exh. cat. New York: Museum of Modern Art, 1941.

Oles, James. *South of the Border: Mexico in the American Imagination, 1917–1947.* Washington, DC: Smithsonian Institution Press, 1993.

Ortega, Cristina Garcia. "Lina Bo Bardi: móveis e interiores (1947–1968) — interlocuções entre moderno e local." PhD diss., University of São Paulo, 2008. http://www.teses.usp.br/teses/disponiveis/16/16134/tde-20092010-092353/.

Palacios, María Fernanda, et al. *Jugando con tierra: la vida en el arte de María Luisa Zuloaga de Tovar.* Caracas: Editorial Ex Libris, 2007.

Pereira, Juliano Aparecido. "Desenho industrial e arquitetura no ensino da FAU USP (1948–1968)." PhD diss., University of São Paulo, 2009. http://www.teses.usp.br/teses/disponiveis/18/18142/tde-30042010-101031/.

Pineda, Rafael. *La tierra doctorada.* Caracas: E. Armitano, 1978.

Porset, Clara, et al. *El diseño de Clara Porset: inventando un México moderno.* Madrid: Turner Eds., 2006.

Queiroz, Rodrigo Cristiano. "Oscar Niemeyer e Le Corbusier: encontros." PhD diss., University of São Paulo, 2007. http://www.teses.usp.br/teses/disponiveis/16/16138/tde-27042010-135104/.

Rivas Pérez, Jorge F. "Latin America, 1900–2000." In *History of the Decorative Arts and Design, 1400–2000*, ed. Pat Kirkham and Susan Weber. New York: Bard Graduate Center; New Haven, CT: Yale University Press, 2013, pp. 581–593.

Rubino, Silvana, and Marina Grinover. *Lina por escrito: textos escolhidos de Lina Bo Bardi*. São Paulo: Cosac Naify, 2009.

Sakurai, Tatiana. "Memorabilia: critérios para o design de mobiliário doméstico para a experiencia." PhD diss., University of São Paulo, 2012. http://www.teses.usp.br/teses/disponiveis/16/16134/tde-24072012-153550/.

———. "Interações — critérios para o desenho de mobiliário doméstico contemporâneo." Master's thesis, University of São Paulo, 2005.

Salinas Flores, Oscar. *Clara Porset: una vida inquieta, una obra sin igual*. Mexico City: Universidad Nacional Autónoma de México, Facultad de Arquitectura, 2001.

Santi, Maria Angélica. *Mobiliário no Brasil: origens da produção e da industrialização*. São Paulo: Editora Senac, 2013.

Sato, Alberto. *Detrás de las cosas: diseño industrial en Venezuela*. Exh. cat. Caracas: Centro de Arte La Estancia, 1995.

Tozzi, Lissa Carmona, ed. *De Sérgio para Adolpho*. São Paulo: Editora Olhares, 2014.

Vasconcellos, Marcelo, and Maria Lúcia Braga, eds. *Móvel brasileiro moderno*. Rio de Janeiro: Aeroplano Editora: FGV Projetos, 2011.

Villanueva, Carlos R. *Caracas En Tres Tiempos*. Caracas: Ediciones Comisión Asuntos Culturales del Cuatricentenario de Caracas, 1966.

———. *La Integración De Las Artes*. Caracas: Facultad de Arquitectura y Urbanismo, Universidad Central de Venezuela, 1957.

Villanueva, Paulina, Maciá Pintó, and Paolo Gasparini. *Carlos Raúl Villanueva*. New York: Princeton Architectural Press, 2000.

# CHECKLIST

**Genaro Álvarez (Mexican, active 20th century)**

1. Coffee table, 1960
Wood, metal, glass mosaic; 14 ³⁄₁₆ x 48 x 9 ¹⁄₁₆ in.
Guillermo Martínez-Cesar/Urbanity Mobiliario,
Mexico City

**Miguel Arroyo (Venezuelan, 1920–2004)**

2. Bowl for Tienda Gato, c. 1949
Ceramic; 2 ¹⁄₁₆ x 7 ¹⁄₁₆ (diameter) in.
Private Collection, New York

3. *Pampatar butaca* prototype, 1953
Mahogany and cedar; 33 ⅞ x 31 ⅞ x 24 ⁷⁄₁₆ in.
Manufactured by Pedro Santana, Carpintería
Colectiva
Collection of Claudio Mendoza

4. Design panel for the *Pampatar butaca,* 1953
Photography on board; 18 ½ x 8 ½ in.
Private Collection

5. Design panel for the Pampatar dining armchair, 1953
Photography on board; 18 ½ x 8 ½ in.
Private Collection

6. Study for Inocente and Josefina Palacios dining room,
Quinta Caurimare, Caracas, 1955
Pencil on Lana Docelles paper; 19 ⅞ x 25 ¹³⁄₁₆ in.
Private Collection

7. Mendoza coffee table, 1956
Wood; 14 x 47 ¹⁄₁₆ x 44 ½ in.
Manufactured by Pedro Santana, Carpintería
Colectiva
Emilio Mendoza Guardia Collection

8. Design for Mrs. Dagnino's vanity chest, 1957
Pencil and crayon on notebook paper; 12 x 18 ⅛ in.
Private Collection

**Arte Nativa Aplicada (Brazilian, f. 1976)**

9. Upholstery fabric with pre-Columbian figures,
c. 1970s
Cotton; 63 x 53 in.
Manufactured by Arte Nativa Aplicada
Private Collection

**Odilón Ávalos (Mexican, 1881–1957)**

10. Table lamp, c. 1950s
Blue glass, iron; 27 ⁹⁄₁₆ x 15 ¾ (diameter) in.
Manufactured by Gran Fábrica de Vidrio de Odilón
Ávalos
Private Collection, Mexico City

**Lina Bo Bardi (Brazilian, b. Italy, 1914–92)**

11. *Cadeira de beira de estrada* [Roadside Chair], 1967
Wood, rope, iron nails; 77 ⁹⁄₁₆ x 35 ⁷⁄₁₆ x 24 ⁷⁄₁₆ in.
Instituto Lina Bo e P. M. Bardi, São Paulo

12. Lina Bo Bardi sitting in the *Cadeira de beira de
estrada,* 1967
Gelatin silver print; 6 ½ x 8 ½ in.
Instituto Lina Bo e P. M. Bardi, São Paulo

13–15. Drawings for the *Cadeira de beira de estrada,* 1967
Felt tip pen on paper; 9 x 6 ⅛ in.; 4 x 5 ⅞ in.;
and 6 x 8 ⁷⁄₁₆ in.
Instituto Lina Bo e P. M. Bardi, São Paulo

16. Drawing for the *Cadeira de beira de estrada,* 1967
Ballpoint pen on paper; 7 ¾ x 7 ⁵⁄₁₆ in.
Instituto Lina Bo e P. M. Bardi, São Paulo

**José Carlos Bornancini (Brazilian, 1923–2008) and
Nelson Ivan Petzold (Brazilian, b. 1931)**

17. Picnic flatware set, 1973
Stainless steel; 1 x 1 ½ x 8 in.
Manufactured by Hércules SA, Brazil
Collection of Claudio Farias

**Roberto Burle Marx (Brazilian, 1909–94)**

18. Bowl, c. 1970
Glazed ceramic; 5 ½ x 4 ⁵⁄₁₆ x 3 ¹¹⁄₁₆ in.
Collection of Jacques Leenhardt

19. Plate, c. 1970
Glazed ceramic; 7 ⅞ in. diameter
Collection of Jacques Leenhardt

**Geraldo de Barros (Brazilian, 1923–98)**

20. Telephone bench, c. 1960s
Enameled steel, wood, vinyl upholstery;
17 ⅜ x 36 ⁵⁄₁₆ x 15 ⁹⁄₁₆ in.
Manufactured by Unilabor
Collection of Mauro Claro

21. *Chaises Unilabor,* 1954
Exhibition copy, 2015
Courtesy Acervo Instituto Moreira Salles

**Felipe Derflingher (Mexican, 1931–2013)**

22. *Bambú* pendant lamp, c. 1970s
Pressed glass, enameled steel; 13 ¾ x 11 ⁷⁄₁₆ in.
Manufactured by Vidrio Artístico Cuernavaca SA
de CV for Taller Studio Feders
Collection of Galería Trouvé

**José Feher (Mexican, b. Hungary, 1902–88)**

23. Zoomorphic pitcher, c. 1960
Ceramic; 11 ⁷⁄₁₆ x 10 ⁵⁄₈ x 6 ⁵⁄₁₆ in.
Manufactured by Cerámica Artística de Texcoco
Collection of Daniel and Pablo Feher

**Gego (Gertrude Goldschmidt, Venezuelan, b. Germany, 1912–94)**

24. *Catalogo de la Fábrica de Lámparas y Muebles Gunz*
(Gunz Lamp and Furniture Factory catalogue), c. 1943
Booklet; 6 ⁵⁄₈ x 6 ⁵⁄₈ in.
Collection of the Fundación Gego Archive

25. Chair, c. 1948
Wood; 36 x 16 ⁵⁄₈ x 15 in.
Private Collection

**Óscar Hagerman (Mexican, b. Spain 1936)**

26. *Silla Arrullo* (Lullaby Chair), 1963
Pine, tule or palm; 27 ⅜ x 18 ⅛ x 20 ¹⁄₁₆ in.
Courtesy of the designer

**Klaus Heufer (Venezuelan, b. Germany, 1923–2013)**

27. Design for a bookshelf for Joh Johannson's apartment
in Caracas, c. 1960s
Graphite on tracing paper; 14 ³⁄₁₆ x 26 ⅜ in.
Private Collection, New York

**Los Castillo (Mexican, f. 1934)**

28. Jar with a parrot handle, c. 1950
Silver-plated metal, brass, abalone shell;
9 ³⁄₁₆ x 5 ¹⁵⁄₁₆ x 7 ¹⁄₁₆ in.
Guillermo Martínez-Cesar/Urbanity Mobiliario,
Mexico City

29. *Metales casados* (married metal) tray with geometric
designs, c. 1960
Silver, copper, brass; 11 ⁹⁄₁₆ x 13 ⁹⁄₁₆ x ¹³⁄₁₆ in.
Private Collection

30. Jar with a mockingbird, date unknown
Silver, copper, brass, green stone;
10 ⁵⁄₈ x 5 ⅞ x 3 ½ in.
Collection of Juan Rafael Coronel Rivera

**Aldemir Martins (Brazilian, 1922–2006)**

31. *Cangaceiro* dish, c. 1966
Melamine; 7 ⅞ x 7 ⅞ in.
Manufactured by Goyana Melcrome
Private Collection

**Paulo Mendes da Rocha (Brazilian, b. 1928)**

32. Study for the *Paulistano* armchair, date unknown
(chair designed 1957)
Graphite on paper; 13 ¾ x 12 ⅝ in.
Private Collection

**Cristina Merchán (Venezuelan, 1927–87)**

33. Tea set, 1961
Ceramic, wood; dimensions variable
Colección Mercantil, Caracas

34. Bowl, 1963–65
Ceramic; 2 ⅝ x 6 ⅝ (diameter) in.
Private Collection, New York

35. Elongated ovoid with relief, 1976
Stoneware with olive green glaze;
8 ¹¹⁄₁₆ x 5 ⅛ (diameter) in.
Private Collection

**Rubén Núñez (Venezuelan, 1930–2012)**

36. Bottle-shaped vase, 1958
Blown glass; 12 ¹³⁄₁₆ in. tall
Lent by The Corning Museum of Glass,
Gift of Rubén Núñez

37. Vase, 1958
Glass; 11 x 10 ⅝ (diameter) in.
Colección Mercantil, Caracas

**Alejandro Otero (Venezuelan, 1921–90)**

38. **Alejandro Otero and Miguel Arroyo**

Model for the door of Miguel Arroyo's house, 1953
Colored paper on board; 10 ¼ x 4 ⅛ in.
Collection of Manuel Vegas Chumaceiro

39. Bowl, 1958–60
Enamel on copper; 2 ¾ x 6 ⅛ (diameter) in.
Private Collection, New York

### Arturo Pani (Mexican, 1915–81)

40. Chair, c. 1970
Methacrylate, chrome-plated steel;
41 ¾ x 27 ¹⁵⁄₁₆ x 20 ¹⁄₁₆ in.
Private Collection, Mexico City

41. Bar cart, c. 1970
Enameled steel, glass mirror; 29 ⅛ x 18 ⅛ x 30 ¹¹⁄₁₆ in.
Private Collection, Mexico City

### Miguel Pineda (Mexican, b. 1940)

42. Plate, c. 1960
Enamel on copper; 10 ⅝ x 10 ¹³⁄₁₆ x 1 in.
Galería Julio de la Torre, Mexico City

### Clara Porset (Mexican, b. Cuba, 1895-1981)

43. Interior for Arq. Enrique Langenscheidt, c. 1950
Ink on paper and fabric samples; 14 ⁹⁄₁₆ x 24 in.
Collection of Archivo Clara Porset CIDI/Facultad de
Arquitectura/UNAM, Mexico City

44. **Clara Porset and Xavier Guerrero (Mexican,
1896–1974)**

*Entry Panel for MoMA International Competition for
Low-Cost Furniture Design,* c. 1950
Ink on panel; 19 ¾ x 31 ½ in.
The Museum of Modern Art, New York, Gift of the
designers, 2009

45. *Butaque,* c. 1955–56
Wood, woven cane; 28 ½ x 21 ½ x 25 ⁹⁄₁₆ in.
Collection of the Familia Galvéz, Mexico City

46. Interior design for a living room, c. 1960
Graphite and color pencil on paper; 8 ⅞ x 11 ¹³⁄₁₆ in.
Collection of Archivo Clara Porset CIDI/Facultad de
Arquitectura/UNAM, Mexico City

47. Three-seat sofa, c. 1950
Heliographic print
35 x 24 in.
Private Collection, Mexico City

48. Writing desk vanity, c. 1950
Heliographic print
35 x 24 in.
Private Collection, Mexico City

### Pedro Ramírez Vázquez (Mexican, 1919–2013)

49. *Equipal* armchair, c. 1964
Leather, chromed steel; 31 x 27 x 25 in.
Collection of the Archivo Diseño y Arquitectura,
Mexico City

### Sérgio Rodrigues (Brazilian, 1927–2014)

50. *Mole* armchair, 1957
Wood, leather; 32 ½ x 40 x 29 in.
Manufactured by Oca
Courtesy of Zesty Meyers and Evan Snyderman,
R & Company, New York

### Cynthia Sargent (American, active in Mexico, 1922–2006)

51. *Scarlatti* rug, c. 1969
Wool and mohair on cotton, hand dyed and hooked;
80 x 129 in.
Riggs-Sargent Family Collection

### Mario Seguso (Brazilian, b. Italy 1929)

52. Bottle with stopper, 1978
Mold-blown glass; 6 ½ x 5 ³⁄₁₆ (diameter) in.
Manufactured by Ca D'Oro Ltda., Rio de Janeiro, Brazil
Collection of The Corning Museum of Glass, Gift of
Ca D'Oro Ltda.

### Donald Shoemaker (American, active in Mexico, 1912–98)

53. Coffee table, c. 1960
Wood, leather; 15 x 45 ½ x 21 ½ in.
Manufactured by Señal, SA
Private Collection, Mexico City

### William Spratling (American, active in Mexico, 1900–67)

54. Pitcher, c. 1940
Silver; 8 ¼ x 8 x 7 ½ in.
Marc Navarro Gallery

### Joaquim Tenreiro (Brazilian, b. Portugal, 1906–92)

55. Design for an interior, c. 1945
Graphite and gouache on paper; 10 x 13 in.
Courtesy of Zesty Meyers and Evan Snyderman,
R & Company, New York

56. Three-legged chair, c. 1947
Wood; 27 ½ x 22 x 24 in.
Manufactured by Tenreiro Móveis e Decorações
Courtesy of Zesty Meyers and Evan Snyderman,
R & Company, New York

Félix Tissot (American, active in Mexico, 1909–89)

57. Platter, c. 1950
Glazed ceramic; ½ x 15 x 11 in.
Manufactured by Cerámica de Taxco, SA
Private Collection, New York

58. Vase, c. 1960
Ceramic, hand-painted and fired at a high
temperature; 11 ⁷⁄₁₆ x 13 ³⁄₈ in.
Manufactured by Cerámica de Taxco, SA
Collection of Ione Tissot

Tecla Tofano (Venezuelan, b. Italy, 1927–95)

59. Pitcher, 1963
Earthenware with gray and white slip, gas fired;
8 ¼ x 6 ⁵⁄₁₆ x 7 ½ in.
Private Collection

60. *Freud, Sexologia,* 1975
Ceramic, sculpted and glazed; 6 ½ x 7 ¹¹⁄₁₆ x 6 ½ in.
Collection of Sagrario Berti

61. Bottle with phallic stopper, early 1970s
Glazed ceramic; 5 ½ x 10 ⁷⁄₁₆ x 10 ⁵⁄₈ in.
Colección Mercantil, Caracas

María Luisa Zuloaga de Tovar (Venezuelan, 1902–92)

62. Vase decorated with pre-Hispanic motifs, 1968
Glazed earthenware; 6 ⁵⁄₈ x 8 ⁷⁄₁₆ in.
Private Collection, New York

Seka Severin de Tudja (Venezuelan, b. Yugoslavia, now
Croatia, 1923–2007)

63. Dish, c. 1950s
Ceramic; ½ x 10 ¾ (diameter) in.
Private Collection, New York

64. *E-4,* 1974
Ceramic; 10 ¼ x 11 ⅞ (diameter) in.
Colección Patricia Phelps de Cisneros

65. *L-13,* 1979
Ceramic; 6 ½ x 7 (diameter) in.
Colección Patricia Phelps de Cisneros

Michael van Beuren (Mexican, b. United States,
1911–2004)

66. Chair and desk, c. 1940
Pine, palm; desk: 29 ½ x 47 ¼ x 19 ⁵⁄₁₆ in.;
chair: 31 ½ x 18 ½ x 17 ⁵⁄₁₆ in.
Manufactured by Van Beuren SA de CV for Domus
Collection of Jan van Beuren

67. Domus bookshelf and chair, c. 1949
(photographer unknown)
Gelatin silver print; 8 ¼ x 10 in.
Collection of Jan van Beuren

68. **Michael van Beuren, Klaus Grabe (b. Germany 1910,
active in Mexico, d. United States 2004), and
Morley Webb (American)**
*Alacrán* (Scorpion) chaise, c. 1940
Primavera wood, fabric straps;
28 x 57 x 25 ½ in.
Manufactured by Van Beuren SA de CV for Domus
Private Collection, Mexico City

69–70. *Entry Panels for MoMA Latin American Competition
for Organic Design in Home Furnishings,* c. 1940
Ink and photo collage on paper; each 19 ¾ x 31 ½ in.
The Museum of Modern Art, New York, Gift of the
designers, 2008.

Paulo Werneck (Brazilian, 1907–87)

71. Mosaic tables, 1950s
Wood, ceramic mosaic; each 10 x 16 x 20 in.
Collection of Gaspar Saldanha

Jorge Zalszupin (Brazilian, b. Poland 1922)

72. *Putskit* wall-mounted organizer, No. 15515, c. 1970–79
Plastic, mirror; 17 ½ x 4 ½ x 26 ½ in.
Manufactured by L'Atelier, São Paulo, Brazil
Courtesy of Zesty Meyers and Evan Snyderman,
R & Company, New York

73. **Jorge Zalszupin and Paulo Jorge Pedreira (Brazilian)**
*Eva* ice bucket, 1976
Plastic; 6 ¹¹⁄₁₆ x 7 ⅞ (diameter) in.
Manufactured by Hevea, Brazil
Collection of Claudio Farias

José Zanine Caldas (Brazilian, 1918–2001)

74. Plant stand, c. 1949
Wood, plastic, laminate; 13 x 21 x 18 in.
Courtesy of Zesty Meyers and Evan Snyderman,
R & Company, New York

Gottfried (German, active in Venezuela, b. 1929) and
Thekla Zielke (German, active in Venezuela, b. 1928)

75.   Decanter and tumbler set, c. 1960
      Ceramic; decanter: 6 ⅞ x 4 ¹⁵⁄₁₆ x 4 ¹⁵⁄₁₆ in.;
      tumblers: 1 ¾ x 2 (diameter) in.
      Manufactued by Gotek, Colonia Tovar
      Private Collection, New York

Cornelis Zitman (Venezuelan, b. The Netherlands 1926)

76.   Model for a chair, 1950
      Enameled steel wire, cotton cord; 3 ⅜ x 2 x 2 ⅛ in.
      Collection of Cornelis Zitman, Caracas

77.   *Chair No. 58,* c. 1952
      Steel rod, laminated wood; 29 ½ x 18 ⅞ x 20 ⅞ in.
      Manufactured by Tecoteca, CA
      Private Collection, New York

78.   **Cornelis Zitman and Vittorio Garatti (Italian,
      active in Venezuela, b. 1927)**
      Maquette for Tecoteca catalogue, with logo
      design, 1957
      7 x 10 x 1 ¼ in.
      Collection of Cornelis Zitman, Caracas

## UNKNOWN DESIGNERS

### Brazil:

79.   Wineglasses, 1950
      Blown glass, enameled, with cloth;
      each 5 ¹⁵⁄₁₆ x 3 ⅜ (diameter) in.
      Manufactured by Figadai, Rio de Janeiro, Brazil
      Lent by The Corning Museum of Glass,
      Gift of Otto Hilbert

### Mexico:

80.   Pitcher and glasses, c. 1970
      Glass, metal; pitcher: 10 ⅝ x 6 ½ x 4 ⁵⁄₁₆ in.;
      glasses: 7 ½, 2 ¹⁵⁄₁₆ (diameter) in.
      Manufactured by Vidrio de Texcoco
      Private Collection, Mexico City

### Venezuela:

81.   *La Burriquita* platter, 1951
      Ceramic; 10 ¼ in. diameter
      Manufactured by Cerámicas Artísticas Nacionales,
      Antímano, Caracas
      Private Collection, New York

## PUBLICATIONS

82.   Instituto Nacional de Bellas Artes, Departamento de
      Arquitectura [National Institute of Fine Arts,
      Architecture Department]. *El arte en la vida diaria:
      exposición de objetos de buen diseño hechos en
      México* [Art in the Daily Life: An Exhibition of Well-
      Designed Objects Made in Mexico]. Exh. cat., text by
      Clara Porset and others. Mexico City, 1952.
      Art & Architecture Collection, The Miriam and Ira D.
      Wallach Division of Art, Prints and Photographs,
      The New York Public Library, Astor, Lenox, and Tilden
      Foundations

83.   *Habitat* no. 1 (October–December, 1950), edited by
      Lina Bo and Pietro Maria Bardi
      Courtesy of Zesty Meyers and Evan Snyderman,
      R & Company, New York

84.   *Habitat* no. 8 (October–December, 1952), edited by
      Lina Bo and Pietro Maria Bardi
      Courtesy of Zesty Meyers and Evan Snyderman,
      R & Company, New York

85.   *Revista Arquitectura México,* no. 34 (June 1951),
      edited by Mario Pani
      Private Collection

86.   *Revista A: Hombre y Expresión* (Sociedad
      Editora "A," Caracas) (January 1954)
      Private Collection

87.   *Acróple, Sâo Paulo* (October 1964), edited by
      Max M. Grunewald
      Private Collection

## ARTWORK

### Elsa Gramcko (Venezuelan, 1925–1994)

88.   *Composición No. 6,* 1957
      Oil on canvas
      Private Collection, Courtesy of Henrique Faria Fine Art

### Alejandro Otero (Venezuelan, 1921–90)

89.   *Tablón de Pampatar* (Pampatar Board), 1954
      Lacquer on wood; 25 ⅜ x 1 ¹⁄₁₆ x 124 ¹³⁄₁₆ in.
      Colección Patricia Phelps de Cisneros

# ABOUT THE AUTHORS

**LOURDES BLANCO** is a curator specializing in pre-Hispanic art, as well as modern and contemporary Venezuelan art and design. She is part of the Advisory Committee for the Sala TAC, Trasnocho Cultural Foundation in Caracas and a member of the Centro de estudios de archivos audiovisuales y artísticos [Center for the Study of Audiovisual and Artistic Archives] in Caracas.

**LUIS M. CASTAÑEDA** is an assistant professor of art history at Syracuse University and the author of *Spectacular Mexico: Design, Propaganda and the 1968 Olympics* (University of Minnesota Press, 2014). His book examines how design became a powerful propaganda tool during the 1968 Summer Olympics celebrated in Mexico City, and examines the global resonance of this event for design culture. Castañeda's research and writing examine multiple aspects of the visual culture and urban history of the Americas, inscribing these spheres within broader horizons of economic, political, and intellectual transformation in the region.

**CHRISTINA L. DE LEÓN** is Assistant Curator of the Visual Arts Program, Americas Society. She has helped organize exhibitions and catalogues on modern and contemporary art. She cocurated the exhibitions *For Rent: Marc Latamie* (2012) and *Cristóbal Lehyt: Iris Sheets* (2013) and has also contributed to the magazine *Review: Literature and Arts of the Americas.* Previously she worked at The Metropolitan Museum of Art and the Cloisters Museum and Gardens, where she helped establish "La Experiencia Medieval," the first series of gallery programs for Spanish-speaking families. De León holds an MA from the Program in Museum Studies at New York University and a BA from Hobart and William Smith Colleges.

**MARIA CECILIA LOSCHIAVO DOS SANTOS** is a philosopher and full professor of Design at the College of Architecture and Urbanism, University of São Paulo. She received an MA and a PhD in Philosophy in Aesthetics at the University of São Paulo, 1975 and 1993, respectively. She has been a visiting scholar in postdoctoral programs at the following universities: University of California, Los Angeles, School of Public Policy and Social Research, 1995-96; University of Campinas, Brazil, Institute of Philosophy and Human Sciences, 1997; Nihon University, Tokyo, College of Design and Arts, 1999; Canadian Center for Architecture, Montreal, 2001. Loschiavo dos Santos has published many articles in Brazilian design magazines and international academic conferences. She is the author of several books on design, among them *Móvel Moderno no Brasil.* Currently she is the chair of the design department at the College of Architecture and Urbanism.

**ANA ELENA MALLET** is a Mexican independent writer and curator specializing in contemporary art and design. She teaches Curatorial Perspectives in Design as part of the Design Studies Degree program at CENTRO in Mexico City. She has worked as a curator at the Museo Soumaya and Museo de Arte Carrillo Gil, Programming Deputy Director at Museo Rufino Tamayo, and Chief Curator at Museo del Objeto (MODO). The more recent design shows she has curated and cocurated include *Inventando un México Moderno: el diseño de Clara Porset,* Museo Franz Mayer, Mexico City (2006); *Thonet. Vanguardias de diseño, 1830–2008* (2008); *Barbie: 50 años de historia, moda y diseño,* Museo Franz Mayer (2009); *Vida y Diseño, 125 años de diseño en México,* Fomento Cultural Banamex (2009); *Huellas de la Bauhaus. Van Beuren, Mexico,* Museo Franz Mayer (2010), and *Mexican Silver Design of the 20th Century,* Fomento Cultural Banamex (2013). She regularly contributes to several cultural magazines, such as: *Chilango, Harper's Bazaar en Español, Open, Luna Córnea, Art Nexus, Código 06140,* and *La Tempestad.*

**GABRIELA RANGEL** Gabriela Rangel is Visual Arts Director and Chief Curator at Americas Society. She holds an M.A. in curatorial studies from the Center for Curatorial Studies, Bard College, an M.A. in media and communications studies from the Universidad Católica Andrés Bello in Caracas, and a B.A. in film studies from the International Film School at San Antonio de los Baños, Cuba. She worked at the Fundación Cinemateca Nacional and the Museo Alejandro Otero in Caracas, and the Museum of Fine Arts in Houston. She has curated and co-curated numerous exhibitions on modern and contemporary art that include Consuelo Castañeda, Carlos Cruz-Diez, Gordon Matta Clark, Arturo Herrera, Paula Trope, and Alejandro Xul Solar. She has also contributed to the art periodicals *Art in America, Parkett,* and *Art Nexus.* Rangel has edited numerous books and has contributed texts to publications *Marta Minujín* (Ciudad de Buenos Aires, 2015), *Javier Téllez/Vasco Araujo, Larger than Life* (Fundação Calouste Gulbenkian, 2012), *Arturo Herrera* (Transnocho Arte, 2009), *Arte no es vida* (El Museo del Barrio, 2008), *A Principality of its Own* (Americas Society-Harvard University Press, 2006), and *Da Adversidade Vivemos: Artistes d'Amérique latine* (Musée d'Art Moderne de la Ville de Paris, 2001).

**JORGE F. RIVAS PÉREZ** is an art historian and industrial designer. He has contributed to and cocurated exhibitions on Spanish Colonial Art and twentieth-century Latin American design, including *Cornelis Zitman: 1947–1957 la década del diseño,* Sala TAC Caracas, Venezuela (2011) and *Interior moderno, muebles diseñados por Miguel Arroyo* (2005). He is the author of several catalogues and articles on decorative arts and design, among which *Spanish Colonial Decorative Arts, 1500–1825,* and *Modern Decorative Arts and Design, 1900–2000* for the Latin American Studies section on Oxford Bibliographies on-line (2011), and "Latin America 1900–2000" in *History of the Decorative Arts and Design, 1400–2000,* edited by Pat Kirkham and Susan Weber (Yale University Press, 2013). Rivas Pérez received his architecture degree from Universidad Central de Venezuela, Caracas, his master's degree in industrial design from Universitá degli Studi di Firenze, Florence, Italy, and his M.Phil from the Bard Graduate Center, where he is pursuing his PhD.

# ACKNOWLEDGMENTS

The editors of this publication want to thank the following people and institutions for their generous collaboration.

Priscilla Abecasis
Rafael Abuchaibe
Beverly Adams
Eddy Almonte
Renato Anelli
Paulo Mauro Mayer de Aquino
Archivo Clara Porset, Facultad de Arquitectura de la Universidad Nacional Autónoma de México (UNAM)
Archivo Diseño y Arquitectura
Joanna Balabram
Alejandra Barajas
Fabiana de Barros
Lenora de Barros
Circe Bernardes
Sagrario Berti
Jan van Beuren
Biblioteca da Faculdade de Arquitetura e Urbanismo da Universidade de São Paulo
Biblioteca y Hemeroteca Nacionales de México
Lourdes Blanco
Tonya Borisov
Graça Bueno
Carla Cabral
Anna Carboncini

Lissa Carmona
Javier Carral
Juan Luis Cebrián Echarri
Manuel Vegas Chumaceiro
Mauro Claro
Colección Mercantil, Caracas
Consejo Nacional para la Cultura y las Artes de México (CONACULTA)
The Corning Museum of Glass
Juan Rafael Coronel Rivera
Nathalia Critchley
Samuel Dezman
Adriana Díaz de Cossío
Alberto Díaz de Cossío
Blanca Espinosa
Facultad de Arquitectura, Centro de Investigaciones de Diseño Industrial (CIDI), Universidad Nacional Autónoma de México (UNAM)
Henrique Faria
Claudio Farias
Daniel Feher
Pablo Feher
Adriana Figueiredo
Angela Figueiredo
Fundación Gego
Galería Julio de la Torre

Galería Marc Navarro
Galería Trouvé
Paul Galloway
Lizeth Galván
Emilia Gálvez
Cristina Gálvez Guzzy
Guillaume Gaubert
Elisa Gomes
Hannia Gómez
Katia González Martínez
Sonia Guarita do Amaral
Barbara Gunz
Tomas Gunz
Óscar Hagerman
Edmundo Hernández
Angélica Hernández Reyes
Hunter College
Instituto Lina Bo e P. M. Bardi
Instituto Moreira Salles
Instituto Nacional de Bellas Artes de México (INBA)
Instituto Sergio Rodrigues
Lily Kane
Lynda Klich
Francisco Kochen
Magdalena Kuri
Ximena Lara
Jacques Leenhardt
Po Shun Leong
Jorge Lestrade

Zeuler Lima
Eunice Liu
Patrick Luna
José Inéz Navarro
Marc Navarro
Otavio Nazareth
Ricardo Niemeyer
Miriam Mamber Czeresnia
Juan Manuel Noguera
Marcelo Mari
Jose Luis Martínez
Guillermo Martínez-Cesar
Carlos Mazari Hiriart
Claudio Mendoza Guardia
Emilio Mendoza Guardia
Zesty Meyers
Rafael Montero
Skye Monson
Harper Montgomery
Luis Muñoz
The Museum of Modern Art
New York Public Library
Pilar Obeso
Cindy Ocampo
Tina Oldknow
Sagrario Pérez Soto
Regina Pozo
Rodrigo Queiros
R & Company, New York
José A. Rangel

Patricio del Real
Joaquim Redig
Fiorella Remus
Enrique Ricalde
Riggs-Sargent Family
   Collection
Stephanie Riggs
Jacqueline Rivera
Tahía Rivero
Héctor Rivero Borrell
Fernando Romero
Dora Ruiz Galindo
José Luis Sainz
Tatiana Sakurai
Gaspar Saldanha
Rafael Santana
Secretaría de Relaciones
   Exteriores de México
Francisco Serrano
Heitor Sette Ferreira Pires
   Granafei
Soumaya Slim de Romero
Irene Small
Evan Snyderman
Miguel Tapia
Ione Tissot
Graciela de la Torre
Julio de la Torre
Dina Uliana
Urbanity Mobiliario

Jorge Vadillo
Pablo Velasco Sodi
Vera Beatriz Veiga Rodrigues
Marcus Vinicius Ribeiro
Sofia Vollmer de Maduro
Carlos Warchavchik
Ricardo Warman
Simone Wicha
Fernando Zalamea
Julián Zalamea
Alejandra Zapata
Madgalena Zavala
Cornelis Zitman
Vera Roos de Zitman

Americas Society is the premier organization dedicated to education, debate, and dialogue in the Americas. Its mission is to foster an understanding of the contemporary political, social, and economic issues confronting Latin America, the Caribbean, and Canada, and to increase public awareness and appreciation of the diverse cultural heritage of the Americas and the importance of the inter-American relationship.

PRINTED AND PUBLISHED BY
SANTILLANA USA
LANGUAGE EDUCATION EXPERTS
2023 NW 84th Ave
Doral, FL 33122

680 Park Avenue, New York, NY 10065
Phone: (212) 249-8950 Fax: (212) 249-5868
e-mail: artgallery@as-coa.org
Web site: www.as-coa.org/visualarts

Phone: (305) 591-9522 Fax: (800) 530-8099
(800) 245-8584
www.santillanausa.com
customerservice@santillanausa.com